Restorative Justice &
Responsive Regulation

RESTORATIVE JUSTICE & RESPONSIVE REGULATION

John Braithwaite

OXFORD
UNIVERSITY PRESS

OXFORD

UNIVERSITY PRESS

Oxford   New York

Auckland   Bangkok   Buenos Aires   Cape Town   Chennai
Dar es Salaam   Delhi   Hong Kong   Istanbul   Karachi   Kolkata
Kuala Lumpur   Madrid   Melbourne   Mexico City   Mumbai   Nairobi
São Paulo   Shanghai   Singapore   Taipei   Tokyo   Tornoto

and an associated company in Berlin

Copyright © 2002 by John Braithwaite

First published by Oxford University Press, Inc. in 2002
198 Madison Avenue, New York, New York 10016

www.oup.com

First issued as an Oxford University Press paperback, 2002

Oxford is a registered trademark of Oxford University Press

Library of Congress Cataloging-in-Publication Data
Braithwaite, John.
Restorative justice and responsive regulation / by John Braithwaite.
p.   cm.—(Studies in crime and public policy)
Includes bibliographical references and index.
ISBN 0-19-513639-X; 0-19-515839-3 (pbk.)
1. Restorative justice.   2. Victims of crimes.   3. Criminals—Rehabilitation.
4. Criminal justice, Administration of.   I. Title.   II. Series.

HV8688 .B73   2001
364—dc21   00-066581

1 3 5 7 9 8 6 4 2

Printed in the United States of America
on acid-free paper

To Ben and Sari

Preface

For informal justice to be restorative justice, it has to be about restoring victims, restoring offenders, and restoring communities as a result of participation of a plurality of stakeholders. This means that victim-offender mediation, healing circles, family group conferences, restorative probation, reparation boards on the Vermont model, whole-school antibullying programs, Chinese *bang jiao* programs, and exit conferences following Western business regulatory inspections can at times all be restorative justice. So long as there is a process that gives the stakeholders affected by an injustice an opportunity to tell their stories about its consequences and what needs to be done to put things right, and so long as this is done within a framework of restorative values that include the need to heal the hurts that have been felt, we can think of the process as restorative justice. This book seeks to ground a set of optimistic propositions (chapters 3 and 4) and of pessimistic claims (chapter 5) about restorative justice by contemplating the global diversity of its practice. The literature is organized to contend that both the optimistic and the pessimistic propositions may capture part of the truth. Regulatory theory (a responsive regulatory pyramid) is advanced as more useful for preventing crime in a normatively acceptable way than extant criminal law jurisprudence and explanatory theory. The responsive regulatory approach is the framework for locating restorative justice in institutional spaces where it can best complement institutions of crime prevention, human and economic development, deterrence, incapacitation, and care and love for the land. An evidence-based approach will be advanced for understanding how the weaknesses of restorative justice might be complemented by the strengths of these other institutions and vice versa. Evidence-based reform will also be advocated toward a more productive checking of restorative justice by liberal legalism, and vice versa.

The book should be read as an attempt to position responsive regulation (chapter 2) as a framework for checking the abuses and limitations of restorative justice diagnosed here. What the book seeks to do, then, is bring together the author's longstanding work on both restorative justice and responsive regulation. My responsive regulation work has tended to focus on areas of business regulation such as occupational health and safety, environmental protection, and nursing home regulation. The restorative justice work has tended to focus on criminal law. In this book the responsive regulatory ideas are translated into arenas such as juvenile bullying and crime generally, and restorative justice is applied to business regulation, the regulatory challenges of sustainable development (chapter 7), peacemaking in international relations (chapter 6), and the transformation of the entire legal system (chapter 8). In short, an integrated theory of restorative justice and responsive regulation is conceived as a worthy pursuit.

The history of this book is that Michael Tonry persuaded me to write a review essay on restorative justice for *Crime and Justice: A Review of Research*, Vol. 25, published by the University of Chicago Press. When I delivered up an essay that was far too long, he cut it while encouraging me to publish the full essay as a book in his capacity as a series editor with Oxford University Press.

This book is more than my original holistic essay restored to its full glory. Of course it has also been updated as a result of an extraordinary explosion of restorative justice innovation and evaluation research in the three years since I completed the original essay. Chapter 3 argues that the 1999 essay, in light of research completed since, may have committed the Type II error of being excessively cautious over the hypothesis that restorative justice can reduce crime. But I also decided to integrate my work on restorative justice with my work on responsive regulation. One reason was that reviewers of the original essay were critical of some of the material therein—mostly material on restorative and responsive business regulation—for being insufficiently relevant to criminology. While the first half of the book is dominated by what we have learned about restorative justice from the core area of criminal justice, throughout there are many lessons from restorative and responsive business regulation. Moreover, chapters 6 through 8 are completely new attempts to move the ideas onto the challenges of regulation for sustainable economic development, international peacekeeping, and transforming the entire legal system.

It seems to me that the reviewers were mistaken in wanting to limit the focus of the original essay to purely criminal matters. First, there is enormous selectivity and arbitrariness in when we react to regulated phenomena as crime. Second, I believe that regulatory theory delivers superior and more general explanations than criminological theory. Crime is a regulatory challenge, as are bullying in schools, educational development in part, and economic development, environmental protection, and world peace. My deeply held suspicion is that restorative justice has really important things to say about all these challenges. And I try to say them here. It is not that restorative justice has answers to all the world's problems; indeed, a message of this book is that restorative justice is only a modest part of the answer to the questions addressed. However, as an IRA ex-prisoner said in a recent conference I attended on restorative justice in Northern Ireland: "Restorative justice is not just about crime, it is about peace and a way of bringing up our children that is less punitive and more decent. It is a holistic philosophy." I suspect he is right that restorative justice has something to say to us about how we live our life as we move through all the institutions we encounter.

This book therefore attempts to correct the bifurcated image of John Braithwaite the criminologist and Braithwaite the scholar of business regulation. They are the same person. The book imports into the study of business regulation the restorative justice ideas that characterize the first Braithwaite and imports into the study of crime the responsive regulatory ideas that characterize the second. And it explores the relevance of both sets of ideas to the governance of the entire legal system, the economy, and international relations. My reading of the evidence of business regulation in this book is that responsive regulation does save lives that would otherwise be lost to breaches of health, environment, and safety laws. My reading of the evidence of restorative justice is that it can reduce criminal violence and school bullying in particular, but other kinds of crime as well.

The reviewers of the original essay also had doubts about the interest of North American and European readers in the amount of material I included from societies with cultures markedly different from those of the North. Here my working hypothesis is that better theories of, say, U.S. crime are likely to be stimulated by broadening our horizons to studying the different patterns of regulatory practices and regulatory outcomes observable in radically different societies and contexts. In particular I believe that both criminology and the social movement for restorative justice have suffered from insufficient openness to learning from Asia and Africa. To assist with nurturing the wider restorative imagination needed, boxes describing specific restorative practices from different times and places are placed throughout the text. This is Norman Davies's (1997) pointillistic technique of giving two ways of seeing the text—one based on the abstractions in the narrative, the other on seeing an array of dots of specificity in our own way.

Finally the reviewers were concerned that I was an advocate of restorative justice and therefore compromised in my capacity to dispassionately review the empirical evidence on its effectiveness. I am an advocate of restorative justice, and I am politically active in the social movement to promote it. It is possible to be passionate about the normative and dispassionate about the empirical: warm values, cold analysis. Yet this does not seem quite the right response. Normatively serious people who engage with a social movement should not be dispassionate about it; they should have a passion for good science to find where its claims are false. If Marxists had been as interested as Marx in data, if Keynesians had been as passionate as Keynes about data (as opposed to equations with no empirical foundation), then Marxists and Keynesians might have done less damage. Indeed, if economic libertarians had the interest in combining economic theory with the passions of moral theory that Adam Smith saw as important, like Keynes and Marx, libertarians might have done less damage, too. Social movement activists ultimately enfeeble their cause by failing to attend to empirical evidence of the limits of their theories. But that does not preclude articulating the kind of inspiring vision of how radical change might open up possibilities for a more decent society that we see in the writings of Howard Zehr, Kay Pranis, and others.

My working hypothesis is that superior explanatory theory (ordered propositions about the way the world is) and superior normative theory (ordered propositions about the way the world ought to be) arise from an explicit commitment to integrating explanatory and normative theory. But for this approach to deliver the goods, what must come with it is a serious commitment to research designed to refute both the normative and the explanatory claims. I will not defend this approach here, as I have done so elsewhere with Christine Parker and Philip Pettit (Braithwaite and Parker 1999; Braithwaite and Pettit 2000). Over time science will judge whether such an approach has marshaled theory and evidence around inferior explanations compared with those advanced by researchers who eschew normative propositions.

Approaches to regulation that seek to identify important problems and fix them (Sparrow, 2000) work better and more humanely than approaches oriented to imposing the right punishment. We can see most clearly how giving wrongdoers their just deserts gets in the way of an effective and morally decent approach to crime. The history of criminology puts the key lessons of how to do regulation well into sharpest relief. Yet the crucial tension in all areas of regulation is between being punishment-oriented and being problem-oriented. Hence all disciplines that study regulation have a lot to learn from the bitter failures of criminology. The crucial tension in raising our children in families and schools is whether to give them what they deserve when they do wrong or to be problem-focused. In international conflict the deepest psychopolitical reality of the choice between peace and war is whether we should give the enemy what we believe he deserves or whether we should look for solutions to problems. While civil suits are not about punishment in a formal legal sense, the psychology of civil litigation is more fundamentally than anything else about whether litigants should give their adversaries what they deserve or whether they should concentrate on fixing the problem.

To juxtapose the orientation to punish with that to fix the problem only scratches the surface of what is at issue with restorative justice and responsive regulation. Regulation is what we do when obligations are not being honored. When people, corporations, or nations fail to meet obligations they owe to us, we get angry. Because we are hurt, there is a need to heal; there is a need for others to listen to the stories of our hurts before we can all move on to solve the problem. When we do not attend to these emotional dimensions of conflicts over obligation, our more coldly rational attempts to regulate fail or, worse, backfire. Restorative practice shows us the practical paths for moving from healing to problem solving. Here not only is there a lot to be learned from restorative justice circles in criminal justice. There also is much to learn from the environmental regulator who invites nongovernmental organizations (NGOs) and citizens who are angry about a shocking case of pollution to sit in the circle with the corporate polluter—both to heal the anger and to harness it to drive the needed corporate transformation. Because restorative justice is conceived in this book as a strategy that often works for building commitment to meet all our obligations, we find it relevant to building voluntary compliance with environmental obligations, with obligations to be peacemakers, with obligations to be caring parents and responsible children who commit to our educational obligations, as well as obligations under all manner of laws. This book therefore concludes that restorative justice has the potential to contribute not only to the creation of a more crime-free society but also to a society where our whole legal system works more efficiently and fairly, to a society where we do better at developing the human and social capital of our young and to a more peaceful world. Because of the empirically grounded promise of restorative justice and responsive regulation for more peaceful and sustainable development, a hope for this book is that opinion leaders at the World Bank and other international development agencies will take its ideas and evidence seriously.

Having made some remarks in response to the reviewers, I must thank them for the precision of their critiques on these and many other fronts. They convinced me I was wrong on many matters, and doubtless it is they who are right on many of the questions where they did not convince me. I owe a particular debt to Michael Tonry for encouraging me to respond in my own way to the critics and to Dedi Feldman of Oxford University Press for her sage editorial advice.

A long list of others made important contributions to my thinking. Among those who made helpful comments on earlier drafts were Valerie Braithwaite, Peter Cane, Harold Crouch, Kathy Daly, Carol Heimer, Carol LaPrairie, Guy Masters, Brenda Morrison, Christine Parker, Hugh Potter, Kent Roach, Tom Scheff, Lawrence Sherman, Heather Strang, and Tom Tyler. My thanks to Leah Dunn, Ellen Foulon, Stephen Free, Clare Guenther, and Chris Treadwell for their diligent research assistance, and particularly to Alison Pilger for her dedication to getting things right. Thanks also to Jean Norman for a fine index and to Dedi Felman of Oxford for many kinds of help. I also especially want to thank my many coauthors over the years whose stimulus has been indispensable to the development of the ideas in this book. Their names are listed in the cited works at the end of the book, and their distinctive ideas are acknowledged as they come up in the text. While some are more important than others to the particular ideas in this book, they all are more important than they think.

Institutionally, I owe a great debt to my colleagues and students in the Research School of Social Sciences, Australian National University, for providing a wonderfully stimulating environment for developing these ideas. I particularly want to acknowledge the influence of my past and present Ph.D. students on the work herein. While they all shape my thinking, there are cites to specific influences of Eliza Ahmed, Geoffrey Barnes, Charles Barton, Sinclair Dinnen, Nathan Harris, Ann Jenkins, Hong Lu, Christine Parker, Patrick Power, and Declan Roche. Jonathan Aleck, Jennifer Balint, Andrew Brien, Eliza Kacyznska-Nay, Robyn Lincoln, Sherif Seid, and Marie Wynter also prompted specific valuable ideas in discussions about their Ph.Ds.

I also thank my family for nourishment and love I cannot fathom.

Some passages have been extracted from the publications listed below and almost all the contents of the third essay have been included. I thank these publishers for permission to use the following works: "Restorative Justice and Social Justice," *Saskatchewan Law Review* 63 (2000): 185–94; "On Speaking Softly and Carrying Sticks: Neglected Dimensions of Republican Separation of Powers," *University of Toronto Law Journal* 47 (1997): 1–57; "Restorative Justice: Assessing Optimistic and Pessimistic Accounts," in *Crime and Justice: A Review of Research*, edited by M. Tonry, vol. 25 (Chicago: University of Chicago Press, 1999); "Reconciling Models: Balancing Regulation, Standards and Principles of Restorative Justice Practice," in *International Perspectives on Restorative Justice*, edited by H. Mika and K. McEvoy (Belfast: Queen's University, 2001); and "Youth Development Circles," *Oxford Review of Education* 27 (2001): 239–52.

Contents

Restorative Justice &
Responsive Regulation

1

The Fall and Rise of Restorative Justice

THE HISTORICAL DECLINE OF RESTORATIVE JUSTICE

This book conceives of restorative justice as a major development in human thought grounded in traditions of justice from the ancient Arab, Greek, and Roman civilizations that accepted a restorative approach even to homicide (Van Ness 1986, pp. 64–68); the restorative approach of the public assemblies (moots) of the Germanic peoples who swept across Europe after the fall of Rome (Berman 1983, pp. 53–56); Indian Hindus as ancient as the Vedic civilization (6000–2000 B.C.; Beck 1997, p. 77) for whom "he who atones is forgiven" (Weitekamp 1989); and ancient Buddhist, Taoist, and Confucian traditions that one sees blended with Western influences today in North Asia (Haley 1996).

Contemporary Nobel Peace Prize–winning Buddhists Aug San Suu Kyi of Burma and the Dalai Lama are reteaching the West that the more evil the crime, the greater the opportunity for grace to inspire a transformative will to resist tyranny with compassion. They follow in the footsteps of Hindus like Ghandi and Christians like Tutu. In the words of the Dalai Lama: "Learning to forgive is much more useful than merely picking up a stone and throwing it at the object of one's anger, the more so when the provocation is extreme. For it is under the greatest adversity that there exists the greatest potential for doing good, both for oneself and for others" (Eckel 1997, p. 135). Or as Saint Paul put it, "Where sin abounded, grace did much more abound." The implication of this teaching for criminologists is that preventing crime is an impoverished way of conceiving of our mission. Crime is an opportunity to prevent greater evils, to confront crime with a grace that transforms human lives to paths of love and giving. The ancient Palestinian restorative justice institution of the Sulha, still practiced in Galilee today, is one of the richest survivals of the ideal of using the lesser evil of crime to build the greater good of a loving community (see Box 1.1).

If we take restorative justice seriously, it involves a very different way of thinking about traditional notions such as deterrence, rehabilitation, incapacitation, and crime prevention. It also means transformed foundations of criminal jurisprudence and of

Box 1.1: The Sulha Today

If a serious crime such as a murder occurs, the first step in a Sulha is that the offender's family approaches a number of different individuals respected as peacemakers and begs for their help. If they offer it, the peacemakers visit the victim's family: "We are asked by the offender and his family to come and pay you a visit in order to have the honor of offering their repentance and to express their sorrow for what has happened and to ask you to be kind—to have a great deal of honor on your own part and to let us take the case into our hands and see how we can help to restore peace between you" (Jabbour 1997, p. 31).

A wise old man is asked in an ancient Arab story, "How do you make peace between people?" The old man answers, "If a bad man and a good man quarrel, I take from the good man and give to the bad man." Then he is asked, "What if it is two bad men who quarrel?" "If it is two bad men," he replies, "then I take from myself and give to both of them" (Jabbour 1997, p. 45). Elias Jabbour then goes on to tell the story from his hometown of women from the family of a murdered man who poured his ashes over the heads of a delegation of peacemakers. "You have the right to do that. Go on, go on," one peacemaker responded. "You are angry? Don't throw it on your enemy—throw it on us. We will take the anger on ourselves."

Accepting the anger of victims with love no matter what they do, of peacemakers sacrificing themselves to absorb that anger, may bring victims to a state of grace. Kay Pranis draws a conceptual parallel for us to consider with Western restorative conferences: "The coordinator not being paid helps make the victim/offender/family feel more worthy."

When the settlement between the families is brokered, it will normally include *diya* (blood money) to "redeem the blood." The peacemaker says, "It's not the price of your man, for there is no price for a human life" (Jabbour 1997, p. 41). The money is symbolic of priceless blood.

When all details of the peace between the two families are negotiated, a process that may take more than a year, the beautiful ceremony of the Sulha occurs. A leader of the victim's family ties a knot in a white flag of peace and gives this flag to the offender, who carries it, surrounded by the peacemakers, as he moves along a line of the victim's family, shaking the hand of each. Community leaders then each make knots in the white flag to symbolize a peace that cannot be untied. Speeches of reconciliation are made by both the victim's and the offender's family. Often the victim family will return the *diya*. Then the mayor or other notable will pronounce something like: "Thank you. You two families were kind and very generous to accept this, and now we are going to open a new chapter . . ." (Jabbour 1997, p. 54). The victim family then takes the offender's family for a cup of bitter coffee. The final step is that the offender's family invites the victim's family to share a meal with them. When all goes well, the violence has become an opportunity to bring a community closer together through each understanding the suffering of the other.

our notions of freedom, democracy, and community, as we will see in chapters 4 through 8.

Restorative justice has been the dominant model of criminal justice throughout most of human history for perhaps all the world's peoples. A decisive move away from it came with the Norman Conquest of much of Europe at the end of the Dark Ages (Van Ness 1986, p. 66; Weitekamp 1998).[1] Transforming crime into a matter of fealty to and felony against the king, instead of a wrong done to another person, was a central part of the monarch's program of domination of his people. Zehr (1995, p. 99) points to the irony that the origins of many of the words of contemporary retributive discourse may have had rather more restorative origins concerning civil wrongs: "The Greek *pune* refers to an exchange of money for harm done. Similarly, *guilt* may derive from the Anglo-Saxon *geldan*, which, like the German word *Geld*, refers to payment." In some parts of Europe where kings were weaker, restorative justice survived the medieval period (see Box 1.2). An important moment in the institutionalizing of restorative ideas was the development in the late sixth century by Celtic monks of a new manner of reconciliation with God—private penance with auricular (told privately in the ear) confession. The penitentials heightened notions of personal responsibility for crime and tackled the ancient idea that failure to exact vengeance was a matter of shame if a member of one's family had been wronged. Continuation of blood feuds became a matter for confession and penance. Specific restorative penances were also instituted. For example, a master who raped his slave was required in certain cases to make amends by freeing the woman from slavery (Rouche 1987, p. 530).

Beyond the parts of the globe ruled by European kings (among the Indigenous peoples of the Americas, Africa, Asia, and the Pacific), restorative traditions persisted into modern times (as did the retributive practices of blood feuds), remaining today as a resource of cultural diversity that can be drawn upon by European peoples whose justice traditions have been more homogenized and impoverished by central state power (see Box 1.3). So in 2001 we saw white South Africans embrace a new youth justice bill that in its preamble set the Indigenous restorative notion of *ubuntu*—the idea that our humanity is relationally tied to the humanity of those we live with—as the fundamental objective of the legislation. *Ubuntu* is the notion that enabled Nelson Mandela to construe even the supporters of apartheid as inextricably its victims. Those who think such African ideas of limited relevance in the West might pause to consider the irony that Abraham Lincoln reinvented his people's identity at Gettysburg with the nation-building idea that all Americans, North and South, black and white, must now transcend their suffering together as victims of slavery (see chapter 6).

While restorative justice may have been the dominant model of justice, it simplifies too much to say that restorative justice remained the dominant practice in societies beyond the direct rule of European kings. Most premodern societies sustained side-by-side restorative traditions and retributive traditions that were in many ways more brutal than modern retributivism. In early medieval Europe, for example, castration was a common modality of private justice against wrongdoers, one that the

Box 1.2: Celtic Persistence with the Restorative

Traditional Scottish disputing retained a reparative character until well into the nineteenth century. It is ironic that a place so near the heart of the British Empire should have been one of the last places to have its restorative traditions crushed by formally retributive state law. Historians seem to think restorative traditions were sustained later in Scotland than in England or on the Continent because Scotland was a place where kings were weak and local kin networks strong. Ian Whyte (1995) in *Scotland before the Industrial Revolution* tells us that for serious crimes, "Settlements often involved formal public reconciliations as part of a religious service and sometimes a marriage between opposing families to try and cement the peace" (p. 217). The reason for reconciliation being highly public was to lock kin in to ending a blood feud.

Jenny Wormwald (1980) documents the widespread sixteenth-century Scottish practice of contractual obligations to submit differences between and within kin groups to "wyss [wise] freindis" or "by siche [sight] of frendis or lawe as they think expedient" (p. 72). Even murder was standardly dealt with by the payment of compensation, apology, masses for the soul of the dead, and pilgrimages. In one case in 1554, William Chalmer of Leidcreif could not pay compensation for a murder he had committed because he had been bankrupted by lawsuits. Instead he offered the kin of the victim his bond of manrent, promising allegiance and service to the family for life. Second, his son and cousin were promised to marry the daughter and sister of his victim, without dowry. The second compensation was the key one, as Wormwald explains: "It was fundamental to the system of compensation that when crime was committed, what mattered was not punishment as retribution or deterrent, but reparation in a form which would as far as possible restore the *status quo* which the crime had upset. In this case Chalmer had deprived his victim's daughter and sister of their natural protector, the head of their family. It was now his responsibility to redress that loss by making provision for them" (p. 74). If the actual outcome seems bizarre to us today—marrying the son of the murderer to the daughter of his victim—the principle of restoration and publicly ending bitterness that can foment further violence should still make sense.

According to Wormwald, all the Stewart kings except James III believed that "the most effective justice was still primarily local justice, and that compromise and compensation might be a better answer to crime than a penal code" (p. 79). Better to secure a "lettre of slanis" than to take a serious crime to the courts in Edinburgh for a state-imposed solution, especially when securing the king's peace without the knowledge of the kin of a slain man meant that the kin still had a right of vengeance. The lettre of slanis was issued by the kin of the victim, stating that full and acceptable assythment had been made. *Slanis* is often thought to derive from the Anglo-Saxon *slean*, meaning "to slay." But Wormwald points out that Irish Celtic origins are more likely, *slan* and its variants "signifying health, safety, wholeness; spiritual salvation" (p. 62). In short, the Celtic institution has a profoundly restorative meaning.

Box 1.3: *The Nanante*

An Afghan criminologist at the University of Edinburgh, A. Ali Serisht, pointed out after the publication *of Crime, Shame and Reintegration* (Braithwaite 1989) that the Pushtoon, the largest ethnic group in Afghanistan, had an institution called Nanante similar to the conferencing notion I discussed in that book. The Nanante is a ceremony in which the criminal offender brings flour and other food and kills a sheep for a community feast. Often this will be held at the victim's house, where the victim will participate in cooking the food the offender brings. At the ceremonial part of the event, the offender will not be told that he is bad and in need of reform, but rather that "you have done an injustice to this person." At the same time the offender will be assured that "you are one of us and we accept you back among us." The police and courts have virtually no presence in communities that rely on the Nanante.

Christian church resisted. Even in the eighth century Charlemagne was finding it difficult to stamp out castration by imposing heavier fines for engaging in the practice (Rouche 1987, p. 456). Long before the Inquisition, church leaders were among those who sought to secure their power through retributive affliction on the bodies of their flock, as in the ninth-century case of the bishop of Le Mans, who was so unhappy with his priests that he had them castrated (Rouche 1987, p. 498). Indeed the canon law constructed in Bologna on the rediscovery of Roman law from the twelfth century laid the foundations for state laws that formally shifted criminal law away from its restorative framework. It was the Church that established prosecution as a central authority to assert its will and crush heresy. The barbarism of the Inquisition was justified because crime was committed not against a victim but against the moral order of the Church. Early Christian practice that had emphasized forgiveness of wrongdoing, reconciliation, and redemption began to lose ground (Zehr 1995, p. 113). The tug-of-war between restorative Christian teachings and insecure rulers who sought to signify their power through vivid displays of inscribing their power on the bodies of felons increasingly favored horrific corporal punishment in early modern times (Foucault 1977). Elsewhere I have hypothesized from the historical literature five stages in the history of Western regulation:

1. A pre-state stage where restorative justice and banishment are dominant
2. A weak state stage where corporal and capital punishment dominate
3. A strong state stage where professional police and penitentiaries dominate
4. A Keynesian welfare state stage where new therapeutic professions such as social work colonize what becomes probation-prison-parole
5. A contemporarily evolving new regulatory state phase of community and corporate policing (with a revived restorative justice) (Braithwaite 2001)

However, in that essay I go on to find that this rather complex sequence, while identifying some important substantive shifts, is in fact too simple. For our purposes here the important point to note is a late modern revival of restorative justice that has its deepest roots in a shift from most regulatory activities having individuals and their bodies as their objects to a world where more of the wrongdoing is done by organizations that are regulated in a mostly restorative fashion.

THE RISE OF A NEW SOCIAL MOVEMENT FOR RESTORATIVE JUSTICE

Interest in restorative justice for individual wrongdoers rekindled in the West from the establishment of an experimental victim-offender reconciliation program in 1974 in Kitchener, Ontario (Peachey 1989). Umbreit (1998) reported that by the mid-1990s there were at least 300 of these programs in North America and over 500 in Europe. By 2000 at the United Nations Congress on the Prevention of Crime and Treatment of Offenders, the Canadian delegation was claiming that there were 400 restorative justice programs in Canada alone.

The 1990s saw the New Zealand idea of family group conferences spread to many countries, including Australia, Singapore, the United Kingdom, Ireland, South Africa, the United States, and Canada, adding a new theoretical vitality to restorative justice thinking. Canadian First Nations' notions of healing circles (James 1993) also acquired wide influence, as did the Navajo justice and healing ceremony (Yazzie and Zion 1996). Less visible was the rich diversity of African restorative justice institutions such as the Nanante. By the 1990s these various programs came to be conceptualized as restorative justice. Bazemore and Washington (1995) and Van Ness (1993) credit Albert Eglash (1975) with first articulating restorative justice as a restitutive alternative to retributive and rehabilitative justice. As a result of the popularizing work of North American and British activists like Howard Zehr (1985, 1995), Mark Umbreit (1985, 1994), Kay Pranis (1996), Daniel Van Ness (1986), Tony Marshall (1985), and Martin Wright (1982) during the 1980s, and the new impetus after 1989 from New Zealand judges such as Mick Brown and Fred McElrea and Australian police, notably Terry O'Connell and northern police leaders converted by O'Connell, such as Thames Valley's Sir Charles Pollard, restorative justice became the emerging social movement for criminal justice reform of the 1990s (Daly and Immarigeon 1998). Since 1995, two organizations, Ted Wachtel's (1997) Real Justice in the United States and John McDonald and David Moore's Transformative Justice Australia have offered training in conferencing to thousands of people worldwide. An evaluation research community also emerged in association with the social movement. This community is much more dominated by Belgians, Germans, Austrians, and Canadians, though Burt Galaway and Joe Hudson (1975) in Minnesota and Canada were the early and persistent role models of this research community. During the 1990s Lode Walgrave, Alison Morris, Gabrielle Maxwell, Kathy Daly, Heather Strang, and Lawrence Sherman were particularly important early leaders of traditions of critical yet constructive research. Even more important are the many local program developers and

Box 1.4: *Postimprisonment Restorative Justice*

"Danny was 15 years old. Late one evening he left home with a can of spirits and a box of matches and set fire to the school library. He had taken great care to see that no people would come to harm, but the damage amounted to £26,000, and the library was out of action for several weeks.

Six days later Danny walked into the police station, saying he wanted to "get something off my chest." His parents were invited to a formal interview where he confessed; he said that he had been worried about forthcoming exams and thought that disrupting the library might buy him more time. He said that he had confessed voluntarily because he realized the damage he had caused and the impact on other people, and was full of guilt and remorse.

Before the case came to the Crown Court, a psychiatrist reported that Danny's behavior could be attributed to acute adolescent depression. Danny was sentenced to two years in a young offenders institution—a shorter sentence than he would have received otherwise, because he had no previous convictions and had given himself up. Just afterward, he commented, "Well, if I've learnt anything from all this, then it's not to tell anyone if I do something wrong!"

He wanted to give an explanation of what he had done, and he was being ridiculed and bullied in the prison for having confessed. Meanwhile, the headmaster had unanswered questions but also wanted to say directly to Danny that it was not the wish of the school that he be sent to prison. Danny's parents, too, were struggling to come to terms and wanted to express a sense of shared responsibility. After several visits to each of the parties, it was agreed that they should meet. The conference took place at the school and brought together Danny (who had been granted special leave from the prison), his parents, one of his friends, the headmaster, and the mediator. The librarian and a prison officer were invited but did not attend. The conference lasted for over two hours: they talked about how people had been affected by the crime, Danny answered questions and described his regret and remorse, and forgiveness was expressed. The head was very moved by Danny's account; after the meeting he walked with his hand on Danny's shoulder to the library building, which had been rebuilt, so that Danny could see the scars that had been healed, and said, "Now we all have to make sure that you can heal from this experience." Danny's father, walking behind them, said, "To be honest with you I couldn't see that this would do any good, and have wondered if it might make things worse . . . but isn't it wonderful to see those two chatting away . . . like the best of friends."

Source: Case notes from Guy Masters in Wright 1999, pp. 187–88

evaluators steering new tributaries that give restorative justice its vitality. It is this localism that makes the restorative movement to justice as jazz is to music.

During the 1980s, there was also considerable restorative justice innovation in the regulation of corporate crime (Rees 1988; Braithwaite 1995b). Clifford Shearing's (1997, p. 12) historical analysis is more about governmentalities of post-Fordist capitalism than village moots: "Restorative justice seeks to extend the logic that has informed mediation beyond the settlement of business disputes to the resolution of individual conflicts that have traditionally been addressed within a retributive paradigm. . . . In both a risk-oriented mentality of security [actuarialism] and a restorative conception of justice, violence loses its privileged status as a strategy to be deployed in the ordering of security." This is a theme I will return to in chapter 8.

The next section of this chapter seeks to conceptualize what restorative justice is against the background of these histories. The final section outlines my engagement with restorative processes in business regulation (nursing homes, corporate crime) and in Asia and the Pacific in an effort to give the reader a grounded feel for restorative justice and the distinctive biography I bring to it.

What Is Restorative Justice, and Why Is It Beginning to Take Off?

Restorative justice is most commonly defined by what it is an alternative to. Juvenile justice, for example, is seen as seesawing back and forth during the past century between a justice and a welfare model, between retribution and rehabilitation. Restorative justice is touted as a long-overdue third model or a new "lens" (Zehr 1995), a way of hopping off the seesaw, of heading more consistently in a new direction while enrolling both liberal politicians who support the welfare model and conservatives who support the justice model.

The appeal of restorative justice to liberals is a less punitive justice system. The appeal to conservatives is its strong emphasis on victim empowerment, on empowering families (as in "family group conferences"), on sheeting home responsibilities, and on fiscal savings as a result of the parsimonious use of punishment. When restorative justice is applied to white-collar crime, pro-business politicians also tend to find the approach more appealing than a retributive approach to business wrongdoing. Every one of these bases of political appeal is subject to horrible perversions, as will be described in chapter 5.

In New Zealand, the country with the most developed programmatic commitment to restorative justice, the mainstream conservative and social democratic parties have been joined by Christian pro-family parties of the Right in their support for restorative justice. In New Zealand (Maxwell and Morris 1993) and Australia (Moore with Forsythe 1995), the evidence is surprising on how supportive of restorative justice can be the police, that traditional ally of law-and-order politicians. The strongest opposition has come from lawyers, including some judges, under the influence of well-known critiques of the justice of informal processing of crime (see chapter 5). At the same time, in both New Zealand and Canada, judicial leadership has been at the vanguard of restorative justice reform. In 2001, the Lord Chief Justice of England became a public supporter of restorative justice.

In the 1990s, restorative justice became a unifying banner, sweeping up various traditions of justice as "making amends" (Wright 1982); reconciliation (Dignan 1992; Marshall 1985; Umbreit 1985); peacemaking (Pepinsky and Quinney 1991); redress (De Haan 1990); relational justice (Burnside and Baker 1994); transformative justice (Morris 1995; Moore with Forsythe 1995, p. 253); and republican justice (Braithwaite and Pettit 1990). During the same period, similar ideas were also being developed by feminist abolitionists (Meima 1990) and in other feminist analyses that emphasized denunciation of the harm and help for victims as more central than punishment (Lacey 1988, pp. 193–94; Harris 1991; Braithwaite and Daly 1994; Roach 1999; Coker 1999). Feminist thinking about crime has been a dialectic of Portia (an ethic of justice) and Persephone (an ethic of care; Heidensohn 1986), out of which some feminists want Portia and Persephone each to check the excesses of the other (Masters and Smith 1998).

The most influential text of the restorative tradition has been Nils Christie's (1977), which defined the problem of criminal justice institutions "stealing conflicts" from those affected. Centuries earlier the philosophies of New Zealand Maori (Pratt 1996), Native American (Krawll 1994; Aboriginal Corrections Policy Unit 1997a), Christian (Van Ness 1986), and Japanese/Confucian/Buddhist (Haley 1996; Masters and Smith 1998) restorative justice became the sources of the deepest influences on the contemporary social movement.

Paul McCold (1997) convened a Delphi process on behalf of the Working Party on Restorative Justice of the Alliance of NGOs on Crime Prevention and Criminal Justice to see if these disparate strands of the emerging alternative might settle on a consensual conception of restorative justice. A Delphi process iteratively solicits expert opinion, in this case on the best way to define restorative justice. The consensus was not overwhelming. The most acceptable working definition was offered by Tony Marshall: "Restorative justice is a process whereby all the parties with a stake in a particular offence come together to resolve collectively how to deal with the aftermath of the offence and its implications for the future." This definition does stake out a shared core meaning of restorative justice. Its main limitation is that it does not tell us who or what is to be restored. It does not define core values of restorative justice, which are about healing rather than hurting, moral learning, community participation and community caring, respectful dialogue, forgiveness, responsibility, apology, and making amends (see Nicholl 1998). I take those who have a "stake in a particular offence" to mean primarily the victim(s), the offender(s), and affected communities (which includes the families of victims and offenders). So restorative justice is about restoring victims, restoring offenders, and restoring communities (Bazemore and Umbreit 1994; Brown and Polk 1996). One answer to the "What is to be restored?" question is whatever dimensions of restoration matter to the victims, offenders, and communities affected by the crime. Stakeholder deliberation determines what restoration means in a specific context.

Some have suggested dimensions of restoration that are found to be recurrently important in restorative justice processes. For example, I have defined the following dimensions of restoration as important from a republican perspective: restoring property loss, restoring injury, restoring a sense of security, restoring dignity, restoring a sense of empowerment, restoring deliberative democracy, restoring harmony based on a feeling that justice has been done, and restoring social support (Braithwaite 1996).

RESTORATIVE VALUES

The process idea of restorative justice as a method of bringing together all stakeholders in an undominated dialogue about the consequences of an injustice and what is to be done to put them right is important. But so is the idea of restorative justice as an alternative that has a very different values framing than punitive justice. A perfect restorative process in which all stakeholders have their say can result in an undominated democratic decision of the conference to impose an extremely punitive outcome. An approach that is impoverished from the perspective of a process definition of restorative justice—for example, mediation between a single offender and victim by shuttle diplomacy (without meeting face-to-face)—might result in a richer result in terms of restorative values such as apology, repairing of harm, forgiveness, and reconciliation. In evaluating how restorative a program is, we need to analyze both the restorativeness of its processes and its values.

My argument in this book will be that in certain respects restorative values must trump restorative process, but in other respects restorative process should trump restorative values. I use republican normative theory (Braithwaite and Pettit 1990) to specify what these different contexts are. From this republican perspective, the first thing we must say is that just as it is dangerous to allow a court to impose a punishment beyond the maximum allowed by law, so it should be forbidden for a restorative justice process to impose a punishment beyond that which would be imposed by the courts for that kind of wrongdoing. If there is not an upper constraint on the punishment that can be imposed in a democracy, then citizens cannot be free in a republican sense. They live in fear of the tyranny of the majority. This constraint imposes no limits on mercy, however, which is in fact a republican virtue, as it is according to most of the world's great religions. So there is no problem with properly constituted restorative justice processes imposing lesser punishments than those courts would impose. In chapters 4 and 5 it will be argued that in fact restorative justice processes should be constrained by all the rights that are foundational to liberal legalism.

The sphere in which restorative process should trump restorative values is where the outcome of the restorative process involves no breach of fundamental rights. We might disapprove of a conference or circle that decides on an unreasonably punitive outcome that is unforgiving and does nothing to repair the harm suffered by victims. But so long as that punishment is not cruel or degrading and does not exceed in quantum what the courts allow, a republican must accept the decision of the conference. The analogy is to democratic elections. When the people elect a tyrant who will undermine democratic values, the republican obligation is not to take up arms but to work for overthrow of the tyrant at the next election and to constrain the tyrant while in power to comply with the Constitution. When we say that a civic republican must accept the decision of a restorative process to flout restorative values, that does not mean that she should be silent about the decision. On the contrary, her obligation is to speak out on why she thinks the decision of this conference or circle was wrong, while defending its right to make it.

I have said that fundamental human rights should set legal limits on what restorative processes are allowed to do. But I also suspect that UN human rights instruments can give quite good guidance on the values restorative justice processes ought to observe. Integrating the rights-constraining and values-guiding requirements for restorative justice under the banner of UN human rights instruments might make for simplicity. It also might make for decent and practical global social movement politics for the movement for restorative justice. This is because while no one thinks these UN rights are perfect, they are the distillation of decades of deliberation in which all nations have participated to build a consensual foundation.

The first clause of the preamble of the Universal Declaration that most states have ratified is "Whereas recognition of the inherent dignity and of the equal and inalienable rights of all members of the human family is the foundation of freedom, justice and peace in the world." Obviously freedom, justice and peace have a lot of appeal to someone who values republican freedom to frame the pursuit of justice and peacemaking in restorative justice. Equally, there is appeal to those like Amartya Sen (1999) and Martha Nussbaum (1995), who value freedom in the Aristotelian sense of freedom to achieve capabilities for human flourishing. On their view consensus around a determinate conception of the good at a high level of generality should be developed from "reasonable procedures" (Nussbaum 1995, p. 74). Nussbaum's "thick, vague conception of the good" requires "rich sensitivity to the concrete context, to the characters of the agents and their social situation" 1995, (p. 94). Citizens are left a lot of latitude to specify concretely how to make sense of the thick, vague and "ever-revisable" (p. 107) conception of the good. In all these senses, freedom as nondomination and freedom as capability for human functioning can be seen as complementary though not mutually exhaustive. They both mean that citizens can make a lot of contextual sense of the highly general yet determinate vision of the good in international human rights.

In its thirty articles the Universal Declaration defines a considerable number of slightly more specific values and rights that seem to cover many of the things we look to restore and protect in restorative justice processes. These include a right to protection from having one's property arbitrarily taken (Article 17), a right to life, liberty, and security of the person (Article 3), a right to health and medical care (Article 25), and a right to democratic participation (Article 21).

From the restorative justice advocate's point of view, the most interesting article is the fifth: "No one shall be subjected to torture or to cruel, inhuman or degrading treatment or punishment." Of course, all states have interpreted Article 5 in a most permissive and unsatisfactory way from a restorative justice point of view. The challenge for restorative justice advocates is to take the tiny antipunitive space this article creates in global human rights discourse and expand its meaning over time so that it increasingly acquires a more restorative interpretation (see Power 2000). This is precisely how successful NGO activists have globalized social justice agendas in many other arenas—starting with a platitudinous initial rights and values framework and injecting progressively less conservative and more specific meanings into that framework agreement over time.

We can already move to slightly more specific and transformative aspirations within human rights discourse by moving from the Universal Declaration of 1948 to the less widely ratified International Covenant on Economic, Social and Cultural Rights of 1976 and the International Covenant on Civil and Political Rights of 1966. The former, for example, involves a deeper commitment to "self-determination" and allows in a commitment to emotional well-being under the limited rubric of a right to mental health. The Second Optional Protocol of the Covenant on Civil and Political Rights of 1989 includes a commitment of parties to abolish the death penalty, something restorative justice advocates would regard an essential specific commitment. Equally most restorative justice advocates would agree with all the values and rights in the United Nations Declaration on the Elimination of Violence against Women of 1993 and the Declaration of Basic Principles of Justice for Victims of Crime and Abuse of Power adopted by the General Assembly in 1985. The latter includes some relevant values not so well traversed in other human rights instruments such as "restoration of the environment" (Article 10), "compassion" (Article 4), "restitution" (various articles), and "redress" (Article 5) and includes specific reference to "restoration of rights" (Article 8) and "informal mechanisms for the resolution of disputes, including mediation, arbitration and customary justice or indigenous practices," which "should be utilized where appropriate to facilitate conciliation and redress for victims" (Article 7).

So my proposal for a starting framework for a debate on the content of restorative justice values (and standards for evaluation and peer review) is as follows.

1. *Restorative justice programs should be evaluated according to how effectively they deliver restorative values, which include:*

    Respect for the fundamental human rights specified in the Universal Declaration of Human Rights, the International Covenant on Economic, Social and Cultural Rights, the International Covenant on Civil and Political Rights and its Second Optional Protocol, the United Nations Declaration on the Elimination of Violence Against Women and the Declaration of Basic Principles of Justice for Victims of Crime and Abuse of Power.

2. *Restorative values include the following values to be found in the international human rights agreements listed in number 1:*

    Restoration of human dignity
    Restoration of property loss
    Restoration of injury to the person or health

Restoration of damaged human relationships
Restoration of communities
Restoration of the environment
Emotional restoration
Restoration of freedom
Restoration of compassion or caring
Restoration of peace
Restoration of empowerment or self-determination
Restoration of a sense of duty as a citizen

As a list of specific restorative values this is unsatisfactorily incomplete, for example, in the noninclusion of the crucial healing values of apology, mercy, and forgiveness, which are nowhere to be found as values in these UN documents. I have argued that these are emergent values of restorative processes, not values we should actively seek to persuade citizens to honor in restorative processes (Braithwaite, forthcoming).

Many will find these values vague, lacking specificity of guidance on how decent restorative practices should be run. Yet standards must be broad if we are to avert legalistic regulation of restorative justice, which is at odds with the philosophy of restorative justice. What we need is deliberative regulation where we are clear about the values we expect restorative justice to realize. Whether a restorative justice program is up to standard is best settled in a series of regulatory conversations (Black, 1998) with peers and stakeholders rather than by rote application of a rule book.

The social movement for restorative justice is so young that it is premature for anyone to have settled views on what should be conceived as restorative values. There has simply not been enough time for sifting through competing views, for the kind of "listening project" that Harry Mika and Howard Zehr with funding from the Open Society Institute, currently are conducting with victims groups across the United States.

I simply want to emphasize one distinction that seems important in this values debate. There are values that we ought to urge participants in restorative justice processes to honor. Respectful listening is an example. But there are other important values where we do not ask anyone to pursue them directly, yet we hope that restorative processes can be designed so that indirectly these values will be realized. Forgiveness is the prime example. Many of us believe that if we can create spaces that give victims an opportunity to discover how they might bring themselves to forgive, this is the most important thing we can do to promote the healing of both the victims themselves and of those who hurt them. Yet it is wrong to ask victims to forgive and very wrong to expect it of them. Forgiveness is a gift victims can give. We destroy its power as a gift by making it a duty. Mercy is another value of this type. In a different way remorse on the offender side has the same quality. Remorse that is demanded is remorse that is destroyed. Creating spaces where wrongdoers might be persuaded of the need for remorse is a good institutional objective. Demanding, coercing, or even expecting remorse or apology may be a bad objective.

The most fraught issue in the values debate is whether values such as retribution, just deserts, and fair punishment should be accommodated in a restorative justice framework. Many of the most distinguished restorative justice thinkers think they should. My own inclination is to think they should not. While all societies seem to have both restorative and retributive values and practices, and while a good case can be made that both have been necessary to the survival of peoples historically (see chapter 6), in this book I argue that in the conditions of late modernity our retributive values are more a hindrance to our survival and flourishing than a help. Hence restorative justice should be explicitly about a values shift from the retributive/punitive to the restorative. Retributive emotions are natural, things we all experience and things that are easy to understand from a biological point of view. But, on this view, retribution is in the same category as greed or gluttony; biologically they once helped us to flourish, but today they are corrosive of human health and relationships. The contrary view is that a more rationalist conception of retribution can be reconciled with restoration, however, and indeed must be if restorative justice is to be a pragmatic program (Daly and Immarigeon 1998; Van Ness and Strong 1997, pp. 27–28).

BROADENING OUR VISION OF RESTORATIVE JUSTICE

While most of the writing on restorative justice focuses on the comparatively small crimes of juvenile delinquents, in this book I emphasize its relevance to adult crime as well, including war crimes and crimes at the commanding heights of business power (as in corporate restorative justice) and political power (as in Archbishop Desmond Tutu's Truth and Reconciliation Commission in South Africa, which he explicitly saw as a restorative justice process). On this view, organizations like Transcend that specialize in peacemaking training for international violence are part of the social movement for restorative justice (see www.transcend.org).

Most restorative justice advocates came to the approach through juvenile crime as a result of evidence of the failures of the welfare and justice models. The path that led me and a number of my colleagues who are experts in corporate crime to restorative justice is quite different and instructive. Many young criminologists began to study white-collar crime after Watergate to resurrect Edwin Sutherland's (1983) project. We wanted to document systematically how the crimes of the powerful were unpunished. What we found, in effect, was that the regulation of corporate crime in most countries was rather restorative. The reasons for this were far from ennobling, being about corporate capture combined with high costs of complex corporate crime investigations that states were unwilling to pay. Nevertheless, some of us began to wonder whether we were wrong to see our mission as making corporate crime enforcement more like street crime enforcement through tougher sanctions.[2] Instead we began to wonder whether street crime enforcement might be more effective if it were more like corporate criminal enforcement.

In my case, engagement with restorative approaches to corporate crime was entangled with my active engagement with social movement politics—particularly the consumer movement, but other social movements as well. In turn, my engagements with regulatory agencies—concerned with nursing homes, occupational health and safety, antitrust, environment, consumer protection, tax, and affirmative action—were as much connected to my history as an NGO activist as with a research background in these domains. I will now describe four examples of restorative justice praxis to open up an understanding of the interface among activism, theoretical innovation, and evaluation: nursing home regulation, Asian community policing, trade practices enforcement, and restorative justice conferences.

Nursing Home Regulation

Valerie Braithwaite, Toni Makkai, Diane Gibson, David Ermann, Ann Jenkins, and I became involved in evaluating nursing home regulation before the Australian federal government took it over from state governments in 1988. Over the next six years we became the government's main consultants in this area. Prior to the change, regulation had consisted of specifying quality of care inputs and prosecuting breaches criminally when enforcement action was required. Since 1988 the move away from the criminal model has been almost total (in our view, it went too far) apart from spectacular cases where multiple deaths from neglect or abuse occurred.

In a radical shift from prescriptive regulation, the old rule books were thrown out and replaced with thirty-one outcome standards (contrast over a thousand standards in most U.S. states) settled consensually between the industry and major stakeholders such as consumer groups, unions, and aged care interests. The new regulatory process was dialogic. While a certain amount of time was spent auditing care plans, quality audit reports, and other records, government inspectors spent more time talking to residents and staff about how the quality of care could be improved. This was a shift to a resident-centered process (victim-centered, in criminal justice discourse); an evaluation showed that this could work, residents could be empowered dialogically, even in nursing homes with the sickest residents (Braithwaite and Makkai 1993). Performance against each of the thirty-one standards was ultimately discussed at a conference of the inspection team and management to which representatives of owners, staff, residents, and relatives were also invited. Occasionally the elected representatives of the residents' committee would invite someone from an outside advocacy group to attend. These functioned in ways quite similar to the family group conferences for juvenile offenders discussed later.

The final evaluation report concluded from a variety of types of data that the new regulatory regime had improved both quality of life for Australian nursing home residents and compliance with the law (Braithwaite, Makkai, Braithwaite, and Gibson 1993), notwithstanding the identification of a large number of problems. Action plans agreed upon at the exit conference to restore residents' rights to quality of care were overwhelmingly implemented, the most common reason for nonimplementation being coming up with a *better* plan subsequent to the inspection. More critically to the evaluation of restorative justice, it was also found that inspectors who treated nursing homes with trust (Braithwaite and Makkai 1994), used praise when improvements were achieved (Makkai and Braithwaite 1993b), and had a philosophy of reintegrative shaming (Makkai and Braithwaite 1994) achieved higher compliance with the standards two years later than inspectors who did not. Jenkins (1997) showed that sustaining the self-efficacy of managers for improving quality of care was critical. While defiance (participation in a business subculture of resistance to regulation) did reduce compliance (Makkai and Braithwaite 1991), disengagement was the bigger problem (V. Braithwaite et al. 1994). Strategies such as praise and avoiding stigmatization were important to sustaining self-efficacy and engagement with continuous improvement.

Hence, within a regime that improved regulatory outcomes by shifting from rule book criminal enforcement to restorative justice, the inspectors who shifted most toward restorative justice improved compliance most (those who used praise and trust more than threat, reintegrative shaming rather than tolerance or stigmatization, those who restored self-efficacy). These results will be discussed again in chapter 4, which considers the theories that predict why restorative justice might work better than punitive justice.

The biggest attraction of research in this field was that we could measure compliance with the law with far greater reliability (assessed through independent ratings by two inspectors) than can be obtained with traditional individual criminal offenses or in other areas of business regulation (Braithwaite and Braithwaite 1995). The limited support in this superior data set for some of the criminological theories that had been influential in our thinking to that point about how to design restorative justice—notably control, differential association, and subcultural theories—shaped our subsequent thinking about restorative justice theory (Makkai and Braithwaite 1991). In the face of all the evidence of the promise of a restorative yet responsively vigilant approach to nursing home regulation, a conservative government in 1997 deregulated the industry, the government inspectors lost their jobs, and Australia's nursing home residents became highly vulnerable under a poorly resourced system of privatized accreditation.

Asian Community Policing

After Brent Fisse and I did some limited fieldwork on how Japanese companies and regulators secured compliance with regulatory laws (Braithwaite and Fisse 1985), I became interested in Japanese social control more broadly. The work of many other scholars suggested that it was based rather heavily on dialogue about collective obligation and relationships as opposed to punishment. This seemed true from social control of the largest corporations (which we were studying) down to the regulation of the petty delinquencies of children in schools. As with nursing homes, Guy Masters's (1995, 1997) work shows that Japanese schools use methods of social control very similar to the family group conferences discussed later (see Box 1.5). There was plenty of degradation and punitiveness in Japanese policing as well, especially when cases move from local *koban* policing (Bayley 1976) to policing by detectives and prosecutors (Miyazawa 1992).[3] Yet it seemed to me then, and still does, that the

---

Box 1.5: Delinquency in the Japanese Classroom

"The students would then be asked by their home room teacher to explain their actions. This would often be done at the child's home in front of the parents. Finally, a meeting with all the students and parents would be arranged, and with any other people that might be involved. For instance if a fight had occurred with students from another school, or an item had been stolen, then these individuals would also be present. The Police might also attend, and make comments. In these meetings, the teachers would start by talking about the student and then the incident. Those involved would be expected to talk about the effect that it had had. The students would be expected to explain why they did it, and to apologise to everybody there. The parents would often then apologise to the injured party, as would the teachers. The students would then have a separate meeting with their home room teacher again, to discuss that meeting, and, as teachers said to me, to stress what the individual student had learnt from the situation. The more serious the incident the more meetings would be arranged . . . For these incidents there was never any specific punishment per se, just the process of the meetings . . . There was a strong feeling that students should not be given up on . . . Even with the persistent trouble makers a common comment was always that, 'This time—I think that they might learn.' . . . When talking about persistent trouble makers one teacher commented that: 'Young children make mistakes. They do bad things, but that doesn't make them bad people. Our job is to look after them when they make these mistakes, until they learn to look after themselves.' It would appear that they look after them by showing them how serious what they have done is, and how it has hurt others" (Masters 1995, pp. 27–29). Lewis (1989, p. 35) identified the following four principles from her observations of discipline in Japanese classrooms: "(1) minimising the impression of teacher control; (2) delegating control to the children; (3) providing plentiful opportunities for children to acquire a "good girl" or "good boy" identity; and (4) avoiding the attribution that children intentionally misbehave."[4]

---

restorative elements of Japanese social control are more influential and sophisticated than in the West. We have much to learn from them (Masters 1997).

In an earlier draft of *Crime, Shame and Reintegration*, I also had a section on Chinese community policing (Braithwaite 1989). I threw it in the bin because Chinese informal justice seemed to involve so much more stigmatization and punitiveness than Japanese justice. Vagg's (1998) Hong Kong data capture well the concerns that beat a path to my wastebasket. Chinese Peoples' Courts, especially as they were projected to us in the Cultural Revolution, seemed a model of how not to do restorative justice.

Yet Hong Lu's (1998) research in Shanghai shows that the most important contemporary restorative justice institution in China, *bang jiao* meetings (*bang* means "help"; *jiao* means "education" and "admonition") tend to start as rather stigmatizing encounters but to end as reintegrative ones (see also Wong 1999). Indeed *bang jiao* often follows upon stigmatization by state punishment, as in two case studies from Hong Lu's dissertation (Box 1.6).

Chinese restorative justice, in both its positive and its negative aspects, deserves more attention because China has by far the largest and most diverse programs: 155,000 local mediation committees, which accounted for over 6 million cases, compared with under 4 million cases that went to court in 1994 (Wong 1999). Many of the mediations were of family or neighbourhood disputes that were not necessarily criminal. China also is the home of Confucius (551–479 B.C.), arguably the most influential thinker about restorative justice the world has known (see Box 1.7).

From the perspective of a European republican philosophy (Braithwaite and Pettit 1990; Pettit 1997), there is much of value to draw on in Confucian thought but also much that might be dangerous. Confucian communitarianism was patriarchal and hierarchic. Perhaps a settled sense of deference was not so dangerous in a stable world where family, village, and a unitary state were the only institutions that mattered. But in a more complex world where there are many levels of government, up to the International Monetary Fund (IMF) and World Trade Organization (WTO), many cross-cutting institutions of civil society to which we belong, a world in which we and our parents are geographically mobile, we need strong, independent individuals as well as strong families and communities. Individuation is vital as a practice of socialization if individuals are to be strong enough to resist tyranny as they move from one site of domination to another in a complex world. Moreover, if we do not move away from the notion of society as a holistic unity to the notion of the separation of powers and an important place for the rule of law, a liberal-republican constitutional order, the lesson of this century's history is that we will get tyranny—"political power out of the barrel of a gun."

Yet we can read the great sweep of Chinese history as a dialectic of learning and unlearning this lesson. I refer in particular to the great historical struggle between the legalists and the Confucians, and to the dialectic between both legalism and Confucianism and the dialectic of freedom in Taoism, to the disastrous abandonment of the rule of law in the Cultural Revolution and the partial return to it since (Gernet 1982; Huang 1988).

One reason it was an intellectual mistake to scrap the China section of *Crime, Shame and Reintegration* is that the study of Chinese history may hold one key to a macrosociology of restorative justice. In the dialectic of Chinese history between the domination of Confucian and legalist ideas, a high-water mark of legalist influence was the Ch'in dynasty. What brought about the fall of the Ch'in empire in 211 B.C.

> was not the alienation and hatred of the scholar class, nor the bitter enmity of the
> surviving remnants of the aristocracy, but the growing popular discontent and mount-
> ing outrage over the cruelty of the system of punishments and the intolerable burden

Case one:

A sixteen-year-old boy was sent to a work-study school for rehabilitation because of repeated thefts. Two years later, after recommendations from his
bang jiao team and work-study school principals, he was transferred to a normal school. Too ashamed to be seen by his neighbors, he went back home
after dark every day. After his mother finally talked to the *bang jiao* team
members, the members visited his neighbors and found that they did not rid-
icule or abhor the boy but wanted to communicate with him, but did not
know how. They then discussed ways to help the boy overcome psychological barriers. A young girl suggested holding a painting exhibition at the activity center because she knew that the boy was good at painting and had won
an award. They approached the boy to ask him to decorate the room and to
collect and select a painting of his own and other paintings to be exhibited at
the room. Three weeks later, a neighborhood painting exhibition was held at
the center. All the neighborhood boys and girls, along with their parents,
were invited. The boy's work was highly praised by the neighbors. This experience has totally changed the boy. Since then, he has been heavily involved in neighborhood activities, writing stories for the newsletter and con-
tributing drawings for the bulletin boards. His mother was so thankful for the
bang jiao team and said that "without their help, my son would not be what
he is today."

Case two:

A twenty-seven-year-old young man killed his own father five years earlier
out of rage at seeing his father beating his mother very badly. He was sentenced to prison for eight years. Due to his good performance in the labor
camp, he was released after serving a five-year sentence. But his brother and
sister-in-law, along with his grandmother, did not forgive him. He slept in the
joint area of the kitchen and the bedroom. *Bang jiao* team members realized
that it was a difficult situation because of mixed feelings about the young
man, in addition to the added burden of an already crowded household.
They made frequent visits to the home and tried to persuade the family to
forgive and accept the young man. Yet, after only two weeks of his release,
he was caught stealing at the local store. When his *bang jiao* team members
arrived at the local police station, he begged them not to interfere, saying
that he would rather go back to the labor camp. After they realized that he
stole because his family members did not give him money and living neces-
sities, *bang jiao* members donated their own money to buy clothes and food
for him and persuaded local police to drop the charges. A month later, they
arranged a job for him at the community-run factory. He saved every dime

(*continued*)

of his salary to buy fruits and nutritious products for his grandmother. And during his sister-in-law's pregnancy, he spent hours upon hours taking care of her. After the birth of a baby daughter, he took care of all three generations because his brother works long hours as a truck driver. *Bang jiao* team members also volunteered their time to help out with the family. After two agonizing years, the family members were finally moved by the young man's sincerity and accepted him as a family member. They were honored with a "model family" award. The young man was grateful for the help of *bang jiao* members, saying that, without them, he probably would have committed suicide.

Source: From Hong Lu 1998

of taxes and levies imposed for the massive public works that the emperor commanded. Crime increased as did the number of those condemned, tortured, mutilated, and exiled to labor gangs. As long as the emperor was alive, fear of his powerful and demoniacal personality held the empire together; after his death all the restraints broke, and the empire exploded in rebellion. (Michael 1986, p. 66)

Today the movement of the Confucian-legalist dialectic is in the reverse direction, with the "rule of law" rebounding as a dominant value. Given the continued trampling of human rights and freedoms in China, this may be a hopeful development, yet part of it is a sharp decline of the proportion of criminal cases dealt with by mediation as opposed to criminal trials. What a pity that so few Western intellectuals are engaged with the possibilities for recovering, understanding, and preserving the virtues of Chinese restorative justice while studying how to check its abuses with a liberalizing rule of law. Whatever its rights and wrongs, the legalist-restorative contest is more central to the dynamic of Chinese history than to the histories of other nations and therefore more central to the development of a macrosociology of the fluctuating fortunes of restorative justice.

Trade Practices Enforcement

Between 1985 and 1995, as a part-time commissioner with Australia's national consumer protection and antitrust agency, I attempted with mixed success to persuade my colleagues on the Trade Practices Commission to experiment in an Australian way with the restorative principles I saw as underlying Japanese business regulation. Ironically, when the commission decided to run its boldest restorative justice conference, I made the mistake of voting against it, believing the conduct to be so serious that formal criminal charges should be laid. It involved the most widespread and serious consumer protection frauds ever to come before the agency. A number of insurance companies were implicated in systematically ripping off consumers through misrepresentations about policies that in some cases were totally useless. The worst abuses occurred in twenty-two remote Aboriginal communities, and these were

---

Box 1.7: *Confucius*

One of Confucius's best-known views is that "if the people be led by laws, and uniformity sought to be given them by punishments, they will try to avoid the punishment but have no sense of shame" (Confucius 1974, p. 16). In opposition to his contemporaries, he was against capital punishment (pp. 92–93, 98). Reciprocity, mutuality, and harmony were central to his ways of seeing.

[XXIII] Tsze-kung asked, saying, "Is there one word which may serve as a rule of practice for all one's life?" The Master said, "Is not RECIPROCITY such a word? What you do not want done to yourself, do not do to others," (p. 123).

Confucius's quest can be read in part as a search for practices of good government that enable people to understand the effects their actions have on one another and that naturally expose the virtue of the virtuous so that others will follow them. Virtue is inculcated by quiet good example rather than by denunciation.

[XXIV] Tsze-kung said, "Has the superior man his hatreds also?" The Master said, "He has his hatreds. He hates those who proclaim the evil of others" (p. 143).

Obversely, it is wise "to find enjoyment in speaking of the goodness of others" (130). For Confucius, then, shame rather than punishment is the key to social control; but shame is not something we do to wrongdoers so much as something wrongdoers discover through the respectful treatment they receive from virtuous people who manifest in the fiber of their being the example of a transparently superior way of living.

---

tackled first. Top management from the insurance company visited these communities for days on end at meetings with the victims, the local Aboriginal community council, the regulators, and local officials of the Department of Social Security in cases where useless policy premiums were being deducted from welfare checks. Some of those executives went back to the city deeply ashamed of what their company had done.

Back in Canberra, meetings were held with insurance regulators and industry associations and even with the prime minister about follow-up regulatory reforms. The plurality of participants led to a plurality of remedies from the first agreement (with Colonial Mutual Life [CML]), which voluntarily compensated 2,000 policyholders and also funded an Aboriginal Consumer Education Fund to "harden targets" for future attempts to rip off illiterate people. It conducted an internal investigation to discover failings in the company's compliance program and to identify officers responsible for the crimes. A press conference was then called to reveal the enormity of the problem. No one recognized quite how enormous it was until a police union realized that its own members were being ripped off through the practices of another company (in this case, there were 300,000 victims and a payout of at least $50 million and perhaps $100 million by the company). As a result of the CML self-investigation, eighty officers or agents of CML were dismissed, including some senior managers and one large corporate agent, Tri-Global. CML also put in place new internal compliance policies. Some procedures relating to welfare checks changed in the Department of Social Security, and there were regulatory and self-regulatory changes concerning the licensing of agents and changes to the law (Fisse and Braithwaite 1993, p. 235). This polycentric problem solving was accomplished without going to court (except with a couple of individuals who refused to cooperate with the restorative justice process). The disparate array of preventive measures was grounded in the different kinds of theories the rich plurality of players involved in this restorative justice process came up with—theories of education, deterrence, incapacitation, rehabilitation, target hardening, moral hazard, adverse publicity, law, regulation, and opportunity theory.

The cynic about restorative justice will say that the Australian insurance cases were unusually sweeping exercises in crime prevention. True, most crime prevention is more banal. Yet this process was so broad in its ramifications precisely because it was restorative. What would have happened if we had prosecuted this case criminally? At best the company would have been fined a fraction of what it actually paid out, and there would have been a handful of follow-up civil claims by victims. At worst, illiterate Aboriginal witnesses would have been humiliated and discredited by uptown lawyers, the case lost, and no further ones taken. The industry-wide extensiveness of a pattern of practices would never have been uncovered; that was only accomplished by the communitarian engagement of many locally knowledgeable actors.

Restorative Justice Conferences

In *Crime, Shame and Reintegration*, I made reference to the desirability of institutionalizing something like the restorative justice conference for criminal offenders (Braithwaite 1989, pp. 173–74). After reading this, John McDonald of the New South Wales police came to me and said this had already been done in New Zealand. Terry O'Connell showed me videotaped interviews with people like Maori chief judge of the New Zealand Youth Court, Michael Brown. These revealed that one of the rationales for restorative justice in the Maori tradition was the simultaneous communication of "shame" and "healing" or "embrace." It was a depressing revelation that what I thought was the only limited originality in *Crime, Shame and Reintegration* had been preceded by several hundred years of Polynesian oral tradition, not just in New Zealand. Indeed, I concluded that Maori ways of thinking about *whakama*, or shame, were in some important ways an advance on my own thinking. After *Crime, Shame and Reintegration* became a widely read book, many people from Africa, Melanesia, Asia, and the Americas contacted me about restorative justice conferences that were part of their tradition. I learned that the Native American healing circle seeks to institutionalize equality rather than hierarchy and "puts the problem in the center—not the person" (Pranis 1996, p. 46, quoting Melton 1995). These stories challenged assumptions I strongly held until the mid-1990s, for example, that traditional Western criminal process was superior at fact-finding with justice than restorative processes (see Box 1.8).[5]

New Zealand remained of preeminent importance, however, because it main-streamed the conferencing innovation into a Western juvenile justice system (and into the care and protection of abused and neglected children as well). The impor-tance of New Zealand was not its adoption of Maori restorative philosophies; indeed, Pakeha (non-Maori) New Zealanders tended to reject much of both the restorative and retributive aspects of Maori philosophy, initially justifying the practice of "family group conferences" in terms of a move from the welfare model to the Western justice

---

Box 1.8: Hollow Water

Healing circles in the Manitoba Ojibway community of Hollow Water began to deal with what many thought of at first as an epidemic of alcohol abuse. As citizens sat in these circles discussing the problems of individual cases, they realized in 1986 that there was a deeper underlying problem, which was that they lived in a community that was sweeping the sexual abuse of children under the carpet. Through setting up a complex set of healing circles to help one individual victim and offender after another, in the end it had been dis-covered that a majority of the citizens were at some time in their lives vic-tims of sexual abuse.[6] Most of the leading roles in this process were taken by women of Hollow Water (Bushie 1999). Fifty-two adults out of a community of 600 (Jaccoud 1998) formally admitted to criminal responsibility for sexu-ally abusing children, 50 as a result of participating in healing circles, 2 as a result of being referred to a court of law for failing to do so (Ross 1996, pp. 29–48; Lajeunesse 1993). Ross (1996, p. 36) claims that the healing cir-cles have been a success because there have been only two known cases of reoffending. Tragically, however, there has been no genuinely systematic outcome evaluation of Hollow Water.

What is more important than the crime prevention outcome of Hollow Water is its crime detection outcome. When and where has the traditional criminal process succeeded in uncovering anything approaching 52 admis-sions of criminal responsibility for sexual abuse of children in a community of just 600? Before reading about Hollow Water, I had always said that the tra-ditional criminal investigation and trial process is superior to restorative jus-tice processes for justly getting to the truth of what happened. Restorative justice processes were only likely to be superior to traditional Western crimi-nal process when there was a clear admission of guilt. The significance of Hollow Water is that it throws that position into doubt.

model! When its innovation became internationally celebrated, New Zealand wisely and more accurately reinterpreted family group conferences as restorative justice. Indeed, for all of us practice was ahead of theory, and it was well into the 1990s before the North American label *restorative justice* subsumed what had been developing elsewhere for a long time.

The way conferences work is very simple. Once wrongdoing is admitted, the offender and his or her family are asked who they would like to have attend a conference as supporters. Similarly, the victim is asked to nominate loved ones to attend. The conference is a meeting of these two communities of care. First there is a discussion of what was done and what the consequences have been for everyone in the room (the victim's suffering, the stress experienced by the offender's family). Then there is a discussion of what needs to be done to repair those different kinds of harm. A plan of action is agreed upon and signed by the offender and usually by the victim and the police officer responsible for the case. Conferencing advocates believe that asking the offender to confront the consequences of his wrongdoing (and talking them through in the presence of those who have suffered them) has a variety of positive effects in terms of taking responsibility, experiencing remorse, and offering practical help and apology to the victim and the community to right the wrong.

Beyond this common core, conferences vary from place to place in how they are run. In Australia, Wagga Wagga was the first conferencing program from 1991 and an important site of early research and development on a culturally pluralized conferencing process suitable for both Western and Australian Aboriginal cases. This R and D is being carried forward by the RISE Experiment in Canberra in which 1,300 adult and juvenile cases have been randomly assigned to conference versus court by Lawrence Sherman and Heather Strang (Sherman et al. 1998). Drunk driving, property crimes, and violent crimes are covered by the experiment.

LEARNING FROM PLURALITY

Western nations need to open themselves to learning not only from the restorative practices of their own Indigenous peoples but also from Asian, Polynesian, African, and other cultural traditions of restorative justice. Of course one reason they should do this is that they have large numbers of citizens from these other parts of the world who crave a more meaningful experience of justice. But another is that out of seeking to understand diversity in the practice of justice, we acquire a richer understanding of how justice becomes real in the lived experience of citizens. The same point applies to learning lessons from nursing home regulation on how better to regulate burglary (and vice versa). We get richer theory from a more plural inductive base. Yet that theory must be adapted and tested in a way that makes sense in a local cultural context.

This book will argue that in most cases justice works best by empowering affected communities to deal with the consequences of injustice and transform private troubles into public issues, as by advocacy of preventive measures. We will enrich crime prevention and enable healing by empowering plural deliberation about the injustice.

But what do we do when this fails, as it often will? What is our theory of when not to use restorative justice? Chapter 2 begins to develop such a theory.

NOTES

1. Barnett (1977, p. 352) cites Diamond's (1935) research as sustaining his conclusion that of the 50 to 100 tribal communities from which data are available, 73 percent call for a pecuniary penalty for homicide, while only 14 percent demand death. In Europe all the Early and Middle Codes to A.D. 1100 called for pecuniary penalties for homicide, while all of the Late Middle Codes made death the exclusive sanction for intentional homicide.
2. Critics indeed might enjoy the irony that Watergate offender Charles Colson, now of Prison Fellowship Ministries, is a prominent restorative justice advocate.
3. I am indebted to Christopher Murphy for pointing out that on the basis of his considerable observation of Japanese policing, Bayley and Miyazawa may both be right in this way, like the blind Hindus in the legend, feeling different parts of the elephant. That is, Japanese policing may be more reintegrative at the *koban* level, more stigmatizing in the hands of detectives and prosecutors.
4. On the greater commitment to restoration in Japanese versus American conceptions of justice and responsibility, the work of Hamilton and Sanders (1992) is instructive.
5. A conversation with Gale Burford about his work on conferencing family violence with Joan Pennell also has me wondering. In a third of their cases, sexual abuse of children came out during conferences. Gale said: "So violence programs that exclude sexual abuse don't really. They just say if they have sexual abuse don't talk about it or you'll be out of the program."
6. LaPrairie (1994, p. iii), in a sophisticated study of this problem from a restorative justice perspective in another context, found that 46 percent of inner-city native people in Canada had experienced child abuse. For an outline of the Hollow Water procedures for dealing with sexual abuse, see Aboriginal Corrections Policy Unit 1997b, especially pp. 221–30. At Canim Lake, the site of another innovative Canadian First Nations healing circle approach to sexual abuse, "The research showed us that up to eighty percent of our people had been sexually abused at one point in their lives" (Warhaft, Palys, and Boyce 1999, p. 171).

2

Responsive Regulation

THE BASIC IDEA OF RESPONSIVE REGULATION IS THAT GOVERNMENTS SHOULD BE RE-sponsive to the conduct of those they seek to regulate in deciding whether a more or less interventionist response is needed (Ayres and Braithwaite 1992). In particular, law enforcers should be responsive to how effectively citizens or corporations are regulating themselves before deciding whether to escalate intervention. Responsive regulation is not only something governments can do; private actors in civil society can also regulate responsively, indeed, even regulate governments responsively (Gunningham and Grabosky 1998).

Regulatory formalism is the important contrast to responsive regulation. The formalist says to define in advance which problems require which response and write rules to mandate those responses. The formalist might say, for example, that armed robbery is a very serious evil. Therefore it should always be dealt with by taking it to court, and if guilt is proven, the offender must go to jail. Responsive regulation requires us to challenge such a presumption; if the offender is responding to the detection of her wrongdoing by turning around her life, kicking a heroin habit, helping victims, and voluntarily working for a community group "to make up for the harm she has done to the community," then the responsive regulator of armed robbery will say no to the jail option.

The problem many have with responsive regulation is that it is not designed to maximize consistency in law enforcement. Indeed, the idea of responsive regulation grew from dissatisfaction with the business regulation debate—some arguing that business people are rational actors who only understand the bottom line and therefore must be consistently punished for their lawbreaking, others that business people are responsible citizens and can be persuaded to come into compliance. In different contexts there is a lot of truth in both positions. This means that both consistent punishment and consistent persuasion are foolish strategies. The hard question is how to decide when to punish and when to persuade (Braithwaite 1985). What makes the question such a difficult one is that attempts to regulate conduct do not simply succeed or fail. As we will see in chapter 4, often they backfire, making compliance with the law much worse. So the tragedy of consistent punishment of wrongdoers of a certain type is that our consistency will regularly cause us to make things worse for future victims of the wrongdoing. In business regulation circles these days, there is not much contesting of the conclusion that consistent punishment of business noncompliance would be a bad policy, that persuasion is normally the better way to go when there is reason to suspect that cooperation with attempting to secure compliance will be forthcoming. But with individual criminal offending, there are still many who defend a consistent punishment policy, even though the meta-analyses of the effects of punishment suggest that increasing our investment in expanding criminal punishment increases somewhat the reoffending of those punished (Gendreau, Goggin, and Cullen 1999).

THE REGULATORY PYRAMID

The most distinctive part of responsive regulation is the regulatory pyramid. It is an attempt to solve the puzzle of when to punish and when to persuade. At the base of the pyramid is the most restorative dialogue-based approach we can craft for securing compliance with a just law. Of course if it is a law of doubtful justice, we can expect the dialogue to be mainly about the justice of the law (and this is a good thing from a civic republican perspective). As we move up the pyramid, more and more demanding and punitive interventions in peoples' lives are involved. The idea of the pyramid is that our presumption should always be to start at the base of the pyramid, then escalate to somewhat punitive approaches only reluctantly and only when dialogue fails, and then escalate to even more punitive approaches only when the more modest forms of punishment fail. Figure 2.1 is an example of a responsive business regulatory pyramid from Ayres and Braithwaite (1992, p. 35). The regulator here escalates with the recalcitrant company from persuasion to a warning to civil penalties to criminal penalties and ultimately to corporate capital punishment—permanently revoking the company's license to operate.

The crucial point is that this is a dynamic model. It is not about specifying in advance which are the types of matters that should be dealt with at the base of the pyramid, which are the more serious ones that should be in the middle, and which are the most egregious ones for the peak of the pyramid. Even with the most serious matters—flouting legal obligations to operate a nuclear power plant safely that risks thousands of lives (see chapter 3)—we stick with the presumption that it is better to start with dialogue at the base of the pyramid. A presumption means that however serious the crime, our normal response is to try dialogue first for dealing with it, to override the presumption only if there are compelling reasons for doing do. Of course there will be such reasons at times—the man who has killed one hostage and threatens to kill another may have to be shot without a trial, the assault offender who during the criminal process vows to go after the victim again and kill her should be locked up.

As we move up the pyramid in response to a failure to elicit reform and repair, we often reach the point where finally reform and repair are forthcoming. At that point

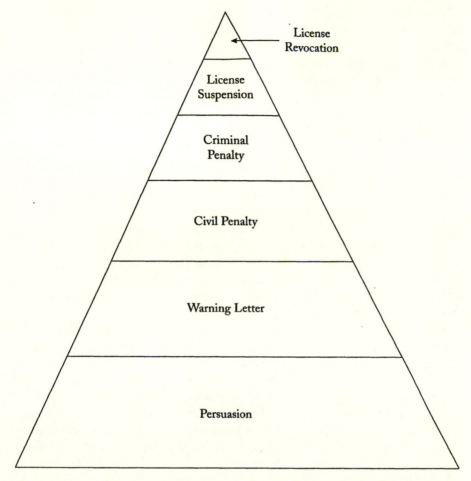

Figure 2.1   An example of a Regulatory Pyramid (from Ayres and Braithwaite 1992)

responsive regulation means that we must put escalation up the pyramid into reverse and de-escalate down the pyramid. The pyramid is firm yet forgiving in its demands for compliance. Reform must be rewarded just as recalcitrant refusal to reform following wrongdoing will ultimately result in punishment.

WHY THE PYRAMID WORKS WITH BUSINESS REGULATION

Business regulatory agencies all over the world are today deploying the idea of the responsive regulatory pyramid. It is an influential policy idea because it comes up with a way of reconciling the clear empirical evidence that sometimes punishment works and sometimes it backfires, and likewise with persuasion (Braithwaite 1985; Ayres and Braithwaite 1992). The pyramidal presumption of persuasion first gives the cheaper and more respectful option a chance to work first, and there is empirical experience in some areas of business regulation that it does work in the majority of cases. The more costly punitive attempts at control are thus held in reserve for the minority of cases where persuasion fails. Yet it is also common for persuasion to fail. When it does, the most common reason is that a business actor is being a rational calculator about the likely costs of law enforcement compared with the gains from breaking the law. Escalation through progressively more deterrent penalties will often take the rational calculator up to the point where it will become rational to comply. Quite often, however, the business regulator finds that they try restorative justice, and it fails; they try escalating up through more and more punitive options, and they all fail to deter. This happens for a number of reasons. One is the so-called deterrence trap, discussed in chapter 4, where no level of financial deterrent can make compliance economically rational. Perhaps the most common reason in business regulation for successive failure of restorative justice and deterrence is that noncompliance is neither about a lack of goodwill to comply nor about rational calculation to cheat. It is about management not having the competence to comply. The manager of the nuclear power plant simply does not have the engineering know-how to take on such a demanding level of responsibility. He must be moved from the job. Indeed, if the entire management system of a company is not up to the task, the company must lose its license to operate a nuclear power plant. So when deterrence fails, the idea of the pyramid is that incapacitation is the next port of call (see Figure 2.2).

This design responds to the fact that restorative justice, deterrence, and incapacitation are all limited and flawed theories of compliance. What the pyramid does is cover the weaknesses of one theory with the strengths of another. The ordering of strategies in the pyramid is not just about putting the less costly, less coercive, more respectful options lower down in order to save money and preserve freedom as nondomination. It is also that by resorting to more dominating, less respectful forms of

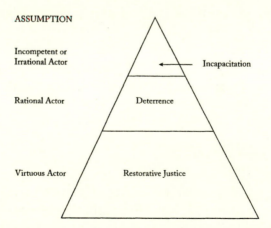

Figure 2.2   Toward an Integration of Restorative, Deterrent and Incapacitative Justice

social control only when more dialogic forms have been tried first, coercive control comes to be seen as more legitimate. As we will see in chapter 4, when regulation is seen as more legitimate, more procedurally fair, compliance with the law is more likely. Astute business regulators often set up this legitimacy explicitly. During a restorative justice dialogue over an offense, the inspector will say there will be no penalty this time, but that she hopes the manager understands that if she returns and finds the company has slipped back out of compliance again, under the rules she will have no choice but to refer it to the prosecutions unit. When the manager responds that this is understood, a future prosecution will likely be viewed as fair. Under this theory, therefore, privileging restorative justice at the base of the pyramid builds legitimacy and therefore compliance.

There is also a rational choice account of why the pyramid works. System capacity overload (Pontell 1978) results in a pretense of consistent law enforcement where in practice enforcement is spread around thinly and weakly. Unfortunately, this problem will be at its worst where crime is worst. Hardened offenders learn that the odds of serious punishment are low for any particular infraction. Tools like tax audits that are supposed to be about deterrence are frequently exercises that backfire by teaching hardened tax cheats just how much they are capable of getting away with (Kinsey 1986, p. 416). The reluctance to escalate under the responsive pyramid model means that enforcement has the virtue of being highly selective in a principled way. Moreover, the display of the pyramid itself channels the rational actor down to the base of the pyramid. Noncompliance comes to be seen (accurately) as a slippery slope that will inexorably lead to a sticky end. In effect what the pyramid does is solve the system capacity problem with punishment by making punishment cheap. The pyramid says that unless you punish yourself for lawbreaking through an agreed action plan near the base of the pyramid, we will punish you much more severely higher up the pyramid (and we stand ready to go as high as we have to). So it is cheaper for the rational company to punish themselves (as by agreeing to payouts to victims, community service, paying for new corporate compliance systems). Once the pyramid accomplishes a world where most punishment is self-punishment, there is no longer a crisis of the state's capacity to deliver punishment where it is needed. One of the messages the pyramid gives is that "if you keep breaking the law it is going to be cheap for us to hurt you because you are going to help us hurt you" (Ayres and Braithwaite 1992, chap. 2).

Paternoster and Simpson's (1996) research on intentions to commit four types of corporate crime by MBA students reveals the inefficiency of going straight to a deterrence strategy. Paternoster and Simpson found that where the MBAs held personal moral codes, these were more important than rational calculations of sanction threats in predicting compliance (though the latter were important, too). It follows that for the majority of these future business leaders, appeals to business ethics (as by confronting them with the consequences for the victims of a corporate crime) will work better than sanction threats. So it is best to try such ethical appeals first and then escalate to deterrence for that minority for whom deterrence works better than ethical appeals.

According to responsive regulatory theory, what we want is a legal system where citizens learn that responsiveness is the way our legal institutions work. Once they see the legal system as a responsive regulatory system, they know there will be a chance to argue about unjust laws (as opposed to being forced into a lower court production line or a plea bargain). But they will also see that game playing to avoid legal obligations, failure to listen to persuasive arguments about the harm their actions are doing and what must be done to repair it, will inexorably lead to regulatory escalation. The forces of law are listening, fair and therefore legitimate, but also are seen as somewhat invincible. The deterrence superiority of the active deterrence of the pyramid, as opposed to the passive deterrence of a fixed scale of penalties that are consistently imposed for different offenses, will be further developed in chapter 4.

CORRUPTING RESTORATIVE JUSTICE WITH COERCION?

In the punishment-versus-persuasion debates among business regulatory scholars, while advocates of consistent punishment argued that cynical businesses abuse offers of cooperation (which they do if cooperation is not backed up by enforcement capability), advocates of consistent persuasion argued that punishment and persuasion involve incompatible imperatives. Theorists of this second sort believe that threat and coercion undermine goodwill and therefore the trust that makes cooperative compliance work. This, indeed, can also be pointedly true. Restorative justice advocates will be reading this chapter with very much the latter concern. How can we but corrupt the restorative justice values discussed in the previous chapter if we seek to coerce them?

The first point to make is a factual one. Very few criminal offenders who participate in restorative justice processes would be sitting in the room absent a certain amount of coercion. Without their detection and/or arrest, without the specter of the alternative of a criminal trial, they simply would not cooperate with a process that puts their behavior under public scrutiny. No coercion, no restorative justice (in most cases).

The question seems not one of how to avoid coercion, but how to avoid the escalation of coercion and how to avoid threats. A paradox of the pyramid is that to the extent that we can absolutely guarantee a commitment to escalate if steps are not taken to prevent the recurrence of lawbreaking, then escalation beyond the lower levels of the pyramid will rarely occur. This is the image of invincibility making self-regulation inevitable. In contrast, when it is seen as common that there are no escalatory consequences when young offenders flout their obligations under a restorative justice process, young offenders will often flout them. When the consequences of this become sufficiently serious, criminal enforcement will be belatedly mobilized in many of these cases. Without locked-in commitment to escalation where lives are not turned around, the system capacity crisis will rebound. The fundamental resource of responsive regulation is the belief of citizens in inexorability.

This does not mean that an offender should go to court as soon as he reoffends after a conference or fails to honor his undertakings at the conference. These are normally grounds for reconvening the conference. Until we get into the area of really serious sanctions—incarceration, confiscation of assets like houses and cars—conferences have a superior capacity to escalate remedies in any case. So at least the first few rungs of most enforcement pyramids will normally be restorative justice rungs. Arguments for attendance in a drug rehabilitation program or an anger management program will become more insistent, victims will insist on greater efforts at compensation, community service hours will be increased, curfews might be imposed until behavior improves. Again the message the restorative justice conference should give is that it is better to put your best self forward at the bottom rung of the pyramid because if you don't, you will end up going through this again, and next time it will be a bigger production, and the conference will be more demanding. And, ultimately, if again and again I fail to satisfy the conference agreement, I will end up in court, which will be more demanding again.

This inexorability is the reverse of the reality of current Western justice systems. In these systems, as a result of overload, it is the offenders who wear the system down rather than the reverse. The enforcement response is to hang back on confronting lawbreaking in a credible way early on, wait until really serious cases land in your lap, and then impose through the courts the harsh punishments that the media and a frustrated public demand in egregious cases. When the young offender finally ends up in jail, she is often genuinely shocked—after years of getting away with all manner of infractions with ten-minute appearances in court and good-behavior bonds, all of a sudden prison strikes like a bolt from the blue. The whole deal seems arbitrary and illegitimate, a perception reinforced by the prison culture offenders enter.

Many wrongly see inexorability as a responsive regulatory objective that requires participants in restorative justice processes to issue threats: the police officer who says, "Next time I'll be taking you to court and you'll probably go to jail." What is required is quite the reverse. It is for conference participants to identify with the offender as someone they are working with to prevent inexorable outside forces from taking over the case and putting it on a more punitive track. Inexorability is a societal accomplishment of the legal system—under a responsive regulatory regime everyone can see that it works inexorably. It is not an accomplishment of the issuance of threats in individual cases, which will only amount to bluff if there is in fact no inexorability in the system.

Threat is counterproductive because it increases a psychological process called *reactance* (Brehm and Brehm 1981), which undermines compliance. I discuss reactance further in chapter 4. It is argued there that what is needed to achieve deterrence without reactance is societal inexorability of escalation (supporting deterrence) combined with offers of help without threat to avert that escalation—offered by others with whom one identifies (knocking out reactance). This is the way to improve compliance in a world where the impact of sanctions on compliance is the sum of a deterrence effect and a reactance effect.

Put another way, my hypothesis is that restorative justice works best with a specter of punishment in the background, threatening in the background but never threatened in the foreground. Where punishment is thrust into the foreground even by implied threats, other-regarding deliberation is made difficult because the offender is invited to deliberate in a self-regarding way—out of concern to protect the self from punishment. This is not the way to engender empathy with the victim, internalization of the values of the law and the values of restorative justice, the sequences of remorse, apology, and forgiveness that I will argue can transform lives in permanent ways. In contrast, contingent threats at best could only change lives in immediately contingent ways. The job of citizens in restorative justice is to treat offenders as worthy of trust. That is why the primary selection criterion for invitees to restorative justice conferences should be that these are the people offenders and victims nominate as those they most trust. Even though it might be trust in the shadow of the axe, there is nothing baffling about offenders actually feeling trusted in these circumstances. The fact is that it is in the nature of human beings to want to be trusted and to want to trust those they are close to. Chapter 4 will discuss some research showing that when lawbreakers believe they are treated as trustworthy by those who regulate them, they are more likely to comply with the law in future. Chapter 4 also develops a restorative theory of deterrence, which is more threatening in the background than threatened in the foreground, more active than passive, and that shows the strength of weak sanctions targeted on those with preventive capabilities.

RESTORATIVE AND RESPONSIVE REGULATION OF THE HARDEST CRIMINAL CASES

These ideas seem plausible to many with respect to business regulation or juvenile justice but not so with "hardened" adult street criminals. I happen to think the approach has a lot of potential with the most serious repeat criminal offenders, and so I will outline in some detail how it might work there. The analysis starts with three propositions:

1. Most serious common crime (e.g., burglary) is perpetrated by a small proportion of the criminal population who commit very large numbers of offenses (Kelling and Coles 1996, pp. 244–45; Kennedy 1997).
2. Competent police services have the intelligence capability to know who most of those serious repeat offenders are (Kleiman 1997, p. 4).
3. But most police services do not have the resources to act on this widespread intelligence in any serious way.

The third of these points is the system capacity problem again. If the police really want to catch someone who is known to be a serious repeat burglar, they can. They can have him followed twenty-four hours a day, and when he ultimately goes a-burgling they can catch him in the act. But twenty-four-hour surveillance is terribly expensive—four shifts of police doing nothing but pursue one property criminal until he is caught. Police would never have the resources to touch many of the known repeat offenders this way, so instead they opt for reactive policing. Every now and then one of these people gets caught in the act for more fortuitous reasons, and the police settle for grabbing these opportunities when they come to them. Intensive surveillance and serious detective work are reserved for categories of serious offending that are more limited in numbers, particularly murders, though murderers are generally not offenders who will offend again.[1]

So here is the restorative and responsive option. Assuming proposition 2 is right, the police approach each of the known serious repeat offenders of a certain type—for example, those believed to commit a lot of burglaries. The offender is approached by a police officer who, in an unthreatening but authoritative manner, says something like the following:

> My name is Constable Bloggs, and I regret to inform you that you have been targeted for the Serious Repeat Offender Program. There are only two ways you can get off this program, John. One is that as a result of the police Serious Repeat Offender group having you under intensive surveillance (taking effect now), serious offenses will be proven against you, and you will be put behind bars. The other is that you desist from crime.
>
> That is where I come in, John. My job is to be available to help you if you choose to get yourself dropped as a Serious Repeat Offender Program target. I work for the Restorative Justice Group. If you choose to work with me, I will set up a restorative justice circle of your loved ones, the people you most trust, those who care about your future. The objective of that circle will be to try to keep you out of jail, to give your life a new direction, and help you to open up new opportunities for yourself. If you genuinely convince everyone in the circle that you are going straight and will stay straight, then the circle has the power to recommend to the judge who approved putting you under surveillance that he should order that you be dropped as a Serious Repeat Offender Program target. To be convinced, the circle and the judge will normally want you to make concrete commitments. In your case, John, one of the things that would involve is your heroin habit. You see, the judge found that there was reasonable suspicion of a pattern of offending that justified your being a suitable target for special surveillance. So, between us, we have to convince the judge that this is not true. To accomplish that we would need to work together as a team with your family and closest friends.

The deepest worry about this strategy is arbitrariness or prejudice in the selection of targets. The most promising approach to limiting such abuse would be the development of criteria for independent judicial approval of targeting.

My assumption is that these police visits themselves would have a small short-term effect on crime. That is, many of the targeted citizens who were intending to commit a crime in the next twenty-four hours would pause, considering their position before doing so. Perhaps in a day or two many of them would reject the offer of working with the Restorative Justice Group. Then they would have to be targeted for intensive surveillance, though not necessarily immediately. The important thing would be for the police to mobilize resources to secure arrests of some of these people and publicize the convictions. All targeted offenders should be advised by mail of convictions of other targeted offenders when they occur, have explained to them that the arrest of this high-priority target means that there will now be more resources for surveillance on remaining targets, and be reminded of the telephone number of the Restorative Justice Group should they want to get off the target list. For this group, there should be a reduction in crime both among those arrested and among those who are not arrested but who decide to reduce their risks by reducing their offending. These reductions in offending will have been achieved at considerable cost in policing resources, however.

There can be a further escalatory element within the targeting option. Most known serious offenders are vulnerable. They commit a lot of minor offenses (like buying drugs) for which they can easily be charged, as well as a steady flow of major ones. They often breach probation or parole conditions; they often have outstanding warrants for things like failure to file a tax return or other infractions. They are accustomed to being allowed to get away with breaching parole or buying drugs because so much of that goes on that credible enforcement again confronts the system capacity problem. So the police understandably do not even try to make enforcement credible in these minor areas. However, the first arrest of targeted offenders has a new meaning as a step up the enforcement pyramid. They now realize that they are in a different category from others who buy drugs or breach parole. So targeted offenders are given another opportunity to respond to the inexorable fact that they will prove to be in a different category from other major burglars. They ponder the next rung of an enforcement pyramid that leads to prison.

Another kind of step up the enforcement pyramid can be to put temptation into the path of the target:

> [A] decoy-car program was established . . . The decoy car was a sports model chosen because of its popularity with thieves. Youths were enticed into it by leaving it running. When youths seated themselves in the car, the ignition system shut down and a remote control was used to automatically lock the door. Arrests and charges followed. (Ericson and Haggerty 1997, p. 273)

I assume that most offenders would opt for the restorative justice process. For many, perhaps most, of these, this might be a purely strategic decision. That is, it would be a decision to try to get themselves dropped as a target without desisting from crime. While it is difficult to be optimistic about these hard cases, as a result of the program some of them may listen to the emotional pleas of family members that they opt for a different life, some of them may go to a new drug rehabilitation program and kick their habit for a period, others will take up an offer of a new job found for them as a result of the engagement of a specialized job placement agency with the process. Most will not do any of these things. Many of this group will con the conference into believing that they have changed their ways when actually they have not. The process will have no impact on this group. In summary, it is hypothesized that such a restorative and responsive regulatory program would have the following effects:

All targeted offenders	Initial twenty-four-hour fall in crime while they consider their position
Those who refuse restorative justice and are not convicted	Modest reduction in crime as a result of increased caution while targeted
Those who refuse restorative justice and are convicted	Significant reduction in crime
Those who accept restorative justice and con the conference	No impact on crime
Those who accept restorative justice and are reformed	Major impact on crime
Those who accept restorative justice, try to reform, but fail	Only short-term reduction in crime

Clearly, if most offenders opted to reject the restorative justice option, the program would fail totally because it would not solve the system overload problem—too many serious offenders committing too many crimes to be able to target a credible proportion. However, because it would be irrational even for the offender who has an iron determination to continue with a life of crime to opt for targeting in preference to restorative justice, we assume the greater problem would be insincere cooperation with the conference. This would cause only partial failure of the program. But it would enable a strategic solution to the system capacity problem. An interesting strategy for lending credibility to the targeting would be for it to be announced that a neighboring police service had a hundred police on call to supplement local police in targeting the serious repeat offenders. This offer could be reciprocated when the other police service launched its targeting program. Hopefully the announcement effect would lend sufficient credibility to drive offenders into the restorative justice option, making it unnecessary to import the extra police. A visible complementary change would be to shift normal enforcement to the targeting of geographical hot spots where a lot of crime occurs and which are frequented by the targeted offenders (see Sherman 1998).

In a jurisdiction with too many serious repeat offenders to be able to resource either the surveillance targeting or the intensive restorative justice conferences required, the solution is to apply the strategy first to an A-list of serious repeat offenders, and much later move on to B- and C-lists. The enforcement pyramid, both by rationing the targeting of punishment and by making it rational for offenders to punish themselves, can solve what Mark Kleiman (1993) has called the "enforcement swamping" problem. Here is how David Kennedy describes this enforcement swamping problem:

> Imagine a neighbourhood in which the capacity of authorities to punish offenders is fixed. If the crime rate in that neighbourhood goes up, the punishment per offence

must necessarily fall. If the new, lower level of punishment attracts new offenders, induces old offenders to offend more frequently, or both, there will be more offending, an even lower rate of punishment, and thus still more offending. When authorities' capacity to punish falls too low to prevent this kind of positive feedback cycle, we have enforcement swamping. A common contemporary example is street drug markets. As a stylized example of this process, when the volume of drug transactions in a particular location gets high enough, the authorities lose their capacity to control the location. Their lack of control attracts more drug dealers, which further weakens control capacities. The market attracts more buyers, cementing the commitment of dealers to do business there. The result is the common phenomenon of flagrant street markets that appear utterly impervious to normal enforcement approaches: they have "tipped to the wrong side of the enforcement swamping divide." (1997, p. 476)

The phenomenon of crossing a tipping point into enforcement swamping is a further reason that the attempt to create the appearance of equal opportunity enforcement is bad policy. It is better to start with an A-list and push those individuals back past the tipping point: "If you can't get past the crossover point for everybody, get past it for somebody and work outward" (Kleiman 1999, p. 21).[2] When we are swamped with enforcement opportunities, zero tolerance amounts to zero credibility. At the same time, equal opportunity enforcement is equal neglect.

Then, of course, the critical question is whether restorative justice programs can be effective with hard-core repeat offenders. Bonta, Rooney, and Wallace-Capretta's (1998) study of serious offenders, 90 percent of whom were subject to a prosecution recommendation of prison sentences over six months and who went through a restorative justice program, found that their reoffending rate was about half that of a sample matched on risk who were sentenced to probation by the court. Burford and Pennell's (1998) study of serious cases of family violence found that abuse/neglect incidents halved in families that went through a restorative family conferencing process compared with a matched control group of families. Chapter 4 outlines some of the theoretical reasons that the comparative effectiveness of restorative justice might be greater with serious than with minor offenders. In chapter 7 I flesh out the possibilities of using the responsive targeting approach developed here with serious corruption, and I outline the research program to this end of the Centre for Tax System Integrity with tax evasion and avoidance by wealthy individuals and corporations.

Programs with considerable similarities to the responsive targeting part of the program proposed here, but without the restorative justice part, were the Boston and Minneapolis youth homicide projects, which were associated with almost a halving of youth homicides in Minneapolis and a two-thirds reduction in Boston (Kleiman 1999). The context was a familiar one—youth gang killings where everyone knew which gang had perpetrated the latest murder, but where proving anything in court was impossible. In Boston the Inter-Agency Operation Ceasefire group gave gang members the following message:

> We know who you are. We know what you're doing. Most of it is illegal. You sell drugs, you carry weapons, you drive unregistered cars, you are truant from school,

you are in breach of your probation terms, you drink alcohol from open containers. We can't crack down on everyone at once, but we can crack down on any group we choose. If we crack down on your group, you can't live your (mostly illegal) life.

Here are the new rules: no deadly violence. Here are the consequences of breaking the rules: concentrated attention until the whole group says "uncle" and turns in its guns. No deal: you break the law at your own risk. But if you or any member of your group shoots someone, the risks will become, and remain, intolerable.

The first Operation Ceasefire intervention involved the Vamp Hill Kings in 1996 after a quick succession of three homicides. Street drug markets were disrupted, warrants were served, probation conditions enforced, and some indictments launched. Compliance did not come readily. A further homicide occurred during the intervention, but eventually sit-down forums with gang members got the message through.

Chapter 4 discusses gang retreats and surrenders in Colombia and New Guinea, much more violent contexts than Boston or Minneapolis. Restorative justice is not a utopian option even for the most serious and organized of criminals, even for the most powerful corporate criminals, as we will also see in the next chapter. However, for restorative justice to be effective with such tough nuts, it must be backed by an enforcement pyramid that is seen as having credibility and inexorability. Even the toughest nuts are capable of being surprised by someone treating them with respect, a person who cares about the effects offenders have on others. As Ayres and Braithwaite (1992, pp. 30–35) report, regulatory ethnographies show regulated actors to have contradictory multiple selves. Even the worst of us have a caring, socially responsible self as well as an exploitative self. The idea of starting at the bottom of the pyramid with the most ruthless criminals is to surprise them with a show of trust and respect, to give them a chance to put their best self forward:

INSPECTOR TO NURSING HOME ADMINISTRATOR: What you want and what we want more than anything else is to improve the quality of care your residents are getting . . .

(later) INSPECTOR TO BRAITHWAITE: When you say to them that we all agree that the care of the resident is what we are all concerned about, you know that's not true, that they're concerned about making money. But what are they going to say? They can't turn around and say, "Hell no, I don't care about the residents; all I care about is profits."

Mafia bosses (some of whom own nursing homes), tobacco executives and other kinds of drug barons, serial wife beaters (Braithwaite and Daly 1994), professional hit men, perhaps even Saddam Hussein,[3] can be surprised by being given an opportunity to put their socially responsible self forward, to be touched by the love of those who care for them most, and in particular to be touched by the way those they love suffer for the evils they do. As Hollywood teaches us, it is with drug barons and Saddam Husseins that we are willing to tolerate good cops who do bad things to protect us from a greater evil or marines who commit war crimes. The philosophy of restorative justice does not allow us to do this. We must always remember that the constraining values and fundamental human rights considered in the previous chapter and again in chapter 5 are our first priority. If they are the only priority we can accomplish in confronting a great evil, then it is them we must honor. That said, restorativists must not duck the responsibility to work through how they can respond to intransigent evils to which we must respond, both with credible clout and determination and with even more credible commitment to imposing a new set of checks and balances on the kind of freewheeling cops so valorized by our folklore.[4]

EVALUATING THE ELEMENTS OF RESPONSIVE REGULATION

I have conceived responsive regulation here as a presumption in favor of trying restorative justice first, then deterrence when that fails, then incapacitation when that fails. In successive chapters I will evaluate the prospects of efficacy at these three levels. Chapter 3 will evaluate whether restorative justice works on the basis of the evidence we have at this time. Yet really the question to be answered here is more demanding from a responsive regulatory perspective. Does restorative justice work so much better and more decently than deterrence to justify a general presumption for trying it before resorting to deterrence? Chapter 4 considers a restorative and responsive account of deterrence. It will be argued there that the active deterrence of escalation from restorative to punitive justice is likely to be much more effective than traditional passive deterrence as conceived in criminological theory since Bentham. And chapter 4 will argue both that restorative justice is generally more effective than the punitive incapacitation of selective incapacitation theory in criminology and that a restorative and responsive account of incapacitation might make for a superior model of incapacitation.

Hence, what the restorative and responsive theoretical position argues is not just that restorative justice is more effective than punitive justice. It is that restorative justice at the base of a regulatory pyramid increases the efficacy of punitive justice as well. It accomplishes the latter by increasing the effectiveness of both deterrence and incapacitation. All this, according to the theory, is especially true with the most hardened, sophisticated, and powerful criminals. The radical implication of the theory is that for no type of offending is imprisonment the normal response that is needed; for all types of offending we are best to have a presumption in favor of restorative justice first, combined with an expectation that restorative justice will often fail. Most of our prisons can be closed and sold. The conservative implication of the theory is that we cannot be abolitionists; restorative justice must be backed up by deterrence and incapacitation options that sometimes must include imprisonment.

NOTES

1. In some parts of the world, notably the United States, there are substantial numbers of repeat murderers who are hit men or gang leaders; these are suitable targets for the kind of program I describe.

2. Also relevant here is what we know about salience and conditional probabilities: "Tax-payers focus on the most salient link in the chain of conditional probabilities that influence the likelihood of getting caught, rather than on the overall probability. Thus a 10 percent chance of getting caught and punished is treated as a lower risk than a combined 50 percent chance of getting caught and a 20 percent chance of being punished if caught, even though the actual risk in both siuations is the same ($.5 \times .2 = .10$). The salience of the higher probabilities leads people to overcompensate in determining the joint effect on risk, a heuristic that has been called the 'conjunctive effect.' Given this effect, compliance levels increase when the salience of high-probability links is increased, even when the under-lying risk is unchanged" (Scholz 1998, p. 143).

3. UN Secretary-General Kofi Annan to Saddam Hussein: "Your're a builder, you built modern Iraq. It was destroyed once. You've rebuilt it. Do you want to destroy it again? Look how you talk about the suffering of your people. It's in your hands, we can do something about this. If we can work out an agreement that will prevent military action and you would undertake to comply, it will save the day" (Shawcross 2000, p. 241).

4. The beginnings of an attempt to work through my favored civic republican way of accomplishing this can be found in Braithwaite and Pettit (1990) and in chapter 5 of this book. In this chapter the important point I am emphasizing is judicial approval of targeting, so judges are guardians of rights and limits. Hence, controversial tactics like the use of decoy cars to catch car thieves are not precluded, but are subjected to a new form of judicial regulation that limits their application to cases of reasonable suspicion of serious repeat offenders who have been warned. Being warned, they can appeal any injustice of the targeting to the judge.

3

Does Restorative Justice Work?

THIS CHAPTER SUMMARIZES THE NOW CONSIDERABLE EMPIRICAL EVIDENCE ABOUT the effectiveness of restorative justice. The literature review is organized around three broad and simple hypotheses:

1. Restorative justice restores and satisfies victims better than existing criminal justice practices
2. Restorative justice restores and satisfies offenders better than existing criminal justice practices
3. Restorative justice restores and satisfies communities better than existing criminal justice practices

These propositions are corollaries of the theories developed in chapter 4. It may seem odd to present evidence for the corollaries of the theories before the theories themselves. The reason for proceeding this way is that I read the evidence that restorative justice works in restoring victims, offenders, and communities as more encouraging and somewhat clearer than the evidence supporting any of the theories. So my way of tackling this book has been to explain the idea of restorative justice in chapter 1, to review evidence suggesting that it might work in this chapter, and then in the next chapter to consider a variety of theories that give an account of why it might work in restoring victims, offenders, and communities.

RESTORATIVE JUSTICE PRACTICES RESTORE AND SATISFY VICTIMS BETTER THAN EXISTING CRIMINAL JUSTICE PRACTICES

A consistent picture emerges from the welter of data reviewed in this section: it is one of comparatively high victim approval of their restorative justice experiences, though often lower levels of approval than one finds among other participants in the process. So long as the arrangements are convenient, it is only a small minority of victims who do not *want* to participate in restorative justice processes. Consistent with this picture, preliminary data from Lawrence Sherman and Heather Strang's Canberra experiments show only 3 percent of offenders and 2 percent of community representatives at conferences compared with 12 percent of victims disagreeing with the statement: "The government should use conferences as an alternative to court more often" (Strang 2000). Most of the data to date are limited to a small range of outcomes; we are still awaiting the first systematic data on some of the dimensions of restoration discussed in chapter 1. On the limited range of outcomes explored to date, victims do seem to get more restoration out of restorative justice agreements than court orders, and restorative justice agreements seem to be more likely to be delivered than court orders even when the former are not legally enforceable.

Operationalizing Victim Restoration

There is a deep problem in evaluating how well restorative justice restores. Empowerment of victims to define the restoration that matters to them is a keystone of a restorative justice philosophy. Three paths can be taken. One is to posit a list of types of restoration that are important to most victims, such as those discussed in chapter 1. The problem with this is that even with as uncontroversial a dimension of restoration as restoring property loss, some victims will prefer mercy to insisting on getting their money back; indeed, it may be that act of grace which gives them a spiritual restoration that is critical for them.[1] The second path sidesteps a debate on what dimensions of restoration are universal enough to evaluate. Instead, it measures overall satisfaction of victims with restorative justice processes and outcomes, assuming (without evidence) that satisfaction is a proxy for victims getting restoration on the things that are most important for them. This is the path followed in the review of the next section, largely because this was the kind of information available when the earlier version of the review was published in 1999. The third path is the best one but also the most unmanageable in large quantitative evaluations. It is to ask victims to define the kinds of restoration they were seeking and then to report how much restoration they attained in these terms that matter most to them.

As this book goes to press, Heather Strang (forthcoming) has completed a manuscript that pulls off something close to this third approach. Strang reviewed the empirical literature on what victims said they wanted out of the criminal justice process and then confirmed the accuracy of that list of aspirations on Canberra crime victims whose cases were randomly assigned to court versus restorative justice conferences. The set of victim preferences she identified were:

- A less formal process where their views count
- More information about both the processing and the outcome of their case
- To participate in their case
- To be treated respectfully and fairly
- Material restoration
- Emotional restoration, including an apology

Strang then went on to show that indeed these victim aspirations were more consistently realized in cases randomly assigned to conferences as opposed to court:

> Feelings of anger, fear and anxiety towards their offender fell markedly after their conference while feelings of security for themselves and sympathy for their offender increased. The conference usually had a beneficial effect on victims' feelings of dignity, self-respect and self-confidence and led to reduced levels of embarrassment and shame about the offence. Overall, victims most often said their conference had been a helpful experience in allowing them to feel more settled about the offence, to feel forgiving towards their offender and to experience a sense of closure. (Strang 2000, pp. iv–v).

Strang's most striking result concerns the capacity of conferences to deal with the feelings of revenge that so often eat away at victims. More than half of court-assigned violence victims said they would harm their offender if they had the chance, compared with only 7 percent of those assigned to restorative justice.

Notwithstanding the strong affirmation overall that victims were more likely to have their needs, especially their emotional needs, met in conference than in court, Strang found a subset of victims who were worse off as a result of their case being assigned to conference. She concluded that these were not so much cases that refuted principles of restorative justice as cases that revealed bungled administration of justice (see Box 3.1). One group of victims who were more dissatisfied than victims whose case was sent straight to court were those whose case was assigned to a conference, but the conference fell through and actually ended up going to court. The lesson here is that badly administered programs that do not deliver on their restorative promises to victims can actually make things a lot worse for them. Overall, Strang's results are extremely encouraging, especially since no one today would suggest that the Canberra program is the best one in Australia. Canberra is a first-generation program, and the evidence reviewed here suggests higher levels of satisfaction of victims and others in the later Australian programs that learned from some of its mistakes.[2]

Victim Participation and Satisfaction

While traditional criminal justice practices are notoriously unsatisfying to victims, it is also true that victims emerge from many restorative justice programs less satisfied than other participants. Clairmont (1994, pp. 16–17) found little victim involvement in four restorative justice programs for First Nations offenders in Canada. There seems to be a wider pattern of greater satisfaction among First Nations leaders and offenders than among victims for restorative projects on Canadian Aboriginal communities (Obonsawin-Irwin Consulting Inc. 1992a, 1992b; Clairmont 1994; La-Prairie 1995).

Early British victim-offender mediation programs reported what Dignan (1992) called sham reparation, for example, Davis's (1992) reporting of offers rather than actual repair, tokenism, and even dictated letters of apology. In some of these programs victims were little more than a new kind of prop in welfare programs: the "new

Box 3.1: Scapegoating: Procedural Injustice and the Forgotten Victim

Matthew, the 24 year old victim in this assault matter, was drinking on licensed premises when a fight broke out involving one of his friends. He said that in the general melee he tried to pull his friend out of the fight, when a "bouncer" hit him over the head and ejected him into the car park, where the fighting continued involving both patrons and security staff. Subsequently Charlie, aged 18 and employed on security at the pub, attended the police station and made full admissions about having punched Matthew in the face. In the view of the apprehending officer, other staff were directing blame at Charlie and it appeared that he had been offered as the sole offender because he was young with no prior convictions and likely not to be prosecuted.

The conference was attended by a large number of supporters of both Matthew and Charlie. As soon as it began, Matthew said that Charlie could not have been the person who assaulted him because he did not look anything like that person. Charlie's employer and workmates insisted that it was Charlie who was the assailant (though his family did not appear to believe that he had been involved). There were many claims and counter-claims in the course of the conference flowing from poor police investigation into the incident, including allegations that the victim and his friends had provoked the brawl. It was complicated by poor and untrusting relations between the licensee and the police, who frequently attended incidents at his premises. After about an hour of acrimonious discussion, the conference was abandoned as it was apparent that there was no agreement on what had happened and no likelihood of reaching an outcome acceptable to all the parties.

After further enquiries the police decided to take no further action with the case. Matthew was very angry and disappointed: his rage at the injustice of having effectively nothing happen following the assault led to his carrying a knife for several months, and in fact to pull it out when the same friend again got into a fight. He spontaneously said at interview that if he "ran into" his assailants from the original incident he would probably attack them in revenge for what happened to him. He had been very upset at the way the conference unfolded, although he believed that the police had been fair and that he had had an opportunity to express his views. He wished the case had gone to court because he believed that way all the co-offenders would have been prosecuted and punished (in fact this could not have happened as only Charlie had been identified as being involved). Two years after the incident he remained extremely angry because he saw the licensee and his security staff as having "got away" with assaulting him.

Source: From Strang 2000, p. 168

48

deal for victims" came in Britain to be seen as a "new deal for offenders" (Crawford 1996, p. 7). However, Crawford's (1996) conclusion that the British restorative justice programs that survived into the 1990s after weathering this storm "have done much to answer their critics" (p. 7) seems consistent with the evidence. Dignan (1992) reports 71 percent satisfaction among English corporate victims and 61 percent among individual victims in one of the early adult offender reparation programs.

In New Zealand, victims attended only half the conferences conducted during the early years of the program[3] and when they did attend were less in agreement (51 percent satisfaction) with family group conference outcomes than were offenders (84 percent), police (91 percent), and other participants (85 percent; Maxwell and Morris 1993, pp. 115, 120). About a quarter of victims reported that they felt worse as a result of attending the family group conference. Australian studies by Daly (1996) and Strang and Sherman (1997) also found a significant minority of victims who felt worse after the conference, upset over something said, or victimized by disrespect, though they were greatly outnumbered by victims who felt healing as a result of the conference. Similarly, Birchall, Namour, and Syme (1992) report 27 percent of victims feeling worse after meeting their offender and 70 percent feeling better in Western Australia's Midland Pilot Reparation Scheme. The Ministry of Justice, Western Australia (1994), reports 95 percent victim satisfaction with their restorative justice conference program (Juvenile Justice Teams). Chatterjee (2000, p. 3) reports that 94 percent of victims in Royal Canadian Mounted Police convened family group conferences were satisfied with the fairness of the agreement. McCold and Wachtel (1998) found 96 percent victim satisfaction with cases randomly assigned to conferences in Bethlehem, Pennsylvania, compared with 79 percent satisfaction when cases were assigned to court and 73 percent satisfaction when the case went to court after being assigned to conference and the conference was declined. Conferenced victims were also somewhat more likely to believe that they experienced fairness (96 percent), that the offender was adequately held accountable for the offense (93 percent), and that their opinion regarding the offense and circumstances was adequately considered in the case (94 percent). Ninety-three percent of victims found the conference helpful, 98 percent found that it "allowed me to express my feelings without being victimized," 96 percent believed that the offender had apologized, and 75 percent believed that the offender was sincere. Ninety-four percent said they would choose a conference if they had to do it over again. The Bethlehem results are complicated by a "decline" group as large as the control group, where either offenders or victims could cause the case to be declined. In the Canberra RISE experiment, victim participation is currently 80 percent (Strang 2000). Reports on the Wagga Wagga conferencing model in Australia are also more optimistic about victim participation and satisfaction, reporting 90 percent victim satisfaction and victim participation exceeding 90 percent (Moore and O'Connell 1994). Trimboli's (2000, p. 28) evaluation of the NSW Youth Justice Conferencing Scheme finds even higher levels of victim satisfaction than with the Wagga Wagga model conferencing programs, though lower levels of victim participation of 74 percent than in Wagga and Canberra.

Trimboli's NSW victims were much more satisfied than the Canberra victims over being kept informed about what was happening, and were more likely to feel that they were treated with respect, that they had the opportunity to express their views in the conference, and that these views actually affected the decision on what should be done about the case. The highest published satisfaction and fairness ratings (both 98 percent) have been reported by the Queensland Department of Justice conferencing program (Palk, Hayes, and Prenzler 1998). Seventy-eight percent of victims felt the conference and the agreement helped "make up for the offence," and only 6 percent said they would be "concerned if you met the young person in the street today" (Hayes, Prenzler, with Wortley 1998, pp. 26, 27). A high 90 percent of offenders made verbal apologies, and a further 12 percent made written apologies in this program. One reason for the program's exceptionally positive results is that it excludes conferencing from cases where victims do not wish to participate, meaning that no data are collected from the least cooperative victims who just want to walk away.

McGarrell et al. (2000, p. 45) not only found markedly higher levels of satisfaction among victims in cases randomly assigned to a restorative justice conference but also found that 97 percent of conference victims "felt involved," compared with 38 percent of control group victims, and that 95 percent of conference victims felt they had the opportunity to express their views, compared with 56 percent of control group victims.

Umbreit and Coates's (1992) survey found that 79 percent of victims who cooperated in four U.S. mediation programs were satisfied, compared with only 57 percent of those who did not have mediation (for earlier similar findings, see Umbreit 1990b). In a subsequent study Umbreit (1998) found victim *procedural* satisfaction at 78 percent at four combined Canadian sites and 62 percent at two combined English mediation sites. Victim satisfaction with *outcomes* was higher still: 90 percent (four U.S. sites), 89 percent (four Canadian sites), and 84 percent (two English sites). However, victim satisfaction was still generally lower across the sites than offender satisfaction. Eighty-three percent of U.S. mediation victims perceived the outcome as "fair" (as opposed to being "satisfied"), compared with 62 percent of those who went through the normal court process. Umbreit and Coates (1992) also report reduced fear and anxiety among victims following mediation, a finding Strang (2000) has replicated on Canberra conferences. Victims afraid of being victimized again dropped from 25 percent prior to mediation to 10 percent afterward in a study by Umbreit and Coates (1992), again results comparable to those obtained by Strang on conferences. A survey of German institutions involved in model mediation projects found that the rate of voluntary victim participation generally ranged from 81 to 92 percent and never dropped below 70 percent (Kerner, Marks, and Schreckling 1992).

McCold and Wachtel (2000) compared systematically thirty-nine program samples (including most of those discussed here) according to whether they were "fully restorative," "mostly restorative," or "not restorative," where restorativeness was operationalized in terms of stakeholder participation. On average, victim perception of both fairness and satisfaction was highest for fully restorative programs and lowest for nonrestorative programs.

In summary, while many programs accomplish very high levels of victim participation, programs vary considerably on this dimension. Consistently, however, across disparate programs victims are highly satisfied with the fairness of procedures and outcomes—more satisfied than victims whose cases go to court, though not as satisfied as offenders and other participants in restorative justice processes. In a meta-analysis of 13 evaluations with a control group, Latimer, Dowden and Muise (2001) found victim satisfaction to be significantly higher in the restorative justice group. Victims also experience reduced fear and increased emotional restoration after the restorative justice process. Heather Strang's (2000) data suggest, however, that one group whose satisfaction and emotional well-being are adversely affected by the offer of a restorative justice conference is victims whose conference falls through. This points up a methodological deficiency in most of the studies reviewed here (that does not apply to Strang's work): they measure satisfaction levels among victims whose conferences actually come to pass, failing to correct for the reduced levels of satisfaction that would apply if cases were included where conferences were offered but not delivered. Trimboli (2000) actually compares NSW results from completed conferences with RISE results of cases randomly assigned to conference (many of which actually ended up in court).

HONORING OF OBLIGATIONS TO VICTIMS

Haley and Neugebauer's (1992) analysis of restorative justice programs in the United States, Canada, and Great Britain revealed between 64 and 100 percent completion of reparation and compensation agreements. I assume here, of course, that completion of undertakings that victims have agreed to is important for victim restoration. Marshall's (1992) study of cases referred to mediation programs in Britain found that over 80 percent of agreements were completed. Galaway (1992) reports that 58 percent of agreements reached through mediation in New Zealand were fully complied with within one year. In a Finnish study, 85 percent of agreements reached through mediation were fully completed (Iivari 1987, 1992). From England, Dignan (1992) reports 86 percent participant agreement with mediation outcomes, with 91 percent of agreements honored in full. Trenczek (1990), in a study of pilot victim-offender reconciliation projects in Braunschweig, Cologne, and Reutlingen, West Germany (see also Kuhn 1987), reports a full completion rate of 76 percent and a partial completion rate of 5 percent. Pate's (1990) study of victim-offender reconciliation projects found a rate of noncompletion of agreements of between 5 and 10 percent in Alberta, Canada, and less than 1 percent in the case of a Calgary program. Wundersitz and Hetzel (1996, p. 133) found 86 percent full compliance with conference agreements in South Australia, with another 3 percent waived for near compliance. Fry (1997, p. 5) reported 100 percent completion of agreements in a pilot of twenty-six Northern Territory police-coordinated juvenile conferences, and Waters (1993, p. 9) reported

91 percent payment of compensation agreed in Wagga Wagga conferences. In another Wagga-style program, McCold and Wachtel (1998, p. 4) report 94 percent compliance with the terms of conference agreements. McGarrell et al. (2000, p. 47) found 83 percent completion of conference agreements in Indianpolis, compared with 58 percent completion of diversion programs in the control group.

Umbreit and Coates (1992) compared 81 percent completion of restitution obligations settled through mediation to 58 percent completion of court-ordered restitution in their multisite study. Ervin and Schneider (1990), in a random assignment evaluation of six U.S. restitution programs, found 89 percent completion of restitution, compared with 75 percent completion of traditional programs. Most of Ervin and Schneider's restitution programs, however, were not restorative in the sense of involving meetings of victims and offenders. Latimer, Dowden and Muise (2001, p. 17) found in a meta-analysis of 8 studies with a control group that restitution compliance was 33 percent higher in the restorative justice cases than among controls. In summary, the research suggests high levels of compliance with restorative justice agreement, substantially higher than with court orders.

Symbolic Reparation

One reason that the level of satisfaction of victims is surprisingly high in processes that so often give them so little material reparation is that they get symbolic reparation, which is more important to them (Retzinger and Scheff 1996). Apology is at the heart of this: preliminary results from the RISE experiment in Canberra show that 71 percent of victims whose cases were randomly assigned to a conference got an apology, compared with 17 percent in cases randomly assigned to court; while 77 percent of the conference apologies were regarded as "sincere" or "somewhat sincere," this was true of only 36 percent of apologies to victims whose cases went to court (Strang 2000). Sixty-five percent of victims felt "quite" or "very" angry before the Canberra conferences, and 27 percent felt so afterward. Obversely, the proportion of victims feeling sympathetic to the offender almost tripled (from 18 to 50 percent) by the end of the conference (Strang 2000). We will see that there is a large body of research evidence showing that victims are not as punitive as the rather atypical victims whose bitter calls for brutal punishment get most media coverage. Studies by both Strang and Sherman (1997) and Umbreit (1992, p. 443) report victim fear of revictimization and victim upset about the crime as having declined following the restorative justice process.

In Goodes's (1995) study of juvenile family group conferences in South Australia, where victim attendance ranges from 75 to 80 percent (Wundersitz and Hetzel 1996), the most common reason victims gave for attending their conference was to try to help the offender, followed by the desire to express feelings, make statements to the offender, or ask questions like "why me?" (what Retzinger and Scheff [1996] call symbolic reparation), followed by "curiosity and a desire to 'have a look,' " followed by "responsibility as citizens to attend." The desire to ensure that the penalty was appropriate and the desire for material reparation rated behind all of these motivations to attend. The response rate in the Goodes (1995) study was poor, and there may be a strong social desirability bias in these victim reports; yet that may be precisely because the context of conference attendance is one that nurtures responsible citizenship cognitions by victims. Eighty-eight percent of Goodes's (1995) victims agreed with the conference outcome, 90 percent found it helpful to them, and 90 percent said they would attend again if they were a victim again (Goodes 1995).

With all these quantitative findings, one can lose sight of what most moves restorative justice advocates who have seen restorative processes work well. I am not a spiritual enough person to capture it in words: it is about grace, shalom. Van Ness (1986, p. 125) characterizes shalom as "peace as the result of doing justice." Trish Stewart (1993, p. 49) gets near its evocation when she reports one victim who said in the closing round of a conference: "Today I have observed and taken part in justice administered with love." Psychologists are developing improved ways of measuring spirituality—self-transcendence, meaning in life beyond one's self. So in the future it will be possible to undertake systematic research on self-reported spirituality and conferences to see whether results are obtained analogous to Reed's (1986, 1987, 1992) findings that greater healing occurred among terminally ill individuals whose psychosocial response was imbued with a spiritual dimension.

For the moment, we must accept an East-West divide in the way participants think about spiritual leadership in conferences. Maori, North American, and Australian Aboriginal peoples tend to think it important to have elders with special gifts of spirituality, what Maori call *mana*, attend restorative justice processes (Tauri and Morris 1997, pp. 149–50). This is the Confucian view as well. These traditions are critical of the ethos Western advocates such as myself have brought to conferences, which has not seen it as important to have elders with *mana* at conferences. Several years ago in Indonesia I was told of restorative justice rituals in western Sumatra that were jointly conducted by a religious leader and a scholar—the person in the community seen as having the greatest spiritual riches and the person seen as having the greatest riches of learning. My inclination then was to recoil from the elitism of this and insist that many (if not most) citizens have the resources (given a little help with training) to facilitate processes of healing. While I still believe this, I now think it might be a mistake to seek to persuade Asians to democratize their restorative justice practices. There may be merit in special efforts to recruit exemplars of virtue, grace, *mana*, to participate. Increasingly, I am tempted to so interpret our experience with RISE in recruiting community representatives with grace to participate in drunk driving conferences where there is no victim. However, as Power (2000) and Miller and Blackler (2000) correctly point out, the Canberra experience with community representatives has been far from universally positive. Many have been decidedly short on *mana* and long on punitive speech. Nevertheless, a research and development program for restorative justice that still appeals to me is how to do well at locating elders with grace to act as community representatives in restorative justice programs in Western cities.

54

RESTORATIVE JUSTICE PRACTICES RESTORE AND SATISFY OFFENDERS BETTER THAN EXISTING CRIMINAL JUSTICE PRACTICES

This section concludes that offender satisfaction with both corporate and traditional individual restorative justice programs has been extremely high. The evidence of offenders being restored in the sense of desisting from criminal conduct is extremely encouraging with victim-offender mediation, conferencing, restorative business regulatory programs, and whole-school antibullying programs, though not with peer mediation programs for bullying.[4] However, only some of these studies adequately control for important variables, and only five randomly assigned cases to restorative versus punitive justice. The business regulatory studies are instructive in suggesting that (1) restorative justice works best when it is backed up by punitive justice in those (quite common) individual cases where restorative justice fails and (2) trying restorative justice first increases perceived justice.

Fairness and Satisfaction for Offenders

As we will see in the next chapter, offenders are more likely to respond positively to criminal justice processing when they perceive it as just. Moore with Forsythe's (1995, p. 248) ethnographic work concludes that most offenders, like victims, experienced quite profound "procedural, material and psychological justice" in restorative justice conferences. Umbreit (1992) reports from his cross-site study in the United States an 89 percent perception of fairness on the part of offenders with victim-offender mediation programs, compared with 78 percent perceived fairness in unmediated cases. Umbreit (1998) reports 80 percent offender perception of fairness of victim-offender mediation across four Canadian studies and 89 percent at two combined English sites. The Ministry of Justice, Western Australia (1994), reports 95 percent offender satisfaction with its restorative justice conference program (Juvenile Justice Teams). McCold and Wachtel (1998, pp. 59–61) report 97 percent satisfaction with "the way your case was handled" and 97 percent fairness in the Bethlehem police conferencing program, a better result than in the four comparisons with Bethlehem cases that went to court. McGarrell, et al., (2000, p. 45) report that conference offenders in Indianapolis were more likely than control group offenders to have "felt involved" (84 percent versus 47 percent) and to feel they have had an opportunity to express their views (86 percent versus 55 percent). Coats and Gehm (1985, 1989) found 83 percent offender satisfaction with the victim-offender reconciliation experience based on a study of programs in Indiana and Ohio. Smith, Blagg, and Derricourt (1985), in a limited survey of the initial years of a South Yorkshire mediation project, found that 10 out of 13 offenders were satisfied with the mediation experience and felt that the scheme had helped alter their behavior. Dignan (1990), on the basis of a random sample of offenders (N = 50) involved in victim-offender mediations in Kettering, Northamptonshire, found 96 percent were either satisfied or very satisfied with the process. As reported in the next chapter, Barnes

(1999) found higher perceptions of a number of facets of procedural and outcome fairness in RISE conferences compared with Canberra courts. However, Trimboli (2000, pp. 34–54) has reported even higher levels of offender perceptions of fairness and outcome satisfaction in NSW compared with RISE conferences. The strongest published result was again on 113 juvenile offenders in the Queensland Department of Justice conferencing program, where 98 percent thought their conference fair and 99 percent were satisfied with the agreement (Palk, Hayes, and Prenzler 1998). Ninety-six percent of young offenders reported that they "would be more likely to go to your family now if you were in trouble or needed help" and that they had "been able to put the whole experience behind you."

McCold and Wachtel (2000) compared systematically thirty-four program samples (including most of those discussed here) according to whether they were "fully restorative," "mostly restorative," or "not restorative," where restorativeness was operationalized in terms of stakeholder participation. As with victim perceptions, offender perception of both fairness and satisfaction was highest for fully restorative programs and lowest for nonrestorative programs. For 13 studies with a control group, Latimer, Dowden and Muise's (2001, p. 14) meta-analysis found restorative justice offenders to be more satisfied about how their case was handled compared with controls.

Reduced Reoffending as Offender Restoration

Meta-analyses of restitution programs suggest that these have some (modest) effect in reducing reoffending (e.g., Gendreau, Clark, and Gray 1996; Cullen and Gendreau 2000; see also Butts and Snyder 1991; Schneider 1986; Geudens and Walgrave 1998; Schiff 1998; Bazemore 1999b). I do not consider this literature here because most of these programs do not involve a restorative *process* (i.e., the restitution is usually imposed by a traditional court, often as punishment rather than in pursuit of any restorative *values*).

Pate (1990), Nugent and Paddock (1995), and Wynne (1996) all report a decline in recidivism among mediation cases. Umbreit, with Coates and Kalanj (1994) found 18 percent recidivism across four victim-offender mediation sites (N = 160) and 27 percent (N = 160) for comparable nonmediation cases at those sites, a difference that was encouraging but fell short of statistical significance. However, a follow-up in 2000 on these and several other programs on a much expanded sample of 1,298 again found mediation recidivism to be one-third lower than court recidivism (19 percent vs. 28 percent), this time a statistically significant result after entering appropriate controls (Nugent et al. forthcoming). Similarly, Marshall and Merry (1990, p. 196) report for an even smaller sample than Umbreit, with Coates and Kalani (1994) that offending declined for victim-offender mediation cases, especially when there was an actual meeting (as opposed to indirect shuttle diplomacy by a mediation), while offending went up for controls. However, the differences were not statistically significant. A German study by Dolling and Hartman (2000) found reoffending to be one-third lower in cases where victim-offender mediation was completed compared with a control group. The effect was significant after entering controls. However, including cases where mediation was not successfully completed reduced the p value to .08, which would not normally be accepted as significant.

In an experimental evaluation of six U.S. restitution programs, Schneider (1986, 1990) found a significant reduction in recidivism across the six programs. This result is widely cited by restorative justice advocates as evidence for the efficacy of restorative justice. However, all but one of these programs seem to involve mandated restitution to victims without any mediation or restorative justice deliberation by victims and offenders. The one program that seems to meet the process definition of restorative justice, the one in Washington, D.C., did produce significantly lower rates of reoffending for cases randomly assigned to victim-offender mediation and restitution compared with cases assigned to regular probation.[5]

There is no satisfactory evidence on the impact of the New Zealand juvenile family group conferences on recidivism. The story is similar with Wagga Wagga. Forsythe (1995) shows a 20 percent reoffending rate for cases going to conference, compared with a 48 percent rate for juvenile court cases. This is a big effect; most of it is likely a social selection effect of tougher cases going to court, as there is no matching, no controls, though it is hard to account for the entire association in these terms given the pattern of the data (see Forsythe 1995, pp. 245–46).

Another big effect with the same social selection worry was obtained with only the first sixty-three cases to go through family group conferences in Singapore. The conference reoffending rate was 2 percent, compared with 30 percent over the same period for offenders who went to court (Chan 1996; Hsien 1996).

McCold and Wachtel's (1998) experimental evaluation of Bethlehem, Pennsylvania's, Wagga-style police conferencing program involved a more determined attempt to tackle social selection problems through randomization. Unfortunately, however, this study fell victim to another kind of selection effect as a result of unacceptably high crossover rates on the treatments assigned in the experiment. For property cases, there was a tendency for conferenced cases to have higher recidivism than court cases, but the difference was not statistically significant. For violence cases, conferenced offenders had a significantly lower reoffending rate than offenders who went to court. However, this result was not statistically valid because the violent offenders with the highest reoffending rate were those who were randomly assigned to conference but who actually ended up going to court because either the offender or the victim refused to cooperate in the conference. In other words, the experiment failed to deliver an adequate test of the effect of conferences on recidivism both on grounds of statistical power and because of unsatisfactory assurance that the assigned treatment was delivered.

Clearer results were obtained from McGarrell et al.'s (2000) Indianapolis Restorative Justice Experiment, which involved random assignment of young first offenders to a Wagga-style conference convened by the police versus assignment to the normal range of diversion programs. Rearrest was 40 percent lower in the conference group than in the control group after six months, an effect that decayed to a 25 percent reduction after twelve months. At the Winchester conference in 2001 McGarrell reported that the analysis of further cases revealed a decay to higher than this 25 percent reduction, but these results are not yet published.

Preliminary reoffending results have been put up on the Web (aic.gov.au) by Sherman, Strang, and Woods (2000) from the RISE restorative justice experiment in Canberra. In this experiment 1,300 cases were randomly assigned either to court or to a restorative justice conference on the Wagga model. While the experiment showed a sharp decline in officially recorded repeat criminal offending for violent juvenile and young adult offenders randomly assigned to conference in comparison to those assigned to court, the results were not encouraging on adult drunk drivers and juvenile property offenders (though not all the latter results were discouraging). Sherman, Strang, and Woods (2000, p. 20) conclude that compared with court, the effect of diversionary conferences is to cause the following:

- Big drop in offending rates by violent offenders (by 38 crimes per 100 per year)
- Very small increase in offending by drink drivers (by 6 crimes per 100 offenders per year)
- Lack of any difference in repeat offending by juvenile property offenders or shoplifters (though after-only analysis shows a drop in reoffending by shoplifters)

The drunk driving results are particularly disappointing. These are conferences without a victim, as all cases involve nonaccidents detected by random breath testing. Sherman, Strang, and Woods (2000, p. 11) interpret the pattern of the results as suggesting that courts reduce reoffending through their power to suspend drivers' licenses, a power not available to conferences in the experiment. However, more detailed decomposition of results is yet to be done on this question.

One conferencing program that has dealt convincingly with the social selection problem without randomization is a Royal Canadian Mounted Police program in the Canadian coal mining town of Sparwood, British Columbia. For almost three years from the commencement of the program in 1995 until late 1997, *no* young offender from Sparwood went to court.[6] All were cautioned or conferenced. Three youths who had been conferenced on at least two previous occasions went to court in late 1997. No cases have been to court during 1998 up until the time the data could be checked (20 October 1998). In the year prior to the program (1994), sixty-four youth went to court. Over the ensuing three years and nine months, this net was narrowed to eighty-eight conferences and three court cases. This was probably not just a net-narrowing effect, however. It looks like a real reduction in offending. According to police records, compared with the 1994 youth offending rate, the 1995 rate was down 26 percent, and the 1996 was rate down 67 percent. Reoffending rates for conference cases were 8 percent in 1995, 3 percent in 1996, 10 percent in 1997, and 0 percent for the first nine months of 1998, compared with a national rate of 40 percent per annum for court cases (which is similar to that in towns surrounding Sparwood). Reoffending rates for Sparwood court cases prior to 1995 have not been collected. While social selection bias is convincingly dealt with here by the universality of the switch to restorative justice for the first three years, eighty-eight conferences are only a modest basis for inference.

Burford and Pennell's (1998) study of a restorative conference-based approach to family violence in Newfoundland found a marked reduction in both child abuse/neglect and abuse of mothers/wives after the intervention. A halving of abuse/neglect incidents was found for thirty-two families in the year after the conference compared with the year before, while incidents increased markedly for thirty-one control families. Pennell and Burford's (1997) research is also a model of sophisticated process development and process evaluation and of methodological triangulation. While sixty-three families might seem modest for quantitative purposes, this is actually a statistically persuasive study in demonstrating that this intervention reduced family violence. There were actually 472 participants in the conferences for the thirty-two families, and 115 of these were interviewed to estimate levels of violence affecting different participants (Pennell and Burford, 2000). Moreover, within each case a before and after pattern was tested against thirty-one types of events (e.g., abuse of child, child abuses mother, attempted suicide, father keeps income from mother) where events can be relevant to more than one member of the family. Given this pattern matching of families by events by individual family members, it understates the statistical power of the design to say it is based on only sixty-three cases. Burford and Pennell (1998, p. 253) also report reduced drinking problems after conferences. The Newfoundland conferences were less successful in cases where young people were abusing their mothers, a matter worthy of further investigation.

While the universality of the New Zealand juvenile conferencing program has made it difficult to evaluate the impact on recidivism compared with a control group, Maxwell, Morris, and Anderson (1999) have now published an important evaluation of two adult programs, which they describe as sharing enough of the core principles of restorative justice to serve as case studies of restorative justice. Te Whanau Awhina (a program only for Maori offenders) and Project Turnaround refer adult offenders to a panel (rather akin to the Vermont Reparation Boards). However, family and social service providers for the family, victims and victim supporters, and the police also frequently attend. For 100 offenders referred to each of these schemes, both reoffending and the seriousness of reoffending were significantly reduced under both schemes compared with 100 controls matched for criminal history, demographic factors, and offense characteristics who went to court. Twelve-month reconviction rates were 16 percent for Project Turnaround compared with 30 percent for controls. For Te Whanau Awhina, reconviction was 33 percent, compared with 47 percent for controls.

Another important recent adult evaluation is of the John Howard Society's Restorative Resolutions program in Winnipeg (Bonta, Rooney and Wallace-Capretta, 1998). The seriousness of the offending gives special importance to this evaluation: there was 90 percent success in reserving entry to the program to serious adult offenders who were facing a prosecutorial recommendation of at least six months prison time (and preferably having histories of incarceration and probation violation). Like the New Zealand programs discussed in the previous paragraph, Restorative Resolutions secured enough of the principles of restorative justice to be accepted as a test of the approach without securing all of them: notwithstanding good-faith consultation with victims, most offenders did not actually meet their victim, and eighteen offenders had their restorative resolution accepted by the court but then with a judicially imposed sentence on top of it. Since this initial report was published, there has been follow-up over three years of a control group of seventy-two offenders, carefully matched on a variety of risk factors; the seventy-two Restorative Resolutions serious offenders had half the criminal reoffending of the control group.

The most recent study by Michael Little (2001), yet to be published as this book goes to press, is of particular importance in that it applies restorative justice to the most persistent offenders. Little's study was conducted in Kent, England. It applied to juvenile offenders who either had been previously sentenced to custody or had failed to complete a community sentence. A second condition for entry was being charged or cautioned on three or more occasions for offenses that would permit a court to sentence to custody. Basically they were the most persistent young offenders in Kent. Twenty-four offenders were randomly assigned to a multisystemic approach that involved a family group conference, joint and heightened supervision by police and social services staff, and improved assessment combined with an individual treatment plan and mentoring by a young volunteer. This was called the Intensive Supervision and Support Program. Fifty-five young offenders were assigned to two control groups. The reduction in rearrest during two years of follow-up was substantial and statistically significant. Because the treatment was multisystematic, however, there was no way of assessing whether it was restorative justice, some other component of the program, or a general placebo effect that produced the success. In the next chapter we consider the theoretical reasons why a combination of restorative justice and intensive rehabilitation in hard cases may be more effective than restorative justice and intensive rehabilitation alone. The results of this randomized trial are compelling because part of the intervention was more intensive police surveillance. This should have produced an increase in the number of offenses detected by the police in the restorative justice group.

Restorative antibullying programs in schools, generally referred to as *whole-school* approaches (Rigby 1996), which combine community deliberation among students, teachers and parents about how to prevent bullying with mediation of specific cases, have been systematically evaluated with positive results (Farrington 1993; Pitts and Smith 1995; Pepler et al. 1993; Rigby 1996) the most impressive being a program in Norway where a 50 percent reduction in bullying has been reported (Olweus 1993). Gentry and Benenson's (1993) data further suggest that skills for mediating playground disputes learned and practiced by children in school may transfer to the home setting, resulting in reduced conflict, particularly with siblings. The restorative approaches to bullying in Japanese schools, which Masters's (1997) qualitative work found to be a success, can also be read as even more radically "whole-school" than the Norwegian innovations (see Box 3.2).

Box 3.2: *Pig, Pig, Pig!*

The incident began during the morning roll call when the boy in charge
called a girl by her (unappreciated) nickname of "pig." The girl was offended and refused to answer, so the boy raised his voice and yelled the
word several times. . . . Later that morning during the break several children
gathered around the girl and chanted, "Pig, pig, pig." Deeply hurt . . . she
ran away from the group. For the remainder of the school day she did not
speak a word; that afternoon she went home and would refuse to return for a
week. The teacher in charge of the class had not been present during the
periods when the girl was insulted, so she did not appreciate what had happened.

Later that day the girl's mother called to ask what had gone on. Immediately the principal began a quiet investigation in co-operation with the
teacher. By that evening, parts of the story were known, and the principal
visited the child's home to apologise to her parents. The next day, and on
each successive day until the problem was solved, special teachers' meetings
were held with all present to seek a solution. On three occasions the principal or the girl's homeroom teacher went to the girl's home and talked with
her. The final resolution involved a visit by the entire class to the girl's
home, where apologies were offered along with a request that the insulted
girl forgive her friends. Two days later she returned to school, and two weeks
later the teacher read a final report to the regular teachers' meeting and then
apologised for having caused the school so much trouble.

Source: Cummings 1980, pp. 118–19, cited in Masters 1997

However, Gottfredson's (1997) and Brewer et al.'s (1995) reviews of school peer
mediation programs that simply train children to resolve disputes when conflicts arise
among students showed nonsignificant or weak effects on observable behavior such
as fighting. Only one of four studies with quasi-experimental or true experimental
designs found peer mediation to be associated with a decrease in aggressive behavior.
Lam's (1989) review of fourteen evaluations of peer mediation programs with mostly
weak methods found no programs that made violence worse. It appears a whole-
school approach is needed that not just tackles individual incidents but also links incidents to a change program for the culture of the school, in particular to how seriously
members of the school community take rules about bullying. Put another way, the
school not only must resolve the bullying incident; but also must use it as a resource
to affirm the disapproval of bullying in the culture of the school.

Statistical power, randomization, and control have been weak in much of the research reported here. Fairly consistently encouraging results from these weak designs, however, should be combined with the reduced reoffending evident under

stronger designs in the studies by Schneider (1986), Olweus (1993) and the other antibullying researchers, Burford and Pennell (1998), the Sparwood police, Maxwell, Morris, and Anderson (1999), Bonta Rooney and Wallace-Capretta, (1998), McGarrell et al. (2000) and Little (2001). However, the research with the strongest design, by Sherman, Strang, and Woods (2000), is encouraging only with respect to violent offenders. My own reading of the three dozen studies of reoffending reviewed is that while restorative justice programs do not involve a consistent guarantee of reducing offending, even badly managed restorative justice programs are most unlikely to make reoffending worse. After all, restorative justice is based on principles of socializing children that have demonstrably reduced delinquency when parents have applied them in raising their children (in comparison to punitive/stigmatizing socialization) (Braithwaite 1989; Sampson and Laub 1993). If we invest in working out how to improve the quality of the delivery of restorative justice programs, they are likely to show us how to substantially reduce reoffending. That investment means looking below the surface to understand the theoretical conditions of success and failure, a challenge I begin to open up in the next chapter.

Restorative justice advocates are frequently admonished not to make "exaggerated claims" for the likely effects on recidivism of a one- or two-hour intervention. Yet when it is modest benefits on the order of 10 to 20 percent lower levels of reoffending that are predicted, it can be equally irresponsible to cite a study with a sample size of 100 (which lacks the statistical power to detect an effect of this order as statistically significant) as demonstrating no effect. If we are modest in our expectations, we should expect reviewers like Braithwaite (1999) to report a study by Umbreit (1994) on a small sample finding a nonsignificant reduction in offending and then in this review to have Braithwaite report an expanded sample by Umbreit and his colleagues to now be strongly significant. In the last two years there has been a surge of positive recidivism results from the United States, Canada, Germany, the United Kingdom, Australia, and New Zealand. At the time this book goes to press, most of these very recent positive results are not incorporated into the meta analysis of thirty-two studies with control groups conducted for the Canadian Department of Justice by Latimer, Dowden and Muise (2001). Equally, Latimer, Dowden and Muise have uncovered unpublished evaluations of a dozen recent restorative justice programs not covered by the review in this chapter. Across their thirty-two studies Latimer, Dowden and Muise found a modest but statistically significant effect of restorative justice in reducing recidivism (effect size 0.07). This means approximately seven percent lower recidivism on average in the restorative justice programs compared to controls or comparison groups. This is indeed a modest accomplishment compared to effect sizes for the best rehabilitation programs. During R and D on first and second generation programs, however, our interest should not be on comparing average restorative justice effect sizes with those of the best rehabilitation programs. It should be on the effect sizes we might accomplish by integration of best restorative justice practice with best rehabilitative practice, an R and D agenda joined in chapter 5. One important difference in the conclusions reached from the set of studies reviewed in this chapter is that Latimer, Dowden and Muise found a bigger tendency for victim satisfaction to be higher in cases that went to restorative justice (effect size 0.19) than the tendency for offender satisfaction to be higher in restorative justice cases (effect size 0.10).

So now we must remember that it is possible to make Type II as well as Type I errors; we can make the error of wrongly believing that "nothing makes much difference." In recent criminological history we have seen this Type II error institutionalized in the doctrine that "nothing works" with respect to offender rehabilitation. Restorative justice clearly has the promise to justify a huge R and D effort now. Certainly there are some notable research failures. Here we might remember the often-quoted retrospective of medical texts that it was not until the advances in medicine during World War I that the average patient left an encounter with the average doctor better off. The question at the beginning of the twentieth century was whether there was enough promise in medicine to justify a huge research investment in it. Clearly there was, notwithstanding a lot of mediocre results from mediocre practice. The results in this section show that there are very strong reasons to think that funding restorative justice R and D will be a good investment for the twenty-first century, especially when, as I argue in chapter 4, restorative justice is conceived as a superior vehicle for delivering other crime prevention strategies that work, and conceived holistically as a way of living rather than just an eighty-minute intervention.

It may be that the key to explaining why the Indianapolis Juvenile Restorative Justice Experiment had a major effect on reoffending while the RISE adult drunk driving experiment did not can be understood in terms of the potential for restorative justice to be a superior vehicle for prevention to be realized in the former case but not the latter. Eighty-three percent of those randomly assigned to conferences in Indianapolis completed their diversion program, whereas completion occurred for only 58 percent of the control group assigned to the standard suite of diversion options (McGarrell et al., 2000, 47). For reasons I will discuss in chapter 4, restorative justice is potentially a superior vehicle for getting offenders and their families to commit to rehabilitative and other preventive measures. The RISE drunk driving conferences generally did not confront underlying drinking problems, with police encouraging the view that drunk driving, not drinking, is the offense. Court did not do any better in this regard, but at least the Canberra courts took away driver's licenses, a preventive measure that was not available to conferences and that probably worked.

Reduced Reoffending in Corporate Restorative Justice Programs

In chapter 1, I recounted how corporate crime researchers like myself began to wonder if the more restorative approach to corporate criminal law might actually be more effective than the punitive approach to street crime. What made us wonder this? When we observed inspectors moving around factories (as in Hawkins's [1984] study of British pollution inspectors), we noticed how talk often got the job done. The occupational health and safety inspector could talk with the workers and managers responsible for a safety problem, and they would fix it—with no punishment, not even threats of punishment. A restorative justice reading of regulatory inspection was also consistent with the quantitative picture. The probability that any given occupational health and safety violation will be detected has always been slight and the average penalty for Occupational Safety and Health Administration (OSHA) violations in the post-Watergate United States was $37 (Kelman 1984). So the economically rational firm did not have to worry about OSHA enforcement: when interviewed, its representatives would say it was a trivial cost of doing business. Yet there was quantitative evidence that workplace injuries fell after OSHA inspections or when inspection levels increased (Scholz and Gray 1990).

There was even stronger evidence that Mine Safety and Health Administration inspections in the United States saved lives and prevented injuries (Braithwaite 1985, pp. 77–84; Lewis-Beck and Alford 1980; Perry 1981a, 1981b; Boden 1983). Boden's data showed that a 25 percent increase in inspections was associated with a 7 to 20 percent reduction in fatalities on a pooled cross-sectional analysis of 535 mines with controls for geological, technological, and managerial factors; these inspections took place at a time when the average penalty for a successful citation was $173 (Braithwaite 1985, p. 3). They were inspections ending with an "exit conference" that I observed to be often quite restorative. Boden (1983) and the Mine Enforcement and Safety Administration (1977) found no association between the level of penalties and safety improvement, however.

This was just the opposite of the picture we were getting from the literature on law enforcement and street crime. On the streets, the picture was of tough enforcement, more police, and more jails failing to make a difference. In coal mines we saw weak enforcement (no imprisonment) but convincing evidence that what Julia Black later came to call "conversational regulation" (Black 1997, 1998) can work—more inspectors reduced offending and saved lives (Braithwaite 1985).

My book was called *To Punish or Persuade: Enforcement of Coal Mine Safety*, and it concluded that while persuasion works better than punishment, credible punishment is needed as well to back up persuasion when it fails. Writing the book was a somewhat emotional conversion to restorative justice for me, as I came to it as a kind of victims' supporter, a boy from a coal mining town who wanted to write an angry book for friends killed in the mines. My research also found strong empirical evidence that persuasion works better when workers and unions (representing the victims of the crime) are involved in deliberative regulatory processes.[7] Nearly all serious mine safety accidents can be prevented if only the law is obeyed (Braithwaite 1985, pp. 20–24, 75–77); the great historical lesson of the coal industry is that the way to accomplish this is through a rich dialogue among victims and offenders on why the law is important, a dialogue given a deeper meaning after each fatality is investigated. The shift from punitive to restorative justice in that industry and the results of that shift have been considerable. During the first fifty years of mine safety enforcement in Britain (until World War I), in a number of years a thousand miners lost their lives in the pits. Fatalities decreased from 1,484 in 1866 to 44 in 1982–83, after which the

British industry collapsed. In the years immediately prior to World War I, the average annual number of criminal prosecutions for coal mine safety offenses in the United Kingdom was 1,309. In both 1980 and 1981 there were none (Braithwaite 1985, p. 4).

The qualitative research doing ride-alongs with mine safety inspectors in several countries resolved the puzzle for me. Persuasion worked much of the time; workers' participation in a dialogue about their own security worked. However, the data also suggested that persuasion worked best in the contexts where it was backed by the possibility of punishment.

In the United Kingdom during the 1970s, fifty pits were selected each year for a special safety campaign; these pits showed a consistently greater improvement in accident rates than other British pits (Collinson 1978, p. 77). I found the safety leaders in the industry were companies that not only thoroughly involved everyone concerned after a serious accident to reach consensual agreement on what must be done to prevent recurrence but also did this after "near accidents" (Braithwaite 1985, p. 67), as well as discussing safety audit results with workers even when there was no near accident. In a remarkable foreshadowing of what we now believe to be reasons for the effectiveness of whole-school approaches to bullying and family group conferences, Davis and Stahl's (1967, p. 26) study of twelve companies that had been winners of the industry's two safety awards found one recurring initiative was "safety letter to families of workers enlisting family support in promoting safe work habits." That is, safety leaders engaged a community of care beyond the workplace in building a safety culture. In *To Punish or Persuade* I shocked myself by concluding that after mine disasters, including the terrible one in my hometown that had motivated me to write the book, so long as there had been an open public dialogue among all those affected, the families of the miners cared for, and a credible plan to prevent recurrence put in place, criminal punishment served little purpose. The process of the public inquiry and helping the families of the miners for whom they were responsible seemed such a potent general deterrent that a criminal trial could be gratuitous and might corrupt the restorative justice process that I found in so many of the thirty-nine disaster investigations I studied.

Joseph Rees (1988, 1994) is the scholar who has done most to work through the promise of what he calls *communitarian regulation*, which we might read as restorative regulatory justice. First Rees (1988) studied the Cooperative Compliance Program of OSHA between 1979 and 1984. OSHA essentially empowered labor-management safety committees at seven Californian sites to take over the law enforcement role, to solve the underlying problems revealed by breaches of the law. Satisfaction of workers, management and government participants was high because they believed the program "worked." It seemed to. Accident rates ranged from one-third lower to five times as low as the Californian rate for comparable projects of the same companies, as the rate in the same project before the cooperative compliance program compared with after (Rees 1988, pp. 2–3).

Rees's next study of communitarian regulation was of U.S. nuclear regulation after the incident at Three Mile Island. The industry realized that it had to transform the nature of its regulation and self-regulation from a rule book, hardware orientation to one oriented to people, corporate cultures, and software. The industry's CEOs set up the Institute of Nuclear Power Operations (INPO) to achieve these ends. Peers from other nuclear power plants would take three weeks off from their own jobs to join an INPO review team that engaged representatives of the inspected facility in a dialogue about how they could improve. Safety performance ratings were also issued by the review team; comparative ratings of all the firms in the industry were displayed and discussed at meetings of all the CEOs in the industry and at separate meetings of safety officers. Rees (1994) sees these as reintegrative shaming sessions. The following is an excerpt from a videotape of a meeting of the safety officers:

> It's not particularly easy to come up here and talk about an event at a plant in which you have a lot of pride, a lot of pride in the performance, in the operators . . . It's also tough going through the agonizing thinking of what it is you want to say. How do you want to confess? How do you want to couch it in a way that, even though you did something wrong, you're still okay? You get a chance to talk to Ken Strahm and Terry Sullivan [INPO vice presidents] and you go over what your plans are, and they tell you, "No, Fred, you've got to really bare your soul." . . . It's a painful thing to do. (Rees 1994, p. 107)

What was the effect of the shift in the center of gravity of the regulatory regime from a Nuclear Regulatory Commission driven by political sensitivities to be tough and prescriptive to INPO's communitarian regulation (focused on a dialogue about how to achieve outcomes rather than rule book enforcement)? Rees (1994, pp. 183–86) shows considerable improvement across a range of indicators of the safety performance of the U.S. nuclear power industry since INPO was established. Improvement has continued since the completion of Rees's study. For example, more recent World Association of Nuclear Operators data show scrams (automatic emergency shutdowns) declined in the United States from over 7 per unit in 1980 to 0.1 by the late 1990s.

In chapter 1, we saw that shifting nursing home regulation from rule book enforcement to restorative justice was associated with improved regulatory outcomes and that the inspectors who shifted most toward restorative justice improved compliance most (those who used praise and trust more than threat, those who used reintegrative shaming rather than tolerance or stimatization, those who restored self-efficacy). These results will be discussed again in the next chapter as it considers the theories that predict why restorative justice might work better than punitive justice. For the moment, I simply report that communitarian regulation has had considerable documented success in restoring coal mining firms, nuclear power plants, and nursing homes to a more responsible approach to compliance with the law. Equally, writers such as Gunningham (1995) and Haines (1997) have shown that there are serious limits to communitarian regulation—rapacious big firms and incompetent little ones that will not or cannot respond responsibly. Deterrence and incapacitation are needed, and needed in larger measure than these regimes currently provide, when restorative justice fails (see also Ayres and Braithwaite 1992; Gunningham and Grabosky 1998).

Carol Heimer pointed out in comments on a draft of this chapter, "If high-level white collar workers are more likely to get restorative justice, it may be because their corporate colleagues and other members of the society believe that their contributions are not easily replaced, so that offenders must be salvaged" (see Heimer and Staffen 1995). This is right, I suspect, and a reason that justice is most likely to be restorative in the hands of communities of care that can see the value of salvaging the offender and the victim.

RESTORATIVE JUSTICE PRACTICES RESTORE AND SATISFY COMMUNITIES BETTER THAN EXISTING CRIMINAL JUSTICE PRACTICES

In every place where a reform debate has occurred about the introduction of family group conferences, two community concerns have been paramount: (1) while victims might be forgiving in New Zealand, giving free rein to victim anger "here" will tear at our community; (2) while families may be strong elsewhere, "here" our worst offenders are alienated and alone; their families are so dysfunctional and uncaring that they will not participate meaningfully. But as Morris et al. (1996, p. 223) conclude from perspectives on this question summarized from a number of jurisdictions: "Concerns about not being able to locate extended family or family supporters, to engage families or to effectively involve so-called 'dysfunctional' families, about families forming a coalition to conceal abuse and about families' failing to honour agreements do not prove to have been well-founded in any of the jurisdictions reported in this book."

In his discussion of the Hollow Water experience of using healing circles to deal with rampant sexual abuse of children in a Canadian First Nations community, Ross (1996, p. 150) emphasizes the centrality of restoring communities for restoring individuals: "If you are dealing with people whose relationships have been built on power and abuse, you must actually *show* them, then give them the experience of, relationships based on respect . . . [so] . . . the healing process must involve a healthy *group* of people, as opposed to single therapists. A single therapist cannot, by definition, do more than *talk* about healthy relationships."

The most sophisticated implementation of this ideal that has been well evaluated is Burford and Pennell's (1998) Family Group Decision Making Project to confront violence and child neglect in families. Beyond the positive effects on the direct objective of reducing violence, the evaluation found a posttest increase in family support, concrete (e.g., baby-sitting) and emotional, and enhanced family unity, even in circumstances where some conference plans involved separation of parents from their children. The philosophy of this program was to look for strengths in families that were in very deep trouble and build on them. In chapter 6, building on the work of Mary Kaldor (1999), I argue that this is the restorative justice prescription to the nature of contemporary armed conflict—find the islands of civility in the war-torn nation and build out from the strength in those islands of civil society.

Members of the community beyond the offender and the victim who attend restorative justice processes tend, like offenders, victims, and the police, to come away with high levels of satisfaction. In Pennell and Burford's (1995) family group conferences for family violence, 94 percent of family members were "satisfied with the way it was run"; 92 percent felt they were "able to say what was important"; and 92 percent "agreed with the plan decided on." Clairmont (1994, p. 28) also reports that among native peoples in Canada the restorative justice initiatives he reviewed have "proven to be popular with offenders . . . and to have broad, general support within communities." The Ministry of Justice, Western Australia (1994) reports 93 percent parental satisfaction, 84 percent police satisfaction, and 67 percent judicial satisfaction, plus (and crucially) satisfaction of Aboriginal organizations with its restorative justice conference program (Juvenile Justice Teams). In Singapore, 95 percent of family members who attended family group conferences said that they benefited personally from the experience (Hsien 1996). For the Bethlehem police conferencing experiment, parents of offenders were more satisfied (97 percent) and more likely to believe that justice had been fair (97 percent) than in cases that went to court (McCold and Wachtel 1998, pp. 65–72). Parental satisfaction and perceptions of justice were similarly high in the Indianapolis experiment (McGarrell et al., 2000). Eighty percent of the conference parents "felt involved," compared with 40 percent for the children who were randomly assigned to other diversion programs. Ninety percent of the conference parents felt they had the opportunity to express their views, compared with 68 percent in the control group.

A study by Schneider (1990) found that *completing* restitution and community service was associated with enhanced commitment to community and feelings of citizenship (and reduced recidivism). While the evidence is overwhelming that where communities show strong social support, criminality is less (Cullen 1994; Chamlin and Cochran 1997), it might be optimistic to expect that restorative justice could ever have sufficient impacts in restoring microcommunities to cause a shift in the macro impact of community on the crime rate (cf. Brown and Polk 1996). On the other hand, Tom Tyler's most recent book with Yuen Huo (Tyler and Huo, 2001) finds that procedural fairness by authorities quite strongly increases trust in authorities, and trust in authorities in turn has considerable effects in increasing indentification with one's community and society and ultimately participation in the community. In the discussion of Tyler's work in the next chapter, we will see there is consistent evidence that restorative justice is perceived as more procedurally fair in a number of ways compared with courtroom justice. Tyler's work opens up exciting new lines of research on why restorative justice might contribute to community building.

Building the microcommunity of a school or restoring social bonds in a family can have important implications for crime in that school or that family. Moreover, the restoring of microcommunity has a value of its own, independent of the size of the impact on crime. The previous section described how whole-school approaches can halve bullying in schools. There is a more important point of deliberative programs to give all the citizens of the school community an opportunity to be involved in deciding how to make their school safer and more caring. It is that they make their schools more decent places to live while one is being educated. Evidence from Australia suggests that restorative sexual harassment programs in workplaces may reduce sexual harassment (Parker 1998). Again, more important than the improved compliance with the law may be the more general improvements in the respect with which women are treated in workplaces as a result of the deliberation and social support integral to such programs when they are effective.

We have seen restorative justice conferences where supporters of a boy offender and a girl victim of a sexual assault agreed to work together to confront a culture of exploitative masculinity in an Australian school that unjustly characterized the girl as "getting what she asked for" (Braithwaite and Daly 1994). Conversely, we have seen conferences that have missed the opportunity to confront homophobic cultures in schools revealed by graffiti humiliating allegedly gay men and boys (Retzinger and Scheff 1996). After one early New Zealand conference concerning breaking into and damaging the restaurant of a refugee Cambodian, the offender agreed to watch a video of *The Killing Fields* and "pass the word on the street" that the Cambodian restaurateur was struggling to survive and should not be harassed. A small victory for civil community life, perhaps, but a large one for that Cambodian man.

One of the most stirring conferences I know of occurred in an outback town after four Aboriginal children manifested their antagonism toward the middle-class matriarchs of the town by ransacking the Country Women's Association Hall. The conference was so moving because it brought the Aboriginal and the white women together, shocked and upset by what the children had done, to talk to each other about why the women no longer spoke to one another across the racial divide in the way they had in earlier times. Did there have to be such an incivility as this to discover the loss of their shared communal life? Those black and white women and children rebuilt that communal life as they restored the devastated Country Womens' Association Hall, working together, respectfully once more (for more details on this case, see the Real Justice Web site at http://www.realjustice.org/).

One might summarize that the evidence of restorative justice restoring communities points to very small accomplishments of microcommunity-building and of modest numbers of community members going away overwhelmingly satisfied with the justice in which they feel they have had a meaningful opportunity to participate. Maori critics of Pakeha restorative justice such as Moana Jackson (1987) and Juan Tauri (1998) point out that it falls far short of restoring Maori community control over justice. Neocolonial controls from Pakeha courts remain on top of restorative justice in Maori communities. This critique seems undeniable; nowhere in the world has restorative justice enabled major steps toward restoring precolonial forms of community among colonized peoples; nowhere have the courts of the colonial power given up their power to trump the decisions of the Indigenous justice forums.

At the same time, there is a feminist critique of this Indigenous critique of community restoration. I will return to at least one case where male Indigenous elders in Canada have used control over community justice as a resource in the oppression of women complaining of rape by dominant men. In this case the community was torn asunder to the point of a number of women leaving it.

With all the attention we have given to the microcommunity-building of routine restorative justice conferences, we must not lose sight of historically rare moments of restorative justice that reframe macrocommunity. I refer, for example, to the release of IRA terrorists from prison so that they could participate in the IRA meetings of 1998 that voted for the renunciation of violent struggle. I refer to much more partially successful examples, such as the Camp David mediations of President Carter with the leaders of Egypt and Israel (more partially successful because they excluded the Palestinians themselves) and to more totally successful local peacemaking such as that of the Kulka Women's Club in the highlands of New Guinea (see Box 3.3).

CONCLUSION

There do seem to be empirical grounds for optimism that restorative justice can "work" in restoring victims, offenders, and communities. When the restorative practice helps bring a war-torn nation to peace, as in the civil wars of the Solomons and Bougainville (see Box 3.3: Kulka Womens' Club, Peacemaking, and chapter 6), we might say restorative justice works with dramatic effect. As the endeavors of the Truth and Reconciliation Commission in South Africa and those of a number of other nations now demonstrate, "working" in terms of healing a nation is more important than working simply conceived as reducing crime. At a more micro level, "working" as healing a workplace after sexual harassment (Parker 1998), a school after bullying (Rigby 1996), and a family after violence (Burford and Pennell 1998) are exceptionally important outcomes that have been considered in this chapter. In chapter 4, we will even conceive of restorative justice as working in terms of strengthening democracy. Finally, to conceive "working" in the traditional criminological way of reducing crime forgets victims. We conclude, following Strang (2000), that restorative justice mostly works well in granting justice, closure, restoration of dignity, transcendence of shame, and healing for victims.

All that said, we have found that restorative justice shows great promise as a strategy of crime reduction. A mistake criminologists could make now is to do more and more research to compare the efficacy of restorative justice, statically conceived, with traditional Western justice. Rather, we must think more dynamically about developing the restorative justice process and the values that guide it. In my view, this chapter demonstrates that we already know that restorative justice has much promise. The research and development agenda now is to enlarge our understanding of the conditions under which that promise is realized. It will become clear that my own theoretical position inclines me to believe that restorative justice can work better if it is designed to enhance the efficacy of deterrence, incapacitation, and particularly rehabilitation and community prevention. Obversely, these strategies of crime reduction can work better if they are embedded in a responsive regulatory pyramid that enhances the efficacy of restorative justice. It follows that comparing the efficacy

---

Box 3.3: Kulka Women's Club Peacemaking

Alan Rumsey (2000) has documented the extraordinary intervention of the Kulka Women's Club to end a New Guinea highlands tribal war. The context is that, after an initial period of colonial pacification, in many parts of the New Guinea highlands tribal fighting has become worse, and more deadly, in recent decades, with guns replacing spears and arrows. What the Kulka Women's Club did on 13 September 1982 was to march between two opposing armies under the national flag, exhorting both sides with gifts to put down their arms, which they did. Note that as in so many of the important non-Western forms of restorative justice, the victims move the offenders by giving them gifts rather than asking for compensation (see Box 1.1: The Sulha), the Javanese case at note 1, and the Crow practice of buying the ways (Austin 1984, p. 36).[8] The distinctive peacemaking intervention of the Kulka Women's Club seems to have been unique, rather than a recurrent Melanesian cultural pattern. Its importance is that it had a long-lasting effect, the peace having held until the present, during two decades when hostilities among surrounding tribes escalated. Though the intervention seems unique, Maev O'Collins (2000) links it to peace and reconciliation meetings organized by women in war-torn Bougainville and women marching in Port Moresby to protest against male violence. In June 2000 a group of seventy women wearing scarfs in the colors of the national flag approached the two warring groups in the Solomon Islands civil war, asking them to talk peace, which they did (*The Dominion*, 17 June 2000). Rumsay's (2000, p. 9) work is important because it shows the need for highly contextualized analysis of the macrotransformative moments of restorative justice: "The very factors that make one area relatively conducive to peacemaking are the same ones that make it more difficult in the neighbouring region."

---

of a pure restorative justice strategy with that of a pure punishment strategy is not the best research path for the future.

In moving in the next chapter to the theories that give an account of why restorative justice might "work," we will discover a number of further dimensions of what "working" might mean beyond those canvassed in this chapter.

NOTES

1. I am reminded of a village in Java where I was told of a boy caught stealing. The outcome of a restorative village meeting was that the offender was given a bag of rice: "We should be ashamed because one from our village should be so poor as to steal. We should be ashamed as a village."

2. The evidence reviewed below also in fact suggest lower levels of victim satisfaction and participation than in its predecessor the Wagga Wagga program, a difference I attribute to

the extraordinary gifts Terry O'Connell brought to that program and the extraordinary way the Wagga community got behind the program.

3. The evidence seems to be that this was due mainly to limitations in the program administration that made it difficult for victims to attend, not to the fact that most victims did not want to attend; only 6 percent did not want to meet their offender (Maxwell and Morris 1996).

4. The word *extremely* has been added to this sentence since my 1999 review of the evidence, indicating an accumulation of encouraging results.

5. This test is reported in Schneider 1986, but for mysterious reasons Schneider 1990 reports only the nonsignificant differences between before and after offending rates for the control and experimental groups separately, rather than the significant difference between the experimental and control group (which is the relevant comparison).

6. I am indebted to Glen Purdy, a Sparwood lawyer in private practice, for these data. The data until early 1997 are also available at www.titanlink.com.

7. For example, DeMichiei et al.'s (1982, p. i) comparison of mines with exceptionally high injury rates with matched mines with exceptionally low-injury rates found that at the low injury mines: "Open lines of communication permit management and labor to jointly reconcile problems affecting safety and health; Representatives of labor become actively involved in issues concerning safety, health and production; and Management and labor identify and accept their joint responsibility for correcting unsafe conditions and practices."

8. Cree elder Roland Duneuette tells the story of the father and mother of a homicide victim taking in the offender as a son to teach him the Cree ways. Alan Rumsay tells me that in the highlands of New Guinea more widely, when one tribe is owed substantial compensation by another that has wronged them, the process that leads to the paying of that compensation starts with the wronged tribe offering a gift to the wrongdoer. In New Guinea, even when the offender acts first by offering compensation to a victim, the preserving of relationships will often also involve the expectation of a smaller but significant reciprocal gift back to the offender by the victim. Such a way of thinking is not unknown in the West. We see it in *Les Misérables*, part of the Western literary canon, and in Pope John Paul visiting and presenting a gift to the man who shot him.

4

Theories That Might Explain Why Restorative Justice Works

THE REVIEW OF EVIDENCE IN THE LAST CHAPTER CONCLUDED THAT THE FIRST OF the new generation of restorative justice programs of the 1990s may have had some effects in reducing reoffending and enhancing restoration in other ways. Some of these programs seemed to be somewhat effective, even though we look back on them in the new century as flawed first-generation efforts. We think we can and are doing better now as we look back on all the mistakes we learned from those earlier programs. Yet to do better in a significant way, the argument of this chapter is that we must commit to sustained research and development of restorative justice that tests theories of the conditions where it is productive and counterproductive.

This chapter shows first that a set of theories that increasingly seem to have strong relationships with one another—theories of reintegrative shaming, procedural justice, unacknowledged shame, defiance, and self-categorization—offer an explanation for why restorative justice processes might be effective in reducing crime and accomplishing other kinds of restoration. Then the chapter argues that restorative justice has the makings of a better theory of crime prevention than the situational crime prevention tradition, a better theory of rehabilitation than the welfare model provides, a better theory of how deterrence can reduce crime than the deterrence model, a better theory of incapacitation than the theory of selective incapacitation, a better approach to cost-effectiveness in crime prevention than the economic analysis of law provides, and a better theory of justice than the justice model and one with richer roots in democratic theory.

Some of these claims are sure to be proved untrue by the kind of R and D advocated here. Equally, where these theoretical claims turn out to be true, we will find that the potential of this truth has not been sufficiently built into the design of restorative justice programs.

REINTEGRATIVE SHAMING THEORY

> *ma te whakama e patu!*
> "Leave him alone he is punished by shame."
>   Maori saying

Crime, Shame and Reintegration (Braithwaite 1989) gives an account of why restorative justice processes ought to prevent crime more effectively than retributive practices. The core claims are (1) that tolerance of crime makes things worse; (2) that stigmatization, or disrespectful, outcasting shaming of crime, makes crime worse still; and (3) that reintegrative shaming, or disapproval of the act within a continuum of respect for the offender and terminated by rituals of forgiveness, prevents crime (see Box 4.1).

In developing the theory of reintegrative shaming, I was much influenced by the restorative nature of various Asian policing and educational practices, by what I saw as the effectiveness of restorative regulatory processes for dealing with corporate crime in both Asia and the West, and by the restorative nature of socialization in Western families that succeed in raising law-abiding children. That child development literature will not be reviewed again here. Essentially, what it shows is that both laissez-faire parenting that fails to confront and disapprove of childrens' misconduct and punitively authoritarian parenting produce a lot of delinquents; delinquency is less likely when parents confront wrongdoing with moral reasoning (Braithwaite 1989). One implication for restorative justice advocates of this substantial body of empirical evidence is that the justice system will do better when it facilitates moral reasoning by families over what to do about a crime as an alternative to punishment by the state.

Restorative justice conferences work by inviting victims and supporters (usually family supporters) of the victim to meet with the offender and the people who care most about the offender and most enjoy the offender's respect (usually including both the nuclear and the extended family, but not limited to them). This group discusses the consequences of the crime, drawing out the feelings of those who have been harmed. Then it discusses how that harm might be repaired and any steps that should be taken to prevent reoffending. Attendances over forty can occur, but average reported attendances, beyond the offender or offenders, are six in New Zealand (Robertson 1996), six in Victoria (Ban 1996), five in Bethlehem (McCold and Wachtel 1998, p. 30), eight in Canberra (unpublished RISE data), and twenty-three in Manitoba (Longclaws, Galaway and Barkwell 1996). Wachtel (1997, p. 73) reports a five-hour conference in Pennsylvania with an attendance of seventy-five.

In terms of reintegrative shaming theory, the discussion of the consequences of the crime for victims (or consequences for the offender's family) structures shame into the conference; the support of those who enjoy the strongest relationships of love or respect with the offender structures reintegration into the ritual. It is not the shame of police or judges or newspapers that is most able to get through to us; it is shame in the eyes of those we respect and trust. These are not new ideas. They have existed

Box 4.1: Destigmatizing Sex Offenders

Circles of Support and Accountability bring together volunteers in an alternative network for sex offenders, who typically have little in the way of family or social support and are often intellectually deficient. Sex offenders are at greatest risk of committing new offences when they're experiencing stress in their lives or feeling isolated, so Circle volunteers provide a friendly ear when the offender needs to sound off. They help him find solutions to problems like finding an apartment or looking for work. They offer advice and encouragement and help celebrate milestones like anniversaries and birthdays. And they watch for signs that he might be at increased risk of reoffending—drinking, for instance, or hanging around schools or parks.

The support is proving effective. Sex offenders as a group are at a high risk of reoffending, but the rate among Circle members is significantly lower, said Corrections Canada psychologist Robin Wilson. In a survey of 30 Circle offenders who had been in the community for an average of just over two years, Wilson found that two had committed new offences (one was charged with sexual assault and one with making an indecent phone call). Statistically, one would expect seven men to have reoffended over that period, Wilson said.

. . . Circles of Support and Accountability have been formed for about 55 released offenders, mainly pedophiles and rapists who were forced to serve their full sentences and thus were not eligible for halfway programs to help them adjust to life outside prison. . . .

Budreo's Circle currently includes two members of his alcohol-recovery program as well as a retired United Church minister—and an unlikely member in the form of Det. Wendy Leaver of the Metropolitan Toronto Police sexual-assault squad. The first time Leaver met Budreo was in November 1994, a few days after his release from Kingston Penitentiary and right after he fled Peterborough, Ont., for Toronto. She went to advise him that Toronto police were applying to have a peace bond placed on him subjecting him to various conditions, as provided in the Criminal Code in the case of sex offenders. About a week later, [Rev. Hugh] Kirkegaard called her to sit on Budreo's Circle. "My initial response to myself was, 'I put these people in jail. I don't support them when they come out of the system,' " Leaver said in an interview. She wondered, "Do these individuals (forming Circles) have any idea what they're dealing with, or are they just a bunch of tree-huggers?" But if she was part of the Circle, she figured, she would at least have some control over Budreo. It would be one way she, as an individual, could help keep her community safe.

Since then, she has joined two other Circles. "I go as a volunteer, but I'm still a police officer. They're well aware that if they step over the line, I'll be the first to turn them in." Circle meetings are held weekly when the of-

(continued)

fender first gets out of prison. During those early days, Circle members also take turns contacting him daily, either in person or over the phone. With time, as the man's needs diminish, the formal meetings are held less frequently. But some of the volunteers often will maintain a presence in the person's life. And the offender can always call a meeting if he is having a problem, or call an individual volunteer if he needs someone to talk to. . . .

A released pedophile in Hamilton turned to his Circle for emotional support after one of his relatives refused to let him hold her newborn baby . . . If someone shows signs of reverting to high-risk behavior, the Circle will challenge him . . . "The community itself has to have some kind of ownership," he said. Psychologist Wilson said: "For a change, you have ordinary, common people taking a reasonable approach rather than just being afraid." But it takes a special commitment. Some volunteers said in interviews they initially felt so repulsed by the crime committed that they weren't always sure they could work with the offender, despite believing strongly in restorative justice.

"I found the actual offence so awful, I wasn't sure I could be part of it," said Norma Johnston, a Hamilton churchgoer. . . . Johnston committed herself only to trying it for three months instead of the year that volunteers are normally asked for. A year later, she continues to sit on the Circle, with no plans to leave. These days, its members are busy trying to get the man tested for possible learning disabilities.

Just the other week, Johnston took him and his wife out to dinner.

"You know, I really like him," she said.

Source: Debbie Parkes, *Montreal Gazette*, 16 April 2000

for hundreds of years in Maori philosophies of justice. Maori thought about *whanau* conferences repeatedly uses the words *shame* (*whakama*) and *healing* or *embrace* in similar ways to Braithwaite's *shaming* and *reintegration*. In Maori thinking, it is the shame of letting one's extended family down that is particularly important to discuss. The advantage of this sort of shame over the individual guilt/shame one is expected to experience as one stands alone in the dock of Western justice is that it is readily transcended when family members extend forgiveness to the offender.

Evidence from the first 548 adult and juvenile cases randomly assigned to court versus conference in Canberra, Australia, indicates that offenders both report and are observed to encounter more reintegrative shaming in conferences than in court, that conference offenders experience more remorse and more forgiveness than court offenders, and are more likely to report that they have learned from the process that there are people who care about them (Sherman and Strang 1997c; see also Harris 2001). Data such as these call into doubt what was a common early reaction to *Crime, Shame and Reintegration*, namely, that contemporary urban societies are not places with the interdependence and community to allow the experience of shame and re-integration to be a reality (see Braithwaite 1993a).

Makkai and Braithwaite's (1994) test of the theory in the domain of compliance of Australian nursing homes with quality of care standards has the attraction of test-retest reliabilities of the measure of compliance with the law between .93 and .96, obtained by having an independent inspector check compliance. Makkai and Braithwaite found that homes checked by inspectors with a reintegrative shaming philosophy experienced improved compliance with the law in a follow-up inspection two years later. Nursing homes inspected by stigmatizing inspectors suffered an equivalent drop in compliance two years later, while homes checked by tolerant and understanding inspectors suffered an intermediate fall in compliance (see Figure 4.1). I am involved in another book (Ahmed et al. 2001), assessing the state of play with further empirical work on the theory of reintegrative shaming. It argues for some adjustments to the theory, but that the theory can continue to focus a productive

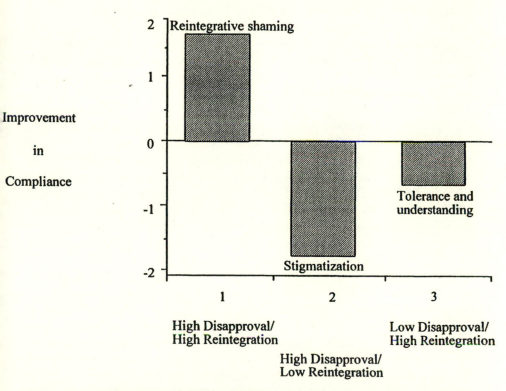

Figure 4.1   Mean Improvement in Compliance for Nursing Homes Where Inspectors Used High Disapproval and High Reintegration Styles; High Disapproval and Low Reintegration Styles; Low Disapproval and High Reintegration Styles (N = 129; F-value = 3.58; p = .03) (From Makkai and Braithwaite 1994)

program of research and development on what makes for effective and ineffective restorative justice processes.

PROCEDURAL JUSTICE THEORY

The idea of reintegrative shaming is that disapproval is communicated within a continuum of respect for the offender. A key way to show respect is to be fair, to listen, to empower others with process control, and to refrain from bias on the grounds of age, sex, or race. More broadly, procedural justice communicates respect (Lind and Tyler 1988; Tyler 1990). Conferences do not have all the procedural safeguards of court cases, yet there are theoretical grounds for predicting that offenders and victims will find them fairer. Why? Conferences are structurally fairer because of who participates and who controls the discourse. Criminal trials invite along those who can inflict maximum damage on the other side; conferences invite those who can offer maximum support to their own side, be it the victim side or the offender side. In other words, those present are expected to be fair and therefore tend to want to be fair. They tend not to see their job as doing better at blackening the character of the other than the other does at blackening theirs.

Citizens are empowered with process control rather than placed under the control of lawyers. In the same study of nursing home regulation discussed earlier, Makkai and Braithwaite (1996) found that of the various facets of procedural justice, perceived process control on the part of citizens is the one that predicts subsequent compliance with the law. Other research suggests other dimensions of procedural justice may be important, however. For example, in the Milwaukee domestic violence experiment (Bridgeforth 1990, p. 76), "arrestees who said (in lockup) that police had not taken the time to listen to their side of the story were 36% more likely to be reported for assaulting the same victim over the next 6 months than those who said the police had listened to them" (Sherman 1993, p. 463; see also Paternoster et al. 1997). More broadly, in *Why People Obey the Law*, Tyler (1990) found that citizens were more likely to comply with the law when they saw themselves as treated fairly by the criminal justice system. Sherman (1993) reviewed subsequent supportive evidence on this question, as did Tyler and Huo (2001).

The key questions are whether citizens feel they are treated more fairly in restorative justice processes than in courts and whether they are more likely to understand what is going on. The answer seems to be yes. Early results from the Canberra conferencing experiment show that offenders were more likely to understand what was going on in conferences than in court cases; felt more empowered to express their views; had more time to do so; were more likely to feel that their rights were respected, that they could correct errors of fact, and that they were treated with respect; and were less likely to feel that they were disadvantaged due to "age, income, sex, race or some other reason" (Barnes 1999; Sherman and Barnes 1997; Sherman et al. 1998). The NSW Youth Conferencing Scheme seems to be even more successful than the Canberra program on these dimensions (Trimboli 2000). Without the randomized comparison with court, a number of other studies have shown absolutely high levels of citizen satisfaction with the fairness of restorative justice processes, with such perceptions being higher the more restorative the programs are (see the studies cited in chapter 3).

Given that there is now strong evidence that restorative justice processes are perceived to be fairer by those involved and strong evidence that perceived procedural justice improves compliance with the law, it follows as a prediction that restorative justice processes will improve compliance with the law.

THE THEORY OF UNACKNOWLEDGED SHAME

Scholars working in the affect theory tradition of Sylvan Tomkins (1962), most notably Donald Nathanson (1992) and David Moore with Forsythe (1995), have a theoretical perspective on why restorative justice should reduce crime based more on the nature of shame as an affect than on shaming, reintegration, and stigmatization as practices. According to this perspective, shame can be a destructive emotion because it can lead one to attack others, attack self, avoid, or withdraw (Nathanson's [1992] compass of shame). All of these are responses that can promote crime. A profound deficiency of Braithwaite's (1989) theory is that it is just a theory of shaming, with the emotion of shame left undertheorized.

From this perspective, therefore, a process is needed that enables offenders to deal with the shame that almost inevitably arises at some level when a serious criminal offense has occurred. Denial, for example, being "ashamed to be ashamed," in Scheff's words, is not an adaptive response. Shame is a normal emotion that healthy humans must experience; it is as vital to motivating us to preserve social bonds essential to our flourishing as is fear to motivating us to flee danger. Indeed, Scheff (1990, 1994), Retzinger (1991), and Scheff and Retzinger (1991) finger bypassed shame as the culprit in the shame-rage spirals that characterize our worst violence domestically and internationally.

The evidence these authors offer for the promotion of anger through bypassed shame is voluminous but of a quite different sort from the more quantitative evidence adduced under the other propositions in this and the previous chapter. It consists primarily of collections of clinical case notes (preeminently Lewis's [1971] research) and microanalyses of conversations (preeminently Retzinger's [1991] marital quarrels). Yet the thrust of this work is also supported by Tangney's (1995) review of quantitative studies on the relationship between shame and psychopathology: guilt about specific behaviors, "uncomplicated by feelings of shame about the self," is healthy. The problem is "chronic self-blame and an excessive rumination over some objectionable behavior" (Tangney 1995, p. 1141). Scheff and Retzinger take this further, suggesting that shame is more likely to be uncomplicated when consequences that are shameful are confronted and emotional repair work is done for those damaged. Shame will become complicated, chronic, and more likely to descend into rage if it is not fully confronted. If there is nagging shame under the surface, it is no permanent solution to lash out at others with anger that blames them. Then the shame and rage will feed on each other in a shame-rage spiral. Consistent with this analysis, Ahmed (2001) has shown in a study of bullying among 1,200 Canberra schoolchildren that bullies deal with shame through transforming it (into anger, for example), and victims acknowledge and internalize shame so that they suffer persistent shame, while children who avoid both bullying and being victimized by bullies have the ability to acknowledge and discharge shame so that it does not become a threat to the self. Ahmed concludes that restorative processes may reduce crime because they create spaces where there is the time and the tolerance for shame to be acknowledged, something that is not normally facilitated in the formal courtroom context.

According to Retzinger and Scheff's work, if we want a world with less violence and less dominating abuse of others, we need to take seriously rituals that encourage approval of caring behavior so that citizens will acquire pride in being caring and nondominating. With dominating behavior, we need rituals of disapproval and acknowledged shame of the dominating behavior, rituals that avert disapproval–unacknowledged shame sequences. Retzinger and Scheff (1996) see restorative justice conferences as having the potential (a potential far from always realized) to institutionalize pride and acknowledged shame that heals damaged social bonds. Circles in this formulation are ceremonies of constructive conflict. When hurt is communicated, shame acknowledged by the person or persons who caused it, respect shown for the victim's reasons for communicating the hurt, and respect reciprocated by the victim, constructive conflict has occurred between victim and offender. It may be that in the "abused spouse syndrome," for example, shame is bypassed and destructive, as a relationship iterates through a cycle of abuse, manipulative contrition, peace, perceived provocation, and renewed abuse (see Retzinger 1991). Crime wounds, justice heals, but only if justice is relational (Burnside and Baker 1994).

Moore with Forsythe (1995, p. 265) emphasize that restorative justice should *not*, in the words of Gipsy Rose Lee, accentuate the positive and eliminate the negative; rather, it should accentuate the positive and confront the negative. Sylvan Tomkins (1962) adduces four principles for constructive management of affect: "(1) That positive affect should be maximised. (2) That negative affect should be minimised. (3) That affect inhibition should be minimised. (4) That power to maximise positive affect, to minimise negative affect, and to minimise affect inhibition should be maximised" (Moore with Forsythe 1995, p. 264). Nathanson (1998) links this model to a hypothesized capacity of restorative justice processes to build community, where community is conceived as people linked by scripts for systems of affect modulation. Community is built by

> 1) Mutualization of and group action to enhance or maximize positive affect; 2) Mutualization of and group action to diminish or minimize negative affect; 3) Communities thrive best when all affect is expressed so these first two goals may be accomplished; 4) Mechanisms that increase the power to accomplish these goals favor

the maintenance of community, whereas mechanisms that decrease the power to express and modulate affect threaten the community. (Nathanson 1998, p. 86)

In the most constructive conflicts, shame will be acknowledged by apology (reciprocated by forgiveness; Tavuchis 1991). Maxwell and Morris (1996) found in New Zealand family group conferences that the minority of offenders who failed to apologize during conferences were three times more likely to reoffend than those who had apologized. Interpreting any direction of causality here is admittedly difficult.

Moore (1994, p. 6) observes that in courtroom justice shame is not acknowledged because it is "hidden behind impersonal rhetoric about technical culpability." Both Moore with Forsythe (1995) and Retzinger and Scheff (1996) have applied their methods to the observation of restorative justice conferences, observing the above mechanisms to be in play and to be crucial to shaping whether conferences succeed or fail in dealing with conflicts in ways that they predict will prevent crime. For Retzinger and Scheff (1996), conferences have the ostensible purpose of material reparation; but underlying the verbal and visible process of reaching agreement about material reparation is a more nonverbal, less visible process of symbolic reparation. It is the latter that really matters according to their theoretical framework, so the emphasis in the early restorative justice literature on how much material reparation is actually paid becomes quite misguided.

The evidence now seems strong that unacknowledged shame contributes to violence; Sherman and Barnes's (1997), Sherman et al.'s (1998, pp. 127–29), and Harris's (2001) admittedly preliminary evidence suggests that in conferences offenders may accept and discharge shame more than when they go through court cases. If both propositions are correct, conferences might do more than court cases to reduce crime. Nevertheless, there remain real disputes among scholars who see shame acknowledgment as crucial to effectiveness in restorative justice:

> [These cases illustrate why] Scheff's argument that successful conferencing depends upon "making sure that all of the shame connected with the crime is accepted by the offender . . . acknowledging his or her complete responsibility for the crime . . ." is misconceived. Far preferable is the view that "a condition of successful reintegration ceremonies is that they leave open multiple interpretations of responsibility while refusing to allow the offender to deny personal responsibility entirely. (Braithwaite and Mugford 1994, p. 160)." (Young 2000, p. 245)

DEFIANCE THEORY

"Disrespect begets disrespect," claims Howard Zehr (1995), and few things communicate disrespect as effectively as the criminal exploitation of another human being. Lawrence Sherman (1993) has woven propositions from the foregoing sections about procedural justice, reintegrative shaming, and unacknowledged shame into an integrated theory of defiance. It has three propositions:

1. Sanctions provoke future *defiance* of the law (persistence, more frequent or more serious violations) to the extent that offenders experience sanctioning conduct as illegitimate, that offenders have weak bonds to the sanctioning agent and community, and that offenders deny their shame and become proud of their isolation from the sanctioning community.
2. Sanctions produce future *deterrence* of law breaking (desistance, less frequent or less serious violations) to the extent that offenders experience sanctioning conduct as legitimate, that offenders have strong bonds to the sanctioning agent and community, and that offenders accept their shame and remain proud of solidarity with the community.
3. Sanctions become *irrelevant* to future law breaking (no effect) to the extent that the factors encouraging defiance or deterrence are fairly evenly counterbalanced. (Sherman 1993, pp. 448–49)

Sherman hypothesizes that restorative justice processes are more likely than traditional punitive processes to meet the conditions of proposition 2. The evidence to date supports this suggestion. We have already seen that restorative processes are accorded high legitimacy by citizens, that they are better designed to empower those with strong bonds with the offender, and that they outperform court in inducing the acknowledgment and discharging of shame for wrongdoing.

While Sherman (1993) reviews some suggestive evidence that lawbreaking might increase under conditions that induce defiance, a systematic test of defiance theory remains to be undertaken. Results from the RISE experiment are still very preliminary here, only laying the foundations for the test of this theory. One published early result encouraging to defiance theory, however, was that while 26 percent of drunk drivers randomly assigned to court felt bitter and angry after court, only 7 percent of offenders felt bitter and angry after a conference (Sherman and Strang 1997b).

Hagan and McCarthy (1997, pp. 191–97) have tested Sherman's defiance theory against the prediction that children who have been humiliated, treated unfairly, and had bonds severed by virtue of being victims of sexual abuse or physical violence (with bruising or bleeding) will have their criminal behavior amplified by traditional criminal justice processing more than offenders who have not been abused. Their data, collected among homeless children in Toronto and Vancouver, supported the defiance theory prediction.

Sherman's defiance theory is not an armchair theory but one grounded in the preliminary R and D on conferencing in Australia. It is therefore important to illustrate the kind of case that motivated the prediction that restorative justice will prevent crime by reducing defiance. Box 4.2 presents a case from the RISE experiment in Canberra.

SELF–CATEGORIZATION THEORY

Self-categorization theory (Turner et al. 1987) explains the conditions under which a social self-concept or social identity becomes salient through an individual cate-

Box 4.2: Rage and Restorative Incapacitation

One man assaulted another very seriously; the victim was left lying in a liter and a half of his own blood and required $3,000 in dental work. The outcome of the conference was simply an agreement for the offender never to go within an agreed distance of the victim. On the face of it, this seems a totally inadequate remedy for a life-threatening assault; a court would likely have imposed prison time for it. But the participants in the conference would have seen such a court outcome as less just.

The victim asked for compensation for his dental bills from the offender. The offender had no money and no job, so he felt he could not agree to this. He had just come out of prison for another offense and was about to go back to prison for a third matter. A court, given his record, would likely have extended this sentence for such a serious assault. During his last prison term, the offender cultivated a spiral of rage against the victim of the assault. He believed the victim had raped his fiancée. The fiancée did not want to press charges, partly because all involved were part of a heroin subculture in which one simply did not press charges against others. Second, the circumstances of the alleged rape were that the rape victim had been having sex with another friend of her fiancé, which her alleged rapist took to be a signal that it was okay for him to do the same. It seemed plausible to our observer and to the police that this rape had occurred, especially when the assault victim said during the conference, "I didn't go out of my way to rape her." However, others at the conference did not believe that the rape had occurred.

It seemed to be the case that the victim and offender were thrown into regular contact because they purchased heroin from the same place, though this was never explicitly said. The victim was terrified that the offender would get angry again back in prison, come out, and kill him the next time. If the offender got an extra few months in jail for the assault, this would make such rage even more likely. So the victim and his supporters were well pleased with an outcome that guaranteed him a secure distance from the offender. The offender never rationally planned to do such damage to the victim. He had "lost it" and knew he was strong enough to kill the victim if he did the same again. He and his supporters wanted to secure him against a shame-rage spiral that would put him back in prison for a third term. While the conference failed to restore harmony, it did restore peace in a way that both sides saw as just in the circumstances. My hypothesis is that the participants are right; this was better justice than the court would have delivered, and a justice that may have prevented a murder by defusing defiance and putting in place a permanent voluntary segregation regime that was more effective incapacitation than the temporary compulsory segregation of a prison. In the four years since the conference, neither the victim nor the offender has been arrested for anything.

gorizing his or her self as having a similar identity to that shared by various social groups. These emergent identities shape what we are and how we act. I act the way I do because I am an Australian, male, a criminologist, a consumer advocate, a republican, and so on. According to self-categorization theory, group identities matter more than group interaction. I do not have to spend time going to Australian Republican Movement meetings for my identity as a republican to affect how I act.

In his more recent work Tom Tyler has forged important theoretical links between the procedural justice tradition and social identity (see Tyler and Blader 2000). Through an impressive series of empirical studies, Tyler and his collaborators have shown that procedural fairness increases cooperative behavior by giving people who are treated fairly the message that that they are respected by the group. This increases their pride in or identity with the group and therefore increases willingness to cooperate to secure its norms. Just as Sherman's (1993) work on defiance theory shows the possibility of integrating reintegrative shaming, procedural justice, and the theory of unacknowledged shame, Tyler's recent work opens up the prospect of integrating self-categorization theory as well into an account that can explain why restorative justice might better secure compliance with the law than punitive justice.

Another developing theoretical bridge is the work of Natalie Taylor (2000), which integrates self-categorization theory with Brehm's theory of psychological reactance (and therefore Sherman's defiance theory). According to Taylor (2000), identification with in-groups delivers "conversion" to in-group norms without a need for the norm violator to be known. Hence, a person who has shoplifted without this being detected may be converted to the norm against shoplifting by a conference with her in-group in which disapproval is mobilized against an act of shoplifting by someone else. "Compliance" is conceived as a purely strategic shift toward a group norm without "conversion" to ethical identification with the norm. When we move up the enforcement pyramid discussed in chapter 2, out-groups can be effective in securing compliance through triggering motivations to avoid averse consequences. But because they are out-groups, they secure only compliance and not conversion. Finally, both "resistance" (refusing to move one's position at all) and "reactance" (moving away from the group's normative position) must be understood in terms of the motivation of people to avoid a negative self-perception. In the case of reactance, a particularly important negative self-perception that defiance averts is that we lack independence or freedom to control our destiny.

The notion of group influence in self-categorization theory is different in emphasis from that proposed in the theory of reintegrative shaming, which emphasizes interdependence. Like most criminological theories, Braithwaite's (1989) is sloppily theorized on this question, slipping back and forth between interaction-based and identity-based accounts of how criminal subcultures influence action. This is true of Sutherland's (1983) theory as well. Headlined as a theory of differential *association*, it actually defines differential association cognitively rather than interactively: "an excess of definitions favourable to violations of law over definitions unfavourable to violation of law" (Sutherland and Cressey 1978, p. 81).

Albert Cohen's (1955) subcultural theory is more incipiently a self-categorization theory than other classic criminological theories. For Cohen, children who fail in the status system of the school have a status problem. They can solve that problem by identifying with other groups that invert the values of the school. If the school values being "square," there is attraction to being "cool," feeling membership in a cool group. If the school values control of aggression, then there is attractiveness in a group that values free expression of aggression. While there is evidence that children experience Cohen's reaction formation (Koh 1997), there is more evidence in more contexts for Matza's (1964) view that delinquents drift between law-supportive and law-neutralizing identities, though some studies do not find a lot of drift away from law-supportive identities among delinquents (Ball 1983; Thurman 1984; Box 1981, pp. 107–8; Agnew and Peters 1986; Anderson 1999; Koh 1997). Sykes and Matza (1957) have suggested five techniques of neutralization that make drift possible: (1) denial of victim (e.g., "we weren't hurting anyone"); (2) denial of injury (e.g. "they can afford it"); (3) condemnation of the condemners (e.g., "they're crooks themselves"); (4) denial of responsibility (e.g., "I was drunk"); and (5) appeal to higher loyalties (e.g., "I had to stick by my mates").

Restorative justice conferences may prevent crime by facilitating a drift back to law-supportive identities from law-neutralizing ones. How might they accomplish this? At a victim-offender mediation or conference when the victim is present, it is hard to sustain *denial of victim* and *denial of injury*. In contrast, these techniques of neutralization are fostered by criminal justice institutions that sustain separation of victims and offenders. Admittedly, victims often do not convince the offender in a conference that they were hurt in a way they could ill afford. Yet when this occurs, victim supporters will often move offenders through the communicative power, the authenticity, that comes from their love of the victim. An upset daughter explaining how frightened her mother now is in her own house can have a more powerful impact on the offender than direct expressions of concern by the victim.

Condemnation of the condemners is also more difficult to sustain when one's condemners engage in a respectful dialogue about why the criminal behavior of concern to them is harmful. Katz, Glass, and Cohen's (1973) research shows that out-group derogation is the preferred way of handling shame when the victim is a member of an out-group. Conferences and healing circles are designed to make the condemners members of an in-group rather than an out-group by two moves: (1) inviting participants from all the in-groups that matter most to offenders and (2) encouraging victims and victim supporters to be respectful, even forgiving, of offenders as persons, thus rendering their out-group location more ambiguous. One of the advantages of the presence of victim supporters is that if the victim is irrevocably a member of an out-group, the consequences of the crime might be effectively communicated by a victim supporter who happens to be a member of an in-group.

The evidence suggests that the transience of in-group and out-group categorizations is contextually responsive to variables like politeness and respectfulness, the very modes of interaction that restorative justice processes seek to nurture (Turner et al. 1987, pp. 55–56). From a self-categorization perspective, an advantage of Chinese social structuring is the relative lack of clear boundaries in defining an in-group, for example, in the elastic definition of *chia*, or family, depending on the problems at issue (Bond and Wang Sung-Hsing 1983, p. 68).

Denial of responsibility is tested at a conference. The presence of supporters who know and care for an offender risks that a denial of responsibility like "I was drunk" might lead to a discussion of his responsibility for recurrent drunkenness that has induced irresponsible behavior in the past. Obversely, criminal trials test only those denials of responsibility legally relevant to mitigating guilt. Even for that legally relevant subset of the psychologically relevant denials, they are tested in ways that are least likely to be persuasive to the offender—by attacking his credibility as a person in the eyes of a judge and/or jury. The restorative conference supports him as a person while questioning the usefulness of his denials to him as a person and to clearing things up for those who have been hurt. The restorative process, by showing a path to redemption, provides an alternative to denial (see Box 4.3). This contrasts with the two paths the court proffers—guilt and punishment or innocence and impunity—a choice that makes denial an attractive posture.

Criminal offenders are criminal offenders partly because they are good at denial. When shame is projected across the room from victim to offender, the offender may have a shield that deflects the shame, only to find the deflected shame spears through the heart of his mother who sobs quietly beside him. What I have observed in many conferences is that it may be the shame of the offender's mother, father, or sister that gets behind his shield of denial. This only happens when he loves one of these intimates (see Harris 2001). There are some useful tactics available in restorative justice processes that begin from a determination of all participants to deny responsibility. Wachtel and McCold (2001) suggest asking participants before the conference to consider showing leadership by asking themselves whether there is any element of responsibility for what happened that they would feel able to own. Moore and McDonald (2000, p. 80) suggest asking the following questions of people who have

---

Box 4.3: Father-Son Identity in Japan

The boy was a troublemaker in school who intimidated his classmates and extorted money from them. His father, who was a former school principal, went to see the son's homeroom teacher in response to the latter's request. When he was told of his son's robbery, "he apologised with a deep bow, saying 'I am very sorry.' Watching his father thus apologizing on his behalf, the offender was moved to tears. This was a turning point for him that changed his way of life completely."

Source: T. Lebra and a letter to the editor of the *Asahi Shinhum*, quoted in Haley 1999, p. 105

difficulty accepting that they may have acted inappropriately: "With the benefit of hindsight, how might you have done things differently?" and "Is it possible that some of the things you have been doing/saying might not have been that helpful?"

Appeals to higher loyalties, such as loyalties to one's friends, is the neutralization technique of greatest interest from a self-categorization perspective. Emler and Reicher's (1995) interviews with delinquents reveal that they are simultaneously concerned about having a reputation for whatever it is their delinquent group values (say, toughness) and concerned about maintaining a different reputation with their families. These delinquents worked hard at keeping families unaware of the different values and conduct they manifest in the delinquent group. Delinquents' parents rarely met their peers. Delinquents were more likely than nondelinquents to keep peers and parents apart (Emler and Reicher 1995, p. 204). Koh (1997, p. 376) found that incarcerated Singaporean delinquents endorsed neutralization techniques to a lesser extent when their family identity was salient and when confrontation with authority was seen to be public rather than private.

Goffman (1956) is the preeminent theorist of what he calls strategies for matching audience segregation to role segregation. In the nineteenth-century village, all roles were played out for the same audience. The condition of modernity, however, is one of a proliferation of group identities—mother, criminologist, golfer, Christian, cat breeder—but with those groups scattered across global space. Most of us are actually not more alone in the modern city, but our togetherness is not unified with place (Braithwaite 1993c). This means, as Benson (1989) shows empirically, that the white-collar criminal in the contemporary world is peculiarly vulnerable to shame if only his business activities might be revealed to his church group. Restorative justice conferences are designed to do just this—to bring together the audiences the criminal would most want to be segregated.

This design can and sometimes does backfire. On rare occasions, we have had restorative justice conferences in Australia where a delinquent gang, or two rival gangs on the victim and offender sides, have dominated the conference numerically and persuasively (in neutralizing shame). On many occasions, we have observed adult restorative justice conferences for drunk driving where the offender's drinking group has dominated the conference with denials of victim, of injury, and of responsibility (Mugford and Inkpen 1995).

Overall, my observation from sitting through more than a hundred conferences of different types is that such cases are in the minority. Why? One reason is that Matza (1964) was right that drift toward and away from rejection of the law's moral bind is more common than outright rejection of moral commitment to the law. For example, while parents of serious delinquents are more likely to have been delinquents themselves (Wilson and Herrnstein 1985, pp. 95–103), they are not Fagins. Criminal parents almost always disapprove of their children's delinquency (West and Farrington 1973, p. 116). Even when we put together a conference dominated by multiproblem families concerning a violent offense, we find empirically that very few of the utterances are approving of violence. One reason for this is that philosophers in the Aristotelian tradition of truth-finding through undominated dialogue, like Habermas

(1996), are right that the closer we get to conditions of undominated speech, the more overwhelmingly it will be the case that evils such as violence will be nearly universally condemned. That is, there is a moral fact of the matter that gratuitous violence is wrong, and undominated dialogue will converge on consensus about contextual judgments of the wrongness of specific violent acts.

A nice moral feature of restorative justice from this perspective is that restorative justice might work only with crimes that ought to be crimes. If a group of citizens cannot agree in an undominated conference that an act of obscenity is wrong, then (1) the obscenity should not be a crime, and (2) the conference will fail in controlling obscenity. But most criminal offenses brought to justice in democratic societies are more like the violence case than the obscenity case: they are unambiguously wrong to most citizens attending a conference.

Put another way, when a victim comes to a conference with a broken nose, *denial of victim* and *denial of injury* are likely to be revealed as bad arguments. From a Habermasian perspective, techniques of neutralization for violence can only be sustained by avoiding undominated dialogue about their justice. Restorative justice breaks through that avoidance. The social psychological research literature supports the interpretation that self-interested egoistical neutralizations are vulnerable to group dialogue: "In situations without strong social bonds [courtrooms?], people are egoistical. Once a group identity is created, however, people are increasingly responsive to group-centered motives" (Tyler and Dawes 1993, p. 102). The challenge for a circle is to forge a common group identity in the face of the other identities that divide the participants; they are a group committed to achieving restoration. While there are differences in identity that divide them, they share the superordinate identity of being a group committed to solving this problem that has been put in the center of the circle.

Of course, circles are never free of domination, so the degree of truth of the Habermasian analysis is contingent. However, some of the ineradicable dominations of social life systematically conduce to law-abiding in-groups having more power in the long haul than law-neutralizing ones, at least with juveniles. It is well documented that delinquency declines beyond a certain age; one reason is that collective support for delinquency declines from about age sixteen (Emler and Reicher 1995). However much delinquent peer groups dominate a young person, she is not unaware that these peers are not going to be around forever; she knows that when they go off the scene, family will still be there lending money, caring, giving emotional support. At least she knows this in those cases where the conference facilitator has succeeded in getting communities of care to the conference (including nonfamily ones) beyond the delinquent peer group, communities of care that will stick by the offender for the long haul.

Where the offender's domination by a delinquent peer group is so strong that it is not trumped by the longer term nature of family bonds, a restorative justice strategy still has time on its side. Empirically, the peer group is more likely than the family to disintegrate when the offender is between the ages of thirteen and twenty. Very few of the gang members in Esbensen and Huizinga's (1993) Denver survey reported being in a delinquent gang for more than one year. Many members indicated that they would like *not* to be members and expected to leave the gang in the future. If we just hang in with one unsuccessful conference after another in which delinquent peers dominate family, eventually the balance will shift in the other direction. Restorative justice rewards the patient. As Siti Hamidah of the Association of Muslim Professionals said of Singaporean conferences: "Many want to change but don't know how, so it's a time to make concrete plans, like returning to school or finding a job" (Hsien 1996).

It is often the case in the short term that peer influences dominate family influence because, though the delinquent group "is characterized by a lack of intimacy or affection, there is a strong sense of belongingness" (Koh 1997, p. 201). Yet where that belongingness is grounded in its provision of an alternative status system to that of a school and this alternative fails them, removal of the original cause by dropout from school may undermine a belongingness so grounded. Indeed, there is evidence of reduced delinquency following school dropout (Elliott and Voss 1974).

An unattractive way of applying the lessons of self-categorization theory to restorative justice would be to exclude delinquent peers from the conference and to exclude drinking mates in the difficult case of the shameless Australian drunk driver. There is little point persuading a delinquent during an hour stacked with the law-abiding when she will spend the next thousand hours in a world surrounded by the law-violating. Better to confront the whole delinquent group or the whole drinking group with the indefensibility of their techniques of neutralization. Better to win the conscience of the delinquent in the presence of his delinquent peers than to win a Pyrrhic victory in their absence. What one must guard against, however, is allowing a law-neutralizing group to dominate a conference. Where the law-neutralizing group is strong, a lot of work is needed to balance it with a plurality of law-abiding citizens who also enjoy the respect and trust of the offender (Mugford and Inkpen 1995). A plurality of attractive law-abiding identities embodied in trusted supporters at the conference is perhaps the best hope for turning away from a law-neutralizing identity. Ross (1996, p. 182) finds special virtue in the participation of healed victims and healed victimizers of sexual abuse who can cut through the (often shared) neutralizations that they had to cut through in confronting their own abuse:

> In Hollow Water, ex-offenders are not shunned forever, but seen as important resources for getting under the skin of other offenders and disturbing the webs of lies that have sustained them. Better than anyone, they understand the patterns, the pressures and the ways to hide. As they tell their personal stories in the circle, they talk about the lies that once protected them and how it felt to face the truth about the pain they caused. It is done gently but inflexibly, sending signals to offenders that their behaviour has roots that can be understood, but that there are no such things as excuses. (Ross 1996, p. 183)

Indeed, at Hollow Water, before they met their own victim in a healing circle, sexual abusers met other offenders and other offenders' victims, who would simply tell their stories as a stage in a process toward breaking down the tough guy identity that pervaded the dominating relationship with their own victim. Note what an interesting strategy this is from a defiance theory perspective as well. Averting defiance is about getting offenders to put their caring identity rather than their defiant self in play.

I can summarize by suggesting that self-categorization theory might be read to make the following predictions about restorative justice:

1. Restorative justice prevents crime when:
   a. justice rituals are structured so that condemners are harder to condemn because they are members of an in-group;
   b. if condemners are irrevocably members of an out-group, condemnation still influences intermediaries who are in-group members present at the conference (who can pass that influence on to the offender);
   c. discussion of consequences reveals that denial is a coping strategy that blocks in-group acceptance;
   d. justice rituals break down the segregation of law-abiding and law-neutralizing in-groups in circumstances where the law-abiding groups will (i) have more persuasive arguments to the extent that speech is undominated and (ii) be more dominant to the extent that speech is dominated.
2. Restorative justice will more often achieve conditions a to d than traditional trials because trial lawyers have a trained competence at exaggerating evil, at condemning condemners, at denying victim, injury, and responsibility, at blackening gray—in short, in consolidating offenders and victims into opposed out-groups.
3. Even when victims and offenders do not share a common identity, restorative justice can search for some superordinate identity (member of the school community, citizens committed to solving together the problem in the center of the circle) that opens a space to empathy. (Eggins 1999)

CRIME PREVENTION THEORY

Lon Fuller (1964, p. 33) suggests that only two types of problems are suited to full judicial-legal process: yes-no questions like "Did she do it?" and more-less questions like "How much should be paid?" Polanyi (1951, pp. 174–84): distinguishes these from polycentric problems, which require reconciliation of complex interacting consequences of multidimensional phenomena. Polycentric problems are not well suited to the judicial model. Because most crime problems beyond the determination of guilt are polycentric, courts are rather ineffective at preventing crime.

In response to the recognition that courts cannot be expected to be competent at crime prevention, crime prevention has expanded as a largely police-facilitated alternative to expending criminal justice resources on dragging cases through the courts. From a restorative justice perspective, an uncoupling of crime prevention from case processing amounts to lost opportunity in two ways. First, every police officer knows that the best time to persuade a householder to invest in security is after a burglary; every business regulator knows that the best time to persuade a company to invest in a corporate compliance system is after something goes wrong and someone gets into trouble. They also know that they do not have the resources to get around and persuade all households and businesses to invest in security or compliance systems. Given that the police or the regulator must make contact with victims and offenders when an offense is cleared, it is a suboptimal use of resources not to seize that opportunity for crime prevention. Moreover, it brings finite crime prevention resources to bear at the moment when motivation for implementing demanding preventive measures is at its peak and at its peak for good reason: one study has shown prospects of another burglary four times as high as in houses that had not been burgled before (Bridgeman and Hobbs 1997, p. 2). Hence, a project in Huddersfield that focused resources such as temporary alarms on prior victims reduced domestic burglary by 24 percent and in a Rockdale project by 72 percent (Bridgeman and Hobbs 1997, p. 3). Focusing crime prevention on existing cases of victimization (Pease 1998b) also mainstreams crime prevention to where the resources are—street-level enforcement—rather than leaving crime prevention ghettoized in specialist areas. Among the reasons for the effectiveness of this strategy is the fact that "victimisation is the best single predictor of victimisation" (Pease 1998b, p. v).[1] This of course is not to deny that there will always be circumstances where crime prevention is best deployed before any offense occurs.

Restorative justice resolves the tension between the incapacity of the court for polycentric problem solving and the imperatives for mainstreaming crime prevention into case management. It also resolves the most fundamental tension between crime prevention theory and practice. The theory says "involve the community"; the practice says "citizens don't turn up to Neighborhood Watch meetings except in highly organized communities that don't need them" (see Box 4.4). I don't go to Neighborhood Watch meetings, even though I think I should. But if the boy next door gets into trouble, if my secretary is a victim, and they ask me to attend to support them, I attend. I am touched by the invitation, that they have chosen me as one whose support they value in a time of stress.

Corruption and capture are worries with problem-oriented policing that leaves discretion totally with law enforcement agencies to decide the preventive measures required. This is especially true with business regulation—be it police regulating prostitution or drug markets or antitrust agencies regulating competition policy. Ayres and Braithwaite (1992, chap. 3) have shown game-theoretically and in terms of republican theory how transforming the crime prevention game from a bipartite game between state and business into a tripartite state-business-community game prevents corruption and capture. "Community" is the ingredient needed to prevent the crimes that arise from crime prevention; and restorative justice may deliver community to deliberative forums better than alternative strategies. At the same time, abuse of police powers in mainstream processes of arrest is rendered accountable to a com-

---

Box 4.4: *Walter Mikac, Restorative Values, and the Australian Gun Buyback*

An extraordinary thing happened in Australia in 1996. The people nearly universally accepted a 1 percent income tax increase for one year only to pay for a gun buyback. Across the country, guns were purchased with these taxes and destroyed. The "trigger" of this political phenomenon was the murder of thirty-five innocents at Port Arthur by Martin Bryant. The emotional heart of the appeal for the gun buyback was the activism of Walter Mikac, whose wife and two young children were gunned down. Margaret Scott (1997, pp. 188–89) has grasped the nub of Mikac's contribution to the prevention of future gun violence:

"The country's mood was volatile. In Hobart there had been threats against the medical staff who had treated Bryant's burns, even bomb threats against the hospital where he was held despite the fact that his fellow patients included many of those injured in the shooting. So, if Walter Mikac had chosen to call for vengeance or for the restoration of the death penalty for murder, he might well have unleashed a fury that would have been difficult to contain. As it was he displayed a degree of forbearance towards his family's killer that left those who heard or read his message amazed and abashed: 'Remember,' he said, 'that the power of love and creation will always triumph over the power of destruction and revenge.'

"Pastor Allan Anderson, who conducted the Mikac funeral service, called for changes in Australia's gun laws so that life might be more effectively protected. . . . If Bryant's acts remained incomprehensible, at least it was clear that he could not have created such mayhem without guns. So Pastor Anderson's words reverberated around the nation and Walter Mikac became the face, the embodied justification of a campaign that the gun-lobby never had any real hope of withstanding."

---

munity when a mother complains during a conference that the police used unnecessary force on her son. I have observed mothers to do this in conferences (because they are polycentric) but not in courtrooms (because they are not).[2]

Crime prevention is a preeminently important area of criminal justice practice and evaluation research, but it is hardly the theoretical cutting edge of the field. In some respects this is a good thing because one should want prevention practitioners not to be theoretically committed, to be interpretively flexible, searching to read situations from the different angles illuminated by multiple theories. Plural understandings of a crime problem stimulate a disparate range of action possibilities that can be integrated into a hedged, mutually reinforcing package of preventive policies (Braithwaite 1993a). Plural understandings are best generated out of a dialogue between crime prevention professionals, such as police, and community members with disparate perspectives from their direct experience with the problem phenomenon.

In the discussion of the Colonial Mutual Life (CML) case in chapter 1, a disparate array of preventive measures was discovered grounded in the different kinds of theories proposed by the rich plurality of players involved in this restorative justice process—theories of education, deterrence, incapacitation, rehabilitation, target hardening, moral hazard, adverse publicity, law, regulation, and opportunity theory.

Restorative justice rituals can be a lever for triggering prevention of the most systemic and difficult-to-solve crimes in contemporary societies, like sexual abuse in families (Hollow Water) and the crimes of finance capital (CML). We should take seriously the possibility of family group conferences with leaders of Colombian cocaine cartels. How do we know they are beyond shame? How do we know they would not like to retire at seventy instead of fear violent usurpation by a rival? Even common thieves retire because they find that managing a criminal identity takes its toll: "You get tired. You get tired trying to be a tough guy all the time. People always expecting this and that" (Shover 1996, p. 137). How do we know that organized crime bosses might not find very attractive an agreement that allowed them to pass on some of their wealth to set up legitimate businesses for their children so they did not need to bequeath to the children the life they had led (see Rensselaer 1992)? How do we know that they do not actually hate killing other human beings in order to survive themselves? An incipient and only very partially successful model here is the Raskol gang surrenders and gang retreats in Papua New Guinea, which have involved surrenders of up to 400 alleged gang members (Dinnen 1996; Box 4.5).

One of the more stimulating recent contributions to thinking about crime prevention is a book by James Jacobs with Coleen Friel and Robert Radic, *Gotham Unbound: How New York City Was Liberated from the Grip of Organized Crime* (1999). After decades of failed punitive law enforcement against members of organized crime

---

Box 4.5: Raskol Gang Surrenders

Papua New Guinea political leaders up to the justice minister and prime minister and leaders of the church and other organizations in civil society have participated in ceremonial gang surrenders and retreats. The leaders receive from gangs apologies, surrendered weapons, undertakings to do community work and work for the rehabilitation of their own members and for youth gangs that have been their recruitment base. Dinnen (1996, p. 121) lists just the documented surrenders in a society where little is documented—thirteen rituals involving 913 alleged gang members. In fact one of the few successful antigang programs (Sherman et al. 1997) in one of the few places where the gang problem is as bad as in New Guinea, Los Angeles, involved hiring older gang leaders as consultants to assist with the negotiation of truces and the mediation of feuds. Homicides and intergang violence fell among the targeted gangs but not between the targeted gangs and others.

Source: Torres 1981, cited in Klein 1995, p. 149

groups who could simply be replaced when arrested, the strategy that Jacobs describes as finally working could not be described as restorative. However, it could be described as a responsive regulatory strategy. Criminal prosecutions leading to imprisonment remained important in the New York strategy of the 1990s. But what did the real work was a business regulatory strategy, particularly one that targeted licenses. A way to stop the mob from fixing prices in the New York garbage collection cartel was to withdraw the garbage collection licenses of mob associates. In some markets corrupted by the mob, suppliers were required to hire an auditing firm that specialized in certifying that the business was mob-free. Court appointment of trustees to clean up (restore worker democratic control to) mob-controlled unions was another important strategy. The effectiveness of such preventive strategies compared with purely retributive enforcement comes as no surprise to those of us who work on business regulation. Jacobs's findings reminded me of U.S. coal mine safety enforcement where locating a resident inspector at the least safe mines in the country to reform their management practices has been shown to improve safety dramatically (Braithwaite 1985, pp. 82–83).

The research shows that a responsive regulatory approach with business regulatory licensing, monitoring, auditing, and restructuring moving up from the base of an enforcement pyramid that has long terms of imprisonment at its peak can work against the most entrenched, sophisticated, and ruthless organized criminal groups in the world. My question is might all of this work even more cost-effectively if there were a restorative process at the very base of the pyramid—somewhat like the retreats organized by church leaders with Raskol gang leaderships in Papua New Guinea or Operation Ceasefire with Boston gangs as discussed in chapter 2. The lesson organized crime prevention can learn from organizational crime prevention is that when the fact of life is that the regulator can persuade a court to appoint a trustee to take over a criminogenic organization and can launch prosecutions that will put many of its principals in prison, those facts of life mean that when the regulator sits down with the principals, there is a chance they will voluntarily let the trustee in. The implied deal is that if you cooperate with the regulatory outcome that we can force on you through the courts, you will both save yourself a fortune in legal costs and be able to sell your business to a legitimate businessperson (who will cease enforcing the cartel) as a going concern at a better price than you would get if the court shuts you down. What the public gets in this kind of win-win deal is lower prices and an end to the violence of standover tactics. Hopefully the public also gets employment growth through the legitimate wealth that future generations of mob families create by embracing honest business as an alternative to racketeering. This can never make sense under a retributive philosophy, but it can under a restorative philosophy.

Ross Homel et al.'s (1997) research on reducing violence around pubs and clubs in Australia is another good example of what works with a more mundane kind of violence. Community organizing rather than the criminal law of assault was the key instrument of state regulation here. Community meetings of concerned local citizens and pub and club owners came up with a package of self-regulatory measures. These included requirements for training bar staff in how to defuse violence peaceably rather than through strong-arm tactics, responsible serving practices to prevent excessive drunkenness, and so on. The police did not patrol these pubs and clubs during the self-regulatory project. As a result of the self-regulatory program, assaults per 100 hours of observation were reduced by 53 percent. But when funding for the program ended and the police moved back in with standard criminal law enforcement, violence returned to the old levels. One way of motivating such programs is to wait for an assault that might shock the community at a hot-spot bar, set up a restorative justice conference that might resolve to publicize it, and call for the need for a preventive self-regulatory program at this and other bars.

In summary, restorative justice can remove crime prevention from its marginal status in the criminal justice system, mainstreaming it into the enforcement process. It can deliver the motivation and widespread community participation crime prevention needs to work and to protect itself against corruption and capture by organized interests (including the crime prevention industry itself). It can sometimes deliver the political clout to crime prevention that it needs to tackle systemic problems systemically. For example, a key to motivating non-criminal justice bureaucracies (e.g., business corporations, housing departments) to engage in and fund crime prevention is to give them a seat in the circle when the emotional force from a specific crime, a specific life that might be restored, is confronted. Ken Pease (1998a) has argued that the real problem of the failure of crime prevention is that it is assumed that a demonstration that something works in preventing crime will mean that it will be done. This is false because crime prevention is not a priority for non-criminal-justice bureaucracies and not even the primary motivation of criminal justice bureaucracies, which tend to be more interested in detecting wrongdoers to punish. My main argument here is that linking restorative justice to crime prevention can supply that missing motivation, an argument that will also be deployed in the next section on rehabilitation.

THE THEORY OF REHABILITATION

In chapter 3 we saw that there is quite a bit of evidence that restorative justice processes may prevent reoffending better than traditional criminal justice processing. The qualitative literature on restorative justice is certainly littered with case studies of offenders who have been rehabilitated as a result of the deliberation at conferences.

What is clear from the criminological literature is that when rehabilitation of criminal behavior does occur, it is at the hands of families more than any other institution. Obversely, family dysfunction correlates as consistently with delinquency as any variable. Hence, the Maori critique of the Western justice system that led to the New Zealand restorative justice reforms of 1989 have a strong empirical foundation: Western justice weakens families because it takes away their responsibility for dealing with crime and preventing recurrence. Weaken family responsibility, especially for cultures with deeply embedded traditions of family responsibility, and you destroy the fabric of crime control (Hassall 1996). Some Australian Aboriginal peoples articulate a similar critique—in a culture where the father of an adolescent's future wife has the primary role in social control, a justice system that wrenches young offenders away from any influence by that person or other relevant elders will destroy, has destroyed, a large part of the basis for social control. Bazemore (1999a) distinguishes the "relational rehabilitation" that is the stuff of restorative justice from individual treatment, with its emphasis on identifying and correcting offender deficits. The relational approach identifies strengths and builds out from those strengths in families and communities that are struggling to help a lawbreaking member.

One reason that restorative justice ought to do better at rehabilitation than rehabilitative justice is that it does not have rehabilitation as its aim. Rehabilitation is like spontaneity as an objective: when you try to be spontaneous, you are not very spontaneous. When the criminal justice system is seen as setting out to change people, even by offering rewards, that can engender reactance, though reactance to reward does not seem as great as to punishment (Brehm and Brehm 1981, p. 229).

The practical focus on the consequences of the crime and the needs this creates for victims and the community—more act-focused and less focused on the offender as a person, more victim-focused and less offender-focused—means that the process is less stigmatizing and more dignified for the offender. It is hard for the communication of disapproval to be respectful when the focus is on the twisted psyche of the offender or his defective conscience. By definition, stigmatic labeling is not averted when words like *sociopath* are bandied around with the family.

However good the diagnosis, however good the rehabilitation program it commends, the very fact that it comes out of a program designed to deliver a diagnosis and a treatment renders the process stigmatic. This means that the crime reduction effects of the rehabilitative program have to be very strong before they can outweigh the crime-instigating effects of the stigmatization. Any program where social workers, psychologists, or psychiatrists come in to do things to or for people risks stigmatization by the very fact of professionalized doing or helping. Retributivist critics of rehabilitation are right when they say rehabilitation strips the offender of dignity in this way (Murphy and Hampton 1989); they are wrong to suggest that punishment confers dignity; a space that gives the offender an opportunity to choose to put things right is what restores dignity. It is such a choice to put things right that most nurtures a continuing commitment to keep things right, that nurtures rehabilitation.

Of course offenders are often desperately in need of a drug rehabilitation program, face-to-face counseling, job training, remedial education, and all manner of rehabilitative programs. If that need is desperate, citizens should speak up for the need in a restorative justice program, and the offenders should see committing to it as part of putting things right. This empowerment of the offender, together with his or her community of care, to choose from rehabilitative programs offered by health and welfare professionals in the state, private, and voluntary sectors is different from state monopolies of social work and health care provision in the traditional welfare model.

I must confess to seeing these as empty ideals in most of the restorative justice programs of which I have experience. I have seen many drunk driving conferences where the offender is a tottering alcoholic, but no one in the community of care mentions the need for a drug treatment program, sometimes because most supporters are also excessive drinkers. In New Zealand, the rhetoric of citizens being empowered to choose rehabilitation programs without having them forced down their throat by the state is impressive; yet this occurs in a context where the retrenchment of the once-exemplary New Zealand welfare state by successive conservative governments means there are no programs left to choose (cf. Maxwell and Morris 1996). Australia is almost as bad in this respect.

It therefore seems highly doubtful that restorative justice conferences are having major rehabilitative effects at this time. They may, however, be averting some of the disempowerment of traditional "corrections," the stigmatization of rehabilitation oriented to changing pathology.

My restorative theory of rehabilitation is that restorative justice programs can achieve great success at rehabilitation, greater success than programs grounded in welfarist models of monopoly state provision selected by professionals, for five reasons:

1. Restorative justice can build motivation.
2. Restorative justice can mobilize resources.
3. Restorative justice reinforces the social cognitive principles that have been shown to be hallmarks of effective rehabilitation programs.
4. Restorative justice can foster plural deliberation that delivers "responsivity."
5. Restorative justice can improve follow-through.

1. Restorative justice builds motivation

The previous section introduced Ken Pease's (1998a) fallacy of crime prevention that bureaucracies will be motivated to implement programs that work. The same is true of rehabilitation programs, where the evidence is now clear that many do work (Cullen and Gendreau, 2000; Andrews 1995), but where just deserts continues to be defended on the spurious grounds that "nothing works." I will not repeat the arguments on how restorative justice can build individual, community, and bureaucratic commitment to do what is needed for prevention. Some of the more restorative drug courts (most are not restorative) are realizing that the best time to tackle an entrenched drug habit is at the time of arrest for a crime to support the habit. Involvement of loved ones who want to keep the offender out of prison can create the motivation for effective rehabilitation in the community so long as they are actively involved and so long as the offender is kept out of prison.

Consider the drunk driver who has a serious alcohol problem. We have found in Canberra that court processing has little to offer in the way of the needed motivational dynamic here. The average duration of a drunk-driving case in Canberra is seven minutes of lawyer talk. Drunk-driving restorative justice conferences average eighty-seven minutes. There is time to consider the underlying problems. The data suggest there is also quite a deal of acknowledgment of shame and guilt (Harris 2001).

A ritual in which trouble with the police has to be dealt with is a unique opportunity for a family member who wishes to make an issue of an underlying alcohol problem. The seriousness and family shame of trouble with the police can motivate the confrontation of a touchy matter that has been swept under the carpet many times before. Unfortunately, the police in Canberra were somewhat discouraging of this kind of confrontation, their attitude being that the offense was drunk driving, not drinking, and "drinking problems are not police business." This is part of the error in current restorative justice practice of failing to seize the motivational opportunity to get rehabilitation moving to deal with underlying causes.

2. Restorative justice can mobilize resources

The previous section also argued that linking crime prevention to existing cases of victimization mainstreams crime prevention to where the policing resources are—street-level enforcement—rather than leaving it ghettoized in specialist prevention units. Police services are famous for presenting rhetoric about community policing and crime prevention and then setting up special units for the purpose that attract a minuscule proportion of the police budget. Governments are famous for saying they believe in community crime prevention and then giving over 90 percent of the crime prevention budget to the police. As David Bayley and Clifford Shearing (1996) have pointed out, the remedy here may be to abandon the police budget in favor of a policing budget, so that citizen groups can contest police control over crime prevention resources. In the meantime, however, linking crime prevention and rehabilitation to case management by the police may be a way to mainstream them. For cases beyond a given level of seriousness, judges should have the power to order expenditure on rehabilitative services recommended by a restorative justice process (up to a specified fraction of the cost of imposing the maximum prison term available for the offense). It follows from the philosophy of restorative and responsive justice that just as judges should be able to order expenditure on imprisonment, they should also be able to order more cost-efficient expenditure on rehabilitation that emanates from restorative justice processes.

3. Restorative justice reinforces the social cognitive principles that have been shown to be hallmarks of effective rehabilitation programs

Many criminal offenders have poor cognitive skills about understanding how to behave in a pro-social fashion. Their antisocial behavior has often been "nattered" at rather than confronted, and pro-social alternative behaviors have not been discussed (Patterson 1982). They get into fights by bumping into people because they have not learned simple scripts like "excuse me." The meta-analyses of effectiveness in rehabilitation programs show that social cognitive programs in corrections with the following features reduce reoffending substantially:

> The predominant anti-social beliefs of the offender in question are identified. In a
> firm yet fair and respectful manner, it is pointed out to the offender that the beliefs
> in question are not acceptable. If the anti-social beliefs continue, emphatic disap-
> proval (e.g., withdrawal of social reinforcers) always follows. Meanwhile, the of-
> fender is exposed to alternative pro-social ways of thinking and behaving by concrete
> modeling on the part of the therapist in one-on-one sessions or in structured group
> learning settings (e.g., courses in anger management). (Cullen and Gendreau, 2000,
> p. 147)

It is equally true that these same social cognitive principles are the stuff of effective child rearing in the community (Baumrind 1973, 1978; Braithwaite 1989). Indeed, their effectiveness in correctional institutions becomes necessary only when
they are not present in the community. Restorative justice aspires to confront wrongdoing, to communicate understanding about why it is wrong through a discussion of
its consequences and to discuss the pro-social alternative courses of conduct. And it
is about nurturing loved ones to take responsibility for such communication. It can
also create a space where loved ones can appeal for professional help in meeting these
responsibilities. So restorative justice can and should be designed to reinforce both
social cognitive processes for pro-social learning within communities of care and to
call up professional help with social cognitive skill development. The restorative theory of rehabilitation predicts that a combination of reinforcing pro-social learning
among loved ones and seeking professional help in the community will be more effective than the demonstrated effectiveness of professional help of that kind in a
correctional institution. In reaching this conclusion the restorative theory of rehabilitation in part relies on the evidence from within the welfarist tradition that rehabilitation within the community tends to be more effective than rehabilitation within
correctional institutions (Lipsey 1990; Cullen and Gendreau 2000, p. 150).

4. Restorative justice can foster plural deliberation that delivers "responsivity"

Plurality of deliberation is another of the virtues of restorative justice that is as
relevant to the broader crime prevention concerns of the previous section as it is to
the rehabilitative concerns of this section. Indeed, it must be said that one of the
limitations of the psychologism of traditional rehabilitation is that its vision of responsive selection of preventive options is limited to selection of rehabilitation programs,
rendering its responsiveness profoundly truncated. Most crime problems have multiple causes and can be prevented in multiple ways. The burglary is caused by the
offender's drug habit or unemployment, by the poor security of the targeted house,
and by the fact that the citizen who saw it happening just walked on by. It follows
that we need the capacity to read criminal situations from the different angles illuminated by different explanations. Elsewhere I have argued that plural understandings of a crime problem are needed to stimulate a disparate range of action possibilities
that can be integrated into a hedged, mutually reinforcing package of preventive

policies (Braithwaite 1993a). Discussion of the problem by a group with local knowledge derived from being affected by the crime in different ways is a good path to a nuanced understanding of the crime. The previous section argued that courts are not capable of the polycentric problem solving at issue (illustrated with the CML and Hollow Water cases) and that restorative justice processes can be more capable of it. Nor are state monopolists of rehabilitation alone capable of it, though within that arena the meta-analytic evidence is consistent with the analysis advanced here: "multi-modal programmes" (Losel 1995) that "use more than one treatment modality to target multiple problems offenders may be experiencing" are more effective (Cullen and Gendreau 2000, p. 139).

In a case like CML (chapter 1), the disparate array of preventive measures employed were grounded in the different kinds of theories suggested by the rich plurality of players involved in this restorative justice process. So I have argued (Braithwaite 1998, p. 29) that what happens with the best crime prevention practice is that:

1. Dialogue about restoration motivates the engagement of a wide plurality of stakeholders in their analysis of why this crime occurred and how recurrence might be prevented.
2. The polycentric problem is thereby grasped via commonsense versions of a variety of theories, used as metaphors to arrive at a nuanced understanding of the crime by seeing it as many things at once (Braithwaite 1993a).
3. Professionals table with the stakeholders their analysis of the advice available from the research literature on what has worked and what has failed in the past with this kind of problem.
4. Prevention professionals design with stakeholders an integrated strategy that is redundantly responsive to the theoretical relevances understood under point 2, the research findings in point 3, and the contextual differences from the situations in which the research was conducted as revealed by the discussions in point 1.

The award-winning Health Canada video *Widening the Circle: The Family Group Decision Making Experience*, based on Burford and Pennell's (1998) work with family violence, advances best restorative justice practice in this regard. We see on the video a social worker list on butcher paper the range of options available locally for dealing with family violence. Later the experts leave but are called in to explain some other kinds of treatment options that the family members think might help in their situation.

My hypothesis is that the plurality of deliberation in restorative justice conferences will increase the effectiveness of rehabilitation programs. This plurality would push out one-size-fits-all pet psychotherapeutic programs often spewed up by state monopolies of welfare provision. The experts under the restorative model have to persuade the affected communities of care that this really will be the best option for them. Most critically, they must persuade the offender or the victim who is to be helped. I hypothesize that this will increase the odds of the help being effective (in comparison with coerced help). While the evidence is not clear that this hypothesis is correct, it is far more clear that commitment to rehabilitation in a context of family and·community support is more effective (Cullen 1994).

In the meta-analyses of correctional programs, "responsivity" is found to be one of the principles that explains what works. Responsivity means matching the nature of help to the needs and learning styles of offenders (Andrews and Bonta 1998, p. 245; Gendreau 1996). While it is comforting to know that responsivity increases the effectiveness of correctional treatment, from a restorative justice perspective this is a limited and impoverished way of theorizing the diverse ways crime prevention should deploy plural deliberation to attempt responsive regulation of the problem.

Restorative justice does not involve a rejection of the rehabilitative ideal in the way articulated by Levrant et al. (1999). It does mean reframing it. Instead of state professionals in social work or psychotherapy deciding that their approach is what is best for the family, the family is empowered with knowledge of a range of rehabilitative options and with the right to choose among a variety of competing public, private, and charitable providers of rehabilitative services. This disempowering of state therapeutic monopolies, like dismantling the police monopoly of the policing budget, is not only democratically superior for republicans who believe in freedom as nondomination (Braithwaite and Pettit 1990; Pettit 1997). My hypothesis is that the marriage of rehabilitation programs to restorative justice will increase their effectiveness. Delivering on this potential is unlikely to be demonstrated at the moment when the welfare state is being dismantled, even as it requires the dismantling of welfarist justice monopolized by state correctional professionals. Admittedly the hypothesis that a marriage of restorative justice and rehabilitation will increase the effectiveness of treatment is a conjecture of theory rather than evidence. But so is Andrews's (1995, p. 58) "Principle of Professional Discretion" that decision making should be in the hands of "sensitive and psychologically informed clinicians." This when the evidence from his own research tradition is that only "about 10 to 20 percent" of real-world professionals who monopolize correctional decision making exercise their discretion to meet the principles of high-quality treatment that the likes of Don Andrews and Paul Gendreau have demonstrated (Gendreau 1998, p. 74).

Professional discretion seems likely to be a principle of ineffectivenss (and plural deliberation the principle of effectiveness) because the most important choice is whether the most promising intervention will involve offender rehabilitation, environmental prevention, target hardening, advice for the victim, changes in police procedures, reconstructing power relationships between men who batter and women who are battered (Coker, 1999, p. 106) and so on, or rather what kind of combination of these. For example, one option for a repeat drunk driving offender is an alcohol rehabilitation program, another is to reform the habits of drinking groups who attend the conference so that there is a designated driver. Other possibilities are surrender of license or surrender of the car on Friday and Saturday nights; commitments at the conference by the proprietor of the pub or club where the offender drinks to reform serving practices (join a "responsible serving" self-regulatory program), agreement to drink at home instead of at the pub, or a move to low-alcohol beer or some other kind of moderation commitment to be supported by drinking mates. The hypothesis is that dialogue between professionals with special competence and a community of care with special contextual wisdom, where the latter make the final choices, will result in wiser choices than professional discretion.

5. Restorative justice can improve follow-through

In chapter 3 we saw that the evidence is that agreements reached out of restorative justice processes are more likely to be implemented than the orders of courts. The reason according to the theory of restorative justice is that voluntary commitment works better than state orders, that the open discussion of consequences that need to be put right motivates that commitment, and that when aunts and uncles offer to monitor implementation of an agreement they are generally more capable of doing so than the police. A drinking mate is more capable of enforcing a designated driver agreement for a drunk driver than the police are able to enforce a license suspension on drivers who persist with driving in most of the researched cases (Ross and Gonzales 1988, Robinson 1977, cited in Barnes 1999). The drinking mates are present when the temptation to drink and drive arises, and they feel an obligation to follow through on their agreement to enforce the undertaking. Follow-up conferences are an important part of many restorative justice programs (see Box 4.6). We assume that rehabilitative initiatives that are followed through to ensure they actually happen are more likely to be effective than those that are conceived and then not followed through to execution.

DETERRENCE THEORY

Bentham would be disappointed at the current state of the evidence on how well deterrence works (Sherman et al. 1997). I will not review here the vast literature on the limited effectiveness of criminal punishments as deterrents. In another essay (Braithwaite 1997b), I have reviewed some of the reasons that deterrence does not work as well as it ought. Deterrence is shown to fail as a policy not so much because it is irrelevant (though it is for many) but because the gains from contexts where it works are canceled by the losses from contexts where it backfires. The next ten sections of this chapter will develop at some length a rationale for why the deterrence that comes with soft restorative justice is more powerful than that of hard punitive justice. This turns on having a restorative justice that avoids the way deterrence can backfire while extending the range and the vulnerability of the targets that do experience deterrence.

Emotion and Counterdeterrence

We all value our life, so it makes little sense that we would not refrain from acts that put our life at risk as a result of the existence of capital punishment. The first

---

Box 4.6: The North Minneapolis African American Circles

A difference of the north Minneapolis African American circles (run by the northside community justice committee) from other restorative justice programs is that a series of circles are held for each offender. The first is the interview circle at which the offender and his or her parents or guardian meet the circle volunteers and decide whether they wish to participate in the program. The program is described in some detail so as to allow the young person to make an informed choice. The crime itself is not mentioned in this meeting. At this meeting the young person's needs and interests are also considered so that individual members of the circle can begin to act as mentors. So, for instance, in a circle I attended, it was established that the young person was a keen basketballer. Some of the male members of the group were also keen basketballers and said they would come and watch the young offender play. The circle also identified that the young person had a problem with math. Another volunteer said she would assist the young person with his math. If the young person agrees to participate in the program, and the volunteers agree to accept the case, a second circle is held in which the crime is discussed, and a social compact developed (which involves a number of commitments by the young offender). Another circle is held for the victim. A fourth circle is held for the victim and offender—a healing circle. Other circles are then held to monitor completion of the social compact the young person makes, culminating in a celebration circle where the group celebrates the young person's completion of his agreement.

Source: Fieldwork notes of Declan Roche

---

step to understanding how it can make sense is to see how the protection we get from some of the worst crimes does not involve calculative deliberation.

For most of the people who caused us problems last week, we did not deal with those problems by killing them. We did not refrain from murder because we weighed up the benefits against the probability of detection and likely punishment but because murder was right off our deliberative agenda. Murder was simply unthinkable to us as a way of solving our problems. It is understanding what constitutes that unthinkableness that is the key to crime prevention. Whether the penalty for murder is death or something else is mostly quite unimportant to that understanding.

Moreover, when murder does become thinkable, it often does so in a way that is not rationally deliberative in a way the deterrence model assumes. It sometimes becomes thinkable in the context of emotions temporarily hijacking those more calculative processes in the brain on which deterrence depends.[3] This emotional short-circuiting of rational calculation in our brain had survival value in the history of our species. The emotion of anger sends blood rushing to our hands so we are ready to fight, to grasp a weapon. The emotion of fear sends blood to our feet so we are ready to flee. The emotion of lust sends blood rushing to a place in between. The short circuit gives our bodies the capacity to exploit windows of opportunity to attack, defend, flee, or procreate before the opportunity has passed.

In the contemporary world, as opposed to the world of our biological creation, the means of risk management and procreation are institutionalized in ways that make more doubtful the survival value of a brain that is liable to have its faculties for rational deliberation preempted by emotion. So the plight of modern humans is to experience regular regret for things we do during those moments when the emotions hijack the brain. For most of us, this is a weekly occurrence, for some a daily one.

It does not take something as drastic as a man attacking us with a spear for threat to trigger anger; the brain makes connections of lower level threats like an angry voice to fire up our anger. This is why emotional defiance to regulatory threats is relevant not only to "crimes of passion" like murder. Overbearing threats by a government official can engender emotional defiance to what economists would expect to be rational business compliance with regulatory laws. Makkai and Braithwaite (1994b) examined compliance by chief executives of 410 Australian nursing homes with thirty-one regulatory standards. They found that the subjective expected level of punishment did not predict compliance in any of a variety of more simple and more complex multivariate models they were able to construct. Figure 4.2 shows, however, that this result conceals the fact that there were contexts where deterrence worked and other contexts where it not only failed to work, but where there was a counter-deterrent effect. A scale to measure the psychological trait of the emotionality of the chief executive was the only variable that specified when the deterrence model would work and when it would not. When managers were low on emotionality, they responded to perceived increases in threat in a "cold and calculating" way. But the CEOs who were high on emotionality responded to escalated threats by getting mad rather than by ceasing to be bad. In Figure 4.2 if deterrence simply failed for high-emotionality managers, the high-emotionality line would be flat. In fact it slopes downward, meaning that for emotional managers, the stronger the deterrent threat, the less compliance. Deterrence fails as a policy not so much because it is irrelevant (though it is for many) but because the gains from contexts where it works are canceled by the losses from contexts where it backfires.

Perhaps the most concentrated research effort criminology has seen was on the deterrence of domestic violence.[4] It tends to bear out a similar picture. In a first randomized experiment, Sherman and Berk (1984) found that arrested domestic violence offenders were less likely to reoffend than those dealt with less punitively. This study had a major effect on public policy. However, subsequent experiments found no net effect of arrest in reducing violence. Again, this overall result concealed the fact that for employed men arrest reduced subsequent violence, while for unemployed men it escalated violence. Sherman (1992) interprets this as a result of underclass men who have experienced repeated stigmatizing and unfair experiences with the criminal justice system responding with anger and defiance when they are arrested. How to interpret the various methodological weaknesses of these studies is

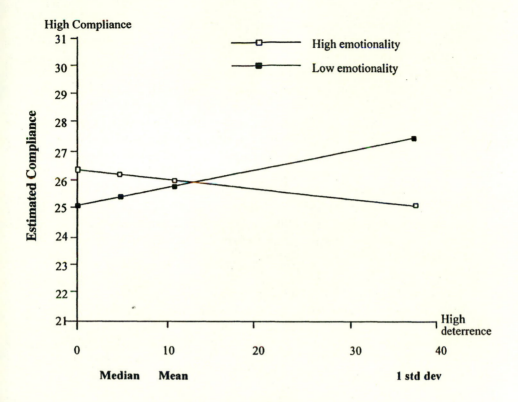

Figure 4.2   Effect of the Interaction Between Emotionality and Deterrence on Compliance with the Law (Makkai and Braithwaite 1994b)

riddled with controversy (see Stanko 1995). What is clear, however, is that we are unlikely to see such a large investment of public money again in systematic random-ized tests at multiple sites of a deterrence hypothesis. If we are not likely to get better data than these at least we need to settle on the conclusion that it is problematic to claim that deterrence is more likely to produce negative than positive effects.

Cognition and Counterdeterrence

Sherman's (1993) invocation of the literature showing that compliance is more likely when actors perceive regulation to be procedurally fair suggests that the rea-sons big sticks rebound are to be found in the psychology of cognition as well as the psychology of emotion. More police can increase crime if police are systematically procedurally unfair or stigmatizing in the way they deal with an underclass; more police can reduce crime if they are procedurally fair and reintegrative in their polic-ing. When we increase the number of police, one reason we do not generally achieve

a measurable reduction in crime is that we put on the beat a mixture of extra stigmatizing police who make things worse and extra fair and reintegrative police who
make things better.

The cognitive mechanisms that produce a "reactance" against threat have now
been the subject of an enormous experimental research effort. This work shows how
foolish it is to follow the institutional design advice of Hobbes (1949) and Hume
(1963) of preparing for the worst—assuming that people are knaves. Unfortunately,
when we treat people as knaves, they are more likely to become knaves. The less
salient and powerful the control technique used to secure compliance, the more likely
that internalization of the virtue of compliance will occur. Experimental research on
children and college students demonstrates the counterproductive effect salient rewards and punishments can have: long-term internalization of values like altruism
and resistance to temptation are inhibited when they view their action as caused by
a reward or punishment (Lepper 1973; Lepper and Greene 1978; Dix and Grusec
1983; Hoffman 1983).

> Over 50 studies examining the effect of extrinsic incentives on later intrinsic moti-
> vation indicate that inducements that are often perceived as controlling (e.g. tan-
> gible rewards, surveillance, deadlines), depending on the manner in which they are
> administered, reduce feelings of self-determination and undermine subsequent mo-
> tivation in a wide variety of achievement-related activities after the reward is re-
> moved. (Boggiano et al. 1987)

These findings seem to be of fairly general import, being supported in domains
including moral behavior, altruism, personal interaction, aggressive behavior, and resistance to temptation (Lepper 1973; Dienstbier et al. 1975; Dix and Grusec 1983;
Boggiano et al. 1987). Just as strong external incentives retard internalization, using
reasoning in preference to power assertion tends to promote it (Cheyne and Walters
1969; Parke 1969; Hoffman 1970; Baumrind 1973; Zahn-Waxler, Radke-Yarrow, and
King 1979).

Reactance

Such findings are an important part of an empirical grounding for why we should
have a first preference for restorative justice dialogue over coercion for dealing with
crime. Brehm and Brehm (1981) constructed a theory of psychological reactance on
the basis of the kinds of studies we have been discussing. Figure 4.3 shows that the
net effect of deterrent threats[5] is the sum of a deterrence effect and a reactance
effect. According to this theory, intentions to control are reacted to as attempts to
limit our freedom, which lead us to reassert that freedom by acting contrary to the
direction of control. Figure 4.3 also shows that reactance is least when we seek to
restrict freedom to do something that is not very important to us and greatest when
the freedom subjected to control is something the regulated actor deeply cares about.
Tom Tyler might suggest that naked attempts to control us give us some negative

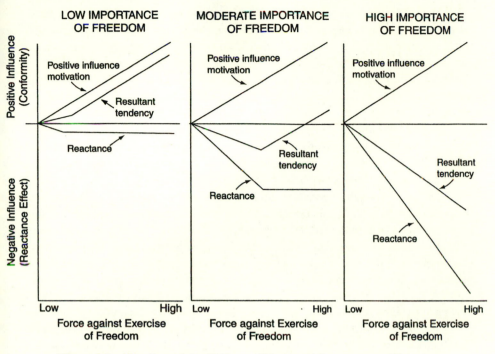

Figure 4.3   The Interactive Effects of Force and Importance of Freedom

information about our identity—that we have a subordinated identity, that we are a slave to the will of another—and this is an identity we do not want.

Hence, if freedom to park our car where we want is not an especially important freedom, the way we react to the size of parking fines will be rather like the left-hand panel in Figure 4.3. The net effect of threat on compliance will be close to the prediction of a crude rational actor model. If freedom of religion is a vitally important freedom to Christians, then throwing more Christians to the lions may only strengthen their commitment to martyrdom, adding rather than detracting from the growth of Christianity, as in the right-hand panel of Figure 4.3.

This insight motivates a fundamental reframing of deterrence theory. Because deterrence works well (without reactance) for people who care little about the freedom being regulated, what we need to do is search for such people who do not care about the particular freedom being regulated. They are the ones in a position to prevent the crime. Later we will find that such deterrable soft targets with the capacity to prevent injustice can usually be uncovered by restorative justice processes.

Rational Counterdeterrence

In addition to reactance effects that have emotional and cognitive dimensions not captured by rational choice models (rage, defiance, perceived procedural injustice, stigmatization, devaluation of the intrinsic virtue of compliance), the stronger deterrents are, the more rational actors will find countermeasures that effectively undermine the deterrents. Hence, in Figure 4.3, we need to discount the rational deterrence effect not only by the reactance effect but also by measures that rationally subvert the deterrent effect. These grow with the size of the deterrent because the more severe the deterrents, the more reason regulated actors have to invest in counterdeterrence.

Capacity to mobilize counterdeterrence also grows with the power of the criminal. Large corporations have a well-documented capacity to organize their affairs so that no one can be called to account. The larger and more powerful the organization, the more inherently complex and hard to prove are its abuses of power. But more than that, complexity is something powerful actors are able to contrive into their affairs. This includes organizational complexity as to who is responsible for what, jurisdictional complexity as to the nation in which each element of the offense occurs, complexity of the accounts, and complexity that repeat corporate players have been able to contrive into the law on previous occasions when they have "played for rules" rather than for outcomes. The more punitive a regulatory regime is, the more worthwhile it is for large corporations to have "vice presidents responsible for going to jail" and for Mafia bosses to have fall guys.[6] Lines of responsibility and reporting are drawn in the organization so that if someone has to be a scapegoat for the crimes of the CEO, it will be the vice president responsible for going to jail. Individuals are promoted to this position on the basis of assuming this risk. After a period of faithful service in the role, they would be moved sideways to a safe vice presidency.

The Deterrence Trap

Precisely when the stakes are highest with a crime, the law enforcer is likely to fall into a "deterrence trap" (Coffee 1981). Because of the inherent and contrived complexity associated with the biggest abuses of organizational power, probabilities of detection and conviction fall. Imagine, for example, that the risks of conviction for insider trading are only one in a hundred for a corporate stock market player that can afford quality legal advice. (In fact, in Australia they had been zero until recently when the first private actor was convicted of this crime.) Imagine that the average returns to insider trading are $1 million. Under a crude expected utility model, it will then be rational for the average insider trader to continue unless the penalty exceeds $100 million. That would be a large enough penalty to bankrupt many medium-sized companies, leaving innocent workers unemployed, creditors unpaid, and communities deprived of their financial base. This is what is required to deter the average insider trader under these crude assumptions. But the criminal law cannot be designed to deal simply with the average case. It should be designed so it can deter the worst cases, which, with sophisticated corporate crime, involve not millions but billions. Here the deterrence trap seems inescapably deep. It also seems inescapably deep with other kinds of crimes of organizational power—such as the terrible overspills of deterrence onto the innocent children of Iraq that we have seen with the imposition of economic sanctions that have still not been strong enough to deter Saddam Hussein's war crimes and human rights abuses.

Braithwaite (1997b) advances two counterintuitive strategies for beating the emotional and cognitive reactance, the rational countermeasures, and the deterrence traps that make deterrence of our biggest crimes difficult at best and counterproductive at worst:

1. Replace narrow, formal, and strongly punitive responsibility (the "find the crook" strategy) with broad, informal, weak sanctions.
2. Separate enforcement targeting from identification of the actor who benefits from the crime.

This is what restorative justice processes can deliver.

The Strength of Weak Sanctions

These two strategies for beating reactance rely on an obvious fact about crimes of the powerful: the more serious the abuse, the more likely it is that many people will be involved. The most egregious abuses of power arise when whole armies, police forces, bureaucracies, or transnational corporations can be mobilized to prosecute the exploitative conduct at issue. Fisse and Braithwaite (1993) have concluded from their various empirical studies that a feature of corporate crime is that it is over-determined, as the philosophers say, by the acts and omissions of many individuals, organizations, and subunits of organizations. While only a small number of people may be involved in committing a corporate crime, Fisse and Braithwaite's empirical work shows that a much larger number usually have the power to prevent it. These people vary in the degree they care about the freedom being regulated and therefore in their susceptibility to reactance.

It may be that rational dollar-maximizing actors need a fine of $100 million if they are to be deterred from insider trading from which they benefit. But they, the beneficiaries of the crime, are not the only potential deterrence targets. They may have a boss; their boss may have a boss who is in a position to stop the misconduct. They may have a variety of subordinates who can prevent the wrongdoing by blowing the whistle. Even secretaries are found to commonly do the whistle-blowing that lands their employer in jail for major frauds. Then there are auditors, law firms, consultants, investment bankers, suppliers, and other organizations both upstream and downstream who know what is going on in the criminal organization.[7] Hence, Fisse and Braithwaite (1993, p. 220) concluded:

> In a complex corporate offense there can be three types of actors who bear some level of responsibility for the wrongdoing or capacity to prevent the wrongdoing:
>
> 1. hard targets who cannot be deterred by maximum penalties provided in the law;
> 2. vulnerable targets who can be deterred by maximum penalties; and

3. soft targets who can be deterred by shame, by the mere exposure of the fact that they have failed to meet some responsibility they bear, even if that is not a matter of criminal responsibility.

So my empirical work with Brent Fisse on corporate crime led to the conclusion that the way to deter crime was not to seek to deter the criminal who benefits most from the crime but to look for a softer target who has preventive capabilities. The paradigm-transforming moment in our praxis with this insight was the Solomons Carpet case (Fisse and Braithwaite 1993). Solomons had committed a false advertising offense. There were problems of proof, and the penalty likely to be imposed by the courts was light. At the Trade Practices Commission we conferenced it without success. Involving even the CEO in successive conferences did not work; he was a hard target for deterrence, calling our bluff to take the case to court. In a final attempt, when we involved Mr. Solomon, the chairman of the board, he turned out to be a soft target who was ashamed that his company was flouting its legal obligations. He sacked the CEO and put in place a remarkable program of compensation for consumers and industry-wide preventive (self-regulatory) measures. So we learned that a good regulatory strategy was to conference, conference again and again with ever wider circles of executives with preventive capabilities until we found the soft target. We moved up the organization until we found the soft target who could be moved by reason or deterred by fear of a personal sense of shame.

Solomons was a minor restorative justice watershed for the Trade Practices Commission. There were subsequent cases like the insurance cases discussed in chapter 1, where some of the insurance executives were soft targets who came away from these encounters deeply ashamed of what their company had done. In fact, many subsequent cases were handled through a process of working up the organization until a soft management target was found who would trigger a dialogic process of responsive reform among those below the soft target. Fisse and Braithwaite (1993) developed this strategy into an accountability model that seeks to mobilize corporate private justice systems to hold responsible all who are responsible (generally at subcriminal levels of responsibility). While holding the axe of law enforcement over an organization's head, the company is required, generally with an independent law firm, to produce a self-investigation report identifying all the persons and procedures responsible for the wrongdoing and proposing remedies. Again, the idea is that some of the persons identified as having a responsibility under this process will be soft targets who will initiate responsive processes of reform, recompense, and prevention for the future.

Generalized Restorative Justice and Soft Targets

The accountability model might have less force in relation to simpler corporate wrongdoings that are less overdetermined by the causative and preventive capabilities of many hands and minds. However, the same restorative justice ideas are being found to have relevance to individual crimes committed in a social context as opposed to a formal organizational context. In Canberra drunk driving conferences, loved ones, drinking mates, and friends from work express their support for the offender and her commitment to responsible citizenship. They also become key players in suggesting ideas for a restorative plan of action. This may include preventive agreements that draw on the capacity of many hands to prevent. Drinking mates may sign a designated driver agreement. Bar staff at the drinker's pub may undertake to call a taxi when the offender has had too much and make him take it. Uncle Harry may undertake to ensure that the car is always left in the garage on Friday and Saturday nights. Even with an offense as seemingly solitary as drunk driving, often there are many individuals with preventive capabilities who can be rendered responsible for mobilizing those capabilities through a restorative justice dialogue. While reactance may be strong with the young male drunk driver who is a "petrol head," proud of his capacity to hold his drink, there may be no reactance from any of the other targets at a restorative justice conference. Indeed, when there is a collective reaction of nonreactance, we observe this to calm the anger of a young offender.

Common garden varieties of juvenile crime are even more collective, proffering more soft targets than drunk driving (Zimring 1981). This is why dialogic, "whole-school" approaches to confronting bullying have reduced bullying, in the seminal Norwegian study, by 50 percent (Farrington 1993; Olweus 1993; Pepler et al. 1993). These approaches include responsibilities of all children and teachers to step in and prevent bullying before it gets out of hand (Rigby 1996, p. 131).[8] In the theoretical frame being developed here, these other children have preventive capabilities within the social organization of the school, yet they are softer targets than the bullies themselves. The victimization of a child by a fourth-grade bully can be prevented by the intervention of every child in the playground in grade five or above who observes it. This may be why whole-school approaches to bullying work, whereas peer mediation programs that target only the bully do not (see chapter 3). The sanctioning that counts is not that directed at the bully but the softer sanctions of disapproval directed at those who fail to intervene to prevent bullying before it gets out of hand.

Most juvenile crime is a collective phenomenon. This points up another limitation of the punishment model. By locking up some members of a juvenile gang, or a drug distribution network, we can cause the group to recruit replacements from law-abiding peer groups (Reiss 1980). The more we move toward more serious crime involving more complex organizational forms (from schoolyard bullies to motorcycle gangs to the Mafia), the more force in this analysis of the limits of deterrence and the overdetermined causative and preventive capability of multiple actors. Of course, some might say that the code of silence makes everyone a "vice president responsible for going to jail" in the Mafia. No soft targets here? Prosecutorial experience proves this not to be the case. Even in the most systematically ruthless and disciplined criminal organizations—the Colombian drug cartels, for example—there are defectors who are sick of the killing and insecurity, who are sufficiently ashamed of what they have done to not want this life for their children (see, e.g., Rensselaer 1992). The fact is that such soft targets will do deals, particularly if they are allowed to pass on to their children the parts of their ill-gotten wealth that are invested in law-abiding businesses, that will enable them to lead the respectable and secure life the criminal has been denied.

Unfortunately, systematic empirical testing of whether restorative justice works better than punitive justice is more possible with juvenile bullying, young adult violence, property crime, and drunk driving, where we can randomly assign hundreds of cases to the two kinds of justice. There are not enough detected cases of the biggest abuses of power[9] for quantitative empirical work that compares outcomes.

We have seen, however, that in one domain of corporate lawbreaking, regulation of the quality of care of nursing home residents, systematic quantitative work on a sample of 410 organizations has been possible. In that domain, as discussed earlier, Makkai and Braithwaite (1991, 1994) failed to find support for a simple deterrence hypothesis. However, they did find support for the effectiveness in increasing compliance of a dialogic approach to regulation based on the proffering of trust, praise, and the nurturing of pride in corporate social responsibilities (Makkai and Braithwaite 1993b), and reintegrative shaming.

The way Australian nursing home regulation used to work was that at the end of an inspection, a meeting occurred between the inspection team and the home's management team. The owner, or a representative of the board in the case of a church or charitable home, was invited, as were representatives of the residents' committee. A dialogue proceeded for about an hour on the positive things that have been accomplished, what the problems are, and who will take responsibility for what needs to be done. In this process, most participants turned out to be soft targets, wanting to put their responsible self forward, volunteering action plans to put right what had been found wrong. This is why it succeeded in improving compliance with the law (Braithwaite et al. 1993).

At the same time, it is clear from our data that there were cases where dialogic regulation failed—where the hardest of targets were in charge, dominating and intimidating softer targets who worked under them. Empirical experience gives good reasons for assuming that even the worst of corporate malefactors have a public-regarding self; we can appeal to a self-categorization as "responsible business," for example (Ayres and Braithwaite 1992). However, when trust is tried and found to be misplaced, there is a need to escalate to deterrence as a regulatory strategy. When deterrence fails—because of reactance or a deterrence trap, or simply because noncompliance is caused by managerial incompetence rather than rational calculation of costs and benefits—then there is a need to move higher up an enforcement pyramid to an incapacitative strategy (see chapter 2). Incapacitation can mean withdrawing or suspending a license for a nursing home that has proved impregnable to both persuasion and deterrence.

Hence, there are increasingly solid empirical grounds for suspecting that we can often reduce crime by replacing narrow, formal, and strongly punitive responsibility with broad, informal, weak sanctions—by making the many dialogically responsible instead of the few criminally responsible. By dialogically responsible I mean responsible for participating in a dialogue, listening, being open to accountability for failings and to suggestions for remedying those failings. The theory I have advanced is that this is more likely when there are many actors with causative or preventative capability with respect to that abuse. Where we can engage all those actors in moral reasoning and problem-solving dialogue, the more of them there are, the more likely one or more will be a soft target. When even only one player with causative responsibility or with a powerful preventative capability turns, empirical experience shows that many other actors who had hitherto been ruthlessly exploitative suddenly find a public-regarding self that becomes surprisingly engaged with a constructive process of righting the wrong. For example, Fisse and Braithwaite's (1983, pp. 144–60) interviews at Lockheed following the foreign bribery scandals of the 1970s showed that once Lockheed's auditors, Arthur Young, put their responsible corporate self forward by refusing to certify the company's annual report, other senior managers switched to responsiveness, to public-regarding deliberation and corporate reform. As a result of this domino effect of public-regarding deliberation, Lockheed became, in the words of Boulton (1978), "a born again corporation." This case also instantiates the second mechanism for beating reactance, which is about the strategic significance of gatekeepers like auditors to making restorative justice feasible.

Separating Enforcement Targeting from the Actor Who Benefits from the Abuse

In the Lockheed example, Arthur Young was a gatekeeper (Kraakman 1984). By refusing to let Lockheed's annual report through the gate it guarded, Arthur Young brought the company's bribery of defense ministers and heads of state to an end, not to mention the careers of the company's chairman and president. Large corporations have many kinds of gatekeepers, such as the general counsel, environmental auditors, underwriters, insurers, board audit or ethics committees, and occupational health and safety committees. Each has the power to open and close gates that give the organization access to things it wants.

A gatekeeper like Arthur Young surely had an interest in doing Lockheed's bidding so it could keep the company's account. Yet Arthur Young was much more deterrable than Lockheed itself, which benefited so directly from the bribery (as did Lockheed's senior managers). Arthur Young, as a nonbeneficiary of the bribes, had less to lose from stopping them; as a gatekeeper that was not responsible for paying bribes, but only for failing to detect them, it also had less to lose from the truth than did those who were handing over the cash. Yet it had much to lose in reputational capital (Lin 1996) as a gatekeeper of hundreds of other corporate clients if someone else blew the whistle. In this case, Arthur Young was the comparatively soft target that opened up a can of worms that led to the demise of some of the hardest targets one could find in the world at that time—such as Prime Minister Tanaka of Japan.

Most people's intuition would be that we should design enforcement systems to target the beneficiaries of wrongdoing. They are the actors who make the criminal choice on the basis of the benefits of lawbreaking exceeding its costs. So from a simple rational choice perspective we should target increased costs of lawbreaking on them, the choosing criminals, not on their guardians. Not so, according to my restorative theory of deterrence.

The most powerful empirical demonstration of the power of targeting gatekeepers rather than beneficiaries of the wrongdoing comes from the most global of regulatory problems—pollution from ships at sea. Ronald Mitchell has demonstrated how the International Convention for the Prevention of Pollution from Ships (MARPOL) was an utter failure (Mitchell 1993 1994a, 1994b). Signatories were required under the convention to impose penalties for intentional oil spills. The most important targets— petroleum-exporting nations—were committed to not enforcing these laws. Most nations simply did not care to invest in proving offenses that were difficult to detect. Only a few petroleum-importing nations, such as the United States, took the require- ment seriously. This simply meant that ships had to be somewhat careful to discharge pollution outside the territorial waters of these few countries. Noncompliance with the regime was the norm.

Then in 1980 the MARPOL regime was reformed in a way that Mitchell (1994) estimates has generated 98 percent compliance. This was a remarkable accomplish- ment given that the costs of compliance with the new regime were very high for ship owners and that predictions grounded in the economic analysis of regulation were for minimal compliance (Okidi 1978). The key change was a move away from imposition of penalties on ships responsible for spills to an equipment subregime that enforced the installation of segregated ballast tanks and crude oil washing. One reason for the improvement was transparency; it is easy to check whether a tanker has segregated ballast tanks but hard to catch it actually discharging at sea. But the other critical factor was the role of third-party enforcers (1) on whom ship operators are dependent and (2) who have no economic interest in avoiding the considerable costs of the reg- ulation. These third-party enforcers are builders, classification societies, and insur- ance companies. Builders have no interest in building cheaper ships that will not get certification by international classification societies nominated by national govern- ments. Classification societies have no interest in corrupting the standards they en- force, which are the whole reason for the generation of their income. Finally, insurers will not insure ships that have not been passed by a classification society acceptable to them because they have an interest in reducing the liabilities that might arise from oil spills.

The new MARPOL regime therefore achieves 98 percent compliance in large part because the effective target of enforcement shifted from the ship operators that benefit from the pollution to builders, classification societies, and insurance compa- nies that do not benefit from it. However, because the ship operators (and builders) are totally dependent on classification societies and insurers, they have no choice but to accept the regime-compliant ships the classification societies have an interest in ensuring are the only ones that get through the gate.

The best-known example of separating enforcement targeting from the actor who benefits from the abuse is requiring employers to withhold tax from the taxable in- come of their employees, which they report, or banks to withhold and report tax on the interest earned by their customers. Little enforcement is needed against the employers and banks that withhold and report because they do not benefit from any underreporting of income. Tax cheating is only a major problem in those domains where it is impossible to harness such disinterested gatekeepers.

Peter Grabosky has initiated a program of work that continually discovers new species of third-party enforcers of regulatory regimes—from volunteer divers who check compliance with South Australia's historic shipwrecks legislation, to elected worker health and safety representatives (Grabosky 1990a, 1990b, 1992, 1994, 1995). Grabosky's work shows just how disparate are the possibilities for shifting enforcement targeting from actors who benefit from the cheating to actors who do not but on whom the cheat depends for something critical to their welfare. This simple shift is capable of making headway with some of our seemingly most intractable regulatory problems.

Another colleague, Neil Gunningham (1995), has long despaired about how hazardous chemicals regulation succeeds in changing the practices of the top twenty chemicals transnationals but barely touches thousands of little chemical companies that are too numerous, too unsophisticated, and too dispersed to be effectively supervised by state inspectors. More recently, however, Gunningham has realized that most of these little chemical companies are vitally dependent on large corporations as suppliers, distributors, customers, or all three. This has led him to the insight that a private or public regulatory regime that requires a major company to ensure not only that its own employees comply with the regulations but also that the upstream and downstream users and suppliers of its products comply may massively increase the effectiveness of the regime.[10] The reason is that a large corporation that supplies a little chemical company has much more regular contact with them than any government inspector, more intimate and technically sophisticated knowledge of where their bodies are buried, greater technical capacity to help them fix the problems, and more leverage over them than the state.

Privatizing public gatekeeping can be one way of separating powers so that enforcement can be targeted on an actor who does not benefit from the abuse of public power. Most national customs services have a lot of corruption. Both senior managers and street-level bureaucrats benefit enormously from bribes paid for turning a blind eye to the under- or overinvoicing of goods. The fact that public customs services have an organizational interest in continuing to sell favors creates a market opportunity for a private organization set up to "sell trust." This is just what the Swiss company Societé Generale de Surveillance (SGS) set out to do when it took over the customs service of Indonesia and other developing countries. SGS persuades nations to sell large parts of their customs work to it through a reputation for incorruptibility that enables it to deliver huge savings to governments. A 1991 press statement of the Indonesian minister of finance claimed that SGS had saved his country U.S. $4.5 billion of foreign exchange between 1985 and 1990 and earned it U.S. $1 billion in extra duties and taxes. Because it is such testimonials that bring SGS business, SGS has a financial incentive to catch cheats and weed out corruption in its own ranks. A major corruption scandal that would strike everyone as quite normal in the customs service of a developing country might cause financial ruin for SGS. SGS sets up its inspection gates in the country of export (where superior intelligence on over- or underinvoicing is available) rather than in the importing country. It accomplishes this by having over a thousand scrupulously audited offices at all the world's key exporting sites. The company constrains itself from engaging in any manufacturing or in any trading or financial interests that would threaten its independence.

"Selling trust" is profitable, so operatives are well paid. As the company's senior vice president, J. Friedrich Sauerlander, confessed to me, in an organization of 27,000 people his internal security organization had uncovered "some slip-ups." But in all major ways, it had been possible to sustain an organization with an incentive structure to reward trust. The beneficiaries of the old breaches of trust were left where they were. But through building a thousand gates to their power on the other side of the world, and guarding those gates with SGS units that flourished in proportion to how much abuse of trust they stopped, targeting enforcement on the bad guys inside the gates became mostly redundant.

From Lockheed, to polluters from ships, to employers and banks withholding tax, to chemical companies, to outside (instead of inside) directors targeted by public interest groups over corporate abuse of power,[11] to big adolescent boys exposed at family group conferences for assaulting their mothers and sisters,[12] we can see some promise in shifting enforcement targeting from actors who benefit from their abuse to actors who do not but on whom the abuser depends for something critical to their welfare.

Talking with Many Soft Targets and General Deterrence

The implication of the analysis in this section of the book is that punishing crooks is a less efficient deterrence strategy than opening up discussion with a wide range of actors with preventive capabilities, some of whom might be motivated by a raised eyebrow to change their behavior in ways that prevent reoffending. It is to keep expanding the number of players involved in a restorative justice process until we find someone who surprises us by being influenced through the dialogue to mobilize some unforeseen preventive capability. The hypothesis is that creative restorative processes have enormous potential to surprise us as Mr. Solomon did. You don't give up after a first conference because no one turns up who can deliver that surprise. You keep convening new conferences with new carers, new stakeholders, new resource people until someone walks through the door who can pull one of the levers to prevent a criminality that is almost always "overdetermined" (Lewis 1986). Again, restorative justice rewards the patient.

Christine Parker, in commenting on a draft of this chapter, pointed out that I think this because of my view (some would say naive view) of human beings as social animals that are almost always enmeshed in multiple communities when they do what they do: "The Braithwaite argument is that there almost always are many with that capacity because we all live in a community wherein many individuals can pull strings of informal control and evoke bonds of responsibility." The argument draws sustenance from empirical findings such as those of Pennell and Burford (1996, p. 218) in their Canadian study of family group conferences for domestic violence: the conferences "generated a sense of shame across the extended family for not having acted in the past to safeguard its relatives as well as a sense of shared identity because often the problems which their relatives experienced were common in their own lives."

It also draws sustenance from another Canadian experience at Hollow Water. How can we understand the accomplishment of having no fewer than fifty-two child abusers brought to justice in such a small Canadian community? Without the restorative process, could we have expected Western punitive justice to have convicted even three or four, or any? Probably not. It was the restorative process that flushed out those with knowledge of the evil. The fact is that for any kind of crime, the community knows about and is concerned about countless crimes of which the police are ignorant. Karstedt-Henke and Crasmoller (1991) showed in Germany that for every juvenile crime the police detect, parents detect at least four, teachers detect about two, and peers detect more than five. Given the stronger evidence for an effect of certainty of punishment on crime than an effect of severity of punishment, (Sherman et al. 1997), "soft" restorative justice for forty might just accomplish more general deterrence than tough incarcerative justice for four.

With respect to knowledge, restorative justice is a virtuous circle, retributive justice a vicious circle. When the community knows about many crimes and reacts to them restoratively, the benefits of restoration motivate others to speak up, increasing community knowledge of crimes it will want to do something about. When the police know about few crimes and respond punitively, the collateral costs of punishment silence citizens into minding their own business, reducing reporting of crime to the police. Again, in a world where certainty of sanctions matters more than severity of sanctions and where informal sanctions deter more than formal ones, the corollary is that virtuous circles of restorative justice deter more than vicious circles of punitive justice.

So the process implication of my analysis is dialogic regulation of social life of the sort we get in a family group conference or a restorative exit conference such as we see after nursing home or nuclear safety (Rees 1994) inspections. There is a structural implication as well, which is developed in Braithwaite (1997b): more robust separations of powers within and between the private and public sectors. The number of third-party enforcement targets is greater to the extent that we have richer, more plural, separations of power in a polity. By building a thousand gates to the power of Indonesian customs, we increase the feasibility of restorative justice.

Dialogue among a wider range of citizens beyond the offender himself means that ripples of general deterrence spread out more widely. When many types of subcriminal responsibility are known to be at risk of exposure to people we care about in restorative justice conferences, we are all deterred in our many roles. This is why Australian nursing home regulation used to work reasonably well. Whether we were the responsible nurse, the aide, the chaplain, the gardener, or the man who visits the woman in the next bed, if no one raised the alarm about a resident who was being abused, we knew that our inaction might be disapproved in a conference. Restorative justice, in other words, is not just about specific deterrence of the offender: it also widens the scope of general deterrence (albeit a more benign general deterrence).

The benign nature of this general deterrence will be seen by most critics as the greatest weakness of restorative justice. The crunch is that restorative justice sets free many whom deterrence or retributive theories say should go to jail—like the insurance executives from CML (see chapter 1). While it is clear that offenders and others who attend restorative justice processes do not view them as a soft option but rather as a difficult and demanding experience (Schiff 1998; Sherman and Strang 1997a; Umbreit and Coates 1992), of course the agreements reached are softer than prison.

A final qualification about general deterrence arises from the assumption that restorative justice will often fail and fail again and again until deterrent justice must be tried in an attempt to protect the community. Since, for the reasons outlined here (such as the deterrence trap), deterrence will also often fail, we will sometimes need to escalate our response to incapacitation. Figure 2.2 represents this articulation of restorative justice to deterrence and incapacitation. The idea of the pyramid, which was justified in detail in chapter 2 and in Ayres and Braithwaite (1992, chap. 2), is that we start with the restorative strategy at the base of pyramid. The possibility of escalation channels regulatory activity down to the base of the pyramid; in crude utilitarian terms the pyramid makes it rational for criminals to punish themselves in restorative justice processes. This model transcends the limitations of passive deterrence in criminology by learning from the shift to active from passive deterrence in international relations theory. With passive deterrence, one simply calculates the probability of compliance on the basis of the expected size and risk of punishment. Active deterrence, in contrast, is dynamic, open to escalating threats in response to moves by the other player, as well as to graduated reduction in tension (GRIT) strategies.

The pyramid dynamically meets the challenge that unless the threat of punishment lingers in the background, there will be a class of ruthless criminals who will exploit the opportunity of restorative justice with a deceitful pretense of cooperation. Where restorative justice for a first or second offense is backed up by a passive deterrent tariff for a third, the rational actor will cheat for one or two free throws. If enforcement is the product of restorative justice negotiation, Langbein and Kerwin (1985) show game-theoretically that rational actors will avoid immediate compliance. At the least, negotiation delays compliance costs; at the best, concessions are extracted that reduce compliance costs. Langbein and Kerwin's model is only true, however, if deceit, holding back on compliance, does not cause an escalation of penalties. In practice it does; deterrence is active rather than passive, which is why Langbein and Kerwin's prediction is false as a description of most regulatory activity (see, e.g., Bardach and Kagan 1982; Braithwaite 1985).

The reality of active deterrence as a strategy that works, at least in the business regulatory domain, where it has been more systematically studied and theorized than with common crime, commends Fisse's (1983) suggestion of giving it a jurisprudentially principled foundation through implementing "reactive fault" as the core criterion of criminal fault. In its most radical version, this would mean in a case of assault, the alleged assailant would go into a restorative justice conference not on the basis of an admission of criminal guilt but on the basis of admitting responsibility for the *actus reus* of an assault ("I was the one who punched her").[13] Whether the mental element required for crime was present would be decided reactively, on the basis of the constructiveness and restorativeness of his reaction to the problem caused by his act (Braithwaite 1998). If the reaction were restorative, the risk of criminal liability would be removed; only tort liability would remain. However, if reactive criminal fault were found by a court to be present, that would be insufficient for a conviction; the mental element for the crime would also have to be demonstrated before or during its commission.[14] But it would be the reactive fault that would be the more important determinant of penalty than the causal fault. In practice, criminal justice systems vary enormously in the reactiveness versus proactiveness of their criminal law in action, Japan being unusually strong on reactive fault, the United States on proactive fault (Haley 1996; Braithwaite 1998). According to this analysis, this helps Japan enjoy lower crime rates than the United States in a way that has a profound jurisprudential justification.

Encouraging findings on deterrence are emerging as a surprising positive result of the RISE experiment on restorative conferencing in Canberra. The data reveal a "Sword of Damocles" effect, something actually revealed in previous criminological research on mercy that might later lead to punishment (Sherman 1992). To date, offenders randomly assigned to conferences are coming out more fearful that they will be rearrested if they offend again, more fearful of family and friends finding out about rearrest, more fearful of a future conference, more fearful of a future court case, and more fearful of at least one other consequence of a court case than those assigned to court (Sherman and Strang 1997b). In this variety of ways, conferences sharpen perceptions of how bad the punitive consequences would be if one were caught again. This is a somewhat unusual result because much criminological research shows that actual experience of the justice system reduces its terrors. For example, tax audits can have counterproductive effects by teaching many of those who are audited that they can cheat on their tax without going to jail and teaching them "how to avoid being caught when they evade taxes" (Kinsey 1986, p. 416).

What the preliminary RISE data suggest is that changes at the margin to send increasing numbers of offenders to conferences may simultaneously increase the deterrent power of both conferences and court. From the deterrence perspective against which I am measuring restorative justice in this section, this is good news. The problem is that if deterrent threats cause defiance and reactance, restorative justice may be compromised by what sits above it in a dynamic pyramidal strategy of deterrence and incapacitation. For Ayres and Braithwaite (1992), this is the greatest challenge facing responsive regulatory institutions. The challenge is to have the Sword of Damocles always threatening in the background but never threatened in the foreground. The criminal justice system must have an image of invincibility at the same time as it has an image of mercy and forgiveness. Police have a lot to learn here from the wisdom of business regulatory inspectors, such as Hawkins's British pollution inspectors: "Negotiating tactics are organized to display the enforcement process as inexorable, as an unremitting progress, in the absence of compliance, towards an unpleasant end" (Hawkins 1984, p. 153). Here is a New York nursing home inspector's account of how her surprisingly restorative regulatory system keeps cooperation in the foreground while coercion looms in the background:

> You can maintain the same demeanor when confronted with tension and stress, when the facility gets aggressive and unpleasant [in one case this involved putting a gun on the table]. You can be friendly if they don't correct. You just pass it on. You never have to be anything but assured and friendly. The enforcement system will take on the battle . . . The team leader just tells them [representatives of the nursing home] what the repercussions are if you don't correct. You just let the system take over. That's all you have to do. A good team leader is confident, friendly, and explains consequences. She never uses a standover approach. (Braithwaite 1993b, p. 30)

The trick is for deterrence to be always threatening but never threatened (Ayres and Braithwaite 1992, pp. 44–53). It is to enculturate trust in regulatory interactions (Braithwaite and Makkai 1994) while institutionalizing distrust through an enforcement system (Braithwaite 1998). It is to surprise the very worst of people by treating them as trustworthy; because if we can persuade them to put their best self forward (say, in the presence of their mother), we will regularly be surprised to find that the most socially responsible of their many selves is restorative. Restorative justice is not about picking good apples for reconciliation and bad apples for deterrence; it is about treating everyone as a good apple as the preferred first approach.

This implies that to be effective restorative justice requires considerable nuance in administration, yet a nuance most human beings have at their disposal. Just as they know from life experience that it is better to discuss consequences, allowing the offender to discover her own shame rather than saying "shame on you," they also know that direct threat engenders defiance in a way an image of invincibility does not. The prediction here, which will be tested in the RISE experiment, is that conferences will fail if they are either "shaming machines" (Retzinger and Scheff 1996) or threat machines. The widespread understanding of this wisdom in the community is reflected in the fact that the majority of parents of children in societies like the United States succeed in raising nondelinquent children because they do have an "authoritative" rather than an "authoritarian" parenting style (Baumrind 1978). Durkheim (1961, p. 10) understood it as well when he said, "Punishment does not give discipline its authority, but it prevents discipline from losing its authority."

Summarizing the Deterrent Effect of Restorative Justice

From the limited state of our present knowledge, the most reasonable working hypotheses on the deterrent effects of restorative justice for further empirical testing are the following:

1. Given that certainty of punishment predicts compliance better than severity of punishment, and given that the community knows about many more crimes than the police, many informal sanctions will deter more than few formally punitive sanctions.
2. When the community knows about many crimes and reacts restoratively, the benefits of restoration motivate others to speak up, increasing community members' knowledge of crimes they will want to do something about (as in Hollow Water). When the police know about few crimes and respond punitively (as in normal enforcement of the sexual abuse of children), the collateral costs of punishment silence citizens into minding their own business. Hence, given that certainty predicts better than severity, virtuous circles of restorative justice deter more than vicious circles of punitive justice.
3. Dialogic social control in which many affected parties participate will normally deter crime better than punitive social control targeted narrowly on criminals because:
   a. given that criminal conduct in a social world is overdetermined by the actions of many actors, there are many beyond the criminal who can be deterred to prevent the crime; and
   b. many of those third parties to the enforcement game will be soft targets because of their sense of social responsibility, their caring for an affected party, or because they have power to prevent without power to benefit from the crime.
4. To the extent that restorative justice holds many people responsible for a crime at levels of responsibility less than criminal responsibility, many are specifically deterred.
5. All the disparate types of third parties that are specifically deterred are also generally deterred through it becoming common knowledge that third parties who fail to prevent crime can be called to account for that failure in restorative justice processes. This will be more true to the extent that there are many gatekeepers, a rich separation of powers in a society (Braithwaite 1997b).
6. Traditional deterrence targeted on criminals cannot be abandoned under a restorative justice system because in some cases restorative justice will repeatedly fail. Escalation to traditional deterrence may happen often enough for its impact not to be significantly diminished, given the evidence from the deterrence literature that even large changes at the margin (like replacing execution with prison) do not have a major impact. It is doing without criminal deterrence altogether that has a major impact (Sherman et al. 1997).
7. The most important function of deterrence is to channel justice into restoration. This means deterrent penalties must not be fixed and passive but should be dynamically responsive to how restorative the offender is proving. Restorative justice therefore requires a jurisprudence of reactive fault (Fisse 1983).

8. It is possible to administer justice so that restoration is in the foreground of actors' deliberation while threat is in the background. Justice can succeed most of the time by getting the offender to put his socially responsible self forward; most of the rest of the time, it can succeed by switching the appeal to the actor's rationally calculating self. The switch will seem more procedurally just and therefore be more effective when persuasion has been tried and tried again before punishment is used as a last resort.

9. Most punishments are more feared in anticipation than they are once experienced. A criminal justice system that privileges restorative justice ahead of punitive justice thereby increases the deterrent power of punitive justice through a Sword of Damocles effect.

The Theory of Incapacitation

Incapacitation means removing an offender's capacity to reoffend; there are many ways to do this beyond incarceration, execution, and cutting off the hands of pickpockets. A useful feature of restorative justice is that it empowers communities of care to be creative about how to incapacitate. The empirical evidence on selective incapacitation in criminology is almost exclusively limited to a consideration of selecting the most dangerous criminals for incarceration. That evidence suggests that we are not very good at getting the selection right (MacKenzie 1997, p. 9; Gottfredson and Gottfredson 1994). Failures to incapacitate those who commit serious further offenses tend to be well publicized. Less well publicized is the likely more serious problem of false positives whose criminal career might have ended had we not thrust them into daily interaction with criminals in a prison where they learn new skills in the illegitimate labor market or suffer demeaning experiences that engender defiance, shame, and rage.

Through using incarceration much more selectively, restorative justice should be able to avert a lot of damage that makes our crime problems worse. That is mere speculation, however, because there is no empirical evidence to support such a hope. At the same time, the pyramidal theory of restorative justice and responsive regulation outlined in chapter 2 means that there is a willingness to resort to incapacitation when both restorative justice and deterrence repeatedly fail to protect the community from a serious risk.

However, imprisonment is not the principal method of incapacitation to which restorative justice would want to resort. Again, there is much that criminology can learn from business regulation here. When a company continually creates a serious risk to the community, a common alternative to putting the company in jail is to put the jailer into the company. An example was the "resident inspector" program run by the Mine Safety and Health Administration in the United States for repeat-offending high-accident mines. The presence of the inspector in these mines stopped certain unsafe practices from being contemplated, substantially reducing deaths and injuries to well below the national average in mines that had been the least safe in the country (Braithwaite 1985, p. 83). Similar resident inspector programs have been applied in the nuclear industry, the nursing home industry, and more recently in relation to the environmental compliance problems of Consolidated Edison in New York. Earlier this chapter discussed this strategy in relation to court appointment of trustees in New York to reform Mafia-controlled unions (Jacobs 1999). Braithwaite and Daly (1994, p. 200) have outlined how successive restorative justice conferences might escalate incapacitative response for domestic violence: "For example, there could be escalation from weekly reporting by all family members of any violent incidents to the man's aunt or brother-in-law (conference 1), to a relative or other supporter of the woman moving into the household (conference 2), to the man moving to a friend's household (conference 3)."

That paper also makes much of flipping the incapacitation target—incapacitating the male offender by assuring the female victim of the resources and guaranteed shelter to walk out, leaving the offender alone in a house without a victim and therefore without a capacity to victimize.

In cases such as the Aboriginal insurance scandals (CML) and the Mafia in New York discussed earlier, agents who make fraudulent claims or who are Mafia front men can be incapacitated by licensing schemes that deny them a license for this kind of work. Doctors, lawyers, and company directors can be delicensed through either positive or negative licensing schemes.

Drunk drivers can also be deprived of a license to drive, a form of incapacitation that works badly in Australia, where drunks driving without licenses is pandemic. More social and less legal assurances of incapacitation may sometimes have more promise, and restorative justice conferences can deliver these. Drinking mates can sign undertakings that they will prevent the offender from driving after drinking and will make him comply with a designated driver agreement. Uncle Harry can incapacitate him from drinking and driving on Friday and Saturday nights when he goes out with the boys by taking ownership of the car and its keys on those nights. Such incapacitation can be escalated by a conference in response to noncompliance by agreement up front that the consequence of failure to hand over the car at these times is that Uncle Harry will take possession of the car for a year.

The theory of restorative justice here is that Uncle Harrys have a more plural range of incapacitative keys they can turn than does a prison guard, who can turn just one key. Uncle Harry can respond dynamically when his incapacitative ideas backfire, but they are less likely to backfire when the offender voluntarily commits to them. As we have seen, unenforceable restorative justice agreements enjoy higher compliance than enforceable court agreements (see chapter 3). Beyond the greater commitment we all have to undertakings we choose ourselves, the further reasons for superior compliance are that the Uncle Harrys of this world come up with ideas more attuned to the reality of the offender's circumstances than a judge, and are better monitors of their implementation than police officers because one Uncle Harry might have more contacts with the offender in a month than all the police in the city during a year. Intimates, in short, can incapacitate more intensively, more creatively, more sensitively, more consensually, and in a more dynamically responsive way than the criminal justice system. This optimistic account of restorative incapacitation lacks systematic support, but it does map a promising new research agenda for the possibilities of restorative justice.

REFINING THE ECONOMIC ANALYSIS OF LAW

This section argues that restorative justice practices may be more cost-effective than criminal justice practices grounded in the economic analysis of crime. The economic analysis of law (e.g., Posner 1977) provides a more theoretically sophisticated, though transparently false, explanatory structure than the other utilitarian analyses in deterrence, rehabilitation, and incapacitation theory. It makes false predictions because it is myopic. Its models assume that rational choosing of costs and benefits provides a total explanation of compliance when we have seen that emotions and twisted cognitions play havoc with the reality. Makkai and Braithwaite (1993a) found that actual costs of compliance with nursing home laws explained only 19 percent of the variance in the subjectively expected costs that should inform rational choices. While there was a powerful effect of expected cost of compliance on compliance, this was not a monotonically increasing effect. There was a turning point in the relationship explained by the behavior of "disengagers." Their behavior is not to be understood in terms of rational game playing but in terms of dropping out of the enforcement game. Regulatory disengagers, rather like many heroin addicts, are in the regulatory system but not of it and certainly not economically calculative about it.

All this means that the underspecification in economic analyses of law is of a rather fatal sort. It is not that the models are basically right and can be improved by tinkering that includes more of the excluded variables. When a variable like reactance can reverse the direction of a deterrence coefficient, when disengagers come into play in a way that turns an increasing relationship into a decreasing one, advice on the optimal level of deterrence will be not just wrong but very wrong. Moreover, these influences mean it will be wrong in a way that assumes increasing deterrence will deliver more economic benefits than it ever in fact does (to the extent that defiance and disengagement neutralize or reverse deterrence). Finally, even if an empirically correct economic analysis of the optimal level of penalties were discovered, its implementation would lead us into a deterrence trap that would create economic chaos in respect of some of our most serious crimes (Braithwaite 1997b). Coffee's (1981) deterrence trap is that fines of the magnitude required to deter much corporate crime will cause bankruptcies, punishing innocent workers who are retrenched.

It is difficult therefore to imagine the construction of a purely economic model of crime that will not set deterrence at a counterproductively high level. The responsive theory of regulatory deterrence in Ayres and Braithwaite (1992) certainly draws heavily on economic analysis, but it uses the economic analysis as an element in the design of a dynamic model that moves from restorative justice when *experience* proves it a failure and then moves from deterrent justice when experience proves that a failure. That is, there is no reliance on a statically optimal level of deterrence. We do not want to rely on that because, for the reasons we have adduced, it will always be wrong.

A dynamic model based on a regulatory pyramid where restorative justice is privileged at the base of the pyramid is more likely to get it right, albeit clumsily. It iterates through one failed strategy after another until contextual deliberation declares one effective. It can also be cheaper because it averts maximally expensive options like imprisonment and courts staffed by highly paid judges, prosecutors, and other professionals as it privileges the efforts of volunteers from the citizenry.

Systematic evidence on the costs of restorative justice compared with punitive justice is scarce, though Peter Reuter has a study under way as his contribution to the RISE experiment in Canberra. Claims are regularly made about multi-million-dollar savings in New Zealand, particularly as a result of closure of juvenile institutions. When the number of residential places has dropped by almost two-thirds since 1989 (Maxwell and Morris 1996), this seems plausible, but no published studies exist of the magnitude of the claimed savings. It certainly is true that nations such as Germany, Austria, New Zealand, and China, which are vigorously committed to restorative programs for juveniles, pay for extremely modest numbers of institutional beds per capita compared with nations such as the United States, the United Kingdom, and Australia. However, to be maximally effective in the terms of our discussion of rehabilitation and restorative justice, restorative justice requires a more credible investment in the welfare state, and this does not come cheap. Of course, the benefits of a decent welfare state should not be measured primarily in terms of crime prevention.

The most thorough study is of Scottish mediation of disputes largely among neighbors, family, and friends (by Martin Knapp and Ann Netten, in Warner 1992, pp. 105–37). Theoretically, these were supposed to be cases that otherwise would have been prosecuted. In fact, in the comparison group nineteen of the forty-four cases were not prosecuted. Across the two programs, when prosecutions did occur, the average prosecution case costs were just over £200, compared with about £300 for mediation and reparation cases, leading Knapp and Netten to conclude that for comparatively simple matters that would not lead to either a not-guilty plea or imprisonment, mediation and reparation were rather more expensive than prosecution. The other more systematic study of costs was of the New Zealand adult restorative panel programs, Project Turnaround and Te Whanau Awhina by Maxwell, Morris, and Anderson (1999). In both programs, but especially the latter, where the corrections system savings were greatest, there were notable savings compared with a control group.

The Theory of Justice

> Allowing offenders to buy their way out of prison with monetary and nonmonetary compensation to victims unacceptably confounds the private goals of mediation and the public goals of criminal law.
>
> Brown, "The Use of Mediation to Resolve Criminal Cases"

For just deserts theorists, it is unjust that offenders get unequal treatment depending on whether they have a merciful or a punitive victim, a poor one who needs compensation or a rich one who does not, a victim who will cooperate in the diversion from court or one who will not. Some restorative justice advocates turn this around by saying that it is morally wrong to privilege equality of treatment for offenders over "equality of justice [which] means equal treatment of victims" (Barnett 1981, p. 259). Or equal justice might mean equality of opportunity for victims with known offenders to pursue the forms of restoration most important to them in the way of their choosing (see generally Roach 1999). Because equality for victims and equality for offenders are utterly irreconcilable, the more practical justice agenda is to guarantee victims a minimum level of care and to guarantee offenders against punishment beyond a maximum limit. The normative theory of restorative justice illuminates a practical path to those guarantees. Hence, in this section I argue that restorative justice may secure justice more meaningfully than criminal justice practices grounded in "justice" or just deserts theories.

The fundamental problem restorative justice advocates have with the justice model has been most eloquently captured by Martin Wright (1992, p. 525): "Balancing the harm done by the offender with further harm inflicted on the offender only adds to the total amount of harm in the world." As with other parts of this book, the analysis of the justice of restorative justice compared with the so-called justice or just deserts model is influenced by a consideration of white-collar crime that is so often lacking in the work of desert theorists.

There is now, as we have seen, a good deal of evidence that citizens are more likely to feel that restorative processes are just and respect their rights after they have experienced them than are citizens who have experienced the justice of courts (see chapter 3). Desert theorists have to respond to this by saying that citizens in a democracy do not understand what justice entails, do not understand what their own interests in justice should cause them to want. While this response may be largely false, given the worries we ought properly to have about tyrannies of the majority, we must recognize it can sometimes be true. The systematic evidence we have from judicial oversight of New Zealand conferences is not consistent with any widespread tyranny of the majority. Maxwell and Morris (1993) report that 81 percent of family group conference plans were approved without modification by courts, with the overwhelming majority of changes (in 17 percent of cases) being to make orders at a higher level rather than at a lower level (a lower level being what one would expect to see if there were a tyranny of the majority to be checked). Almost identical results have been obtained in the Restorative Resolutions project for adult offenders in Manitoba (83 percent judicial ratification of plans, with five times as much modification by addition of requirements as modification by deletion; Bonta, Rooney, and Wallace-Capretta 1998, p. 16).

There is no consensus within the social movement for restorative justice on what should count as unjust outcomes. Most advocates want restorative justice to be a more modest philosophy than to aspire to settle this question. Rather, restorative justice should settle for the procedural requirement that the parties talk until they feel that peace has been restored on the basis of a discussion of all the injustices they see as relevant to the case. Within that dialogue about justice, Braithwaite and Pettit (1990) and Braithwaite and Parker (1999) have made the case for a republican conception of justice. Most restorative justice advocates do not know or care what is involved in a republican rationale for restorative justice, let alone subscribe to it. The most popular philosophical foundations among advocates for the justice of restorative justice are spiritual (e.g., Van Ness 1986). Yet civic republicanism is one secular philosophical foundation that has a critique of the just deserts model and that enjoys some support among restorative justice theorists. One of the virtues of republican theory is that its justification of restorative justice does not depend on all those involved in restorative justice processes subscribing to a republican conception of justice, in the way that just deserts does depend on a consistent commitment of judges and juries to the conception of justice in its justice model.

The next chapter will assess a number of concerns about the injustice of restorative justice, both procedurally and in terms of outcomes. I conclude that a considerable number of concerns about the injustices of restorative justice are true insofar as we can judge from the current state of the evidence. The truth of that critique, I want to contend, is consistent with the conclusion in this section that restorative justice is more just than just deserts.

Following Campbell (1988, pp. 3–4), Parker (1999b, pp. 45–47) makes a Rawlsian distinction between the concept and the conception of justice in her republic of justice. Parker's concept of justice is "those arrangements by which people can (successfully) make claims against individuals and institutions in order to advance shared ideals of social and political life" (Parker 1999b, p. 46). A *concept* of justice thus conceived as means, formal and informal, by which people seek to secure social and individual relations they think are right will yield different views (*conceptions*) of rightness. Parker's (1999b) republican conception of substantive justice is of freedom as nondomination (following Skinner 1984; Pettit 1993, 1997). The just society then institutionalizes processes of disputing that will maximize freedom as nondomination. So Parker (1999b, p. 49) integrates concept and conception in a definition of justice that I will adapt only slightly here: justice is "that set of arrangements that allow people to make claims against other individuals and institutions in order to secure freedom against the possibility of domination."

Freedom as nondomination is the same republican conception of freedom as a citizenship status that Braithwaite and Pettit (1990) called dominion. Freedom as nondomination is contrasted with freedom as noninterference, which is at the core of the liberal tradition. Republicans from Rome to Montesquieu, Madison, and Jefferson wanted more than liberty in the impoverished individualistic sense favored by the liberals who came to dominate Western political discourse through the nineteenth century. Resilient liberty required community assurance against domination through the guarantees of a rule of law, a separation of powers, uncoerced deliberation in governance, welfare policies that guarantee protection from the dominations of poverty and norms of civic virtue. It required liberty, equality, and fraternity/sorority.

Braithwaite and Pettit (1990) have sought to rework what they consider all the key normative questions in the criminal justice system in accordance with the maximization of freedom as nondomination. They also compare a full retributivist position with a full republican position and conclude that a full just deserts policy would increase injustice while a republican policy would reduce it. This results from certain facts about complex modern societies. These are mostly facts about the distribution of power, which prevent punishment from being imposed on those most deserving of it. A policy of attempting punishment of all those who deserve it (and who can be caught) has the effect of increasing injustice, worsening tendencies to punish most where desert is least. This is because of a tendency for the law to be "the most powerful where the least needed, a sprinkler system that turns off when the fire gets too hot" (Geertz 1983, p. 217).

Braithwaite and Pettit (1990, chap. 9) argue that there are a number of bureaucratic realities about criminal justice systems that conduce to the theorem that where desert is greatest, punishment will be least. One is the problem of system capacity (Pontell 1978; Nagin 1978). Braithwaite and Pettit rely on this literature to show that those locations in time and space where crime is greatest, and those types of crime where offending is most widespread and serious, are precisely where the criminal justice system resorts to leniency in order to keep cases flowing and avert system overload.[15] But bureaucratic pressures are not the main reason for the truth of the theorem. Structural realities of power are more important. Braithwaite and Pettit (1990) claim to show that in the terms of just deserts theory, there are more white-collar criminals deserving severe punishment in any society than blue-collar criminals deserving severe punishment. Attempts to give deserved punishment to all who are guilty, however, successfully impose desert on blue-collar offenders while being systematically unsuccessful with white-collar offenders.

The white-collar crime enforcement system in every country operates on comparatively restorative principles. Braithwaite and Pettit (1990) argue that this is sociologically inevitable as well as desirable. Retributive corporate crime prevention would fail because of deterrence traps, formidable defiance, and the superior capacity of the powerful to deploy rational countermeasures against deterrence—like the appointment of "vice presidents responsible for going to jail" (Braithwaite 1984). The best path to equal justice for equal wrongs is therefore to move blue-collar criminal enforcement down the same restorative path that white-collar enforcement has long followed.[16]

The injustice of the justice model arises from its reactive quality in a world where equal reactions produce unequal results. Parker (1999b) works through the proactive reforms required for republican access to justice. She suggests, for example, that all organizations above a certain size have access to justice plans that, through consultation with stakeholders, (1) identify the various types of injustices (to consumers, workers, minorities, creditors, etc.) that are common consequences of its activities; (2) set up restorative justice forums to correct these injustices when they arise; and (3) deploy preventive law measures to ensure compliance with the law and remove blockages to access to justice. Performance indicators would be required under these plans to demonstrate improved access to justice this year compared with last year (continuous improvement). The results of independent audits against these performance indicators would be made public. Responsively regulated access to restorative justice plans in the large organization sector then frees up more finite legal aid resources for injustices inflicted in small organizations like families and by individuals.

Parker's imagined world of access to restorative justice is one where most victims of the most serious crimes (organizational crimes) that currently get no justice are given access to corporate restorative justice. It is a world of profoundly greater justice than the "justice" model imagines. Of course, justice imagined is not justice accomplished. We can say, however, that the justice model skew of our present system, a skew toward just deserts for the poor and impunity for the powerful, accomplishes profound injustice. Moves in the direction of restorative justice for poor offenders and restorative justice for more victims of corporate offenders are the practical moves toward an amelioration of that injustice. This theme is further developed in chapter 8, where on a wider front we seek to develop the ideal beautifully articulated in Psalm 85: 10: "Mercy and truth are met together; righteousness and peace have kissed each other." Securing peace and doing right requires wrongdoers to accept responsibility. The notion of criminal responsibility is also central to the philosophy of conventional criminal law. Restorative justice not only rejects "What is the right punishment?" as the central question because the right punishment will almost always be the wrong solution to the problem; it also rejects holding criminals responsible as central. The passive responsibility of holding people responsible certainly has a place in restorative thinking, but not a central place because there is a risk that pointing the finger of responsibility will discourage the active responsibility that is more important to restorative justice (Bovens 1998; Braithwaite and Roche 2000). Active responsibility is the virtue of taking responsibility for putting things right. The democratic ideal of the restorative justice conference is that a space is created in which all participants might exhibit the virtue of taking active responsibility for putting things right, for preventing recurrence. Holding another responsible (passive responsibility) not only involves the danger of reactance against the attribution of responsibility (as a perceived act of domination), but also runs the risk that by holding the other responsible we tacitly declare our innocence (Harmon 1995, p. 9). Through blaming the other, we declare ourselves blameless as we abrogate the possibility of us taking active responsibility for righting the wrong. So restorative justice is about nurturing the taking of active responsibility, especially by offenders who are given the most compelling reasons to do so by the discussion of the consequences of a crime. A wrongdoer taking responsibility is a morally superior outcome than being made to be responsible by an imposed sanction. This is so because a wrongdoer wanting to take responsibility for a wrong more potently communicates that an injustice has occurred, that the victim's rights are respected. Imposed condemnation is less effective at this because it so often leads to condemning of the condemners, with resultant disvaluing of the acknowledgment of injustice.

As Heimer (1998, p. 369) puts it: "It is the humanity of other people that inspires responsibility." Retributivists are obsessed with passive responsibility because their priority is to be just in the way they hurt wrongdoers. The shift in the balance toward active responsibility occurs because the priority of the restorativist is to be just in the way they heal.

While active responsibility is the most virtuous kind, we often need resources to be responsible with effectiveness to right and prevent wrongs. Yet "responsibilization without resources" is often the sad reality of restorative justice (LaPrairie 1999).

DEMOCRATIC THEORY AND RESTORATIVE JUSTICE

Christie's (1977) claim is that the king's justice stole conflicts from citizens; it was in fact a significant accomplishment in the progressive consolidation of the domination of monarchs over their people in Europe from the eleventh to the nineteenth century. For much of Europe, justice was centralized under state control, and local restorative justice was substantially extinguished by 1200 (Weitekamp 1998). Yet restorative justice as mainstream disputing between and within clans was not extinguished by the English in Scotland until well into the nineteenth century; it was never extinguished by the Dutch in Indonesia, where *adat* (local) criminal laws work in parallel with a dominant Dutch criminal law of the Indonesian state. As we have seen, Cree, Navajo, and Maori restorative justice survived, though barely. Even in England and France, the greatest imperial extinguishers of restorative justice, restorative justice practices remain profoundly influential in civil society, in schools for example. The globalized centrality of the prison and professional police forces in the statist revolution's new justice model actually came quite late.

While the story of our criminal law is a story of imperial oppression to extinguish restorative justice, its major victories are historically recent enough across most of the globe for there to be substantial residues of more democratic modes of doing justice available to be revitalized. Recent empirical experience in places like New Zealand indicates that the flames of restorative justice can be rekindled surprisingly quickly because citizens find that they like restorative justice, and popular demand for it spreads.

Control over punishment systems (combined with discretion to issue royal or presidential pardons) strengthened the power and legitimacy of rulers (see, e.g., Foucault 1977; Garland 1985, 1990). The new democratic rulers of the past two centuries continued to see their control of the secret police as vital to combating organized threats to their monopoly on the legal use of violence and the control of the regular police as vital to their control of disorganized threats. Yet abuse of that power (executing someone popular and innocent; the Guilford four falsely imprisoned as IRA bombers) proved at times such a threat to their legitimacy that rulers were forced by political opponents to institutionalize certain principles of fairness into the state system. That process started with Magna Carta. These are accomplishments of liberalism that are worth preserving in a civic republican justice system.

At the same time the impression that the state punishes crime in a consistent, politically evenhanded way, so vital to the legitimation of statist criminal justice, is seen by citizens as a pretense. One law for the rich, another for the poor—that is the reality that seems transparent to citizens in totalitarian and democratic states alike. This is another dimension of the democratic appeal of shifting the control over mercy from the monarch back to the people affected, while using state law to constrain excesses of community through defining maximum punishments, rights, and procedural requirements. The theme of how to set up a just interaction between the peoples' justice and the law's justice is one returned to many times in the pages that follow.

There is more to the democratic virtue of restorative justice than returning conflicts to the citizens from whom they have been stolen. Western democratic institutions were planted in the shallow soil of societies where disputing had been taken over by the king. Disputing over daily injustices is where we learn to become democratic citizens. And the learning is more profound when those daily injustices reveal deeply structured patterns of injustice. Engagement with them is de Tocqueville's apprenticeship of liberty. In Benjamin Barber's terms, democratic disputing is educative, central to learning to be free:

> While we root our fragile freedom in the myth that we are born free, we are in truth born dependent. For we are born fragile, born needy, born ignorant, born unformed, born weak, born foolish, born unimaginative—born in chains. . . . Our dependency is both physical—we need each other and cannot survive alone—and psychological; our identity is forged through a dialectical relationship with others. We are inescapably embedded in families, tribes, and communities. As a consequence, we must *learn* to be free. That is to say, we must be taught liberty. We are born small, defenceless, unthinking children. We must be taught to be thinking, competent, legal persons and citizens. We are born belonging to others; we have to learn how to sculpt our individuality from common clay.
>
> The literacy to live in civil society, the competence to participate in democratic communities, the ability to think critically and act deliberately in a pluralistic world, the empathy that permits us to hear and thus accommodate others, all involve skills that must be acquired. Excellence is the product of teaching and is liberty's measure. There is no excellence without freedom . . .
>
> Human association depends on imagination: the capacity to see in others beings like ourselves. It is thus through imagination that we render others sufficiently like ourselves for them to become subjects of tolerance and respect, sometimes even affection. Democracy is not a natural form of association; it is an extraordinary and rare contrivance of cultivated imagination. Empower the merely ignorant and endow the uneducated with a right to make collective decisions and what results is not democracy but, at best, mob rule: the government of private prejudice and the tyranny of opinion—all those perversions that liberty's enemies like to pretend (and its friends fear) constitute democracy. For true democracy to flourish, however, there must be citizens. Citizens are women and men educated for excellence—by which term I mean the knowledge and competence to govern in common their own lives. The democratic faith is rooted in the belief that all humans are capable of such excellence and have not just the right but the capacity to become citizens. Democratic education mediates the ancient quarrel between the rule of opinion and the rule of excellence by informing opinion. (Barber 1992, pp. 4–5)

I remember in 1991, in the early days of restorative justice conferencing in Australia, suggesting to Terry O'Connell that it was a mistake to allow young children to attend and participate in conferences. Sometimes it is, but basically empirical experience has proved me wrong. In conferences, children are learning to be democratic citizens. The adults are mostly wise enough to make allowances for the unsophistication of much of what children say and to support them, help them establish the relevance of their point of view. Often it is the very unsophistication of the child's legitimate perspective that is so moving: "I've listened to what you've said about [my big brother]. It's not true. He is always kind to me; he helps me when I don't know what to do. I don't know any boy who is kinder than my brother."

We might hope for the town we love (I do) that the thousands of children who have now experienced participatory antibullying programs in our schools, the thousands of adults who have experienced restorative justice conferences in our police stations or community halls, will learn how to do justice restoratively and apply those lessons in the families, clubs, and workplaces where they face their sharpest conflicts. Most especially we might hope conferences are educating the police for democracy. Experience is the best educator, more so the more nuanced the skills required. We hope that citizens are learning in conferences and circles how to deliberate respectfully in the face of the greatest provocations of daily life. If they can learn to deliberate wisely and respectfully in the most provocative contexts, then they are citizens well educated for democracy. My observation is that the citizens of my town are learning, however disappointed I become at the slowness of the learning and at the many setbacks restorative justice has suffered in Canberra. The hope is that the seeds of our democratic institutions will be planted in slightly deeper soil in the new century as a result. People in ordinary families and communities can have more of a say in a world dominated by big business, professional politicians, and technocrats, a theme taken further in chapters 6 to 8. Democratic participation requires democratic competence, which must be learned through the exercise of active responsibility. Restorative justice processes can be one crucial vehicle of empowerment where spaces are created for active responsibility in civil society to displace predominantly passive statist responsibility.

Representative democracy with a separation of powers is more sustainable than direct democracy. There are too many of us, and the world is too complex for us to find time to participate in a direct democracy, even in endless citizen-initiated referenda. However, the conference-circle technology of democracy can give us an opportunity to directly participate in certain major decisions that impact our lives and those of our loved ones. Through this engagement with democratic participation in complex problem solving, citizens learn to be actively responsible. This is deliberative theory's response to a representative democracy that, by failing to cultivate relationships in a community, produces a people characterized by selfishness, apathy, and prejudice. Fishkin and Luskin (1999, p. 8) claim to observe among participants in their deliberative polling "a gain in empathy and mutual understanding." Restorative justice processes have produced more systematic evidence of such gains (Strang 2000; Ahmed et al. 2001). The deliberative democracy of restorative justice is a corrective to majority rule democracy, where power can become a numbers game that is insensitive to multiple perspectives and empathy with multiple needs:

If your position has the larger numbers, there is little incentive to seek common ground or ways that the interests of all might be served. In fact, if you can outvote the other position you don't even need to understand that position. Majority rule decision making often leaves a significant number of people feeling left out, alienated, and resentful because no attempt was made to understand their needs . . . Majority rule decision making also encourages parties to exaggerate their differences and to belittle or denigrate the other position in order to recruit more supporters. That process increases the barriers between different perspectives. (Pranis 2000)

Once citizens learn to be actively responsible as opposed to learning to rely totally on protection by a state that enforces passive responsibility, they will become active in social movement politics. NGOs offer the second great avenue for revitalizing meaningful forms of citizen participation in a democracy. They can be as relevant to democratizing global institutions such as the IMF, the World Bank, and the WTO as they can be to redemocratizing the state (Braithwaite and Drahos 2000).

NGO influence can feed back into restorative justice conferences as advocacy of making the personal political, by invoking the possibility of agitating for structural change. The most important way this happens is when the justice of the people puts pressure on the justice of the law to change. This, indeed, is a shared project of the partnerships restorative justice advocates seek to forge with other social movements against domination.

Robert Baruch Bush and Joseph Folger's (1994) transformative mediation provides a microtheory of how to realize these democratic aspirations. Restorative justice is a problem-oriented approach and Bush and Folger contrast this with their approach to transforming relationships. In this book it has been argued that values about solving problems and relational values can and do co-exist in well run restorative justice programs. Bush and Folger urge us to focus on two specific values that I want to construe here as the micro-foundation for building democracy. These are empowerment and recognition. Empowerment gives voice to citizens in a democracy; it transforms them from being weak and alienated to being strong and constructive. Recognition means acknowledgment and empathy for the position of others. Recognition helps us move from being self-absorbed to being responsive. Being responsive at this micro level means being attentive to and open with others, prepared to see their point of view and respond to their good faith with trust. The responsiveness born of recognition and the strength born of empowerment are mutually reinforcing, enabling "compassionate strength." Relationships are shifted from being destructive, alientating, and demonizing to constructive, connecting, and humanizing. Connecting with one another's humanity is the micro-foundation of democracy, just as alienation and demonization are the psychological foundations of totalitarianism. The evidence traversed in this chapter and the last is so far consistent with the conclusion that at least compared to courtroom processes, restorative justice does better in terms of recognition and empowerment, as captured for example in Strang's (2001) data. But much empirical work remains to be done to test the rich theoretical dynamic proposed by Bush and Folger for explaining the exit from alienation to compassionately strong citizenship via recognition and empowerment.

CONCLUSION

In the previous chapter we saw that there are good preliminary theoretical and empirical grounds for anticipating that well-designed restorative justice processes will restore victims, offenders, and communities better than existing criminal justice practices. More counterintuitively, this chapter concludes that a restorative justice system may deter, incapacitate, and rehabilitate more effectively than a punitive system. This will be especially so if restorative justice is embedded in a responsive regulatory framework that opts for deterrence when restoration repeatedly fails and incapacitation when escalated deterrence fails. We find active deterrence under a dynamic regulatory pyramid to be more powerful than passive deterrence in a sentencing grid; community incapacitation is more variegated and contextually attuned than clumsy carceral incapacitation.

In the face of all the discretion that community responsiveness implies, most surprising and confronting of all is the conclusion that restorative justice is more just than the justice of the justice model. Empirical evidence of community perceptions of justice under the two models strongly supports this. Normative theory of a republican cast explains why we should get this result. Restorative justice can deliver freedom as nondomination in a way just deserts cannot, and citizens in democracies have profoundly deep aspirations to freedom and deep distrust of domination. Restorative justice confronts the dilemma that equal justice for offenders is utterly incompatible with equal justice for victims. I have argued that a greater degree of equality for both is delivered by rejecting equality as a goal, guaranteeing victims a minimum level of care and guaranteeing offenders against punishment beyond a maximum. Abandoning equal punishment as a goal better enables us to secure the more fundamental goal in the writing of most great jurisprudential scholars of equal respect and concern for all affected persons (Braithwaite forthcoming). For Declan Roche (2001), if equal respect for the dignity of persons means empowerment, "then it follows that offenders should be allowed to do more than they are required, and victims to demand less than they are entitled. That is, informal justice should allow offenders to show generosity and victims to grant mercy."

Just disputing processes have an important role to play in connecting private troubles to public issues. When communities start taking responsibility for the vulnerabilities of their young offenders and start talking about these vulnerabilities at and after conferences, of course they become more engaged with the deeper institutional sources of the problems.[17] When communities begin taking responsibility for family violence, as at Hollow Water, a profoundly institutional debate is triggered (Ross 1996; Lajeunesse 1993; Aboriginal Corrections Policy Unit 1997a, 1997b; Green 1998). When communities engage with their victimization by powerful corporations, as with the Aboriginal insurance cases (CML), the imagination of prime ministers can be caught up in the aspirations for restructuring the regulation of finance capital.

Finally, we have seen in this chapter that theoretical interconnections are beginning to be understood among a number of at first seemingly unconnected theories of why restorative justice might prevent crime and restore victims, offenders, and communities. These are theories of defiance/reactance, reintegrative shaming, shame acknowledgment, social identity and procedural justice. It is very early days, however, with the development and refinement of these theories, and even earlier days with empirically testing them. And before we wax too optimistic about the promise of restorative justice to deliver more effective and decent criminal justice, we must consider a number of lines of critique of the capacity of restorative justice to deliver these results in the next chapter. Just as the conclusions of the present chapter and the previous one have been that the promise of restorative justice is real, the conclusion of the next chapter will be that the dangers of restorative justice are also real.

NOTES

1. Preventing repeat victimization has at least the following virtues:

    > It fuses the roles of victim support and crime prevention which have been historically separated. Insofar as repeated offences against the same target are the work of the same perpetrator(s), clearance of a series of crimes and linked property recovery is made more likely than was the case when events were seen as independent. It thus explicitly links the police tasks of prevention and detection.
    >
    > Insofar as the provisional evidence is confirmed that repeated crimes are disproportionately the work of *prolific* offenders, the prevention/detection of attempts at repetition provides an uncontentious way of targeting prolific offenders. (Pease 1998b, pp. v–vi)

2. There is another reason. Mothers do not complain in court against the police for the same reason their sons do not—because legal aid lawyers in Australia are fairly systematic in warning clients that complaining about the police is likely to backfire in a way that leads to a longer sentence (see further Roche, 2001).
3. For an account of this phenomenon that is readily digestible, if neurophysiologically dubious in parts, see Goleman 1995.
4. For a review of the research effort by its most central participant, see Sherman 1992.
5. The theory posits the same form of relationship as in Figure 4.3 for reactance to rewards as to punishments. However, the data suggest that reactance to punishment is stronger than to rewards. See Brehm and Brehm 1981, p. 229.
6. These were executives I discovered and interviewed in my research on corporate crime in the pharmaceutical industry; see Braithwaite 1984.
7. Often, they get to know as a result of explicit auditing practices that put them in a better position to regulate malpractice than any government regulator. For example, in analyzing the implications of the chemical industry's Responsible Care program, Neil Gunningham (1996) explains that "Dow insists on conducting an audit before it agrees to supply a new customer with hazardous material, and routinely audits its distributors. The audit involves a team visiting the distributor's operations to examine handling, transportation, storage and terminating techniques and prescribing improvements aimed at achieving environmental standards far in advance of current regulatory requirements. Many large chemical manufacturers go further."
8. It is common for other children to be involved in "holding" the victim for the bully or preventing him from getting away (Rigby 1996, p. 151). Victims themselves have preventive capacities, which research evidence shows can be developed to protect them from bullying (Rigby 1996, p. 226).

9. Cases like the billion-dollar frauds of the Bank of Credit and Commerce International, which Fisse and I have used to argue the comparative advantage of the accountability model (Fisse and Braithwaite 1993).

10. I rely here on personal communications with Gunningham at Australian National University seminars.

11. The leading example here is the "Corporate Campaign" against the J. P. Stevens company over its abusive labor practices. Members of the top management team were very hard nuts here. But the campaign was able to so embarrass outside directors that they resigned from the board, a consequence that really did concern top management. See Fisse and Braithwaite 1983.

12. Here an alternative target is an extended family with capacities to monitor, restrain, and disapprove the conduct of the violent boy. See Braithwaite and Daly 1994. Also see Lajeunesse 1993; Burford and Pennell 1998.

13. Functionally, New Zealand law already accomplishes this result by putting cases into family group conferences not on the basis of an admission of criminal guilt but on the basis of formally "declining to deny" criminal allegations.

14. Fisse is open to the more radical view that if criminal liability is about punishing conduct known to be harmful and if failure to respond responsibly is harmful, then such reactive fault can be sufficient to establish criminal liability.

15. See also the discussion earlier in chapter 2 on enforcement tipping.

16. A related argument is that by maximizing our resort to restorative justice and minimizing the resort to punishment, we minimize the moral error of punishing the innocent:

> No practicable system of punishment can hope to punish only the guilty; in ensuring that we punish a reasonable proportion of the guilty, we will inevitably punish some who are in fact innocent. We could avoid punishing the innocent, by refusing to punish anyone: in maintaining a system which we know will sometimes punish the innocent we therefore cannot claim that we punish the innocent unintentionally; we must admit that we too are abusing it as a system of punishment (Schedler 1980, p. 185).

17. For the profoundly institutional way the citizens of Wagga did this, see City of Wagga Wagga, "Wagga Wagga's Communitarian Response to the Juvenile Justice Advisory Council's Green Paper 'Future Directions for Juvenile Justice in New South Wales.' " Wagga Wagga, 1993.

5

Worries about Restorative Justice

My disposition is transparently optimistic about restorative justice. Partly this manifests a bias, a personality that suffers pathological optimism. But it also represents a considered belief that the criminal justice system needs a new and positive vision, that criminologists became depressingly nihilistic in the 1970s and 1980s. The optimistic bias that gives pessimists something better to shoot at can yet be the kind of optimism that we see among the best natural scientists—the medical researcher whose very optimism about a new theory of disease motivates extraordinary rigor in putting in place randomized controlled trials to refute it. But that is not enough. The scientific optimist is also required to develop and test ideas about the side effects and the contraindications of her new drug. The adverse side effects and contraindications of restorative justice are numerous. Many have already been introduced in the course of qualifying the hopes and claims of the previous chapters. Here I begin with some of the structural impediments to the effectiveness of restorative justice.

RESTORATIVE JUSTICE MIGHT PROVIDE NO BENEFITS WHATSOEVER TO MOST VICTIMS

Most victims of crime are victims of white-collar crimes without ever coming to realize this. They pay higher prices every day for products whose prices have been fixed by criminal price-fixing conspiracies. Even for offenses like burglary, where the victim is acutely aware of victimization, in every country in the world only a small minority of cases are cleared by arrest. Even for offenses like domestic violence, where the victim knows she has been victimized and by whom, reports to the police followed by admissions of guilt are extremely rare. Of course, if restorative justice does reduce the crime rate, many people who would otherwise have been victimized get a benefit. But restorative justice may have nothing to offer the overwhelming majority of citizens who are actually victimized by crime. The documented volume of unapprehended white-collar crime and domestic violence alone (Braithwaite and Pettit 1990, chap. 9) makes it easy to demonstrate that it would be foolishly optimistic to believe that the criminal justice system could do something for the known victims of known criminals for even 10 percent of our crime.

While there are limits on what the state can do to heal when there is no known criminal, these limits are less for organizations in civil society. The battered women's movement can help to heal survivors who will not file a complaint; circles can and do heal victims in the absence of offenders. There can and should be a level of state funding for victim support groups that allows them to provide professional, material, and emotional support at least to all victims of violence who request it. Hence, it is not really correct to suggest that restorative justice has nothing to offer the 90 percent plus of victims for whom there is no apprehended offender. Restorative justice requires the provision of help to such victims at least in cases where they have suffered serious physical or emotional harm. Restorative justice advocates, myself included, can be criticized for neglecting the implications of our theoretical position for aid to victims without offenders. There is also the problem of offenders without victims who are willing to meet with them. In a community consultation on restorative justice in Darwin, Australia, in 2000, one suggestion was that healing circles could be held in prisons for offenders without willing victims and in the community for victims without known offenders, and that every now and then a visitor could move from one circle to the other.

Even If Restorative Justice Works, Will It Really Have a Major Effect on the Crime Rate?

Because more than 90 percent of victimizations will be untouched by meetings between victims and offenders, preventive effects of such restorative justice interventions would have to be massive to register any measurable impact on the overall crime rate. It would take a much bigger conferencing program than exists anywhere in the world to conference 1 percent of all (detected and undetected) criminal offenders. In the unlikely circumstance that conferences halved their reoffending, that would reduce the crime rate by half a percent.

Yet no one thinks that the effects of an eighty-minute conference on days, months, and years of competing influences will be massive. Many of the pessimists reasonably say that even if restorative justice theory is right (which they doubt), the impact of transitory restorative justice interventions are sure to be so small as to be detectable only on a massive (unaffordable) sample. The theory is therefore useless because its benefits (if true) could never be demonstrated by economically feasible scientific research.

Consider the Canberra drunk driving restorative justice experiment being conducted by Lawrence Sherman and Heather Strang. For every officially recorded drunk driving offense that comes into the experiment, the offenders are reporting eighteen other undetected drunk drives during that year. Add to that all the undetected drunk drives of those who are never caught, and it is clear that the 450 RISE drunk driving conferences touch only a tip of the iceberg. On the other hand, it is the really serious repeat offenders who are most likely eventually to be caught. So at least the restorative justice process might eventually get a shot at a good proportion of the worst offenders (one would hope so in Canberra, with as many as 1,500 drunk driving convictions every year in a city of just 310,000!). Here we must remember the argument in chapter 2 that most serious crime is committed by a relatively small number of repeat offenders, and these offenders eventually do get caught. In short, although most crime does not get detected, most serious criminals do. Furthermore, if the analysis in chapter 4 of the *general* deterrent and crime prevention (e.g., culture-changing) superiority of restorative justice over punitive justice is right, there might be a notable impact on the overall crime rate.

RESTORATIVE JUSTICE PRACTICES CAN INCREASE VICTIM FEARS OF REVICTIMIZATION

There is no need to canvass again the studies reported in chapter 3 that clearly establish that restorative justice practices can increase victim fears of revictimization. However, they also establish that reduction of victim fears of revictimization appears to be about twice as common. While victims are mostly surprised to learn how shy, ashamed, and inadequate offenders are, some offenders are formidable and scary. Such cases can destabilize restorative justice programs in the media. Our worst case in Canberra involved an offender who threatened a woman with a syringe filled with blood. The conference was not well run, and feelings between offender and victim deteriorated. Subsequently, the victim found a syringe left on the dashboard of her car, which she took to be a threat from the offender (though this allegation was never proved). The case was covered by a local television station. Out of two thousand Canberra conferences (some with no victims, some with twenty), this is the only case of escalated victim fear that hit the media. But one can be enough! Restorative justice programs need to offer much more comprehensive support to the victims who face such traumas.

A related worry is that restorative justice programs can treat victims as no more than props for efforts to rehabilitate offenders. This concern became acute with a number of British mediation programs during the 1980s where it was common for the offender and victim not to meet face-to-face, but rather for the mediator to be a go-between. Where no meeting occurs, Retzinger and Scheff's (1996) symbolic reparation, which we have seen is more important to most victims than material reparation, is more difficult. In these circumstances we can expect the dissatisfaction of victims to focus on the limits of the material reparation they get: "Projects which claim to provide reparation for victims actually operating to maximise the potential for diversion of children from prosecution" (Haines 1998, p. 6). The British concern about victims being no more than props has not been a major issue in the debate in Australia and New Zealand about the pluses and minuses of restorative justice conferences. This is not to deny that victims used as props by a youth lobby that is concerned only to get a kinder deal for young offenders does not emerge as a deficiency in particular cases.

Jennifer Brown (1994, p. 1274) is concerned that victim anger may be redirected in ways that may be destructive for victims by mediation ground rules that "forbid blaming and extended discussion of past events" in favor of "a more forward-looking, problem-solving outlook." A connected concern is that approaches by state officials, perhaps particularly if they are police, may create pressure on victims to take part in a restorative justice process when they would rather cut their emotional and material losses. Brown (1994, p. 1266) is probably right that at least for a subset of victims, "The very rhetorical appeal of the program may induce a sense of guilt in a reluctant victim." Indeed, the same point might be made of the moral obligation imposed on victim and offender supporters by restorative justice processes. That is the inevitable fallout of a program that seeks to get things done by nurturing citizenship obligations; it comes with a cost.

Victims are often enticed into restorative justice before they are ready. Pressure to achieve "speedy trial" objectives for offenders can be quite contrary to the interests of victims. Indeed, even in terms of the interests of offenders, rushing into a restorative justice meeting can be counterproductive with a victim who with a bit more time would be ready to forgive rather than to hate. Best practice is probably to offer victims of serious crime a healing circle with victims only before proceeding to a victim-offender circle (see Box 1.8: Hollow Water; Box 4.6: The North Minneapolis African American Circles). The key judgment for the victim support circle is whether the victim is ready (if ever) to meet the offender.

RESTORATIVE JUSTICE CAN BE A "SHAMING MACHINE" THAT WORSENS THE STIGMATIZATION OF OFFENDERS

The "shaming machine" concern has been well articulated in Retzinger and Scheff's (1996) essay, "Strategy for Community Conferences: Emotions and Social Bonds," written after their observation of a number of Australian conferences, from which they came away concerned about the damaging effects of sarcasm, moral superiority, and moral lecturing in particular:

> The point about moral indignation that is crucial for conferences is that when it is repetitive and out of control, it is a defensive movement in two steps: denial of one's own shame, followed by projection of blame onto the offender . . . For the participants to identify with the offender, they must see themselves as like her rather than unlike her (There but for the grace of God go I). Moral indignation interferes with the identification between participants that is necessary if the conference is to generate symbolic reparation. In our judgement, uncontrolled repetitive moral indignation is the most important impediment to symbolic reparation and reintegration. But on the other hand, to the extent that it is rechannelled, it can be instrumental in triggering the core sequence of reparation . . . Intentional shaming in the form of sustained moral indignation or in any other guise brings a gratuitous element into the conference, the piling of shame on top of the automatic shaming that is built into the format. This format is an automatic shaming machine . . . in a format that is already heavy with shame, even small amounts of overt shaming are very likely to push the offender into a defensive stance, to the point that she will be unable to even feel, much less express, genuine shame and remorse.

Restorative justice processes are "already heavy with shame" as a result of the simple process of victims and their supporters talking about the consequences of the crime. In effect, that is all one needs. Umbreit (1994, p. 4) makes a similar point on victim defensiveness: "For individual victims, use of such terms as 'forgiveness' and 'reconciliation' are highly judgmental and preachy, suggesting a devaluing of the legitimate anger and rage the victims may be feeling at that point." The ideal in terms of avoiding labels is beautifully articulated from the Canadian First Nations experience by Ross (1996, p. 170):

> How would you react if a victim kept piling judgmental labels on you, one after the other, calling you "vicious, perverted, deranged, vile, sickening" and so forth? Are they the kinds of conclusions you'd want to accept about your "whole" self? Or are they conclusions you'd want to fight about? Or if you didn't feel like fighting, would you simply stop listening to them, let them wash over you, never really let them penetrate? . . . On the other hand, what if you were an offender who sat in a circle with others and listened to someone simply relive their own reactions: their sense of violation and vulnerability, their fear of strangers, their inability to sleep, their sudden eruptions into tears and shaking at work, their sense of isolation from family and friends, their feelings of dirtiness, their gnawing suspicion that there was something so wrong with them that they deserved to be hurt and hated. What if you then heard all the relatives and friends of your victim speak in the same way, from their hearts, painting pictures of their own confusions, their powerlessness to help, their fear for the future of their daughter, sister, aunt or mother? Would you be able to shut that out as easily, to just stop listening? It is the experience of Hollow Water that careful heart speaking, with its nonjudgmental disclosure of feelings, no matter how intense, is ultimately irresistible to the vast majority of offenders.

Braithwaite and Mugford (1994) think that the best protection against the vices of moral lecturing and sarcasm is to do a good job of inviting a large number of caring supporters for both the victim and the offender, a point also discussed by Retzinger and Scheff (1996). If these invitees really do care about the offender, they will counter moral lecturing with tributes to the sense of responsibility and other virtues of the offender. Then, even if the sort of connection with the moral lecturer that would allow productively reparative communication is severed, the bond with the other participant who comes to her defense is strengthened in the same sequence. For Braithwaite and Mugford (1994) this is the genius in the design of a Maori *whanau* conference, a Cree healing circle, or Japanese school discipline that is absent in the design of dyadic Western victim-offender mediation.[1] Of course, training of facilitators to intervene against moral lecturing and ask for respectful discussion of consequences and solutions is also a remedy. Training of citizens through learning how to do restorative justice in school disputes is even more important: reason is more likely to prevail in democratic deliberation when citizens are educated to reasonableness (Barber 1992). Over the next few years there will be a flood of research coming out of the RISE experiment on what predicts the degeneration of conferences into defensive self-righteousness and their elevation into the symbolic reparation Retzinger and Scheff want.

RESTORATIVE JUSTICE PRACTICES RELY ON A KIND OF COMMUNITY THAT IS CULTURALLY INAPPROPRIATE TO INDUSTRIALIZED SOCIETIES

The most common assertion of critics of restorative justice, even in the face of thriving programs in large multicultural cities like Auckland, Minneapolis, Toronto, Sydney, and Singapore, is that it might work well in rural contexts but not in the metropolises of industrialized societies. The theory outlined in chapter 4 really makes a different kind of prediction, however:

> In our cities, where neighbourhood social support is least, where the loss from the statist takeover of disputing is most damaging, the gains that can be secured from restorative justice reform are greatest. When a police officer with a restorative justice ethos arrests a youth in a tightly knit rural community who lives in a loving family, who enjoys social support from a caring school and church, that police officer is not likely to do much better or worse by the child than a police officer who does not have a restorative justice ethos. Whatever the police do, the child's support network will probably sort out the problem so that serious offending does not occur. But when a police officer with a restorative justice ethos arrests a homeless child in the metropolis like Sam, who hates parents who abused him, who has dropped out of school and is seemingly alone in the world, it is there that the restorative police officer can make a difference that will render him more effective in preventing crime than the retributive police officer. (Braithwaite 1996, pp. 18–19)[2]

Hagan and McCarthy's (1997, p. 163) research shows that homeless youth in Toronto and Vancouver were far from alone. A majority speak of their "street families" who look out for them: "You really learn what friendship is . . . If I need them, they're there for me." In other words, part of our stigmatization of the homeless is to view them as somehow asocial, noncommunal.

Certainly the restorative justice movement could be more conscious of helping other peoples to recover their own restorative traditions rather than showing them our own. I have suggested (Braithwaite 1996) the need for culturally specific investigation of how to save and revive the restorative justice practices that remain in all societies. Thence the following two elements for a research agenda:

1. Helping indigenous community justice to learn from the virtues of liberal statism—procedural fairness, rights, protecting the vulnerable from domination.
2. Helping liberal state justice to learn from indigenous community justice—learning the restorative community alternatives to individualism. (Braithwaite 1996)

Ultimately, these two challenges are rephrased as:

1. Helping indigenous community justice to learn from the virtues of liberal statism—procedural fairness, rights, protecting the vulnerable from domination.
2. Helping liberal state justice to learn from indigenous community justice—learning the restorative community alternatives to individualism. (Braithwaite 1996)

Clearly, there can be no return to an imagined authentic past of Indigenous justice. Equally, there can be Orientalism (Blagg 1997) in deciding which bits of Indigenous justice we will take to use ourselves and colonialism in mandating which bits of Western justice Indigenous people will be forced to take. If what we worry about with colonialism is subordination, it may be unexceptionable to use the antisubordination narratives that Coker (1999) finds replete in Navajo justice, just as we choose to use antisubordination resources in Western law to protect Indigenous women from domination by male elders in matters of family violence (See Box 5.1). And it may be equally unexceptionable for Western peoples to draw on the wisdom in both traditions for resisting domination (as required by a republican normative frame; Pettit 1997). In short, cultural borrowings that reduce domination can be valorized; those more common (western) borrowings that increase domination must be resisted.

The design of restorative justice institutions can be rather minimalist. A conference, for example, can be defined by a strategy for who is invited and a small number of procedural rules about advising the defendant of a right to leave and take his or her chances in court, speaking in turn, and so on. Even "speaking in turn" may be too Eurocentric to be a minimal requirement because in some cultures it shows polite engagement to finish another person's sentence or to speak at the same time. Perhaps the ideal is undominated speech. The ideal is certainly not to be culturally prescriptive: to allow participants to begin and end a conference with a prayer if that is their wish, to include noisy babies if they wish or exclude them if they wish, to allow Samoan offenders to kneel at the feet of victims and First Nations Canadians to wash the feet of victims (Griffiths and Hamilton 1996), to communicate by storytelling that may appeal to less formally educated members of a community (Young 1995) more than by a deductive reasoning that appeals to certain dominant men, or to lawyers. The sad fact is that this ideal is often not realized in restorative justice processes. Cunneen (1997), Findlay (1998), and Blagg (1998), for example, are right to point out that the interest of Australian Aboriginal people in participating in restorative justice alternatives was often assumed rather than discovered by reformers through an empowering dialogue with Aboriginal people (and other silenced minorities). Sometimes, we even inflict Maori process on young Maori who say they don't believe in "too much shit about the Maori way" (Maxwell and Morris 1993, p. 126).

Box 5.1: Dialogue Between Brother Pat Howley and John Braithwaite

The following exchange occurred in Vanuatu June 2000 at a conference on restorative justice in Melanesia.

Pat Howley: November 1999, I was in Bougainville conducting training on restorative justice for people in the field. The main process was through role play. At Arawa there was a group of about thirty-six men and women who had come in from the mountains and the coast for the course.

Bougainville is still without courts, and trainers have been using restorative justice for everything from stolen chickens to murder.

While we were discussing the matter of restoration to the offended party, one of our trainers (Sylvester) from Eivo pointed out that in "custom fashion" it was common for the family of a murderer to provide a young woman to the family of the dead man so that she could raise up children in his name. Prior to this, we had looked at the matter of rape, and I had stepped out of my role as a facilitator to make my position clear on this matter: "Mediators must not accept marriage to the rapist, as a solution. The girl is not to be placed under pressure by her (extended) family to marry the rapist, and if the group insists on this, then the mediation is to be broken off at this point and the matter sent to a chief or a court."

Sylvester thought that the Eivo custom was in fact quite different but wanted the matter discussed. He asked me for an answer.

As the facilitator in the training course, I automatically threw the matter back to the group, which carried on a lively discussion. Some felt that this was a really good solution because it avoided future payback and provided for the two clans to live in peace. Some were not so sure that this ancient custom was suitable for today. The position of the woman was not discussed. I wanted to know if the girl would be treated with respect and was told that as the mother of the dead man's children she would be as well respected as any woman in the village. The next question was to find out if she would be second wife (*numba 2 meri*) to one of the dead man's brothers. Again, I was assured that she would not.

At this stage Peter, the chief of Pokpok Island, came back to me and asked me for my opinion. Before the "crisis," Peter was a Christian, but he has now gone back to the traditional beliefs and has since reclaimed land, which the Catholic Church had bought freehold in 1906. I was not sure where Peter was coming from or if it was a hostile question to use against me.

I explained to him that I do not answer questions on "custom" and sent the matter back to the group for further discussion. The group had finished with the matter, and so there was no further discussion. Again, Peter asked

(continued)

me for an opinion. He was in no way antagonistic, but I really don't like answering questions on matters of custom except by asking questions which some may interpret as answers, so again I refused to answer his question. Our relations had been good throughout the training, so I laughingly told him that he was a rogue for trying to trick me. He told me that I was a rogue, too, and we had a good laugh about it.

John Braithwaite: In the context of the civil war in Bougainville, it seems to me, Pat, you were quite right not to tell the Bougainvillians what to do on a difficult question for them, and it was a hard thing for you, given how you feel about this morally, and given the history of expectations on Bougainville that the Catholic Church would offer moral instruction. I did wonder whether a better way of refusing would have been to say: "That is not a question for you to discuss with me but one you should with the women who would be affected." It also occurred to me that while your refusal to answer was right in the context of Bougainville in civil war, if this question had been given to you on the Papua New Guinea mainland a different answer could have been given. "It is not for me to say, but you must remember that your Parliament has written laws which guarantee the human rights of women."

Pat Howley: I would be rather slow to quote the laws of the land as an argument against discrimination. The law of the land is not a significant force in the social conditioning that people have grown up with. This is a male-dominated society, and only a paradigm shift in culture will change it—the law cannot. In our People Skills course we have a chapter on male-female relations in which we use the yin-yang diagram as a metaphor of balance in the individual, the relationship between men and women and the community. We finish up with a discussion on the topic "real men don't beat women." This has not changed the culture yet, but in some places and with some people it has softened it.

One of the trainers who is well educated pointed out to me that this custom exists also in the West, where daughters were married off to cement alliances among royalty and the rich and powerful.

As you see, John, I am a person trying to straddle two different cultures, and I am confused by both. There is much to be learned, and I tread softly where I can.

For all these failings, the design of restorative justice processes is for participant ownership and adaptation, whereas the design of the Western criminal trial is for consistency—to be determinedly unicultural—one people, one law. The complex challenge for restorative justice is to improve the match between plural aspirations of design and unicultural realities of accomplishment.

RESTORATIVE JUSTICE CAN OPPRESS OFFENDERS WITH A
TYRANNY OF THE MAJORITY, EVEN A TYRANNY OF THE
LYNCH MOB

Empowering Indigenous justice in many parts of the world can and does at times
empower communities to kill offenders and more commonly to punish them corpo-
rally. Police in outback Australia are not coy to confess to criminologists that they
allow the latter to happen; they would never let themselves be seen to allow the
former. Liberal justice regimes that turn a blind eye to violent Indigenous justice
succumb to a dangerous kind of cultural relativism. It is one thing to accept the legitimacy of traditional forms of social control in a unicultural traditional society. In a
multicultural society where all people learn to count on the state for protection of
their rights, without state oversight of respect for fundamental human rights there is
no way of being sure that those punished really are members of the traditional society
or, even if they are, that they are not cultural dissidents who wish to call on the protections afforded to all citizens by the state regardless of race. Without state oversight,
there is no way of assuring that the rights of a victim from a different cultural group
than the offender will be protected. Moreover, as Ross (1996, p. 234) points out: "In
many communities, the overnight withdrawal of the Western justice system would
not be followed by the immediate substitution of effective Aboriginal approaches,
but by significant violence."

Some Australian outback police, black and white, show considerable wisdom in
communicating the message that traditional justice processes are encouraged to run
their course so long as they do not cross certain lines. "If you do that, blackfella law
will be pushed aside by whitefella law." Put another way, what such police do is
encourage Aboriginal restorative traditions but, when they want to exercise their retributive traditions with extreme vigor, require them to put their case to a court of
law. No citizens can feel secure in their rights when in some contexts the state is
willing to sacrifice them to the tyrannies of any group.

This is not to say that courts have generally been less tyrannous than the mob. On
the contrary, public executions stopped because the mob booed and pelted execu-
tioners as they carried out the horrors ordered by the courts (Hay 1975, pp. 67–68;
Foucault 1977, pp. 61–67) and because juries refused to convict for minor offenses
that would lead to the gallows (Trevelyan 1973, p. 348). Courts around the world still
order executions (in private) in numbers that surely exceed those imposed by popular
justice tribunals. Today, no popular justice forums impose other sanctions as barbarous
as the imprisonment that Graeme Newman (1983) points out in practice tends to be
considerably more barbarous than corporal punishment. Certainly, contemporary liberal courts have some upper limits on the barbarism they can indulge. However, it
seems empirically wrong, as a matter of both attitude and practice, that courts are
less punitive than victims and restorative justice forums.

In practice, if courts in New Zealand were less punitive than family group conferences, they would be cutting conference agreements for community work and
other sanctions on a regular basis, but we have seen that increments are much more

common than cuts (Maxwell and Morris 1993). The *Clotworthy* case before the Court of Appeal of New Zealand has been more damaging than supportive to the principles of restorative justice (Box 5.2). With the John Howard Society Program in Winnipeg that has been found to be so successful in reducing reoffending, the Canadian courts have still been overturning 18 percent of the program's recommendations for diversion from prison (Bonta, Rooney, and Wallace-Capretta 1998). Declan Roche (2001) concluded from his review of accountability in twenty-five restorative justice programs in five countries:

> It appears based on the available evidence from the programs surveyed, that internal review mechanisms generally intervene to prevent outcomes that are too harsh, while external mechanisms generally intervene to prevent outcomes that are too lenient. In other words, internal review mechanisms tend to enforce upper limits, while external mechanisms enforce lower ones.

Box 5.2: Clotworthy

Mr. Clotworthy inflicted six stab wounds, which collapsed a lung and diaphragm, upon an attempted robbery victim.[3] Justice Thorburn of the Auckland District Court imposed a two-year prison sentence, which was suspended, a compensation order of $15,000 to fund cosmetic surgery for an "embarrassing scar," and 200 hours of community work. These had been agreed at a restorative conference organized by Justice Alternatives. The judge found a basis for restorative justice in New Zealand law and placed weight on the wish of the victim for financial support for the cosmetic surgery and emotional support to end through forgiveness "a festering agenda of vengeance or retribution in his heart against the prisoner." The Court of Appeal allowed the victim to address it, whereupon the victim "reiterated his previous stance, emphasising his wish to obtain funds for the necessary cosmetic surgery and his view that imprisonment would achieve nothing either for Mr. Clotworthy or for himself" (p. 12). The victory for restorative justice was that "substantial weight" was given by the court to the victim's belief that expiation had been agreed; their honors accepted that restorative justice had an important place in New Zealand sentencing law. The defeat was that greater weight was given to the empirical supposition that a custodial sentence would help "deter others from such serious offending" (p. 12). The suspending of the two-year custodial sentence was quashed in favor of a sentence of four years and a $5,000 compensation order (which had already been lodged with the court); the community service and payment of the remaining compensation were also quashed. The victim got neither his act of grace nor the money for the cosmetic surgery. He subsequently committed suicide for reasons unknown.

At the level of attitudes, Sessar (1998) has shown that judges and prosecutors in Germany have more punitive attitudes than the general public. In the United States, Gottfredson and Taylor (1987) found the general public to be no more retributive than correctional policy makers. Doob and Roberts's (1983, 1988) research shows that the more information the public has about particular cases, the less punitive it becomes. Hough and Roberts (1998) use data from the British Crime Survey to suggest that citizens derive their information about punishment primarily from the mass media, underestimate the severity of sentences actually imposed, and approve penalties lower than those actually imposed. Kerner, Marks, and Schreckling (1992) show that while a majority of Cologne victims who had been through victim-offender mediation felt the German justice system was too lenient, only 28 percent felt the treatment of "their" offender was too lenient. When citizens of most Western democracies answer opinion polls, they support capital punishment; when they sit on juries, they are much less supportive. Roberts and Stalans's (1997) literature review suggests that while in response to opinion polls citizens support tougher sentencing in the abstract, on more specific judgments about appropriate punishment they are not more punitive than the status quo and are very supportive of restitution as an alternative (when it is brought to their attention as an alternative). A number of studies find victims to be considerably less punitive than popular stereotypes would have it (Umbreit 1990a; 1994, pp. 9–13; Weitekamp 1989, pp. 83–84; Heinze and Kerstetter 1981; Shapland, Willmore, and Duff 1985; Kigin and Novack 1980; Novack, Galaway, and Hudson 1980; Youth Justice Coalition 1990, pp. 52–54; Sessar, Beurskens, and Boers 1986; Sessar 1990). McCold and Wachtel (1998, p. 35) found victims to be less punitive than victim supporters in Bethlehem conferences and much less punitive than offender supporters (though more punitive than the offenders themselves). This evidence is one reason the social movement for restorative justice has generally moved from seeing victims of crime movements as potential sources of resistance (see Scheingold, Pershing, and Olson 1994) to tangible sources of support.

All of this serves to keep the problem of the tyranny of the majority in perspective. While it is extremely rare for victims to fly into rages of abuse, it does happen in restorative justice processes, and when it does, justice can be compromised. The remedy has to be an absolute right of the accused to walk out of the restorative justice process and try their chances in a court of law.

RESTORATIVE JUSTICE PRACTICES CAN WIDEN NETS OF SOCIAL CONTROL

Polk (1994, p. 134) and Minor and Morrison (1996), among others, have expressed concern about the net-widening potential of conferencing and other restorative justice programs. Systematic data to test such concerns are scarce. Maxwell and Morris (1996) do not find evidence of net widening as a result of the New Zealand restorative justice reforms of 1989. This is especially true at the most intensive end of intervention, with the number of places in residences for young offenders falling from 200 to 76, and sentences that involve custody declining from an average of 374 per year prior to the juvenile justice reforms to 112 in 1990 (Maxwell and Morris 1996, p. 94). Forsythe (1995) found no net widening in the Wagga Wagga juvenile conferencing program and, indeed, found a small decrease in juvenile cases being processed by the justice system after the program's introduction. The Sparwood, British Columbia, police conferencing program discussed in chapter 3 was unique in terms of the net-widening hypothesis because it completely abolished court in favor of conferences, which were held much less frequently than court cases had been held in the past. Yeats (1997, p. 371) associates the introduction of restorative justice conferences and an expanded cautioning program for juveniles in Western Australia with more than a halving of the number of charges heard in the Children's Court in the mid-1990s. Dignan (1992, p. 462) found quite modest net widening in the Kettering evaluation of a British adult victim reparation program; while some experienced higher levels of intervention than they might otherwise have experienced, more experienced lower levels of intervention than they would otherwise have encountered. The John Howard Society's Restorative Resolutions project in Manitoba was designed to be confined to adult cases where the Crown had already recommended a prison sentence of six months or more (this being true in 90 percent of the cases; Bonta, Rooney, and Wallace-Capretta 1998). This approach to restorative probation builds in strong guarantees of net narrowing and has considerable promise for reducing minority overrepresentation in prison.

Net widening is most likely to occur with programs the police do not take seriously and which depend on referrals from the police. The police then refer cases they would not normally bother doing much about, and the restorative justice program is motivated to get more cases by proving to the police that it is a tough option. A reverse of this situation is the New Zealand program. Here police support for conferencing is strong, and in any case the police cannot send a juvenile to court to prevent a family group conference.[4] It is this legislative *mandating* of diversion to restorative justice that explains the larger size of the New Zealand restorative justice program for young offenders compared with other jurisdictions (Power 2000).[5] Indeed, this is the greatest and most neglected accomplishment of the New Zealand reforms.

It is worth considering why net widening is believed to occur in critiques of the welfare model of criminal justice, and whether these factors might not be so worrying in a restorative justice program aimed at securing freedom as nondomination. Walgrave (1995, p. 230) makes the point: "Educative and clinical arguments within a legal system imbue subjective and speculative approaches of the clinical practitioner with the coercive power of justice." With restorative justice, educative and clinical services are options selected by the joint deliberation of offenders and their community of care, who enjoy an absolute right of veto over them. Welfare professionals actually suffer a diminution in coercive state backing of their discretion to intervene under the restorative justice model. As Walgrave (1995, p. 233) puts it, the restorative model is a move from "the state of power" and "the welfare state" to "the empowering state."

On the present limited evidence, restorative justice more often narrows than widens nets of formal state control; but it does tend to widen nets of community control.

Whether the nets that are widened are state or community nets, an assumption that net widening is a bad thing seems wrong. From a republican normative perspective, net widening that increases freedom as nondomination is a good thing (Braithwaite and Pettit 1990). From this republican perspective, it is important to widen nets of social control over white-collar crime and domestic violence. Even with juveniles, we need to widen nets of community control over school bullying because this so demonstrably is oppressive of the freedom of victims, because restorative justice programs aimed at reducing bullying work (Olweus 1993), and because bullying is connected to other problems—victims being more susceptible to suicide than nonvictims and offenders being more supportive of adult wife abuse than children who are not bullies (Rigby, Whish, and Black 1994).

If it is true that restorative justice narrows nets of judicial control and widens nets of community control, then another kind of critique of restorative justice swings into play. Jennifer Brown (1994, p. 129) quotes Barbara Babcock, who in turn is referring to an argument by Thurman Arnold: "The trial is an important occasion for dramatic enactment, the symbolic representation of the community's most deeply held values." Restorative justice advocates see this as the romantic vision of the law of trial lawyers (and Hollywood). The guilty plea cases that are the bread and butter of both criminal courts and restorative justice programs are devoid of courtroom drama; on average Canberra RISE cases that go to court are over in about ten minutes and very few people are present to observe the "drama." (Roche 2001), Yes, then, there is a worry that restorative justice programs can widen nets of community control and even nets of state control for some types of crime. The question is whether they should.

RESTORATIVE JUSTICE FAILS TO PROMOTE SOCIAL JUSTICE

There are reasons for taking seriously three competing hypotheses about the relationship between restorative justice and social justice:

1. Restorative justice is unimportant to struggles for social justice.
2. Restorative justice risks the worsening of social injustice.
3. Restorative justice can be an important strategy for advancing social justice.

I consider these in turn.

Restorative Justice Is Unimportant to Struggles for Social Justice

This is what I used to think. Social justice requires restructuring the economy, confronting unemployment, land rights for indigenous peoples, equal employment opportunities for women and other categories of people subject to discrimination, more effective regulation of corporate power, a different kind of tax system, greater equity at the IMF and the WTO, and a fairer education system. Any kind of reform to the criminal justice system does not seem central to achieving any of these objectives.

Restorative Justice Risks the Worsening of
Social Injustice

Restorative justice, at least in some of its manifestations, has been accused by some critics of Orientalism (Said 1995). According to Harry Blagg (1997, p. 483), "Justice systems have a tendency to generate and reflect mono-culturalist narratives. . . . Orientalist discourses are, primarily, powerful acts of representation that permit Western/ European cultures to contain, homogenize and consume 'other' cultures." So, for example, in the New Zealand Maori context, to interpret the reforms around the Children, Young Persons and Their Families Act (1989) as a shift to "restorative justice" is to frame a local struggle over decolonization and justice of much wider significance into the narrowing discourse of a global Western-led social movement. The deeper significance of the legal struggles between Maori and Pakeha cultures is about whether Maori people are able to do their own justice in ways that connect to their meaning systems, not whether they are enabled to do "restorative justice."

On the other hand, the meaning of restorative justice might be culturally plural— creating spaces where Indigenous peoples (and other minority cultures) can do their own justice in ways that make sense to them. This means a shift from the univocal "consistent" justice of extant Western systems. Sounds simple. But of course this is a complex and difficult prescription in contexts where there is an offender from one culture and a victim from another.

Even when restorative justice is read in a way that is maximally culturally plural, tensions remain between restorative justice and social justice for Indigenous people. Imagine, for example, that research on restorative justice processes reveals what procedures are best to ensure that non-Western cultures—be they Vietnamese, African, or Cree—are given space to transact justice in ways that have most meaning to them. In response we require restorative justice facilitators to undertake training courses in how to assure this plurality. But do we then forbid Indigenous elders who have not been so certified as trained restorative justice facilitators from presiding over Indigenous justice processes? Basically, I think we should not. To do so would be to privilege our restorative justice aspirations over more important social justice aspirations of Indigenous peoples searching empowerment. This is Blagg's caution. But to some degree the tensions here are unavoidable. Most readers who would agree with my position here would not want to persist with it in the context of the rape of an Asian or African woman by an Indigenous man or even perhaps the rape of an Indigenous woman by a man from another culture who does not wish to submit to the justice of the elders. Once colonialism, slavery, and immigration have ruptured the lives of Indigenous peoples, all forms of justice, including the most plural forms of restorative justice, can be a threat to social justice for Indigenous people.

There is no inevitability that disempowering state courts in favor of empowering the people will advance social justice. Peoples' courts and *bang jiao* programs in China have quite often empowered officials of a totalitarian political party rather than the people. Even when the people have been empowered, we have seen tyrannies of the majority oppress homosexual minorities in Cuban Peoples' Courts, among other tyrannies. Indeed, there have been cases where elders of Indigenous peoples have been empowered by restorative justice programs and then used that power as males to protect male friends who have been abusing Indigenous women. In Rwanda we even saw genocide as an upshot of unaccountable power over on-the-spot justice being returned to leaders of a disenfranchised group suffering a terrible colonial legacy.

While there can be no social justice without empowerment for peoples who have suffered dreadful colonial histories, that empowerment can itself worsen social injustices for others. Hence both restorative justice that crushes Indigenous empowerment (as in Blagg's [1997] analysis) and Indigenous empowerment that crushes social justice are complex postcolonial possibilities.

The most forceful critique of restorative justice has been a feminist one. Whatever the limitations of adversarial legalism, a battered woman with a lawyer standing beside her against a batterer and his lawyer is a more equal contest than one-on-one mediation between victim and offender. The question is whether a meeting of two communities of care where both victim and offender are surrounded by supporters involves more or less imbalance of power. A feminist perspective has been that one of the accomplishments of the women's movement in the 1980s was to have violence against women and children treated as a crime (Dobash and Dobash 1979). The worry about restorative justice is that by not taking such crimes to court, restorative justice might fail to treat them seriously (Stubbs 1995). Worse, restorative justice might return family violence to being a private matter rather than a social problem whose dimensions are profoundly public.

Restorative justice advocates reply that court processing of family violence cases actually tends to foster a culture of denial, while restorative justice fosters a culture of apology. Apology, when communicated with ritual solemnity, is actually the most powerful cultural device for taking a problem seriously, while denial is a cultural device for dismissing it. In turn feminists rightly contend that insincere apology is endemic in attempts to regulate family violence: the apology becomes a tactic, a way station toward the ultimate reassertion of violence and domination. Gale Burford and Joan Pennell's (1998) sophisticated research on family group conferences for domestic violence in Newfoundland was, I think, persuasive that family violence was reduced by their interventions. This is the best piece of research done on the topic, and it is significant that one of its authors—Joan Pennell—came out of a background of distinguished contributions to the battered women's movement in North America.

What we have learned from Pennell and Burford and from Hollow Water (see Box 1.8: Hollow Water) is that it is possible that some initial feminist assumptions that restorative justice would be a threat to social justice for women may sometimes be in error—not always in error but sometimes in error (see Strang and Braithwaite forthcoming). Compared with restorative justice, criminal law may prove a blunt instrument for reaching "the myriad controlling behaviors of a battering system" (Coker

1999, p. 58). Restorative justice has potential as a tool for advancing social justice for women and children who are suffering at the hands of violent men. But more careful empirical research is still needed to test this potential (Strang and Braithwaite forthcoming). I will now more systematically explore these possibilities for restorative justice to advance justice for the disadvantaged.

Restorative Justice Can Be an Important Strategy for Advancing Social Justice

I have already said that restorative justice can and should have the meaning of justice that empowers all communities of care for victims and offenders—Indigenous and non-Indigenous. It is possible to design restorative justice so it does not shift power over Indigenous people from the hands of white judges to the hands of police who are not accountable to judges. It is possible for dialogue to occur between Indigenous elders and experts who have learned research lessons from cross-cultural restorative justice experience: Each can learn lessons from the other. I have seen a conference where a trained state restorative justice coordinator handed the facilitation over to an Indigenous elder, taking a backseat from which he would not budge unless some voices were unjustly silenced by the elder. Even when voices are unjustly silenced by an elder (a circumstance I have not seen), the state coordinator can still intervene in a respectful, deferential way: "Uncle Frank, some of the members of the group sound like they want to hear what Mary has to say, and I would like to hear her story myself."

The experience of restorative justice programs in Australia is that they have been quite successful in empowering women's voices in the justice process. Kathy Daly (1996) reports that this has been the experience so far of her extensive observational work, from a feminist theoretical frame, of conferences in South Australia.[6] Mothers are often the most eloquent communicators at restorative justice conferences. One of the most interesting recommendations Richard Young and Carolyn Hoyle have made to the Thames Valley Police conferencing program is: "Where an offender is accompanied by his or her mother it will usually be sensible for facilitators to ensure that the mother is the first person from the offender's supporters to be invited to contribute." Sometimes mothers even speak of the violence they suffer at the hands of their sons, a matter on which they never want to testify in court. In the worst cases of women in violent relationships, however, there remain empirical grounds for the worry that fear of retaliation will induce silence (Hooper and Busch 1996).

Empowerment of young people is often not accomplished: the young are often silenced by "a room full of adults" (Haines 1998, p. 93). However, Canberra offenders randomly assigned to conferences are considerably less likely than offenders assigned to court to say that they were disadvantaged in proceedings due to "age, income, sex, race or some other reason" (Sherman and Barnes 1997). While there was no comparison with court, Joe Hudson's (1998) study of Canadian family group conference participants found 80 percent to be "very satisfied" with the way all conference participants were treated as equals.

Morris et al. (1996, p. 224) conclude from the consideration of the issue across the set of contributions to their volume: "Fears raised by commentators about the disempowerment of women have not been supported by observers and researchers who note their active participation in the process in contrast with their non-participation in judicial processes." Our research group's qualitative observations of restorative justice at various sites is that women's voices in restorative justice conferences are often extremely influential. Pranis (2000), pp. 292–93 has explained how specific aspects of circle processes inspired by North American Indigenous practices reinforce equal voice:

> Participants are seated in a circle which structurally conveys a message of equality. Titles are not used in the circle process, minimizing positional authority as a relevant element of decision making. A talking piece [e.g., a feather] is used to structure the discussion. Participants may only speak when holding the talking piece and the talking piece is passed clockwise around the circle providing an opportunity for every participant to speak. The talking piece creates space for the ideas of participants who would find it difficult to insert themselves into the usual dialog process. In the circle process it is assumed that everyone present has something to contribute to the resolution of the problem. The use of the talking piece reduces the responsibility of the facilitator and increases the responsibility of every participant to guide the dialog toward a good end.

David Moore has argued, "There is something about getting a group of humans together in a circle which tends to make them more dignified than they would otherwise be" (*Sydney Morning Herald*, 18 March 1999, p. 15). Moore argues that the circle makes it difficult for tyrants to exercise tyranny because in a circle they find it harder to divide and conquer.

All this may constitute a kind of empirical response to feminist critics of republicanism and deliberative democracy who fear the pursuit of communitarian consensus, which may be a male consensus (Young 1995; Phillips 1991). At the same time, it opens up another feminist concern about restorative justice, which is that women again bear the burden of all the unpaid caring (Daly 1996). The potential fiscal benefit of conferences that they may be cheaper than courtroom justice is likely to be carried on women's backs. Hughes (1996) explores this concern through considering Campbell's (1993) analysis that in "Britain's dangerous places," it is women who are the "community builders" while men deal with unemployment by indulging a cult of selfish irresponsibility and brute force. In Britain's high-crime communities, "Crime and coercion are sustained by men. Solidarity and self-help are sustained by women. It is as stark as that" (Campbell 1993, p. 319). No, the data do not suggest it is as stark as that. Yet there seems little doubt that women do more of the restoring than men in restorative justice processes. The price tag for communitarian empowerment (which most women say they want in all the interview-based research) is a gendered burden of care.

A related worry about restorative discourses is that they may domesticate violence. Sara Cobb (1997, p. 414) finds that "the morality of mediation itself" can frame the interpretation of action, subsuming, taming the morality of right and wrong so that "the category 'victim' dissolves" (p. 436). Some restorative justice advocates view it as a good thing for the category of victim to dissolve, indeed for the category of crime to dissolve. There is a divide between some mediation advocates who believe the mediator should be "neutral" and some conferencing advocates who see a conference beginning from an assumption that a crime has been admitted about which the facilitator is not neutral but disapproving. Rights are not necessarily domesticated to needs (Minow 1990) by a justice that "erases any morality that competes with the morality of mediation." The right kind of interplay between the justice of the law and the restorative justice of the people might secure rights as trumps against the morality of mediation, a topic to which I will return. One way of thinking about the distinction is that rather than being about the mediation of conflicts, restorative justice is about the righting of injustices; rather than being about neutrality, it is about fairness (Coker 1999). We cannot conceive fairness as only about impartiality to the exclusion of sensitivity and responsiveness.

An opposite kind of claim about disadvantage sometimes made about restorative justice programs is that they are a benefit granted disproportionately to Caucasians. It is not an allegation I have seen made in New Zealand and Canada, where so many of the leading programs have been run by and for First Nation peoples. However, there have been some worrying suggestions of the validity of such a concern in the United States (Gehm 1990; Brown 1994; Schiff 1998) and Australia (Blagg 1997; Daly 1996; Wundersitz and Hetzel 1996). In Australia we have been disappointed by the proportion of our juvenile conferences where the offender is an Aboriginal young person—only 11 percent of the young offenders in the Canberra program which is barely better than the percentage of court cases that are Aboriginal (10 percent).[7] Thus far we have failed badly in Australia to use restorative justice to reduce Aboriginal imprisonment rates. This has been the biggest disappointment to date in the way restorative justice has developed in Australia.

The best restorative justice conferences help young offenders who have dropped out of school or who have been excluded from school to get back to their education; they help unemployed offenders to find jobs. But these accomplishments are rare. Even if they became common, it is hard to imagine restorative justice making a major positive contribution to reducing the injustice of joblessness.

But here it may be important to think of restorative justice in terms of avoiding harm more than in terms of doing good. The evidence is persuasive now that a criminal record is an important cause of unemployment (Hagan 1991). It is even more clear that the criminal justice system is a major part of the social injustice that black peoples suffer in nations like Australia and the United States. In the United States, the prison system is the most important labor market program for young black men—more of them are in it than in the higher education system, for example. In Australia, the prison system is a major cause of suicide in the Aboriginal community. It is also a major cause of rape and drug addiction as afflictions that disproportionately afflict the poor. Then there is AIDS. We also have an epidemic of hepatitis C in Australian prisons, infecting up to 60 percent of male prisoners and up to 80 percent of female prisoners (Parliament of NSW 1998, pp. 69–70). In Russia, up to 50 percent of the prison population is infected with the tuberculosis bacillus—a legacy of overcrowding (Lee 1999).

Ann Stringer (1999) has shown that imprisonment is also a major cause and effect of debt among poor people, be they white or black. Among 121 Queensland prisoners, 80 percent had some debt when they went into prison, with drug use rather than investment in housing being the most important cause of the debt. Forty-nine percent said that they had committed a crime to repay a debt. Imprisonment cut them off from a variety of means of sorting out these debts, leaving their families vulnerable to repossession and other assaults on their circumstances. Inequalities grounded in the indebtedness of poor families to finance companies are greatly worsened by imprisonment.

Hence the most important ways restorative justice may be able to reduce social injustice involve reducing the impact of imprisonment as a cause of the unequal burdens of unemployment, debt with extortionate interest burdens, suicide, rape, AIDS, hepatitis C, and, potentially most important, the epidemic of multiple-drug-resistant tuberculosis, presently worst in Asia and Eastern Europe but soon to be arriving in North America and Western Europe thanks in part to overcrowded prisons. There is not much evidence yet that restorative justice realizes this potential. Early results from the RISE experiments in Canberra are not consistent on this, but there is some encouragement:

> Juvenile Property (Security) offenders who were treated in court significantly more often reported that they had experienced financial pressures in the preceding year and that they had had "serious troubles or problems with people who were close to you." Youth Violence offenders who had been to court significantly more often said that they had changed jobs during the preceding year, while Drink Driving offenders who had been to court significantly more often had dropped out of full time study or been fired or laid off from a job in that period. (Strang et al. 1999, p. 95)

In other words, offenders randomly assigned to a conference rather than a court case as a result of their crime were in some respects less likely to suffer adverse life events such as being fired in the two years after their apprehension.

Finally, chapters 1 through 3 argued that the empirical experience of corporate restorative justice in the finance, nuclear, coal mining, and nursing home industries suggests that it offers an approach to attacking the criminal abuses of corporate power that can be so important to understanding the advantaging of the rich over the poor. In some cases, such as the major frauds against Aboriginal consumers by Australian insurance companies in the early 1990s (the CML case described in chapter 1), restorative process can engage even prime ministers with the need for structural change in the regulation of an industry. My colleagues and I in the ANU Centre for Tax System Integrity are hoping to develop restorative strategies for tax compliance that might turn around some of the stupendous advantaging of the rich over the poor in this arena.

I have rejected the first hypothesis that "restorative justice is unimportant to struggles for social justice." Restorative justice brings with it serious risks of worsening social injustice and potential to reduce it. So far neither possibility has been realized in any significant way because restorative justice has made marginal inroads into the criminal justice system. Which will be realized depends in considerable measure on the centrality of freedom as nondomination as a restorative justice value: whether nondomination prevails to ensure maximum plurality of contesting voices is heard concerning both process and outcome.

Restorative justice has the potential to lift some of the silencing of the voices of dominated groups such as Indigenous people and women and children suffering abuse. Kay Pranis (2000) explains that human beings are storytelling animals, and we can judge the power a person has by how many people listen attentively to her stories. It follows that an underestimated way restorative justice might confer power upon the disenfranchised is simply by listening to their stories and taking them seriously. This is a kind of power that does matter to people and one that can easily be granted with a little time and respect. If restorative justice succeeds in giving voice to dominated Indigenous people, women, and children, the Canadian work of Pennell and Burford and Hollow Water is a basis for cautious optimism that restorative justice might reduce violence and sexual abuse against women and children. And our Australian work suggests potential for reducing criminal abuse of corporate power. But we must be careful that it does not subvert some of the protections courts occasionally afford to such victims of injustice. A right to restorative justice that takes away a right to the formal justice of the courts is unlikely to be progress. But social justice might be advanced by adding a meaningful right to access to restorative justice to effective access to courtroom justice (see chapter 8).

We have also seen in this section that restorative justice has unrealized potential to reduce the imprisonment, unemployment, school expulsion, imprisonment-induced suicide and drug addiction, imprisonment-induced infectious disease, and imprisonment-induced assault that disproportionately afflict the poor.

Criminal offenders and victims who are caught up in the criminal justice system have a lot of things in common. One of them is that they are more likely to be poor than nonvictims and nonoffenders (Hindelang, Gottfredson, and Garofalo 1978; Braithwaite and Biles 1984). A restorative justice strategy that succeeds in empowering both victims and offenders therefore empowers folk on both sides who are disproportionately powerless. If both victims and offenders get some restoration out of a restorative justice process, then that is help with progressive rather than regressive social justice implications. Obversely, a retributive justice system that responds to the hurt of one side by inflicting hurt on the other side is regressive in its distributive impact. It adds to the hurt in the world in a way where those burdens of hurt fall more heavily on the poor. This is more pointedly true when a vicious spiral is triggered by retributive values—where criminals want to hurt victims again, victims want to hurt criminals back,[8] as hurt endlessly begets more hurt. So it could be that the poor will be the greatest beneficiaries of a world where help begets help, grace begets grace, just as the poor are the losers from our present propensity to institutionalize hurt begetting hurt.[9]

RESTORATIVE JUSTICE IS PRONE TO CAPTURE BY THE DOMINANT GROUP IN THE RESTORATIVE PROCESS

Restorative business regulatory practices are frequently captured by business (Clinard and Yeager 1980, pp. 106–9). As Dingwall, Eekelaar, and Murray (1983) have shown, child protection practice is liable to "family capture." As with business regulation, Dingwall, Eekelaar, and Murray show that a "rule of optimism" prevails among family regulators who have a bigger caseload than they can manage. Sandor (1993) even worries that family group conferences might ignite episodes of physical abuse, so common in the lives of serious juvenile offenders. This is a worry that deserves testing by a major empirical study. Indigenous justice can empower elders to tyrannize the young of their tribe. Critics have alleged this in a most alarming way in Canada through allegations by women from a reserve that leaders of a program of Indigenous justice administered by a panel of elders

> manipulated the justice system to protect family members who had committed violent rapes, had intimidated victims and witnesses into withdrawing charges, had perjured themselves during the trial of the project leader's son (for rape), had slashed tires of community members who tried to speak out and sent the alleged "rape gangs" to their homes, and generally had used the project to further their stranglehold on the community and the justice system.[10]

In New Zealand, I saw one tragic conference where the state funded the travel of an offender to another community because his *whanau* (extended family) wanted to separate him from a liaison with a girlfriend it did not want. In pushing for this the youth justice advocate was not an advocate for the youth, who was heartbroken by this outcome, but was captive of the *whanau*, which was the repeat player in the use of his legal services.

Observational work on juvenile justice conferences quite regularly reports lower levels of offender involvement than involvement by their family members. Maxwell and Morris's (1993, pp. 110–12) interviews found fully 45 percent of young offenders, compared with 20 percent of family members, saying they were not involved in making the conference decision. In Canberra and South Australia, Daly (1996) reported 33 percent of offenders not to be engaged with the process. The Maxwell and Morris (1993) data showed family members of the offender having by far the largest influence on the decision, followed by professionals who were present, the young offender, and the victim (not surprising since the victim was absent from a majority of the conferences in this study). Haines's (1998) critique of conferences as a "room full of adults" who dominate a child is therefore often correct. All such failures are relative, however: the RISE experiment in Canberra shows that young offenders are considerably more likely to believe that they could express their views when they went to a conference than when they went to court (Sherman and Barnes 1997; Sherman et al. 1998, pp. 121–22). McGarrell et al. (2000, p. 44) found that 84 percent of young offenders "felt involved" in their conference, compared with 47 percent of the control group who felt involved in their alternative diversion. Eighty-six percent of conferenced youth felt that they had been given a chance to express their views, compared to 55 percent of controls. The least negative results on this question are from the Queensland conferencing program, where Hayes, Prenzler, with Wortley (1998, p. 20) report 97 percent of young offenders as "not pushed into being at the conference" and "NOT pushed into things in the conference" and 99 percent saying both "I got to have my say at the conference" and "People seemed to understand my side of things."

The best remedy to this problem is systematic attention in the restorative justice preparatory process to empowerment of the most vulnerable parties (individual victims and offenders) and systematic disempowerment of the most dominant parties (the police, school authorities, state welfare authorities, and sometimes large business corporations). How is this accomplished? The most critical thing is to give the individual offender and the individual victim the one-on-one power in a meeting in advance of the conference to decide who they do and do not want to be there to support them. Unfortunately, the practice is often to empower the parents of young offenders to decide who should be there. They can certainly have a legitimate say; but on the offender side it is only the offender who should make the final decision about who will make her most comfortable, who she most trusts. To the extent that one is concerned here with imbalances of power between children and adults, men and women, major corporations and consumers, dyadic victim-offender mediation cements an imbalance. Imbalances are muddied, though hardly removed, by conferences between two communities of care, both of which contain adults and children, men and women, organized interests (like Aboriginal community councils in the CML case) and disorganized individuals. To illustrate formally the significance of these cross-cutting matrices of power imbalance, let us assign the arbitrary quantum of power 4 to an adult and 1 to a child. The adult has four times as much power as the child in a dyadic victim-offender mediation. Add to both sides of the dialogue two other adults and one other child. The imbalance of power falls from 4 to 1 to 1.3 to 1.

Simple rules of procedure can privilege less dominant voices over state voices. The police should never be allowed to give their version of what happened in advance of the offender's version. The New Zealand and South Australian practice of giving attending police a right of veto over the conference agreement is a bad practice from this perspective. The victim and the offender should have a right of veto, and should be formally reminded of it at the start of the conference, but perhaps no agent of the state should have such a right as a conference participant. On this view, if the police feel a victim has dominated an offender by requiring excessive punishment, their approach should be to advise the offender of his right to walk away from the agreement and have the matter heard by a court. Against this view is a non-RISE case we had in Canberra where the police did not veto an agreement, enthusiastically crafted by the victim and the mother of the offender, to have a child wear a T-shirt emblazoned with the words *I Am a Thief* (see Box 5.3). Certainly, among the formal negative performance indicators for facilitators should be (1) how much they talk,[11]

Box 5.3: I Am a Thief

At a shoplifting conference in Canberra, a store manager (the victim) and the mother of the offender proposed that a twelve-year-old boy should wear a T-shirt outside the shop emblazoned with the words *I Am a Thief*. The boy did not object, initially wearing it with bravado rather than shame. The police facilitator of the conference thought the agreement unwise but considered it inappropriate to impose this view on the conference. The day I became aware of the case, I was quoted on the front page of the *Canberra Times* and interviewed on a dozen television and radio stations shaming (as reintegratively as I could) the conference outcome, arguing that there should be a guideline prohibiting any degrading or humiliating conference agreement, just as conferences were not allowed to impose physical punishments or incarceration. This was a divisive move for the reform coalition because some police (particularly the union) initially defended the outcome, and some in the Victims of Crime Assistance League were willing to defend it. The debate over the rights and wrongs of the outcome raged in the letters column of the *Canberra Times* and on call in radio for weeks. Unfortunately, the mother of the child and the victim received a great deal of stigmatization in these letters (but also a lot of support); the store manager was disciplined by his company for such a foolish action, and the company apologized, an outcome some in the victims' movement resented. While no one was named in this publicity, neighbors and school friends came to know who the child was. At another level, the publicity was a triumph for restorative principles of deliberation in the public sphere. I was amazed at the extent to which participants in the debate, from the attorney general and editorial writers down to children, were able to articulate the difference between the desirability of disapproving the act of shoplifting and the undesirability of stigmatizing shoplifters as people. The critics of stigmatization decisively won the public debate, so much so that the mother changed her thinking and was moved to propose with the police that the conference be reconvened to burn the T-shirt or take some similar action. The child, who, after all the publicity had had enough, vetoed this. Police training and quality control over officers allowed to be facilitators improved a little after the incident, but not as much as advocates would have liked.

(2) dominating proceedings, and (3) participation in setting the terms of the conference agreement.

With restorative business regulation, Ayres and Braithwaite (1992) have shown game-theoretically the importance of having third parties present during regulatory negotiation to protect against corporate capture. With nursing home regulation, for example, this can mean representatives of the residents' committee, supported by advocacy groups where they want this, relatives, staff, and their unions and outside board members, as well as management meeting with the regulators.

While there are such measures we can take to counterbalance capture, there can be no doubt that capture by dominant groups is an ineradicable reality of restorative justice (just as it is of state justice).

Restorative Justice Can Extend Unaccountable Police Power, Even Compromise the Separation of Powers among Legislative, Executive, and Judicial Branches of Government

Critics such as Danny Sandor (1993) and Rob White (1994) are particularly concerned about conferences facilitated by the police, something now happening in Australia, the United Kingdom, the United States, and Canada and being advocated elsewhere. It is all very well to reply that facilitation is not control, that police should not have a veto power over decisions, but no one can deny that good facilitators have "dramatic dominance" (to use Stephen Mugford's Goffmanesque characterization) even if they exert little direct control. This dramatic dominance ensures, among other things, that the conference is orderly, that everyone has their turn to speak without interruption, that civility triumphs over abuse. Supporters of police conferencing in police stations, such as the Police-Citizens Consultative Committee in Wagga Wagga, claim this lends "gravitas" to proceedings. These citizens and police also argue that police facilitation, indeed, the presence of the police uniform, helps victims feel secure, a critical problem given the evidence that victims often come away from criminal justice processes, including restorative ones, feeling more afraid of their offender (see chapter 3). Interesting and important speculations, but there is no evidence to support the importance of such alleged advantages. Conversely, there is no evidence to support counterclaims that offenders are intimidated by the presence of a police uniform during a conference or by the police station as a venue. It seems unlikely that either is totally false; many young people do distrust the police, and many crime victims distrust "do-gooder social workers" and trust the police.

What does seem true, by definition, is that hard-line views on either side of this debate do disempower and disadvantage participants. A rule that police must or must not facilitate conferences has unfortunate consequences when it precludes someone from taking the facilitator role who is the most gifted person who most enjoys the confidence of the disputants. It has perhaps even more unfortunate consequences when it forces police officers to facilitate conferences when they do not believe this is "police work" (see Hoyle and Young 1998). In New Zealand, where police "do not" facilitate conferences, I saw one conference where a Pakeha official facilitator handed over the effective facilitation of the conference to a police officer because the police officer was Maori and all the participants Maori. A rule that Maori conferences must be held on the traditional Marae (meeting place) might be most unwise if that would terrify a Samoan victim. A rule that it be held on neutral ground is sad if one party is quite stipulative about where she will feel safe about the conference and the other party does not care. In my unsystematic observation on this question, most parties do not seem to care greatly about where conferences are held; but when they do express a strong preference, why not yield to them?

The more fundamental question is whether there is something wrong in principle with police facilitating a conference. Does it make the police investigator, prosecutor, judge, and jury? It is only a very partial answer to reply that the investigator is never the police facilitator in such programs. Even if the police have no veto over the conference decision, they can still dominate it and become a de facto judge and jury. At least a lay facilitator who dominates a conference process does not add that domination to institutional domination over the decision to proceed with the matter. At a lower level, this is also a separation-of-powers argument against facilitation control in the hands of any state agency that already has control over another part of the process—such as control by the courts (as in South Australia) or a juvenile justice or welfare agency. It is not an argument against a prosecutor or judge having a right of veto over the outcome of a conference.

Is there therefore any case for control of facilitation by a state agency rather than facilitator recruitment by an institution in civil society, especially when that civilian facilitator has the power to co-opt a police facilitator if that is what the parties want? There are two cases for state control. One is simply politically pragmatic. Restorative justice reform requires enormous energy and political will to struggle against retributivism and vested interests, not least within police forces. My own position has been politically pragmatic in just this way: to admire those with the courage to take on the battle, wherever they pop up institutionally—in civil society, the police, the courts, prosecutors, or state welfare agencies. During the R and D era of restorative justice, so long as the activists are sensible, competent, and committed, let us encourage openness to research results from their innovation. We really have so few data on who is right about these questions of comparative advantage in institutional location. My own suspicion is to think that success is 70 percent driven by attention to getting implementation detail right and only 30 percent by getting the institutional infrastructure right. Gifted people can run wonderful restorative justice programs in an open field with no infrastructure whatsoever. They seem to have done so for millennia. But that suspicion is itself something that must be open to empirical refutation.

A second argument for institutional location of conferencing in a police service is about the transformation of police cautioning and police culture more broadly. Even in New Zealand, with the largest juvenile conferencing program anywhere, for every juvenile case dealt with by a conference, more than five are dealt with by a police caution. Rendering police cautioning more restorative is more important than rendering conference or court processing more restorative. From the perspective of the theory of reintegrative shaming, if, as seems to be the case (Braithwaite 1995d), stigmatizing interactions do more to increase crime than reintegrative ones do to reduce it, five stigmatizing police cautions will do more damage than any good from one reintegrative conference. Not just in formal cautioning but also in daily interaction on the street, the challenge of transforming police culture from a stigmatizing to a restorative style is important. The hope of the leading police reformers in this area, like Terry O'Connell in Australia, has been that police "ownership" of conferencing would imbue police commitment to restorative justice in wider arenas, including their own internal affairs (corruption, sexual harassment). At this stage, however, I doubt if anyone could plausibly demonstrate that any police service has experienced a major change of corporate culture as a result of restorative justice innovation. Perhaps Thames Valley, England, begins to approach this situation. The evidence is clear that significant police cultural change has not occurred in Bethlehem, Pennsylvania (McCold and Wachtel 1998, p. 3), though the individual police most exposed to conferences did move toward a more restorative and less crime-control-oriented philosophy of policing. But then cultural change is never rapid and always resisted.

If the relationship of any restorative justice program with the police is not well managed, disaster is courted. The police are the gatekeepers to the criminal justice system, and if they shut the gate to restorative justice, it is nigh impossible to push it open against their resistance. All manner of hybrids are possible. One is for a conferencing unit to be located in police stations, pushing internally to divert cases as they come through the station door, caressing and cajoling police cooperation, but with the facilitators actually being employees of an institution in civil society contracted by the justice minister to deliver the service. Some of these facilitators could be respected businesspeople who would have the sophistication to run conferences for complex white-collar crimes, others could have special language skills, others special gifts in gaining the confidence of young people, and others could be elders of a local Indigenous group.

More broadly, from a republican perspective, one wants to see most restorative justice conferencing transacted in civil society without ever going through the police station door—in Aboriginal communities, schools, extended families, churches, sporting clubs, corporations, business associations, and trade unions. Equally, one wants to see those community justice processes subject to state oversight for breaches of citizens' rights and procedural fairness. In such a world, restorative justice would contribute to the building of a republican democracy with a much richer separation of powers. That is not the world we live in yet. For the moment, the restorative justice debate is debilitated by excessively statist preoccupations to the point where the reforms in place do raise some legitimate worries about impoverishing rather than enhancing the separation of powers in our democracies.

RESTORATIVE JUSTICE PRACTICES CAN TRAMPLE RIGHTS
BECAUSE OF IMPOVERISHED ARTICULATION OF
PROCEDURAL SAFEGUARDS

Robust critiques of the limitations of restorative justice processes in terms of protection of rights have been provided by Warner (1994), Stubbs (1995), Bargen (1996), and Van Ness (1998). There can be little doubt that courts provide superior formal guarantees of procedural fairness than conferences.

At the *investigatory stage*, Warner (1994, p. 142) is concerned with the following:

> Will police malpractice be less visible in a system which uses FGCs [family group conferences]? One of the ways in which police investigatory powers are scrutinised is by oversight by the courts. If the police act unlawfully or unfairly in the investigation of a case, the judge or magistrate hearing the case may refuse to admit the evidence so obtained or may criticise the police officer concerned. Allegations of failure to require parental attendance during questioning, of refusal to grant access to a lawyer, of unauthorized searches and excessive force could become hidden in cases dealt with by FGCs.

These are good arguments for courts over restorative justice processes in cases where guilt is in dispute. But the main game is how to process that overwhelming majority of cases where there is an open-and-shut admission of guilt. Here no such advantage of court over conference applies; quite the reverse. As Warner herself points out, a guilty plea "immediately suspends the interests of the court in the treatment of the defendant prior to the court appearance" (Hogg and Brown 1985). In the production line for guilty pleas in the lower courts there is no time for that. In restorative justice conferences there is. Mothers in particular do sometimes speak up with critical voices about the way their child has been singled out, have been subject to excessive police force, and the like. Declan Roche (2001 chap. 7) has documented cases where police accountability to the community has been enhanced by the conference process. And such deterrence of abuse of police power that comes from the court does not disappear, since the police know that if relations break down in the conference, the case may go to court as well.

Police therefore have reason to be more rather than less procedurally just with cases on the conference track than with cases on the court track. The preliminary RISE data from Canberra suggest they are. In about 90 percent of cases randomly assigned to a conference, offenders thought the police had been fair to them ("leading up to the conference" and "during"); but they thought this in only to 48 to 78 percent (depending on the comparison) of the cases randomly assigned to court (Sherman et al. 1998). Offenders were also more likely to say they trusted the police after going through a conference with them than after going through a court case with them.

At the *adjudicatory stage*, Warner (1994) is concerned that restorative justice will be used as an inducement to admit guilt. In this restorative justice is in no different position than any disposition short of the prospect of execution or life imprisonment.

Proffering it can induce admissions. Systemically, though, one would have thought that a shift from a punitive to a restorative justice system would weaken the allure of such inducements. In the preliminary data from the four RISE experiments in Canberra, there is a slight tendency for court offenders to be more likely than conference offenders to agree that "the police made you confess to something which you did not do in this case." But in the preliminary results this difference was statistically significant only in the Juvenile Personal Property experiment (Sherman et al. 1998, pp. 123–24).

Warner (1994) is right, however, to point out that guilt is not always black and white. Defendants might not understand self-defense, intoxication, and other defenses that might be available to them. Even so, it remains the case that such matters are more likely to be actually discussed in a conference lasting about eighty minutes (Canberra data) than in a court case averaging about ten (Canberra data). This may be a simple reason that Canberra offenders who go through a conference are more likely to believe that the proceedings respected your rights than offenders who went through court (Sherman and Barnes 1997; Sherman et al. 1998).

At the *dispositional or sentencing stage*, Warner (1994) makes some good points about the care needed to ensure that sentences reflect only offenses the evidence in this case shows to have been committed and only damage the evidence shows to have been done. We have had conferences in Canberra in which victims have made exaggerated claims of the damage they have suffered, in one case many thousands of dollars in excess of what more thorough subsequent investigation proved to be the truth. Warner (1994) and Van Ness (1998) are both concerned about double jeopardy when consensus cannot be reached at a conference and the matter therefore goes to court, though Warner (1994) concedes it is not "true double jeopardy." Indeed, it is not. The justice model analogue would seem to be to retrial after a hung jury or appeal of a sentence decision (which no one would call double jeopardy) rather than retrial after acquittal. Moreover, it is critical that defendants have a right to appeal in court an unconscionable conference agreement they have signed, to have lawyers with them at all stages of restorative justice processes if that is their wish, and that they be proactively advised of these rights.

Most restorative justice programs around the world do not legally guarantee the American Bar Association's (1994) guideline that "statements made by victims and offenders and documents and other materials produced during the mediation/dialogue process [should be] inadmissible in criminal or civil court proceedings." This is a problem that can and should be remedied by appropriate law reform.

Van Ness (1998) has systematically reviewed the performance of restorative justice programs for juveniles against the United Nations Standard Minimum Rules for the Administration of Juvenile Justice ("The Beijing Rules"). Restorative justice programs are certainly found wanting in the review, though he concludes that they often tend to outperform traditional court processes on rules such as right to a speedy trial. For example, the New South Wales Young Offenders Act (1997) has the following requirement: "43. *Time Limit Holding Conferences*: A conference must, if practical, be held not later than 21 days after the referral for the conference is received." While

Van Ness's work certainly affirms my hypothesis that restorative justice processes can trample on rights, where rights will be better or worse protected after the introduction of a restorative justice program is a contextual matter. For example, when in South Africa prior to the Mandela presidency 30,000 juveniles per year were being sentenced by courts to flogging, who could doubt that the institutionalization of restorative justice conferences might increase respect for childrens' rights, as Sonnekus and Frank (1997, p. 7) argue:

> [Under apartheid] the most common sentence given was corporal punishment and children often preferred a whipping instead of residential care in a reformatory or school of industry. The time children spent in prison while awaiting trial and placement was not applied towards their sentence, thus a child may have served double and even triple sentences.

Nevertheless, rights can be trampled because of the inferior articulation of procedural safeguards in restorative justice processes compared with courts. The conclusion will seek to grapple with how justice might be enhanced in the face of this critique by a creative interplay between restorative forums and traditional Western courts.

CONCLUSION

We have seen that restorative justice can trample the rights of offenders and victims, can dominate them, can lack procedural protections, and can give police, families, or welfare professionals too much unaccountable power. Braithwaite and Parker (1999) suggest three civic republican remedies to these problems:

1. Contestability under the rule of law, a legal formalism that enables informalism while checking the excesses of informalism
2. Deindividualizing restorative justice, muddying imbalances of individual power by preferring community conferences over individual-on-individual mediation
3. Vibrant social movement politics that percolates into the deliberation of conferences, defends minorities against tyrannies of the majority, and connects private concerns to campaigns for public transformation

Lawyers who work for advocacy groups—for Indigenous peoples, children, women, victims of nursing home abuse—have a special role in the integration of these three strategies. Lawyers are a strategic set of eyes and ears for advocacy groups that use specific legal cases to sound alarms about wider patterns of domination. When appropriate public funding is available for legal advocacy, advocates can monitor lists of conference outcomes and use other means to find cases where they should tap offenders or victims on the shoulder to advise them to appeal the conference agreement because they could get a better outcome in the courts. They thus become a key conduit between rule of law and rule of community deliberation. It is a mistake to see their role as simply one of helping principles of natural justice and respect of rights to filter down into restorative justice. It is also to assist movement in the other direction—to help citizens to percolate up into the justice system their concerns about what should be restored and how. A rich deliberative democracy is one where the rule of law shapes the rule of the people and the concerns of the people reshape the rule of law. Top-down legalism unreconstructed by restorative justice from below is a formula for a justice captured by the professional interests of the legal profession (the tyranny of lawyers). Bottom-up community justice unconstrained by judicial oversight is a formula for the tyranny of the majority. When law and community check and balance each other, according to Braithwaite and Parker (1999), prospects are best for a rich and plural democracy that maximizes freedom as nondomination. Mackay (1998, p. 104) puts this aspiration in a Habermasian framework. For him, restorative justice:

> provides the opportunity for citizens to debate and test its claims from the basis of their own experiences and needs in a way that the conventional legal system does not. It brings the social system more into alignment with the communicative culture of the life world, and as such enables law to operate more effectively as a link between the two.

Communitarianism without rights is dangerous. Rights without community are vacuous. Rights will only have meaning as claims the rich can occasionally assert in courts of law unless community disapproval can be mobilized against those who trample the rights of others. Restorative justice can enliven rights as active cultural accomplishments when rights talk cascades down from the law into community justice.

None of the problems discussed in this chapter have been satisfactorily solved, just as none of the hypotheses of chapter 4 are satisfactorily demonstrated. Decades of R and D on restorative justice processes will be needed to explore my suspicion that the propositions of both the optimistic account in chapter 4 and the pessimistic account of this chapter are right. For the moment, we can certainly say that the literature reviewed here does demonstrate both the promise and the perils of restorative justice. It is, however, an immature literature, short on theoretical sophistication, short on rigorous or nuanced empirical research, far too dominated by self-serving comparisons of "our kind" of restorative justice program with "your kind" without collecting data (or even having observed "your kind" in action!). That disappoints when the panorama of restorative justice programs around the globe is now so dazzling, when we have so much to learn from one another's contextual mistakes and triumphs.

NOTES

1. As Mark Umbreit has pointed out to me, much victim-offender mediation is not dyadic. Other participants are often involved. He also rightly points out that dyadic encounters have their advantages, too. Some things might be said one-on-one that could never be drawn out in front of the wider group. In short, some of the most successful conferences

may adjourn for dyadic mediations; some of the most successful mediations may expand into conferences.

2. Put another way, the kind of theory I favor does not have a structurally or culturally determinate explanation of crime: low Japanese crime rates are not about village culture or Japanese culture; to understand them we look to Japanese regulatory practices and provision of opportunities for human development. Changing regulatory practices and development opportunities can explain why Japanese crime rates fell from World War II in a way that it is hard for changing Japanese culture or the demise of village life to explain (Masters 1997).

3. *The Queen v. Patrick Dale Clotworthy,* Auckland District Court T. 971545, Court of Appeal of New Zealand, CA 114/98.

4. The New South Wales Young Offenders Act (1997) empowers a "specialist youth officer" to opt for a conference against the advice of the police and precludes police commencement of proceedings before giving the specialist youth officer an opportunity to consider the conference option.

5. The mandating is pretrial normally, but if the police proceed by arrest and laying of charges, there is mandated court referral to a conference—except for murder, manslaughter, or minor traffic offenses. Section 246, Children, Young Persons and Their Families Act (1989) NZ.

6. Gabrielle Maxwell (1993, p. 292) concludes that restorative justice conferences are "places where women's voices are heard" (see also Burford and Pennell's [1998] findings). Similarly, Rigby (1996, p. 143), with data from 8,500 students, shows that at all ages girls are more interested than boys in talking through bullying problems in school programs. Daly (1996) reports that while a minority (15 percent) of offenders were women in her study of Australian conferences, 54 percent of victims, 58 percent of victim supporters, and 52 percent of offender supporters were women.

7. This 10 percent figure is from 1995 Children's Court appearances in Canberra, the most recent Heather Strang has been able to extract. My appreciation to Strang for providing the data.

8. Heather Strang's data from Canberra find that victims randomly assigned to restorative justice conferences are significantly less likely to say they would harm their offender if they have the chance (21 percent) than victims randomly assigned to court (6 percent). This effect size doubles in violence cases. See Strang 2000.

9. I think I am indebted to Howard Zehr for all this begetting talk from an address I heard him give in New Zealand.

10. This is a quotation that I treat as anonymous with respect to person and place. I was able to confirm the same broad story from four other sources.

11. Perhaps I am partially wrong here, however, if the more general literature on the effectiveness of problem solving in mediation is a guide. Carnevale and Pruitt's (1992, p. 565) review concludes that when disputants are able to resolve the dispute themselves, mediator intrusiveness gets in the way, but when conflict intensity or hostility is high, interventionist mediation can improve outcomes.

6

World Peacemaking

RESTORATIVE AND RESPONSIVE REGULATION OF WORLD PEACE

This chapter argues that both the restorative justice paradigm and the responsive regulation paradigms are useful for reconfiguring how to struggle for world peace. I argue that this is especially true of the conditions since 1989, where war has been widespread but not about confrontations between major powers. While it remains true that major powers can use their clout to mediate disputes in the shadow of a pyramid of coercive interventions, this rarely solves the underlying sources of late modern wars. We find the sources of these wars are often the fragmentation and low legitimacy of weak states, ethnic divisions that are prized open by warmongers who seek to plunder weak states as much as to rule them. The capacity of bottom-up restorative justice, revealed in earlier chapters, to build state legitimacy, heal ethnic division, and undercut hatemongers has a distinctive relevance to these new geopolitical conditions. However, a responsive global regulatory strategy is also needed to complement and connect restorative peacemaking to top-down preventive diplomacy and negotiated cessation of hostilities.

The main conclusions of the chapter are as follows:

1. The wealthy democracies (OECD members) coexist peacefully, transacting their disputes in an increasingly restorative fashion. Democratic governance and economic strength grounded in interdependence are reasons for that peace.
2. Less democratic, economically weak states have been the sites of a proliferation of mostly internal armed conflicts. Failure of democratic governance and poverty are reasons for these wars, which are characterized by plunder of the state, rape of the people, and prizing open ethnic divisions.
3. Important moves in the direction of a restorative diplomacy have been preventive diplomacy, conceived by Dag Hammarskjöld and reinvented

in Boutros Boutros-Ghali's *Agenda for Peace*, and expanded efforts at mediation of disputes since the partial success of President Carter at Camp
David.

4. Both mediation and preventive diplomacy have partially worked in defusing disputes, building the institutional capacity of states, and accomplishing the short-term cessation of hostilities.

5. However, they have failed in dealing with the underlying hatreds and their
deeper causes, so armed conflicts that seem settled regularly reignite.

6. The reason for the unsustained nature of the accomplishments of international mediation and preventive diplomacy is that they have been limited to elite diplomacy—something that UN secretary-generals, U.S. sec-
retaries of state, or former foreign ministers do in dialogue with political
leaders of the warring armies. This elite practice fails to conceive the accomplishment of peace within the OECD as an accomplishment of democracy and the failure of peace elsewhere as a failure of democracy.
Those failures leave the people livid with hatred over abuses of their human rights, ethnically divided, deprived of a sense of identity with a democratic state and its institutions. A diplomatic practice is needed that heals
these hurts of abused peoples. We call this *restorative diplomacy*. The Truth
and Reconciliation Commission in South Africa and hopefully the efforts
to heal the wounds of war in Bougainville may provide clues for how to do
restorative diplomacy that touches the hearts of the people and lays foundations for rebuilding institutional capacity over the long haul.

7. Three theoretical failures of elite diplomacy are defined. First, elite diplomacy ignores the lessons of Robert Putnam's conception of international politics as a two-level game. When strong elites are divided, weak
but unified domestic democratic forces across polities can combine with
peacemaking factions among the elites to win the peace. Second, elite
diplomacy is conceived in terms of rational choices of unitary states to the
neglect of diplomacy as a process of healing the emotions of divided peoples. Humiliation, shame, anger, and hatred are the key emotions restorative diplomacy must heal through diplomatic practices that are face-
saving, identity-restoring, reintegrative, participatory, and deliberative.
Third, elite diplomacy tends to rely on power imbalances to impose solutions. When those power imbalances shift over long periods of history,
unresolved historical resentments supply a political niche for divisive
leaders.

8. A crucial example of a practice that combines a response to these three
theoretical failures of elite diplomacy is working with domestic and international human rights NGOs at UN human rights institutions in alliance
with rights-respecting states to prevent war by healing the hurts of ethnic
groups whose rights have been abused and responsive regulation of the
active accomplishment of continuous improvement in human rights.

9. Given the grounding of late modern war in economic weakness and plunder by elites, of peace in integration into the world economy, the IMF and development banks have crucial roles to play. Their economic diplomacy has also been flawed in its elitism. Elitist IMF diplomacy has been as much a cause of war as a force for peace. Instead of dictating top-down conditionality with national elites, the IMF and development banks should sit in the circle, listen to the good governance and financial restructuring proposals that emerge bottom-up from the islands of civility in domestic polities, then back those of the reforms that will contribute to fiscal and monetary balance. By backing reforms that emerge with democratic support from a dialogue of national healing, banks back sustainable reforms and the forces for democracy more than the elites whose plunder may be the cause of the next war, the next economic collapse.

10. Regional restorative justice institutes might be funded to assist local peacemakers from the islands of civility in war-torn states to prepare restorative justice training manuals appropriate to local conditions, to train local trainers of healing circle facilitators, to advise peacemakers on options for exploiting the crisis of war to coordinate dialogues between elites and the people on how to build new democratic institutions.

11. The movement for an international criminal court risks repeating the mistakes of the post-Watergate attempts at domestic regulation of corporate crime—select trials of demonized individuals that exonerate the collective and that may jeopardize responsive regulation to protect the vulnerable. There is an important role for an international criminal court. It is not one of consistently and proportionately punishing violators of international law.

Expanding the Zone of Interdependence and Restorative Diplomacy

In international relations, I will argue that restorative traditions in the modern world are of increasing value to states and retributive traditions of declining value. Insufficiently retributive societies were often wiped out in the past by more violent cultures.[1] Punitiveness, however, has less survival value for communities that are more interdependent, a lesson North American states finally learned in their dealings with each other during the nineteenth century and European states in the twentieth. Most of the world continue to live in a zone of violence where major political disputes continue to be settled through force of arms. However, North America and Western Europe today constitute a zone of restorative diplomacy, into which the newly economically interdependent states of Asia and Central Europe are being integrated (cf. Goldgeir and McFaul 1992). Within this zone of restorative diplomacy, democracies do not go to war against one another (Burley 1992, pp. 394–95; Doyle 1983, 1986; Maoz and Abdolali 1989) or almost never do. Rather, disputes among the wealthy democratic states of the OECD are mostly settled through conciliation, mediation, conferences, and summits. They are dealt with through processes that approach Tony Marshall's definition of restorative justice (see Laue 1991) discussed in chapter 1, albeit through processes with huge imbalances of power.

One criticism of the theory of reintegrative shaming that we rejected in chapter 5 with respect to crime in the streets is that interdependence no longer exists in modern societies—that the interdependence and community needed to effectively mobilize disappoval of violence existed in premodern but not modern societies. With international crimes of violence, we can reject this critique even more forcefully. International relations theorists grant centrality to the observation that interdependence between nations has increased, especially with the globalization of markets before World War I and after World War II (Keohane and Nye 1987), and that complex interdependence is a resource for warding off war (Kaczynska-Nay 2000). The path Iraq has taken under Saddam Hussein, in cutting itself off from the economic interdependence that creates wealth and employment under modern conditions, is hardly in the interests of the people of Iraq. While totalitarianism allows this to happen, it would be quite an unsustainable policy in a state with genuinely democratic elections. Not only is complex interdependence greater today than it was between the world wars, but there is a more organized sense of international community than there was then. While the United Nations is a disappointment as a peacemaker and peacekeeper, it is less of a failure than the League of Nations and since 1989 has been active as never before in putting peacekeepers into the field. Former UN secretary-general Dag Hammarskjöld first conceived the idea of preventive diplomacy, which has been reinvented in a post–Cold War context by his successor, Boutros Boutros-Ghali's (1992) *An Agenda for Peace: Preventive Diplomacy, Peace-Making and Peace-Keeping.* The idea of preventive diplomacy is to prevent serious disputes from arising between and within states and to prevent such disputes that do arise from escalating into armed confrontation (see Box 6.1). While international community-building through preventive diplomacy has been more an aspiration than an accomplishment, the more profound sense of international community beginning to develop in the world today is in international civil society. This is a theme I wish to develop in this chapter.

MEDIATION OFTEN WORKS

Even in previous centuries, diplomacy has often worked in defusing conflicts that might lead to war. For example, the consummate diplomats of post-Napoleonic Europe such as Metternich and Castlereagh did much to create the conditions for the century of comparative peace up to World War I. Preventive diplomacy and mediation for peacemaking have a long history of both failure and success, enough success to teach us that there are few crafts more important to our survival. But diplomacy in the world of Metternich and Castlereagh was obviously a different practice than today. I will develop the argument that the key differences between the worlds of the nineteenth and twenty-first centuries imply that to be effective, diplomacy must adopt practices and values more akin to those of restorative justice. The most im-

Box 6.1: The South China Sea since 1990: A Regional Approach to Preventive Diplomacy

The problem: The Spratly and Paracel Islands in the South China Sea continue to be subject to disputed territorial claims involving access to resources and control over sea lanes. Most of the friction has been between China and Vietnam, although Taiwan, Malaysia, the Philippines and Brunei have their own territorial claims. The increasing military presence of some claimants has added to concern about the issue becoming a major regional flashpoint.

The response: Since January 1990, a series of "unofficial" workshops has been sponsored by Indonesia, a littoral non-claimant, and supported by ASEAN (with some resource assistance from Canada). Attended by officials from claimant states "in their private capacities," and academics and other experts, they promote an informal exchange of views, without putting claimants into any position which could prejudice their respective claims on sovereignty.

The process is an ongoing one, but the workshops have provided a framework for dialogue, the establishment of basic ground rules, the development of working relationships, and the exploration of options (including joint resource exploration zones) which might allow for joint economic gain if sovereignty issues can be resolved or, perhaps more likely, set aside.

The lessons:

The workshops represent an innovative attempt by an impartial neighbouring state to institute an informal preventative diplomacy process: by redefining the task as a search for options which are of mutual interest to the parties, the process promotes problem-solving and the beginning of a cooperative dialogue.

This kind of Second Track diplomacy provides an excellent basis for later official talks: such a process takes time, but both the process and the substance of such workshops can systematically build momentum towards a peaceful resolution.

Joint projects which come from working group proposals develop mutual goals and working relationships: this has been shown to be one of the best ways of reversing a competitive process.

The workshops provide a positive example of the kinds of thoughtfully-designed regional initiatives which could be undertaken more frequently by regional, sub-regional or unilateral actors.

Source: Reprinted from Gareth Evans, 1999, pp. 60–61

portant difference is that in a world of states without universal democratic suffrage, diplomacy was more a matter of doing deals among elites. How the masses or the media would react to the deals did not count in the way it does today.

Consider mediation in international relations. The most important and effective mediations in the nineteenth and twentieth centuries were not paragons of restorative justice practice. President Carter's Camp David mediation between President Sadat and Prime Minister Begin was his greatest accomplishment. But it failed badly to measure up to the ideals of restorative justice. The mediator had profound self-interests in the outcome and sought to use its greater power, its capacity to offer side payments, to forge an accord that delivered those interests. U.S. political leaders are the most common mediators in the big conflicts that confront the modern world— even big domestic ones as in Northern Ireland. When the mediator is a self-interested and assertive superpower, the empowerment ideal of restorative justice is bound to be at risk. The same point applies when a European Union diplomat mediates in the former Yugoslavia. In terms of restorative justice principles, Camp David also rates poorly because it excluded key stakeholders, though it must be borne in mind that as a historical package the United States went on to conduct other mediations where the Palestine Liberation Organization, Syria, and other stakeholders had a seat across the table from Israel. Restorative justice advocates need to be careful here not to draw a conclusion that throws out the baby with the diplomatic bathwater simply because so many of the most important mediations are not very restorative. We need more, not fewer, Camp Davids in world diplomacy, (see Box 6.2). However, in twenty-first-century conditions, we also need more than this kind of mediation between elites; we also need the democratized peacemaking that is restorative justice.

Box 6.2: Confidence-Building Border Agreements

The 1996 agreement between China and India on CBMs [confidence-building measures] builds on the 1993 agreement on the maintenance of peace and tranquillity along the existing Line of Actual Control (LAC). The CBMs agreement stipulates that neither side shall use its military capability against the other. Instead, they undertake to respect the LAC and seek a fair, reasonable and mutually acceptable settlement of the boundary question (Article II). Both countries agree to reduce military forces in the border areas to levels compatible with friendly and good neighbourly relations. Agreed ceilings are also set for military forces along the LAC. Major types of armaments are subject to ceilings (Article III). Large military exercises in close proximity to the LAC are to be avoided or subject to prior notice (Article IV). Other Articles provide for consultation and exchange of information between border authorities. Both countries also concluded a separate agreement on cooperation in combating drug trafficking and other crimes.

Source: Reprinted from Simon Tay, 1999, pp. 152–53

Touval and Zartman (1985, 1989) have coordinated the most systematic empirical examination of the effectiveness of twentieth-century mediation in international conflicts. It included the following eight case studies:

- Soviet mediation between India and Pakistan, 1966
- Algerian mediation between Iran and Iraq, 1975
- U.S. and British mediation in Rhodesia/Zimbabwe, 1976–79
- Western Five mediation in Namibia, from 1977
- Algerian mediation for the release of U.S. hostages in Iran, 1980–81
- Mediation by the Organization for African Unity
- Mediation by the Organization of American States
- Mediation by the International Committee of the Red Cross

In their analysis, Touval and Zartman (1989) assume that mediators, like the antagonists, are motivated by self-interest, an assumption not wildly at odds with the facts of most of these cases. It would certainly be hard to paint many of these mediators as motivated by restorative justice values. Even so, most of the mediations were found to succeed in reaching agreements that removed the antagonists from each other's throats and helped them to live peaceably together for a time: "Successful though they were, the mediations did not change the basic distrust between Iran and Iraq, the United States and Iran, some blacks and whites in Zimbabwe, Indians and Pakistanis, Moroccans and Algerians, Somalis and Ethiopians" (Touval and Zartman 1989, p. 135).

While we should not belittle the peacemaking accomplishments of these mediations, we might want to assert that the restorative justice peacemaking of Tutu and Mandela *has* changed basic distrust between blacks and whites in South Africa (and among warring black factions) has created the conditions of permanent rather than temporary peace among the armies operating in South Africa. While violence in South Africa is still at an extremely high level, it has stopped rising and now has started to fall, the homicide rate having decreased by 37 percent between 1994 and 2000 (www.saps.co.za/8_crimeinfo/bulletin/2000(4)). Elite mediations by self-interested practitioners of power politics can forge a realist temporary peace, but in late modern conditions they are unlikely to secure the permanent healing that engages the forgiveness of democratic peoples (see Box 6.3). The South African accomplishment seems to be about both healing and justice. Restorative injustice would not have accomplished it. Desmond Tutu made this point when he spoke in Israel in 1999:

> I was able to point out that we had learned in South Africa that true security would never be won through the barrel of a gun. True security would come when all the inhabitants of the Middle East, that region revered by so many, believed that their human rights and dignity were respected and upheld, when true justice prevailed. (Tutu 1999, p. 216)

The position of the United Women Association of Bosnia and Herzegovina, as outlined in Box 6.3, is perceptive according to the Tutu analysis: once the Dayton agree-

When the Dayton Peace Agreement was signed five years ago we had hoped that the following year would bring true peace and investments that had been promised to us, that the economy would recover together with communication lines, that the refugees would return home and that the mutual trust and contacts between people would be established again. None could predict that even with all the effort of the international community so little would have been achieved. The frictions among the three national communities in Bosnia and Herzegovina still exist. . . . There is mistrust and hatred, and the future is very uncertain. Refugees and displaced persons have not returned home, most of them have nowhere to go. The roads lead to nowhere, the economy is on its knees and the dark ideology rules the country. . . . The war has brought unbearable sediment of hatred. It brought disappointment to those who had always been against the war and against the split of the country but as well, it disappointed those who had hoped that in the war they would achieve their nationalistic goals. Currently in our country rule apathy, suspicion, despair, indignation, crime, corruption and amorality. The scale of social values is turned upside down and ordinary citizens do not know how to cope with the situation. The country is being suffocated by unbelievable political, economical, cultural and moral crisis. Besides all of the above-mentioned, there is a period of reconstruction ahead of us. Not only that our needs but as well the worlds of capital insist on the reconstruction. We, the women should not stay aside of the very important events. . . . It is our turn to work on the difficult tasks of the reestablishing of trust, economy, and cultural ties. In order to achieve our goal, the women of Bosnia and Herzegovina ought to be aware of their own social and political importance. . . . We do not support the cold peace that can suddenly break into a conflict. We support the true peace and cooperation. . . . I would like to conclude in the end that the people in Bosnia and Herzegovina have been traumatized through generations. Trauma passes from one generation to another. Three nations in Bosnia and Herzegovina leave their traumas in heritage to their own children, keeping their own points of view upon the matter. If we do not begin to talk openly about our traumas, we will not achieve permanent peace.

ment had been signed to stop the shooting, it should have been the turn of the women to take over from the soldiers, to enjoy the backing of those with the guns and the money to embark on the work of reconciliation on the ground among the people. Beyond South Africa, the civil war on Bougainville (concerning secession of this island from Papua New Guinea and fighting between different local factions) has been a testing ground for a restorative justice approach to peacemaking. The PEACE Foundation Melanesia, funded by Caritas, the New Zealand Overseas Development Agency, and the Princess Diana Fund, has given basic restorative justice training to 10,000 people on Bougainville, 500 as facilitators, including many traditional chiefs, and 50 to 70 as trainers (Howley 1999, 2000). Out of this, the PEACE Foundation Melanesia expects to have some 800 active village-based mediators to deal with the conflicts that have arisen in the aftermath of a civil war, from petty instances of ethnic abuse up to rape and political killings. The Bougainvillians are discovering their own ways of doing restorative justice consistent with their Melanesian principle of *wan bel* (literally "one belly") or reconciliation. Phillip Miller, an Australian volunteer who has done much of the training of peacemakers in the villages "is without doubt the best known and most popular expatriate in Bougainville" (PEACE Foundation 1999b, p. 1). Two indigenous district coordinators for the PEACE Foundation stood in the May 2000 elections and won.

Former PEACE Foundation director Brother Patrick Howley points out that civil war becomes an opportunity for old grievances between people that have nothing to do with the war to be acted out. Unless these conflicts are healed when the shooting stops, they may lie dormant, waiting to contribute to or escalate the next outbreak of hostilities. For example, men used the war to win old disputes over land by making allegations that their adversaries were spies, in an effort to have them killed so the land could be seized. Patrick Howley believes the most damaging new hatreds for long-term peace that must be healed are in the hearts of traumatized children who witnessed their parents being tortured in sadistic and degrading ways, sodomized by a rifle barrel, for example. These children need help to heal so they do not become the avengers that cause the next war. Remarkably, Howley reports that there were cases of the civil war being used to even scores from World War II, when some Bougainvillians helped the Japanese and others the Americans. In Bosnia such failures to heal after World War II atrocities are even more important to understanding the violence of the past decade (Shawcross 2000, p. 47).

Realist international relations theorists might look at a case like the Buin story in Box 6.4 "Now Buin Is Moving Again" and say this is not the stuff of war; this is the settling of an insignificant factional conflict. But perhaps this perception of what is an insignificant conflict juxtaposed against real structural conflicts between a reified Bougainville Revolutionary Army and a reified Papua New Guinean state which are attributed unitary interests is the problem with realist diplomacy that occurs in places like Dayton. This is Clifford Shearing's (1995, 1997, 2001) Hayekian critique of state planning to control violence discussed in chapter 5. The social engineers of statist diplomacy do not have enough local knowledge to understand what are the real conflicts. The conflicts on the ground are always more complex than their reifications,

Box 6.4: "Now Buin Is Moving Again"

In October 1998, Paul Bobby the BRA [Bougainville Revolutionary Army] Commander for Buin was shot dead in his village Kararu in Buin District. Since this incident the situation in Buin had been tense. The peace process not only halted but several ambushes and shoot-outs threatened to return Buin to the conditions of the crisis. In a wave of reprisals and counter reprisals, the ensuing 8 months saw armed clashes between the relatives, soldiers and supporters of Paul Bobby and the followers of Thomas Tarii (the other main BRA Commander in Buin). During this period the BRA splintered into factions and all efforts by the higher BRA commanders to resolve the conflict failed.

The conflict resulted in restrictions of movement especially on the Buin highway to Arawa and the strategic road to Kangu where ships are unloaded. Consequently there was a disruption to the delivery of services to the district. . . . Incidents of lawlessness increased especially in Buin town and a general feeling of fear and uncertainty prevailed. The conflict threatened to spread into neighbouring Siwai and Kieta districts as incidents spread . . . [I]t was generally acknowleded throughout the island that this conflict represented the gravest threat to the peace process. . . .

[A]s the number of incidents escalated, individuals and organisations from outside the BRA became more active in trying to begin the process of reconciliation. Enormous credit should be given to the various women's groups in Buin who initiated discreet dialogue between the factions. Their efforts gradually restored a sufficient level of trust between the factions to allow them to come together for the first time to try to resolve the conflict through discussions rather than violence. With the initiative of the Telei District Peace Committee Chairman (Steven Kopana) and with the support of the [UN-backed] International Peace Monitoring Group (PMG) based in Buin, Francis Kauman and Joe Nakota were requested to mediate in the reconciliation. These two experienced PEACE Foundation Conflict Resolution trainers were recognised both for their skills and neutrality as key people in the meeting.

The reconciliation took place at the "PMG Haus Garamut" (meeting house) in Buin High School on 21/5/99. The meeting started at 9.30 am and concluded at 4.30 pm and was witnessed by hundreds of people who had gathered from the east and the west . . . After moving speeches, tears and the shaking of hands, the reconciliation concluded with the signing of a Memorandum of Understanding by the eleven BRA Company and Platoon commanders involved in the conflict. The seven points agreed to in the Memorandum of Understanding (written in Tok Pisin) state clearly the common desired goal, i.e., "Bai yumi lusim pasin bilong fait na kirapim bek bel sis na trust namel long yumi yet" (We will reject violence and initiate again

(continued)

peace and trust between ourselves). The other points agreed are brief but poignant. Upon close examination they reflect a deep understanding of the root causes of the conflict and possible obstacles in implementing the agreement. This indicates that the Memorandum of Understanding was clearly agreed to after a great deal of honest and assiduous discussion. . . .

Whilst time will be the ultimate test of the Agreement, there is now a general feeling of relief that an encumbrance has been lifted from the people of Buin. Freedom of movement has been restored and the path has now been cleared for the establishment of a Buin Joint Police Force consisting of ex-BRA and resistance [pro-PNG] soldiers . . . In his closing speech at the reconciliation Col. Edgar (CO PMT Buin) remarked that had Francis and Joe not gained these skills there couldn't have been a reconciliation. In thanking Francis for his efforts, Linus Konukun, the newly elected Speaker of the recently established Bougainville Constituent Assembly, remarked "Now Buin is moving again."

Source: Reprinted from PEACE Foundation, 1999a

---

more rapidly changing than their intelligence reports from diplomats in air-conditioned offices of the capital can keep up with. Only Indigenous ordering, in this case in a schoolhouse in Buin, to define the cross-cutting conflicts in local terms will deal with the local drivers of a war. Equally, there may be geopolitical dimensions of the conflict that can only be understood in the language that is spoken in a meeting between major and minor state powers in the Office of the Secretary-General of the UN in New York. If they want to be effective in making peace, the big-men of Buin and of New York both must learn when to defer to the local knowledge of the other.

One of the demands of the Bougainville Interim Government and the Bougainville Revolutionary Army in its peace negotiations with the Papua New Guinea government has been for transformation of the new Bougainville justice system to one based on restorative justice.[2] The Australian and New Zealand military peacekeepers on Bougainville have played a complementary role here as well. Their commanders reward them not so much for military accomplishments, such as completing patrols, but for building relationships with the people through sporting and musical events (the band being a crucial part of the force) where good food and fellowship are provided.[3] This means a military presence that complements a restorative approach to peacekeeping, as illustrated by the role of the Peace Monitoring Group in Box 6.4. The peacekeepers are unarmed, a symbolism that seems to have impressed local warriors. It is the symbolism of a pyramid of restorative and responsive regulation: "Yes we are warriors who can call upon the firepower required to put down challenges to the peace. But we do not need it; we can do the job with good food, good music, good relationships and goodwill." Australian foreign minister Alexander Downer has reported how on visiting Bougainville he was moved by the reciprocal gestures of breaking of spears by warriors and spontaneous singing of women. This signifies the difference between realist elite diplomacy and idealist peacemaking with reconciliation that touches the hearts of ordinary men and women.

NEW AND OLD WARS

From the time of the rise of strong states in the Middle Ages until 1989, the way to understand war and how to prevent it was to grasp shifts in the balance of power among major states. From 1945 to 1989, the key thing to understand about the maintenance of peace between major states was the relationship of those states to the two superpowers. When war broke out in minor states—in Cuba, Korea, Vietnam, Angola, Vietnam, or Afghanistan—it had to be understood in terms of superpower rivalries in the periphery. Of course, there were many other schisms; it is not as if ancient divides such as that between Islam and Christendom had disappeared; it was just that it was clear which was by far the most consequential schism between 1945 and 1989 in shaping the outbreak of wars. This meant that to be effective, diplomacy had to engage superpower elites—telling diplomacy was something Kissinger and Gromyko did. Such men are no longer the principal architects of war and peace:

> Who are the architects of postmodern war, the paramilitaries, guerrillas, militias, and warlords who are tearing up the failed states of the 1990s? War used to be fought by soldiers; it is now fought by irregulars. This may be one reason why postmodern war is so savage, why war crimes and atrocities are now integral to the very prosecution of war. (Ignatieff 1999, pp. 5–6).

Contemporary wars, David Keen (1998) points out, are numerous (engaging fifty-one nations in internal armed conflict between 1994 and 1998)[4] and in many cases seem intractable, with hostilities resurfacing repeatedly after they seem to be resolved. States like Myanmar, Cambodia, El Salvador, and Mozambique have been at war with themselves over decades. The problem, according to Keen, is that in many of the most crippled states in the contemporary world, war is more an economic opportunity than a problem to the protagonists. Securing control of some weak states has less to offer than does pillage, collection of protection money (Mafia style), monopolizing trade of key commodities like oil through violence, forced labor, appropriating depopulated land and mineral resources, selling off the forests or the ivory, stealing foreign aid, or simply setting up roadblocks and making people pay "taxes" to be allowed through. Persistence of conflict can therefore in part be understood by armies on both sides having an interest in keeping the war going, at least at some points during complex shifts in alliances. Relations between warlords can be cordial in such circumstances of cooperative conflict. Keen's (1998, pp. 18–19) analysis can make sense of practices such as avoiding pitched battles (e.g., Liberia) and selling arms and ammunition to the other side (e.g., Cambodia, Chechyna, Sierra Leone, Sri Lanka). 1993 was the first year since the recording of conflicts when armed conflicts over autonomy or independence markedly outnumbered conflicts over the type of political system or government composition (Australian Department of Foreign Affairs and Trade 1999, p. 74). A related statistic is that between 1975 and 1995, un-regulated population movements—forced movement or movement across borders unsanctioned by governments—increased over 1,000 percent, most of them trans-border refugees, most of the rest internally displaced as a result of war or persecution (Dupont 1999, p. 162).

However collaborative warlords are, hatred and fear across the schisms of domi-nated populations are necessary to keep these wars going. Accomplished warlords have cruel skills in prizing apart the fissures in contemporary weak states. Part of my analysis of what is therefore needed in the contemporary world is grassroots peace-making skills for healing these fissures, so that power-hungry, money-hungry, rape-hungry warlords have less fear and division to work with. Late modern warlords need a situation where terrified citizens are saying "Who is to protect us now?" from the other, so that the warlord can say "I will protect you from them." Yugoslavia since Tito is an example of ethnic political-military elites filling a power vacuum in a dis-integrating state by offering protection from other ethnic groups, thereby furthering the disintegration of the state and driving other ethnicities into the arms of their own warlords.

Before pushing too far the late modern nature of the phenomenon, we must see that warlords of one sort or another dominated much of Europe for a millennium after the collapse of the Roman Empire. Consider how the predations of competing princes ravaged Europe during the Hundred Years' War (1338–1453). The great powers of late modernity all suffered considerable domination and fragmentation by warlords before they became great powers. This was the situation in Britain for most of the period from the collapse of Roman control to the end of the Wars of the Roses (1485). Japan was dominated by warring Samurai during the centuries prior to its becoming a fin de siècle major power. In the centuries between China's demise as the most powerful empire in the world and its reemergence as a major power in 1949, it was dominated by warlords. Even in the United States' brief history up to the decades after the Civil War, the period when it was a weak state, a variety of players who could loosely be described as warlords controlled large swathes of the continent, of-fering protection from competing groups—Santa Ana, Sam Houston, George Custer, Crazy Horse, Sitting Bull, Geronimo, Andrew Jackson (before he became president), Jefferson Davis, (Granville) Stuart's Stranglers in Montana and the Regulators in Wy-oming (Johnson 1998, p. 537), Wyatt Earp, various pirates in the Caribbean, even Allan Pinkerton in eastern cities had a murderous private army of sorts. While these are radically different kinds of armed protectors of people who were afraid of other armed groups, what they have in common is the offering of armed protection in spaces where the state was too weak to hold sway. Murderous and pillaging private militias, such as those of Andrew Jackson, were no longer a feature of American warfare once the U.S. state had become sufficiently strong to no longer need or want privateering.

Once these states became major powers, they regularly contested militarily the power of other major states until 1945. But the modern era when war was predomi-nantly an activity of the armies and navies of the strongest states was really only a phenomenon of half a millennium. In both the premodern and post-1989 eras, war was predominantly an activity of irregulars led by leaders I am loosely calling warlords more than by state commanders in chief. Such wars were predominantly intrastate rather than interstate:[5]

> The last forcible territorial acquisition of significance was China's incorporation of Tibet in 1951. Israeli control over the Occupied Territories has been recognised by no state, and is not claimed by Israel to be permanent. The forcible partition of Cyprus is recognized by no one other than Turkey. Indonesia's incorporation of East Timor in 1975 was never accepted by most countries. And Iraq's invasion of Kuwait was not merely repulsed by Kuwait's allies but condemned even by most states otherwise sympathetic to Iraq. (Donnelly 2000, p. 146).

Most major military powers became capitalist democracies. As wars became more expensive in lives and taxes, they became less electorally popular. From the nineteenth century, the Rothschilds, and *haute finance* generally, were advising major states that while their banks were happy to lend for wars in the periphery, wars with other major economies were bad for business (Polanyi 1957). This was a dramatic change in the posture of the dominant European banking families, who in previous centuries had made their fortunes by funding the wars of major states against one another. As democracy spread and integration into global markets deepened after World War II, the incentives for strong states to eschew war in favor of restorative diplomacy strengthened further.

At the same time, globalization increased the rewards of warlordship in weak states. Warlords establish linkages with organized criminal elements in wealthy states; they sell drugs into affluent markets out of the Golden Triangle, Afghanistan, Tadjikistan, Peru, or Colombia and through states like Nigeria (Braithwaite and Drahos 2000, chap. 15); they profit from global markets in arms, even perhaps in parts of the old Soviet empire from diversion of nuclear materials; they hold Western business executives or tourists hostage for ransom payments; they do dirty work for a fee for Western security agencies; they dump toxic wastes on the land of their people in return for large payments from Western business; they plunder foreign aid supplies; they hire their services as enforcers of Western intellectual property rights against pirate manufacturers in the periphery, while themselves replacing real and expensive medicines with valueless counterfeits. The drug situation in AIDS-ravaged nations says something of the ruthlessness of the criminal exploitation of the people of Africa that is occurring. Pharmaciens Sans Frontières estimates that 60 percent of Cameroon's national market in medical drugs is pirated products, sometimes just capsules filled with flour (Hibou 1999, p. 107). The Nigerian government distributed false vaccines during a 1995 meningitis epidemic in the guise of aid.

Hence, the globalization of markets simultaneously increases the costs of warfare to major states and increases the rewards of warlordship and state crime within weak states. Fred Halliday's (1999, p. 326) empirical findings on the particular kind of warfare called revolution mirror this conclusion, even if it is framed a little differently:

Revolutions have occurred in societies that have embarked on, but are at a comparatively early stage of, economic and political development; they express the pressures on traditional societies of international factors, the tensions within societies in transition, the drive for an accelerated development, competitive with other states. Revolutions have not occurred in traditional societies, nor in developed democratic ones.

To understand contemporary African wars, we need to see a process of the criminalization of the state in Africa, symbiotic relationships among official controllers of state and military power, international organized crime, and local warlords (Bayart, Ellis, and Hibou 1999). One of the reasons restorative justice notions developed in criminal justice systems are relevant to late modern wars is that war and state crime are part of the same phenomenon. They coexist in processes of using violence to acquire power for purposes of plunder. State-manufactured counterfeit captures the paradigm of this expanded criminal imagination. In 1994 a number of Lebanese companies were used by President Mobutu of Zaire to smuggle thirty tons of officially sanctioned counterfeit Zaire banknotes printed in Europe and Argentina, loaded into the security vehicles of the central bank, but without the central bank having control over the process. Some of the notes were used to pay soldiers. President arap Moi of Kenya also commissioned counterfeit banknotes that were never registered with the central bank to pay for his election campaign (Hibou 1999, p. 108). Kenya is one country known to have falsified its national accounts to the World Bank and IMF (in 1994) in order to keep international funds flowing—a necessary further criminal expedient for states that create unsustainable monetary imbalances through large-scale state counterfeit (Hibou 1999, p. 79). National accounts are in fact regularly falsified in structural adjustment negotiations to satisfy conditionalities that are known to be a lie by those who negotiate them, conditionalities that are intended only for public consumption so that there is an appearance that the rules of the Bretton Woods institutions are being met (Hibou 1999, p. 109). The problem is that the privatization of the productive sector mandated in structural adjustment packages is taken further to the privatization of sovereignty—sovereignty over central banks and monetary policy, privatization of the military, and privatization of the collection of tax by warlords. The criminalized state has the appearance of free elections, national accounts, a sovereign central bank, an army under constitutional authority, a publicly accountable tax system. But in fact these institutions have been sold to private interests to varying degrees. The army has been sold to the people who printed the money to pay them, or by the general-cum-warlord who organized them to stop cars and collect "taxes"; whether they are "regulars" or "irregulars" is moot.

Wars that have the objective of prolonging the plunder of wealth and women (more than victory over a military adversary for long-term control of a bankrupt state) result in a higher ratio of civilian to military casualties. At the turn of the century the ratio of military to civilian casualties in war was eight to one; for the wars of the 1990s, it was one to eight (Kaldor 1999, p. 8). The level of human rights abuse is so terrible because privatized sovereignty plunders by fomenting hatred of a dehumanized other that easily becomes a denial of all humanity. The following is from the Song of the Sudan People's Liberation Army (quoted in Bayart, Ellis, and Hibou 1999, p. 6).

> Even your mother, give her a bullet!
> Even your father, give him a bullet!
> Your gun is your food; your gun is your wife.

HEALING FOR THE PEOPLE

A paradox of democracy and tyranny is that aspiring tyrants harness hurts felt by the people to political support for retributive policies against out-groups. It follows that lasting peace and lasting democracy depend on preventing and healing those hurts. The nature of these democratic hurts shows why it is so important (as argued in chapter 1) for the social movement against restorative justice to have a value framework of educating people away from retribution and stigmatization. Hitler's tyranny is the best lesson on preventable democratic hurts. Versailles was a degradation ceremony intended to humiliate a defeated Germany in 1919 (Braithwaite 1991; Scheff 1994; Offer 1994). It continued a century-long vicious circle of humiliation: Napoleon humiliated Prussia with financial reparations that inflamed Prussian anger; Prussia humiliated the French with a heavy burden of reparations after defeating them in 1870 (Craig and George 1990, p. 74). The democratic citizens of the Weimar Republic felt the humiliation of Versailles deeply, a sentiment to which Hitler appealed. He referred to the Weimar Republic as "fourteen years of shame and disgrace!" (Scheff 1994, p. 131). Thomas Scheff (1994) has pointed out that every page of *Mein Kampf* bristles with humiliation and rage. Hitler constituted his tyranny by promising a regime to direct that rage against the deserving—Jews, communists, and the Allied powers.

The Allies learned lessons from Versailles. The Marshall Plan after World War II was a restorative approach to reintegrate Germany with respect into the international community—the finest moment of the American century. Even though Emperor Hirohito was a war criminal, the United States showed great wisdom to resist demands from allies such as Australia for his execution. Healing the symbolic relationship with the emperor was the first step to healing the relationship of the West to the democratic Japanese people. By the time of the Gulf War, the United States had forgotten that lesson again. It embarked on a way of dealing with Saddam Hussein that gave him a mandate to give a speech like the following a few days after the Desert Storm invasion:

> Rise up, so that the voice of right can be heard in the Arab nation. Rebel against all attempts to humiliate Mecca. Make it clear to your rulers, the emirs of oil, as they serve the foreigner; tell them the traitors there is no place for them on Arab soil after they have humiliated Arab honour and dignity. (Braithwaite 1991, p. 23)

Another tyrant consolidated through harnessing the shame of a humiliated people to keep democratic institutions out of the reach of that people. In the conditions of the twenty-first century, disrespectful, humiliating posturing in significant international disputes is communicated to ordinary people even when they do not live in democracies; they see their humiliation on CNN and the Internet. Hence, the democratization of communications, even without the democratization of politics, means that unless the hearts of a humiliated people are healed, they will constitute a niche waiting for the occupation of a political predator. Indeed, even where both the democratization of politics and the democratization of communications are limited, as in Rwanda,[6] retreat of the comparatively benign tyranny of colonialism means that there is no check on occupation of a niche made fertile for genocidal tyranny. If Belgian colonialism had been operative, it doubtless would not have tolerated the cycles of Hutu-Tutsi violence. Under the new rules of the game of a democratizing world where colonial gunboat diplomacy cannot sort things out, where the most murderous tyrannies whip up out-group hostilities among the masses, mediation among elites is not enough. Peacemaking must be democratized; it must heal whole peoples, preparing the soil of popular sentiment for peace and democracy rather than for demagogues who would despoil their freedom and plunder their prosperity. Of course one reason that such democratic peacemaking can work is that most peoples fundamentally want peace, prosperity, and freedom more than they want revenge. To consider what democratized peacemaking might mean in practice, the next section considers the contemporary predicament of the world's fourth-largest nation, Indonesia.

The Need for Restorative Peacemaking in Indonesia

The 1997–98 Asian economic crisis unleashed a variety of pent-up democratized sentiments across the Indonesian archipeligo. One was the desire for democracy itself, as realized in the toppling of the Soeharto military regime and the installation of democratic government for the first time. Another was the desire for self-determination in places like East Timor, Irian Jaya, and Aceh, where resentment with the tyranny of the military had been strongest for longest. And another was hatred for out-groups, for the Chinese minority who control a disproportionate share of the wealth, and for one religious group against another—especially between Muslims and Christians in places like Ambon. These hatreds saw burning of shops belonging to Chinese, of houses and cars belonging to Muslims, and rapes and shootings in Christian churches.

Today Indonesian democracy is at risk from aspiring tyrants who would benefit from whipping up these out-group hatreds. These individuals build local and national political support by promising to put the Chinese in their place, to purify government by creating an Islamic state, to establish order and stop rioting in the way only military rule can supply. Aspiring enemies of pluralist democracy all.

Indonesia ironically has been a lead practitioner of preventive diplomacy. It sponsored the innovative South China Sea preventive diplomacy of the 1990s (see Box

6.1) and facilitated the peace settlement between the Philippines government and the Moro National Liberation Front (Djalal 1999). As early as 1968 it led the preventive diplomacy to defuse the competing territorial claims over Sabah by the governments of Malaysia and the Philippines (Acharya 1999, pp. 35–36). Yet while Indonesia itself needs preventive diplomacy today, its predicament reveals the limitations of the preventive diplomacy of friendly foreign ministers to the crises of late modernity. At the national level there is a crisis of certain key institutions such as the banking system; in each Indonesian hot spot there are specific grievances that must be resolved by preventive diplomacy; but there is also a deeper crisis of the politics of identity, the politics of emotion—of honor and humiliation, of running amok (an expression originating in Indonesia). More than an eminent person is needed to persuade an angry populace that they are not justified in running riot. Just as a crisis of disorder can be a pretext for a military takeover, it can also motivate a process of truth and reconciliation concerning the hurts of East Timor or Aceh, concerning the plunder of such places by military officers or the more widespread effects of the corruption of the banking system by relatives and cronies of the ruling elite.

Indonesia is a nation with wonderful resources of intracultural restorative justice. Traditions of *musaywarah*—decision by friendly cooperation and deliberation—traverse the archipeligo. *Adat* law at the same time allows for diversity to the point of local criminal laws being written to complement universal national laws. What is lacking is experience with intercultural restorative justice on a scale needed to ward off the assault on democracy from the demagogues of interreligious and interethnic intolerance. Hence the preexisting intracultural restorative traditions must be harnessed to the new intercultural challenge. Importing Western models of mediation is not the answer; indeed, it could be seen, IMF-like, as more interference of a Western out-group that justifies a usurping of their "Western democracy" in favor of "Asian values," Islamic law, Indonesia for the true Indonesians, or something worse.

Yet the West can play a facilitating role for democratic restorative justice, as it has done in Bougainville, and indeed in South Africa, where Northern Hemisphere legal scholars trained in restorative justice practices played some useful fringe roles in the Truth and Reconciliation Commission. Regional restorative justice institutes can be repositories of R and D expertise. They can be knowledge brokers, generalists, or regionalists with broad research-based knowledge on how restorative justice initiatives have succeeded and failed in forging peace across the world. Dozens of leaders from across Indonesia, from all religious and cultural groups, could be funded to visit a regional restorative justice institute to assist with their development as peacemakers, to learn about the successes and failures of different peacemaking strategies that have been applied in other lands, then to talk and talk and talk with one another about how to combine these lessons with the wisdom of their various indigenous restorative justice traditions to forge a set of intercultural peacemaking strategies appropriate to Indonesian cultural divides.[7] Then those individuals would be equipped to train trainers of peacemakers across Indonesia. With help from such a regional center, they would develop their own peacemaker training manuals that they could use at home. If 10,000 had to be trained in little Bougainville, then perhaps a million peacemakers are needed for vast Indonesia. For each little conflict that breaks out between Muslims and Christians, perhaps two trained restorative justice facilitators would be needed—a Muslim and a Christian elder. The peacemakers not only might decide among themselves how to restore a sense of justice after specific outbreaks of violence or crime but also would convene meetings first within and later between cultural groups to discuss how to build trust locally. A small start has been made by Duane Ruth-Heffelbower and his colleagues in Empowering for Reconciliation who have trained a thousand locals at Indonesian hot spots, restorative justice work that is being joined by Catholic Relief Services, UNICEF, and World Vision.

Peacemaking among elites will not be enough to secure democracy in Indonesia. Peacemaking is needed on the ground, among the ordinary people, in local languages and with local courtesies that connote the respect that tackles feelings of humiliation, anger, hurt, unacknowledged shame, and distrust. Outside peacemakers cannot deliver this. But if local leaders manage to achieve this healing with the democratic participation of all locals who feel grievances acutely enough to bother engaging with the reconciliation dialogue, then aspiring tyrants and outside agitators will find that there are fewer local flames of hatred to fan. In the Indonesian context, as in Rwanda, outside agitators may be important to the destabilization of peace. According to many reports, some among the marauding mobs who executed the Muslim-versus-Christian violence on Lombok in January 2000 were actually imported from Java and other parts of Indonesia in the employ of forces unknown (*Weekend Australian*, 22–23 January 2000, p. 11). Timely restorative justice dialogue by locals on the ground is well designed to cope with this kind of destabilizing tactic. If only local Muslims and Christians can meet and hear each other denounce the violence, can hear Christians tell stories of Muslims who spent the night helping Christians defend their houses from the mob (as they did on Lombok), can come up with plans for sounding of alarms and mutual help should future outbreaks occur. Where there are locals who have joined the mob, local justice can be done, compensation paid, apologies offered, the road to forgiveness and healing opened.

REASONS FOR COMPLEMENTING ELITE MEDIATION WITH DEMOCRATIZED RESTORATIVE JUSTICE

We are now in a position to summarize the circumstances of the twenty-first century that limits the effectiveness of the elite preventive diplomacy and peacemaking of which the likes of Metternich and Castlereagh were such expert practitioners in the nineteenth century:

1. Gunboat diplomacy and other paternalist moves by colonial powers to prevent local demagogues from whipping up genocidal hatreds are less of an option in a postcolonial world.
2. Political elites cannot take for granted the subservience of the masses in a world where slavery and servitude are less common and where trade unions and other NGOs that can call on global support have capacities to undermine subservience.

3. Democratic citizenries who have been humiliated by an out-group, who are suffering unacknowledged shame, are peculiarly vulnerable to hate-mongering tyrants who would destroy democracy.

4. Humiliation of elites at degradation ceremonies like Versailles cannot be politically contained as shame suffered only by elites when citizenries have access to the mass media and the Internet.

5. "Glocalization" means that associated with the centripetal forces of glob-alization are centrifugal forces of localization or political fragmentation that we see in Eastern Europe and even with devolution in Scotland, Northern Ireland, and Wales. Why should the Slovak Republic not go it alone when it no longer need rely on Czech strength for national defense against hostile invaders, when it can rely on collective security in Europe that has been negotiated globally? Glocalization implies that many future wars will be wars of breakup as in Yugoslavia, where violence is fanned from local in-terethnic tensions.

6. Aspiring tyrants in today's world are learning that one way for them to seize power is to fan centripetal intercultural hatreds, to exploit the demise of the gunboats of the Soviet or British empire, to harness the spreading democratic ethos among the masses for the destruction of democracy, to propagate na-tional or subnational humiliations by writing visual *Mein Kampf*s for televi-sion and the Internet.

If these are the emerging twenty-first-century realities of armed conflict, then diplomatic elites will not be able to sort them out simply by meeting at Dayton or Camp David. They will have to engage mass publics with healing as well. In addition to democratized restorative justice, there are also implications for the elite peace-making that remains so necessary to responsive regulation for peace. It remains vital for elite diplomacy to be conducted behind closed doors precisely because the last thing one wants is for the slights, the loss of face, that inevitable occasional blowup to become publicly known in a way that might inflame mass anger. Yet it is also vital once the realist diplomats have done their deals and made their accommodations that the realist deals be translated into the idealist language of peace and justice. In par-ticular, it is important for the leaders on each side to go on television lauding the other side as just and as peacemakers. Especially where there has been humiliation in realist terms, it is most crucial that this is translated into idealism, decency, and generosity in the cause of peace and justice. A degree of hypocritical idealism is necessary to a world without the shame that fuels warfare.[8]

SAVING FACE IN DECISIONS TO GO TO WAR AND DECISIONS TO BACK DOWN

Even in superpower contests, the importance of the politics of identity and the politics of humiliation cannot be overestimated. This is not a new observation: the first law of the Concert of Europe that secured a century of major power peace was, after all,

"Thou shalt not challenge or seek to humiliate another great power" (Richardson 1994, p. 104). This section argues that diplomacy must be based on richly plural deliberation that is attentive to detecting humiliations that might be in play so that opportunities to allow the other to save face are not missed. In Graham Allison's (1971) classic study of the Cuban missile crisis of 1962, he concluded that to have a well-rounded understanding of what happened, it was necessary to look at the crisis through three different lenses. One was a rational actor model. The U.S. state was pursuing its interest as a unitary national actor in preventing World War III. The second was an organizational process model. Actors could be understood as followers of standard operating procedures. For example, when Secretary of Defense McNamara challenged Admiral Anderson, chief of naval operations, on the need for U.S. ships to be politically sensitive in how they managed the naval blockade of Cuba, particularly by avoiding the humiliation of the Russians, there was an angry exchange in which Anderson picked up the *Manual of Naval Regulations* and said, "It's all in there." The third model was a bureaucratic politics model. As a political player, the navy sought to exploit the crisis to show that its "Hunter-Killer" anti-submarine program, which was out of favor on Capitol Hill, was effective. But playing cat and mouse with Russian submarines to prove this point was hardly in the unitary interests of the United States as a rational actor on the brink of nuclear war.

Allison is persuasive in showing that to understand the most dire crisis the world has faced, we need to look at it simultaneously in these three different ways. Looking at it through one lens misleads the eye; using two lenses enables the brain to forge a more holistic stereoscopic vision, and three lenses an even more holistic perception. Ting-Toomey and Cole (1990) have suggested a fourth lens, a face-negotiation model. Robert Kennedy, a key player, wrote in *Thirteen Days: A Memoir of the Cuban Missile Crisis:*

> Neither side wanted war over Cuba, we agreed, but it was possible that either side could take a step that—for reasons of "security" or "pride" or "face"—would require a response by the other side, which, in turn, for the same reasons of security, pride, or face, would bring about a counterresponse and eventually an escalation into armed conflict. (Kennedy 1969, p. 62)

Concomitantly, in his reminiscences, Krushchev says his worry during the crisis was "the maintenance of Soviet prestige . . . the thought kept hammering away at my brain: what will happen if we lose Cuba? . . . It would gravely diminish our stature . . ." (Krushchev 1970, p. 493). Ting-Toomey and Cole (1990, p. 92) quote both President Kennedy and the Soviet leader as having greater respect for one another because each understood the need for the other to escape from the crisis with his face and pride intact.[9] They allowed each other to back down without being seen to be forced into a humiliating retreat. Face-negotiation was utterly tangible in the Cuban missile crisis. More universal are intangible questions of shame management:

> Among the most troublesome kinds of problems that arise in negotiation are the intangible issues related to loss of face. In some instances, protecting against loss of

> face becomes so central an issue that it swamps the importance of the tangible issues at stake and generates intense conflicts that can impede progress toward agreement and increase substantially the costs of conflict resolution. (Brown 1977, p. 275)

The experimental psychological literature on mediation shows that mediator tactics of drawing out proposals that help negotiators beat a graceful retreat are associated with successful agreement (Kressel, Pruitt, and associates 1989, p. 418).

When diplomatic negotiators are perceived as unjustly demanding, unreasonably resistant in making concessions, or punitive, this can be seen as insulting insensitivity to our honor or, worse, as a deliberate attempt to humiliate. Even emotionally healthy people have their moments when the shame that thereby arises is unacknowledged and transformed into externalized anger (Ahmed 2001). Emotionally healthy national leaders quite often transform shame into anger against out-groups. In a serious enough crisis, such as in the Cuban missile crisis, we hope that, like Kennedy and Krushchev, they will acknowledge their fear of shame so that they both prevent their own unacknowledged shame–rage spirals (Scheff 1994) and help with face-work that protects their adversary from needlessly provocative humiliation. Thomas Scheff (1994) shows, however, that the emotional makeup of Hitler and other leading Nazis was quite unlike that I just described with Kennedy and Krushchev. Hitler was unable to acknowledge shame, and he carried a lot of it with him. Perceived insults quickly spiraled into unacknowledged shame, rage, and then more unacknowledged shame about the rage and what the rage led to. At the micro level, as discussed in chapter 4, Eliza Ahmed's work has shown that unacknowledged shame is a powerful predictor of bullying (Ahmed 2001). Reports of the behavior of political leaders suggest that they are far from immune to this psychodynamic (Scheff 1994).

Harris's (2001) work shows that restorative justice processes are a good strategy for eliciting the acknowledgment of shame. The bigger the crisis of war, the more shame there is to be acknowledged. We need processes of deliberation that help leaders maintain the emotional health to acknowledge shame—to be as explicit in acknowledging the potential shame of being responsible for the destruction of humanity as President Kennedy when he began one of his reflections on the Cuban crisis: "If anybody is around to write after this . . ." (Kennedy 1969, p. 127). When Robert Kennedy wrote his seven lessons from the crisis, he was not thinking of shame management. However, one of the benefits of applying his lessons is that the proposed dialogue makes it harder for the leader to fail to acknowledge the shame he feels. Kennedy's lessons are as follows:

1. Take time to plan; don't go with your first impulse;
2. the President should be exposed to a variety of opinions;
3. depend heavily on those with solid knowledge of the Soviet Union;
4. retain civilian control and beware of the limited outlook of the military;
5. pay close attention to world opinion;
6. don't humiliate your opponent;
7. beware of inadvertence. (Kennedy 1969)

These are also prescriptions for restorative justice processes. Restorative justice must be designed to be planful, plural, solicitous of expert advice, democratized, on guard against humiliation, and attentive to inadvertance. Indeed, restorative justice adds a crucial ingredient missing from Kennedy's list—high-quality listening to and dialogue with the adversary and other stakeholders. The assertion that restorative justice processes conduce to the acknowledgment of shame and that shame acknowledgment reduces violence against out-groups is not totally speculative. The empirical work of the ANU Centre for Restorative Justice shows that this can be the case in microcontexts (Ahmed et al. 2001).

Richly plural problem-focused deliberation (the Kennedy policy circle), as opposed to narrow in-group punitive deliberation (the Hitler policy circle), is also likely to acquire better understanding in terms of Allison's original three lenses. The plural problem-focused deliberation of restorative justice is well equipped to draw out the rational calculations of stakeholders, a critical stance on the standard operating procedures they are following, and an appreciation of the games of bureaucratic politics they are playing (in addition to the games of shame and pride management they play). The holism of restorative justice, as developed in chapter 8 (Zehr 1990), gives it great potential for integrating the four views through Allison's (1971) three lenses and Ting-Toomey and Cole's (1990) face-negotiation lens into a holistic quadrascopic perception of a conflict.

GLOBAL CIVIL SOCIETY AND THE SHAMING OF VIOLENCE

One of the classic studies of international relations was of the Bonn economic summit of 1978 by Robert Putnam and his colleagues. This summit secured agreement on crucial elements of the Tokyo Round of the General Agreement on Tariffs and Trade (substantial tariff reductions and a subsidies and countervailing duties code), particularly from a reluctant France, pump-priming commitments by the trade surplus states of Germany and Japan, and oil price deregulation by the United States (Putnam and Bayne 1987; Putnam 1988; Putnam and Henning 1989). According to the Putnam analysis, the summit accord was only possible because *all* key states were internally divided. Influential *minority* factions within the economic policy communities of the key states forged a winning global coalition of minority factions. A coalition of President Carter's international and economic advisers favored oil price decontrol, but this was opposed by the president's domestic policy advisers and a strong majority in Congress. German pump priming was favored by only a small minority of officials in the Economics Ministry and the Chancellery, leaders of labor unions, and the left wing of the Social Democrats but was opposed by the Free Democrats, the Bundesbank, most of the business and banking community, and most economic officials in the government. Expansionism by Japan was supported by a coalition of business interests and Liberal Democrat Party politicians of modest power, but implacably opposed by the Ministry of Finance, the most powerful actor in Japanese government. In each key state, "advocates of the internationally desired policy acted (in the words of one of the Americans) as a kind of benevolent 'conspiracy,' and in each case they signalled to their foreign counterparts that additional international pressure would be welcome" (Putnam and Henning 1989, p. 107). Other empirical research suggests that at least half the time during international crises, top national decision makers are not unified (Snyder and Diesing 1977).

Putnam's (1988) theoretical conclusion from the successful Bonn Summit is that the politics of global negotiation is best viewed as a two-level game: a game of domestic interest group politics and another of international deal making to avert threats to national interests.

> Each national political leader appears at both game boards. Across the international table sit his foreign counterparts, and at his elbows sit diplomats and other international advisors. Around the domestic table behind him sit party and parliamentary figures, spokespersons for domestic agencies, representatives of key interest groups, and the leader's own political advisors. The unusual complexity of this two-level game is that moves that are rational for a player at one board (such as raising energy prices, conceding territory or limiting auto imports) may be impolitic for that same player at the other board. . . . On occasion, however, clever players will spot a move on one board that will trigger realignments on other boards, enabling them to achieve otherwise unattainable objectives. This "two-table" metaphor captures the dynamics of the 1978 negotiations better than any model based on unitary national actors. (Putnam 1988, p. 434)

In the two-level game of global strategic decision making, the peace movement and other antiviolence constituencies in civil society are weak players. However, as in the Bonn summit, it is often possible for these players to prevail because, weak as they are, they have a more unified value position (a pro-peace position) across states than the big players of geopolitics. If the majority factions of the most powerful states have conflicting positions—some pro-war, some antiwar—whereas the social movement players are unified in an antiwar position across all states, then the unified weak players can combine with some of the strong players who agree with them to win the day. Unified subordinate actors defeat divided dominant actors. We see the same political possibility with the debacle of the Seattle WTO meeting's failure to launch a Millennium round of the GATT in November 1999 and the collapse of the Multilateral Agreement on Investment a year earlier. The NGOs were weak but reasonably unified in their agenda; the major states were strong but hopelessly divided.

In the modern world we should not underestimate the capacity of international civil society to mobilize shame against warmongering. As the Vietnam war illustrates, in the two-level game of international relations, even the world's greatest commander in chief can have his prestige at international negotiating tables crippled (indeed, can lose office) at the behest of weak players who unify to shame a warmongering leader domestically.

If we are required to shame some military adventurism of a U.S. President, only in extremis (Vietnam) will this have an effect by driving him from office. Our immediate target with a President Clinton is Chelsea and the rest of his extended family,

his secretary, his golfing buddy—the same targets as in a restorative justice conference. The difference is one of technique more than substance. The need for it arises
from certain realities of political and economic power. Presidents hire public relations
professionals to render them invulnerable to shame. Their worst political enemies
will regard their conduct as shameful no matter what they do. But the opinions of
enemies are not at issue here. Chelsea's is. Most of the time, Chelsea is going to buy
the cover story manufactured by the president's spin doctors and give her dad the
benefit of the doubt. Most of the cut and thrust of politics will deliver very little shame
from people whose respect the president deeply cares about.

Public but respectful shaming is the best we can do with presidents. It mostly will
not work because politicians, like hardened criminals, are professionals at erecting
shields to protect themselves from shame. When it does work, my hypothesis is that
it works mostly through placing a story of human dimensions on the media that
touches the heart of a Chelsea Clinton, that causes someone like her to say, "Dad,
you must pay attention to this story." Again the psychological principles are the same
as with the juvenile offender's conference. The nun's simple television narrative of
the suffering she saw as a result of the bombing has infinitely more power than saying
"Shame on you" for causing this crime.

The history of wartime secrecy shows that under the special kind of darkness of
its cloak extraordinary evil lurks. Schemes too nefarious to be conceived in peace
can be countenanced under the cover of a war footing. Truth and reconciliation commissions following armed conflicts (as opposed to war crimes trials to administer victors' justice to scapegoats) are well equipped to disinfect these practices with sunlight:
the South African Truth and Reconciliation Commission, for example, revealed some
especially nefarious practices of scientists, doctors, and universities:

> Scientific experiments were being carried out with a view to causing disease and
> undermining the health of communities. Cholera, botulism, anthrax, chemical poi-
> soning and the production of huge supplies of Mandrax, Ecstasy and other drugs of
> abuse (allegedly for crowd control) were some of the projects of this programme.
> (Tutu 1999, p. 143)

And then, of course, there was the now abandoned secret nuclear weapons program in South Africa. Truth and reconciliation policies are important to constituting
the shamefulness of war because they reveal to the people the horrors perpetrated
on both sides, and they bring to light the extremes to which protagonists might have
been willing to go (like biological weapons) had they been pushed into a desperate
enough situation. Truth through justice is the ally of peace because the full ugliness
of war does not withstand democratic scrutiny. A future prospect of revelatory truth
will therefore cause leaders to ponder whether the shame of bringing on the war can
be withstood.

Most fundamentally, however, as my colleagues and I have argued elsewhere (Ahmed et al. 2001), the most important implication of the theory of reintegrative shaming is active social movement politics that constitutes the shamefulness of crimes

against humanity and the environment—a social movement against slavery to shame slavery, a labor movement to shame occupational health and safety crimes, a women's movement to shame rape, an environmental movement to shame environmental crimes, a peace movement to shame the violence of war. Domestic politics matters. Just as the domestic politics of ethnic division is a primary tool of warlords, the domestic politics of unity in support for peace is the most elemental resource of peacemakers. Elite peacemaking diplomacy that neglects grassroots democratic politics hands the political advantage to warlords who can be counted on not to neglect populist sentiment.

Responsive International Peacemaking

This chapter has made the case that fully democratized restorative justice has a more important role to play in building peace in today's world compared with the past. This is not to say that nonrestorative forms of diplomacy that do deals among elites without any concern for justice are not also capable of important peacemaking accomplishments. Indeed, the empirical evidence suggests that since World War II power-based elite mediations dominated by major powers have often secured at least temporary peace, though not enduring peace. I have argued that the peace is usually not enduring because unresolved resentments fester in civil society. This is particularly likely because elite mediation usually involves a mediator who acts for a major power. The greater the power imbalances, the more difficult and intractable the conflict, the greater the temptation to resort to an imposed solution. Indeed, power considerations drive most conflicts, and when power disparity is great, the usual result is unilateral imposition of a solution (Laue 1991, p. 326). Those who are imposed upon tend to resent this. If the resentment is deep enough, they will pass it on to their children and into their history books. Over time, power imbalances that led to the imposition tend to shift. When they do, there is an opportunity for an emerging politician to build support by claiming that he is the leader the people have been waiting for to right this historic wrong. The objective of restorative diplomacy is to eliminate such political niches. It is to maximize prospects of a peace settlement that protagonists might not accept as ideal, but that they will accept rather than resent. While we must come to terms with the fact that realities of power cannot be eliminated from the resolution of armed conflict, there are two things we can do to prevent power imbalance from imposing resented solutions. First, we can have a preference for restorative justice in an undominated circle of deliberation as a strategy that we try and try again before resorting to power assertion to secure peace. Second, we work to keep escalation to power assertion as something that is threatening in the background rather than something that is threatened in the foreground. Even if the reality is that the protagonists sit in a circle to restore peace because a major power with the capacity to intervene has summoned them to the circle, threat must be kept out of the circle until all efforts at undominated resolution have failed and utterly failed again.

The theory of restorative and responsive regulation means that our first preference is peacemaking by restorative justice; when that fails and fails again, we should be willing to allow major powers to use their clout as mediators to engage in dominated peacemaking among elites (if necessary by dangling the carrots and sticks that are available only to major powers) (See Fig. 6.1) If that fails, the next step might be an ominous resolution at the General Assembly or Security Council of the United Nations calling upon the cessation of aggression. If that were not heeded, there might be escalation to selective economic sanctions by UN members and then to more comprehensive sanctions. The ultimate escalation would be to UN-approved preventive deployment or military action to deter the aggressor, starting with limited strategic air strikes at military targets where there is near-zero risk to civilians and ultimately the deployment of ground forces.

The theory of the enforcement pyramid is that the clear signaling of willingness to escalate international intervention should lesser interventions fail will motivate the parties to make restorative justice work at the base of the pyramid. Our policy objective, according to this model, is to strive to broaden the base of the pyramid by having a higher and higher proportion of international disputes dealt with by negotiation at the base of the pyramid. It is not the unrealistic objective of having all of the action occur at the restorative base. The paradox of pacifism is that if we lop the top off the enforcement pyramid, if we are left to negotiate from a position of weak-

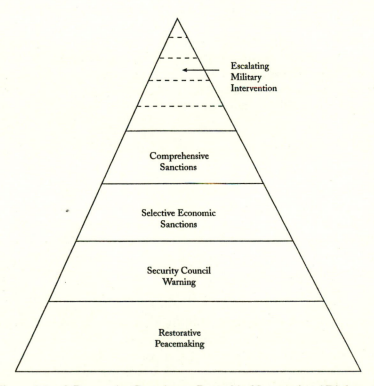

Figure 6.1   A Responsive Regulatory Pyramid of International Diplomacy

ness, then we actually have less capacity to channel dispute settlement into the diplomatic arena at the base of the pyramid. Lop the top off the enforcement pyramid, and we leave the world exposed to the predations of twenty-first-century Hitlers, a world where justice will always succumb to appeasement.

When there is escalation to dominated mediation in which a major power bangs the parties' heads together and the prospect of escalation beyond this is displayed, we create conditions for de-escalation of disputing to democratized restorative justice. Cooperative peacemaking should normally be rewarded by de-escalation down the pyramid. Power-based mediation can sometimes create a temporary peace that opens an opportunity for a restorative justice process to struggle for an enduring peace based on justice, healing, and an ongoing commitment to preventive diplomacy. Arguably the foreign troops of the Peace Monitoring Group in Bougainville have done just that—they created pacified spaces so the Bougainvillian factions could meet and discover for themselves the terms of their reconciliation.

Speaking softly while being able to call upon a big stick that is democratically sanctioned is the greatest hope for maximally peaceful international disputing. A UN that carries a big stick or that is capable of voting to call on others to wave a stick for it is thereby able to speak more softly, with assurance that the injustice of an invasion of a peaceable people simply will not be allowed to stand. As with state justice, so with international justice in the theory of restorative and responsive regulation—the capacity for deterrent escalation motivates restorative problem solving and self-regulation. Violence that is illegal by the standards of international law must be seen as a slippery slope that will inevitably lead to confrontation by the international community. The aspiration is for the international community to have an image of invincibility in confronting violent tyranny. The trick is for escalation to be threatening in the background but not threatened in the foreground—military peacekeepers on Bougainville armed with trombones rather than rifles.[10]

THE LIMITS OF RESTORATIVE AND MARKET VALUES

Prior to 1989, the first ports of call in an attempt to understand prospects for peace were Washington and Moscow. Perhaps today the two constituencies whose analysis we would look to first would be the players on the opposite sides of the barricades at the 1999 Seattle WTO meeting. On one side were the protesting NGOs, on the other the delegates—trade bureaucrats, WTO, World Bank, and IMF officials, technocrats committed to a freer world trading system. Both sides have an analysis of how to create a peaceful world that is right in general yet repeatedly wrong in its particular application.

The missionaries of free trade believe that the best guarantee of peace for developing countries is for them to cease being weak states by fixing their fiscal and monetary imbalances, attracting foreign investment, and increasing interdependence with other states through free and expanded trade, thereby reducing poverty. This does seem right in general because we have seen that national strength through deep integration into the global economy does seem to be a characteristic of nations

that are immune to major wars in contemporary conditions. They are the characteristics of states that are granted legitimacy by their people.[11]

International NGOs tend to see social injustice, poverty, and disrespect for human
rights as causes of war. I have already expressed general agreement with this analysis
in quoting Desmond Tutu's appeal to the nations of the Middle East that the way to
secure lasting peace in the region is to convince people on all sides that their human
rights and dignity are respected and that social justice is being built in the region.
Young men are more likely to join the private armies of warlords for low pay when
there is no remunerative work for them in the legitimate economy.

While the free traders' top-down analysis of global markets and peace is basically
right and the NGOs' bottom-up analysis of social justice, democracy, and peace is also
basically right, in particular contexts the top-down analysis can be too forgetful of
bottom-up realities, and vice versa. Hence, while it may be that fiscal balancing to
reduce the accumulation of debt is absolutely necessary for long-run strengthening
of a weak economy, in the short run a structural adjustment package that cuts funds
to schools and hospitals in a volatile part of the nation may fuel such bottom-up resentment that the state disintegrates into war. The IMF structural adjustment package hands the political agenda to antidemocratic and militaristic forces for ethnic division. If fully implemented, the IMF structural adjustment package for Indonesia
following the 1997 Asian crisis is an example of one that almost certainly would have
so weakened the Indonesian state as to invite pillage by the forces of armed retribution against the religious/ethnic other.[12] Another necessary structural adjustment
was the privatization of Russian state industry. In practice, however, the hasty, corrupt
privatization into the hands of the old nomenclatura and the Russian Mafia fueled
enormously destabilizing bottom-up resentment at the replacement of one monopoly,
one tyranny, with another that left the people poorer. Similarly in Africa we have
seen discount privatizations into the hands of criminal cronies of ruling elites.

Obversely, bottom-up peacemaking with a social justice package that transforms
an angry populace into a harmonious one may be Pyrrhic if top-down forces have
every reason to continue with war. It is not so hard for an angry warlord to orchestrate
an atrocity by one group against another that shatters a new harmony. Elite diplomacy,
pressure from major powers, threats to the foreign bank accounts of warlords, may be
necessary to get them to commit to the peace. "Outside intervention must therefore
fashion a peace that is more attractive than war for the majority of those involved . . .
if economic and social problems are not tackled, bottom-up violence will remain a
strong possibility; but addressing these tensions may prompt top-down violence in the
form of a backlash by endangered elites" (Keen 1998, pp. 57, 70). Realistic economic
alternatives to violence must be enabled for those at both the top and the bottom of
the war-torn society.

In ending war, there can be no purity of commitment to restorative values like
social justice. Nelson Mandela was neither a purist nor a pacifist; he waged a pragmatic struggle for maximally feasible social justice. He believed it was necessary to
be willing to escalate reluctantly to armed struggle against an implacable apartheid.
He believed there could be no peace unless whites felt secure that they could keep

most of their wealth. So he promised them that security; indeed, he promised a return to an internationally respectable South Africa that would attract more investment for wealth creation. Here his philosophy was diametrically opposed to the "one [white] settler, one bullet" philosophy of the Pan-African Congress. A South Africa where most of the wealth of the white invaders was immediately transferred to black Africans would be a more just South Africa, but not one of enduring peace.

HOLISTIC RESTORATION OF SOCIETIES

Giving both elites and the poor a peace in which they are all better off is not such an impossible task when one takes account of the economic costs of late modern war. During the war in Bosnia-Herzegovina, GDP per capita declined from U.S.$2,719 to $250. If a war goes on for long enough, the wealth left to plunder becomes slim. There is a lot of scope for giving up the pillage of 10 percent of a society's normal GDP if negotiators have in prospect the restoration of 90 percent of that GDP through peace. Rational neighboring states also have an interest in helping, not just so they can get refugees off their hands. The GDPs of Serbia/Montenegro, Croatia, and Macedonia fell between 35 and 51 percent during the Bosnian war; those of Albania, Bulgaria, Romania, and Slovenia fell between 10 and 27 percent. Restoring peace can restore a lot of wealth in a circle of nations that suffer negative growth as a result of a war that cuts their trade.

Moreover, much plunder is unsustainable. Printing money, falsifying the national accounts, and borrowing as if the printed money were real wealth is not sustainable. When all the forests are sold, they are beyond renewal. The most vivid story of unsustainable plunder during war in Africa is pouring pesticide into rivers, hauling in the dead fish that float to the surface, and selling them—hardly a path to a sustainable fishing livelihood (Hibou 1999, p. 108).

A restorative justice process is needed to persuade all elements of the society that a combination of predation and ethnic hatred is not the basis for a sustainable future for anyone, not even for the predators. Respect between ethnic groups can be rebuilt in time to the point where wealth-building trade among them can be restored. Once some wealth is restored, people can be persuaded to pay their share of tax on it if it is explained that this is necessary to pay an army that will refrain from extorting private taxes from the people, an army that will disarm pillaging private warlords. A sustainable tax administration that is granted a minimum of legitimacy by the people is absolutely essential to persistent peace because it guarantees the rudiments of social justice to the people—schools, health care, food, clean water, law and order. The crisis of war can be seen as the opportunity to build the legitimacy of fair taxation for a permanent peace.

The trouble with elite diplomacy is that it does not engage civil society with such essentials. UN or U.S. negotiators standardly treat the warring armies as if they are little states at war with each other—representatives of their ethnic group—instead of predators at war with the people. A cease-fire between the armies is a major accomplishment. But unless the peace process addresses the reasons these armies go to war against their people, there are high risks that later they will resume doing so.

If the new identity politics the warlords exploit grew out of the collapse of the legitimacy of postcolonial or postcommunist states, then the peace process must diagnose with the key stakeholders in civil society the reasons for that disintegration issue by issue. If one issue is the corruption of the judiciary, then agreement must be reached on the reform of the judiciary. If another is the independence of the central bank, then that must be guaranteed. The IMF, World Bank, and international investors can be guarantors of such assurances. But elitist peace diplomacy where bankers are the negotiators that insist on such conditions will not normally work. It must in addition be a bottom-up process with the civil societies of the war-torn nations. When they negotiate the conditions of good governance, when they own them, they will grant legitimacy to their state, its laws, its courts, its army, its tax administration. The conditions for peace in weak contemporary states will not be forged by good governance reforms imposed as hated IMF conditionality. Obversely, the IMF agenda of fiscal and monetary balance will gain legitimacy when the IMF is seen to put its weight behind the bottom-up good governance demands of the war-torn civil society. Good governance is not something effectively dictated by foreigners; it is a stumbling process that must be coaxed and caressed out of a legitimacy-building state and a legitimacy-granting civil society. Unless a painstaking policy of winning "hearts and minds" to democratic governance is energized, the strategy of sowing "fear and hate" will over time prevail once more (Kaldor 1999, p. 114).

The civil society strategy of Mohamed Sahnoun as UN special representative to Somalia is particularly commended. He included elders, women's groups, and neutral clans in plural talks: "His strategy was not so much one of marginalizing the warlords as of including the non-warlords in political discussions" (de Waal 1997a, p. 178). Demobilization strategies are most likely to work when they are community-based, involving veteran participation and veteran NGOs. Kaldor (1999, p. 136) commended the Uganda Veterans' Board and the National Demobilization Commission in Somaliland, which worked with the veterans' organization, SOYAAL, as explained by veterans themselves:

> The boys on the "technicals" (pick-up vehicles mounted with machine guns or anti-tank guns) are themselves tired. They see no benefit, only death. They climb the technicals out of need. Some of those in secure jobs now include some who were the worst gangsters. They prefer the $200 that comes with a settled job to the millions they get as bandits. (de Waal 1997a, p. 331)

As argued in chapter 4 about the capacity of restorative justice conferences to get the old men of the Mafia to retire from killing, even the younger and poorer gangsters of Somaliland grow tired of killing—a human kind of tiredness that is an underestimated resource for peace.

The restorative process envisioned here requires much time and patience. A problem is that the United States and the UN do not see things this way. They want a truce, an early date for an election, and an early meeting of the elected government with an IMF official who will tell them what the West demands.[13] This is understandable but not effective. If the conditions that are criminalizing governments in Africa and the postcommunist world are not confronted, then criminals will make their payoffs and win the election. If ethnic healing is not confronted first, then fundamentalists of ethnic hatred will stand for the election and win as in the November 1990 Bosnia-Herzegovina election and again in the election after the Dayton accord. If warlords are not disarmed by a military that is granted democratic legitimacy, they will reassert control in regions where they can most readily use resentment to recruit young soldiers.

Mary Kaldor (1999) has a sophisticated approach to this dilemma of democracy. She finds that islands of civility always survive in ravaged countries. Her strategy is to link those islands of civility to support from transnational institutions—aid organizations, human rights NGOs, pro bono lawyers, the Red Cross, peacekeepers. I would add that these islands of civility in the war-torn civil society should also be linked to support from regional restorative justice institutes and an IMF and World Bank that have been reformed to a strategy of bottom-up consent. Regional experts from specialist institutions like the IMF should be important participants in a quality deliberation not only because they are indispensable stakeholders but also because they have an expert competence that should not be dismissed by their political critics. As UN Secretary-General Kofi Annan is fond of saying, "We can't impose peace." But the UN should be funded to support peacemakers and to support their democratic institution-building.

Of course the worse the war has been, the more decimated the islands of civility will be, and the more outside support they will need. Yet Kaldor (1999, p. 121) argues that there were many cases of locally negotiated peace accords between factions in South Africa, Northern Ireland, Central America, and West Africa that can be enumerated. They are zones of peace that can be expanded outward into the zone of war and repositories of local knowledge about how to heal the conflicts at issue. The appealing thing about Mary Kaldor's approach is that it transcends the barren standoff between those who favor a truce and top-down structural adjustment versus defenders of humanitarianism and neutrality.

Sadly, criminalized governance appropriates humanitarianism to line its pockets. Neutrality—studiously avoiding taking sides on any controversial issue—is fine for the Red Cross, according to Kaldor, but impartiality is the principle she suggests peacemakers should follow. Impartiality means an absence of discrimination on the basis of nationality, race, religion, political party, and the like, but impartiality is not neutral on the law. It stands for justice and protecting the victims of human rights abuses, for being clear that abuses of human rights are wrong and must stop. This mirrors the distinction developed in chapter 5 between neutrality in mediation of "conflicts" and restorative justice to right "wrongs" of injustice. In the worst wars, islands of civility need courage and protection from outside—lawyers promising to launch war crimes prosecutions against anyone who liquidates them, perhaps regular video reports to sister NGOs outside, peacekeeper patrols around their homes. If all we promise is neutrality, then we promise them death. The UN ran when members of the exemplary human rights community in Rwanda were subject to systematic assassination after they predicted "massive atrocities unless named perpetrators were called to account" (de Waal 1997b).

That story needs to be told across international civil society so that such desertion of human rights advocates is constituted as shameful. Kaldor (1999, pp. 124–25) also argues that peacekeeping is not enough. What is needed is capability to enforce international humanitarian and human rights law. In the theoretical frame of this book, what is needed is a capability to escalate up an enforcement pyramid from nonintervention to dialogue and preventive diplomacy to peacekeeping to peace enforcement. This means mostly policing with consent rather than soldiering with force. It is what the British peacekeeping manuals describe as "minimum necessary force," contrasted with the Weinberger-Powell doctrine of "overwhelming force" that failed so spectacularly when applied in Somalia (Kaldor 1999, p. 129). Where there are injustices from breaches of international law and injustices that are root cases of a war, the difference between a restorative justice philosophy and a philosophy of peacekeeping as simply ending the conflict is that the restorative justice approach demands best efforts to right the wrongs, to heal the injustices. It does not mean in principle opposition to impunity for war criminals. If amnesty of a war criminal is necessary to end a war, to begin reconstruction and to right the structural injustices, then such an amnesty can be justified according to our responsive theory of restorative justice. Granting impunity to specific rapists can be necessary to preventing further rape in war; equally, promising war crimes prosecution of rapists if they walk away from the peace negotiations can deter rape. The objectives are healing survivors, prevention of rape, and communication in a morally clear way that rape is never acceptable in war; the restorative objective is not the consistent punishment of rape.

RESTORATIVE AND RESPONSIVE REGULATION OF HUMAN RIGHTS

We have seen that warfare since 1989 has been increasingly about the abuse of the rights of Bosnians by Serbians and vice versa, of Tutsis by Hutus and vice versa. It follows that one of the things the international community must do to prevent war is increase the effectiveness of the international regulation of abuse of fundamental human rights. For the most part, this regulation can be restorative. At the moment, states are not required to demonstrate continuous improvement in their efforts to secure human rights, only to honor specific rights. Responsive regulation for continuous improvement in human rights performance is not the way that human rights lawyers tend to think. It is a paradigm shift worthy of their consideration, however. When states fail to report on their human rights performance to UN agencies, nothing much happens. The UN has very little capacity to put the sort of monitoring teams into the field to check whether states with poor records are improving—compared to the capacity the IMF, the WTO, the International Labour Organization (ILO), and the OECD secretariats have on economic matters. Yet there are reasons for thinking that dialogic international regulatory processes such as the WTO Trade Policy Review Process or being called before ILO committees do have an effect on states (Braithwaite and Drahos 2000).

The kind of preventive diplomacy teams that Gareth Evans (1999) has advocated might pick up cases where UN human rights reports detect serious abuses that might create the conditions for war. Then major powers might be alerted by the preventive diplomacy teams in the cases of greatest intransigence to lean on the state, to mention trade and aid linkages, if this is what is needed. The UN human rights regime can and should be strengthened by an explicit linkage to preventive diplomacy by the major powers. But bottom-up restorative diplomacy should always be the first port of call according to the responsive regulatory strategy. This means review teams that seek to persuade improvement, offers of assistance linked to poor human rights performance in the way the ILO links technical assistance funding to poor performance on labor standards (Braithwaite and Drahos 2000). Carrots more than sticks. But also a degree of shaming at meetings in Geneva might be involved when there is not continuous improvement on the human rights effort or, worse, when there is failure to report on those efforts. And international praise should be involved when states that have been human rights laggards are independently evaluated to have improved their performance.

Informal meetings around tables in Geneva can be effective in applying pressure respectfully and with offers of help. So can informal meetings in the domestic capital between monitoring teams from other states and key domestic players, including local NGOs—both human rights NGOs and NGOs representing ethnic groups that claim their rights are not respected—all invited to sit together in the problem-solving circle. This is what I mean by restorative regulatory processes to continuously improve respect for human rights. But these restorative processes need to be given the clout that should come from the recognition that human rights abuse is an important cause of late modern wars. They should enjoy the clout that comes from linkage of restorative rights enforcement to preventive diplomacy by major powers that recognize a shared interest in preventing such wars.

A start along this path is the postconflict monitoring work of the Human Rights Co-ordination Centre in assessing whether Bosnia and Herzegovina is meeting the human rights obligations necessary to accession to the Council of Europe. It would exaggerate to say that the Centre demands continuous improvement, since it sometimes finds that enacting a law is sufficient to satisfy a standard. Yet it does audit in the field, does frequently report on nonimplementation of laws that are on the books, and does have the backing of international institutions whose support is important to political elites.

Guarding against Retributive Criminalization

The International Criminal Court that will come into existence if enough states ratify the statute to establish it is a good thing from the perspective of restorative and responsive regulation. It is a good thing because criminalization provides a new peak to the enforcement pyramid against war crimes. Its main virtue, however, should not be the internationalization of enforcement but to be there to motivate combatant states to do their own restorative and responsive regulation of compliance with the laws regulating warfare.

From the restorative justice perspective, there is no objection in principle to amnesties following wars, so long as they are amnesties that contribute to the ending of war, so long as all stakeholders are given a voice in the amnesty negotiations, so long as those who benefit from amnesties are willing to show public remorse for their crimes and to commit to service to the new nation and its people to repair some of the harm they have done. What must be objected to from a restorative justice perspective is selective prosecution of those the victors view as most worthy of being demonized, with unconditional amnesty for the rest. The political appeal of the latter approach is often irresistible. Make a few individuals scapegoats for the collective failures of whole armies that have failed to meet their obligations to educate their soldiers to their obligations under the Geneva Convention. In some cases, including Rwanda and Yugoslavia, such criminal scapegoating before the violence has been fully brought under control actually increased resentments in ways that can create more victims of violence (Alvarez 1999).

With complex organizational crimes, there are usually many who are responsible for the loss of life, including some from outside the jurisdiction. The restorative objective is to get as many of those who share some responsibility to own it and commit to changes that will prevent reignition of violence. Forgiveness is the most powerful emotional tool for encouraging the perpetrators of evil and the contributors to evil to own their contribution. Nurturing forgiveness often requires considerable reticence in resorting to selective use of the criminal process.

A truth and reconciliation commission that grants amnesties in these terms might not achieve equal punishment for equal wrongs, but it may dissuade elites from rejecting a peace that will lead to their punishment and may guarantee victims the following minimum conditions of restorative justice: a chance to discover the truth of what happened that is most important to them (often the location of a loved one's grave); officially sanctioned condemnation of the crime; loving social support; citizens who empower them by listening to their story with respect and sympathy; a state that will acknowledge the truth of their suffering (as by President Alwyn of Chile writing personally to every victim with a copy of their Truth and Reconciliation Commission report, or schools named after victims in South Africa); a hearing that assures them of equal consideration of their claims upon limited resources for compensation; and a hearing that takes seriously their ideas for permanently suppressing the political project that led to their victimization (cf. De Grieff 2000). Blanket amnesties cannot guarantee these minimal assurances of justice for victims; in fact, they ignore these kinds of victim claims to justice, as Pablo De Grieff (2000) has argued.

The danger of highly selective criminal enforcement against war criminals is that presidents and generals will learn the lessons large corporations learned when corporate crime enforcement was stepped up in the aftermath of Watergate. Many of the most irresponsible corporate criminals set up scapegoats who would be paid to take the fall if there were a criminal investigation. In many corporations, we heard furtive jokes about their "vice president responsible for going to jail" (Braithwaite 1984). Responsive regulation is a better idea than criminal enforcement against anyone and everyone you can convict to satisfy a public lust for punishment because while the latter creates incentives to invest in setting up scapegoats, responsive regulation creates incentives to invest in complying with the law. The sad thing about complex, covert, organizational crime, including most war crimes, is that it is all too easy for the most evil and powerful to set up scapegoats (Fisse and Braithwaite 1993). We saw this in the Pacific in 1945, where so many junior Japanese officers were hung as war criminals, but not Emperor Hirohito. We see it in the conviction of East German border guards for shooting people climbing over the Berlin Wall when they had no part in the design of the "shoot to kill" policy. Meanwhile the prosecution of Eric Honecker was aborted. Not General Pinochet, not Contreras, the former head of the Chilean secret police whose conviction was reversed by the Supreme Court, but middling criminals of the Pinochet regime may be convicted. The illusion must be resisted that prosecuting as many war criminals as possible is an accomplishment of justice or deterrence. Where there are thousands of criminals and the administrative capacities of a state in transition to peace are limited, selective individual prosecutions are inevitable. Rwanda is the extreme contemporary case, where 125,000 genocide suspects are awaiting trial, and only 2,500 cases were tried between 1996 and 2000 (*New Republic*, 10 April 2000, p. 18). It will take a hundred years to try them at this rate. Selective prosecution inevitably risks what happened in Argentina—"sending the signal that whoever is not charged is innocent" (De Greiff 2000, p. 32) and that there can be impunity for collective and institutional aspects of responsibility that do not throw up soft individual targets.

RESTORATIVE AND RESPONSIVE REGULATION FOR PEACE

Peacemaking, according to this analysis, is rendered more structurally possible by (1) vibrant global peace and human rights movements that render warmongering shameful and politically unpopular in the two-level game of world politics (Putnam 1988); and (2) responsive diplomacy that privileges restorative and preventive peacemaking at the base of a regulatory pyramid yet can escalate to more coercive measures backed by the UN, powerful states, the IMF, banks, and credit ratings agencies.

There is no recipe book for peacemaking. We know it will be costly. If we are serious about regulating war, we had better be able both to escalate up an enforcement pyramid and to reduce tension by de-escalating down the pyramid to less interventionist approaches. Peacemakers need the wisdom to discover deliberatively the contexts where they must create spaces for empowering local knowledge and where they must heed the knowledge of elites who control state and global institutions. Peacemakers need to be contextually wise in how they use a capacity to be responsive to events with a regulatory pyramid. They had better be able to listen and learn from local knowledge so they can craft with others a peace that does not replicate the conditions that caused war. And they must hear the whole range of contrasting perspectives that have a substantial following.

That means a lot of meetings at many different levels, perhaps something like the process of iterated conventions nations go through when they write or rewrite their constitution. This requires patience, eschewing the quick fix in favor of the long haul of restoring an enduring peace that reconstructs governance. It must be a transformation that heals and fixes the injustices, real and perceived, that caused this war and could fuel the next one. Economic security and hope must supplant fear if the peace is to succeed. All this is as true of confronting conflicts through preventive diplomacy before a war has broken out as it is of peacemaking after a war.

Yet the peace cannot be perfect justice because crucial stakeholders in the continuation of late modern wars are so often folk we have loosely called warlords. Their agenda is not social justice but plunder. We cannot arrest them because they hold the guns. We must either kill them or convince them that they will be better off with the peace we craft together. This new diplomacy for late modern wars is bottom-up, instantiating the restorative justice values of deliberation, healing, procedural and social justice, rule of law, protection of fundamental human rights, and building communities. It has much to learn from restorative justice on the value of ritual spaces where emotions like humiliation might heal. But if that fails, responsive diplomacy is willing to resort to economic and military deterrence and top-down coercive imposition to stop the rape and slaughter. Responsive diplomacy makes those morally fraught and complex judgments after learning the lessons the Kennedys drew from the Cuban missile crisis. It heeds Gabriel Kolko's (1994) conclusion that twentieth-century wars were started by men who suffered from "socially sanctioned blindness," who were trapped in an elite consensus that incubated false analysis because it excluded dissenting analyses from below.

We must note that the problem of late modern war is no longer a problem of avaricious acquisition of territory by major powers. It is a problem of weak states whose citizens and armies deny them legitimacy because they fail to deliver in a ruthlessly competitive world system. A fundamental solution is therefore a transformation of global economic institutions toward a world system with greater social justice between nations. Such a pursuit is not a zero-sum game; within limits, all nations can be better off economically, environmentally, and in terms of security if they grasp the conditions for peace at the WTO, IMF, and development banks. Certainly, 99 percent of the world's people would be better off if we solved international strategies of tax evasion/avoidance and money laundering of ill-gotten gains. The superrich few in the North benefit most from international law-evasion strategies. Plugging the holes in the dike through which plunder escapes is hard to do. But to the extent we succeed in doing it, we not only redistribute wealth from the northern superrich but also help fight the plunder of the southern warlord class.

According to our analysis, the contemporary conditions for peace are restorative diplomacy between democratic states integrated into global trade and investment flows and protected from internal plunder by robust separations of powers among institutions of good governance—an army that is not a law unto itself, an independent judiciary and central bank, a public service free of systemic corruption or capture by political faction, a free press and a tax administration that is granted legitimacy by the people.[14] Our conditions for peace are precisely the conditions that make it inconceivable today that the United States and England could wage war with each other for the first time since 1812; or France and Germany, Japan and Holland, Australia and New Zealand.

But these conditions have not easily or quickly been won even in these privileged states. Consider how the ravages of the crash of 1929 propelled not just Germany along the path to totalitarianism. Consider how many decades it took for the United States to heal the wounds of the Civil War between the whites of the North and the South, wounds that are still not fully healed between free whites and the descendants of enslaved blacks, wounds that today have ongoing implications for the level of violence in that society (see note 11). Robert Meister (1999) has insightfully construed the Lincoln of the Gettysburg Address and the Second Inaugural Address as a practitioner of reconciliation akin to Mandela. This is the Mandela of reconciliation who lays the foundations in the hearts of the demos for democratic institution-rebuilding. The Lincolnian reconstruction was more than a matter of constitutional and political settlements. At Gettysburg Lincoln reinvented the polity in a way that attended to the voices he heard bottom-up. This reinvention of America was as a "narrative of common survivorship" (Meister 1999)

> in which identification between victims and victimizers permitted forgiving without forgetting. Abraham Lincoln expressed this most eloquently in his declaration that "We were all slaves to slavery." In this way Lincoln rewrote the history of the American past as a shared narrative that reunited former opponents by casting them as common survivors of shared trauma. (Hesse and Post 1999, p. 25)

A reborn nation would be a survivor of a sundered Union that was itself the victim of slavery. In this Lincoln made the second great American contribution to world political thought after the forging of the Republic itself. Lincoln saw the need for victims and perpetrators to internalize each others' hurts, each others' shame, and to transcend it through a sense of shared survivorship. Americans were Americans because they were survivors of slavery and the war to end it, who together now would "bind up the nation's wounds." Nelson Mandela gave the parallel message in his inaugural address, two of his white jailers seated beside him, that all South Africans had been in some sense victims of apartheid.

While ethnic hatreds, war, and plunder are recurrently characteristic of dozens of weak late modern states, according to our analysis these characteristics are consequences of weak institutions of governance that are denied legitimacy by their people. A peace process is actually a historic opportunity to fix institutions. Germany, Japan, Italy, and Austria seized this opportunity for democratic institution-building between 1945 and 1950 with a lot of reconstruction help. The Marshall Plan was costly to the United States, but through trade and collective security it was one of the best investments U.S. taxpayers ever made in their own peace and prosperity.

Restorative justice seems to have the elements needed to transform a crisis of war into an opportunity for institutional renewal, a potential South Africa is currently beginning to realize. The main reason for this is that it involves a bottom-up process that seeks to engage civil society in a discussion of the institutional renewal required to make the peace just and permanent. Working together to put the institutional problems in the center of the circle is a good start to transcending ethnic hatreds. Global financial institutions need to be in the circle as well—listening. When asked to speak, their obligation is to say that lending and investment will not flow unless bankers see fiscal balance, an independent central bank that resists printing money to pay for private armies. Ultimately, structural adjustment is inevitable, but imposed structural adjustment is not. It can be explained that the new policy of the global financial institutions is for a war-wearied civil society to commit to institutions that will prevent the return of the kleptocratic state, that will replace forever the rule of armies with the rule of law. To get an excellent education system for the new generation, commitment in civil society to this goal, and to a legitimate tax system to pay for it, is essential. Understanding is also essential—understanding among the people that the alternative is an inexorable slide down the slippery slope of a structural adjustment package that will cause retrenchment of teachers.

Just as the family crisis of arrest for a serious crime can be a resource in a restorative justice conference for finding the motivation to lick a heroin habit, so the crisis of war can be a resource for restorative justice conferences to motivate institutional renewal that transcends reliance on tyrants for protection from the ethnic other.

Finally, restorative justice is a valuable philosophy of diplomacy because late modern war is a criminal matter much more than modern and early modern war was. The wars of the 1990s were mostly fought by irregulars who knew nothing about the Geneva Convention, and they were waged more against civilian populations than against other armies. The wars were systemically criminal, and many of their root causes were about the criminalization of the state—the use of the institutions of the state as an apparatus of plunder, impoverishing the people and causing them to withdraw legitimacy from the state. It follows that peace is unlikely unless the people can come to terms with their anger and hatred over those crimes. Rituals are needed to heal the damaged souls of the people, to help them find ways to transform hatred into sorrow or forgiveness, to be able to move forward with hope rather than wallow in the evil of the past. Restorative traditions have been developed through the ages in all the world's cultures to help with that transition. The global social movement for restorative justice is now a rich collective memory file for retrieving bits and pieces of those traditions and putting them to use in helping people deal with their most difficult conflicts in a way that is culturally meaningful to them. Desmond Tutu (1999) is probably right that in a society torn by ethnic war there can be *No Future without Forgiveness*. Rituals of a funereal character have a place in helping survivors put hatred aside to grieve for their people and then resolve to push on in the way their loved ones would have wanted. But if the shame of the survivors' degradations is not acknowledged and discharged, if the hatred festers below the surface when the next national crisis comes along, the political niche will still be there for the demagogue to seek power by blaming the nation's woes on the evil other. Forgiveness cannot be forced; it can only come when survivors are emotionally ready for it. What we can do, what the great global project for peace must do, is provide ordinary citizens with rituals that expose us personally to the sorrows and suffering of the other, and them to ours, rituals that create spaces where apology and forgiveness have a chance to be expressed. That is why the PEACE Foundation Melanesia is on the right track in training Bougainvillian facilitators to move around their villages convening restorative justice conferences to heal the emotional wounds of their war. Then ordinary Bougainvillians can play their part in those rare moments "when hope and history rhyme" (Seamus Heaney, quoted in Asmal 2000, p. 24).

NOTES

1. The most famous example was the razing of Carthage by Rome after Hannibal achieved his tactical objectives and left Rome in peace (when he had it at his mercy).
2. Letter to John Braithwaite from Chris Siriosi, provincial peace co-ordinator, Bougainville Transitional Government, 15 April 1998.
3. Here and in the following sentences I rely on remarks by Brigadier Bruce Oxborn, Colonel Bob Breen, and Australian Foreign Minister Alexander Downer at a seminar, "Monitoring Peace in Bougainville," organized by the State, Society and Governance in Melanesia Project, Australian National University, Canberra, 8 September 1999.
4. The Australian Department of Foreign Affairs and Trade (1999, pp. 73–74) reported eighty-two armed conflicts around the world between 1989 and 1992, seventy-nine of them within states. In 1993, thirty-four of the thirty-four major armed conflicts were intrastate conflicts.
5. Of twenty-seven major armed conflicts in 1999, all but two took place within national boundaries (Collier 2000, p. 1).
6. Though hate radio was used to incite people to genocide in Rwanda (Kaldor 1999, p. 86).
7. Western peacemaking institutes that teach restorative justice already exist. There is the Eastern Mennonite University Peacemaking Institute in the US which draws on the inspiring teaching and knowledge of Howard Zehr among others. The Transcend organization inspired by Johan Galtung has conflict resolution training centres in Norway, Moscow, Budapest, Geneva, Washington, and London. One option is to resource these institutes to assist leaders from countries like Indonesia to draw on the global stock of knowledge about restorative justice innovations so they can discuss and design their own manuals for training local trainers. And then funding them and protecting them at home to train trainers.
8. Regrettably, such hypocrisy is not always the norm: 'Peacemaking between nations in current practice typically involves largely public meetings between two or more opposing groups. In this context, group dynamics and the very architecture of the meeting rooms seem to foster bimodal alienation. The broadcasts of the Madrid conference that I saw showed the Arab and Israeli representatives denouncing each other to visibly large audiences. The speakers' awareness of TV cameras added an even larger audience to their perception of the situation" (Scheff 1994, p. 145).

9. Indeed, a number of studies have concluded that the crisis brought the two leaders closer together and paved the way for the first arms-control agreements (Kaczynska-Nay 2000, p. 87 n. 78).

10. The enforcement pyramid might not seem to be a bad description of the United States' failed policy, with the backing of UN legitimacy, in the Gulf War. My view, however, is that it was a deeply flawed application of this strategy in three ways:

   1. Seemingly in part due to the incompetence of the U.S. ambassador to Iraq, the United States did not, prior to the invasion of Kuwait, clearly signal an enforcement pyramid. Nor did it engage with preventive diplomacy to help resolve the real disagreements Iraq had with Kuwait over disputed oil fields, disputed territory, and war debts. It did not signal clearly to Iraq that it was willing to escalate intervention right up to the point of a counterinvasion to prevent an invasion of Kuwait. The Iraqis did not have their hopes decisively shattered for an East Timor scenario—where the United States would piously condemn the invasion in the UN while sitting on its hands tacitly approving.

   2. Having jettisoned its initial posture of appeasement toward its old ally, the United States overreacted in the other direction by escalating far too quickly through its enforcement pyramid. For example, on its own advice from General Powell and others, five months was not long enough for the naval blockade to effect the Iraqi economy in a significant way.

   3. The United States never signaled a willingness to negotiate de-escalation down its enforcement pyramid. A pause in the air war or even a holding back on escalation to the ground war were options that were ruled out by the United States.

   In practice, then, the U.S. response amounted to a precipitate transition from appeasement to all-out commitment to war rather than the astute deployment of preventive diplomacy backed by an enforcement pyramid. The ruling out of de-escalation led to a policy that was stupid, immoral, and arguably criminal. The latter may seem a provocative claim. My perspective is that while it is a defense of shooting a man to point out that he was confronting you with a knife, it is murder to shoot him in the back after he says, "I give up" and turns around to walk away, even if he walks away with the knife still in his hand. The policy of slaughtering the retreating Iraqi army was stupid because it was motivated by an explicit U.S. policy of humiliating Saddam Hussein. "Humiliation is the name of the game," said one U.S. official on 24 February 1991. "Or to put it more positively, we want to make sure that Saddam cannot emerge as a mystical or heroic creature in the Arab world" (*Canberra Times*, 25 February 1991).

11. While it is true that strong states that are economically competitive are granted more legitimacy by their citizens than states that are the economic losers of the world system, we can see the same basic sociological dynamic at work within strong states. Within a strong state like the United States, it is in the areas that are weakest economically—the impoverished inner cities where *The Truly Disadvantaged* (Wilson 1987) live—that legitimacy is withdrawn from the state. Gary LaFree's (1998) wonderful study shows that the truly disadvantaged withdraw legitimacy from the state most at those times when the gulf between the rich and poor is widest, and it is at these periods of history that surges in the crime rate occur. In the inner cities of the United States, a "war on drugs" is indeed under way, and as a result 2 million U.S. citizens are now in prison, suffering the rape and violence that accompany imprisonment in a way not so dissimilar to the way rape and violence are characteristic of real wars. Similarly, there are outback towns in Australia that have lost their economic base, lost government services, where the legitimacy citizens accord to the state is minimal, violence is at very high levels, and where young black men and the police

are metaphorically at war with each other, indeed, where local police sergeants can be metaphorical warlords.

12. Politics aside, there are economic reasons for doubting fiscal contraction as a prescription while a financial crisis is in train: "It is bad policy to toss out 'the single greatest discovery of the Keynesian revolution, namely the importance of fiscal stabilizers.' Even the IMF has all but admitted by now that its initial policy prescription of fiscal contraction served only to deepen the Asian crisis; and the nations of the region have made a tremendous recovery from the crisis once they pursued expansionist fiscal policies" (Buckley 2000, pp. 19–20).

13. "The television cry 'something must be done' can be irresponsible and fickle. Too many of the efforts I have described were forgotten as soon as victory was declared. (Even Kosovo had virtually disappeared from newspapers and screens by October 1999.) A commitment to peace is as important as a commitment to war, but it is far more difficult to sustain" (Shawcross 2000, p. 374).

14. Why is the legitimacy granted to the tax administration so crucial? Because fiscal balance is a condition for investment, lending, and employment creation. And because foreign imposition of structural adjustment to restore this is ultimately inevitable and usually worsens withdrawal of health and education services, worsens the collapse of law and order, thereby eroding the legitimacy of weak states.

7

Sustainable Development

JUST AS RESTORATIVE PRACTICES AND THE VALUES OF RESTORATIVE JUSTICE HAVE A useful contribution to make to peace in the world, so they have something to offer the sustainable development that is one of the conditions for that peace. Sustainable development is crucial to peace if we frame it as giving priority to those who have been left behind in the economic struggle—the poor of the developing world. Conceived in this way, sustainable development is a political objective that advances social justice. And as argued in the previous chapter, there can be no enduring peace without social justice. Sustainable development is a political objective at odds with radical green philosophies that reject economic growth. Sustainable development conceives economic growth as crucial to creating jobs for the poor in both developed and developing economies. But it contends that development can be accomplished while reducing the impacts the environment currently endures. There are enough examples now of highly successful corporations that outperform the market while substantially reducing the environmental impact of their production to give us confidence that the environmental stewardship required for sustainable development is possible (Gunningham and Grabosky 1998; Parker forthcoming). Sustainable development is not an oxymoron; it is a coherent objective.

The next section considers the way restorative justice might support a rule of law that promotes sustainable development. Then the chapter considers how restorative justice institutions might make a major contribution to the human and social capital development so crucial to economic growth in the late modern world, then how restorative justice and responsive regulation can contribute to combating corruption, to the integrity of tax systems, to sustainability, to assuring that competition is not corrupted by cartels and monopolies, and to preventing the collapse of national, regional or global financial systems. These are the steps we will take through what the IMF and World Bank regard as the good governance agenda necessary for sustainable development.

RULE OF LAW AND SUSTAINABLE DEVELOPMENT

Developed economies cannot flourish without a rule of law that gives a minimum level of predictability to economic life (North 1990). If we cannot put our money in a bank without fear that the banker will abscond with our savings, we will not save; if we cannot trust our money to a stockbroker, we may not invest; if we cannot trust that business partners, suppliers, and creditors will honor their contractual obligations, then we may hold back from entering into productive economic relationships. The rule of law is the ultimate guarantee of these preconditions for economic development. We should not take them for granted. At most places and times in human history since the institution of the stock exchange was invented in the seventeenth century, it has been impossible to make a stock exchange or a futures exchange work (Braithwaite and Drahos 2000, chap. 9). Neither trust in civil society nor the rule of law to enforce contracts was up to enabling market making. Francis Fukuyama (1995, p. 27) argues that nations that depend on formal social control to govern economic and social life impose a tax on all social actions in comparison to societies that can secure governance through informal ties of respect. Hence the arguments developed in chapter 8 about how restorative justice can make the rule of law more effective in areas like contract and corporations and securities law become important arguments as to how restorative justice might promote sustainable development.

This chapter sticks with the more basic argument that a functioning criminal law is essential to sustainable development. There are many developing nations where a basic lack of safety in the streets is a major impediment to investment. This chapter will briefly discuss only two case studies of this phenomenon—Papua New Guinea and Colombia—but many other examples could be used, which would include more developed economies where public safety is a major impediment to investment, such as Russia and South Africa. As LaFree (1998, p. 72) concludes, "Crime can seriously undermine a society's social capital." The history of the development of capitalism in Europe is one of the creation of ever-wider pacified spaces where trade could be transacted without the fear of highwaymen or pirates. During the Hundred Years' War (1338–1453) there was very little of Europe where it was safe to travel any distance with goods for sale. This is a fundamental reason that European economic development lagged so far behind that in China during this period of history. Still today there are parts of Europe where highwaymen chill trade. There is a tendency in the West to see safe streets as a condition for investment as a story about other times and other places. Yet when carjacking becomes a serious problem in a wealthy city, this is not one of the attractive features of the city in the eyes of investors thinking of locating there. In the most advanced capitalist economy, there are many once-flourishing U.S. inner cities that have now been utterly deserted by all but retail investors. A basic absence of safety on the streets is a major reason for the capital flight.

Colombia has one of the highest homicide rates in the world—78 per 100,000, compared with less than 2 for most of Europe. Some parts of Colombia are worse than others. In Medellin the rate was 400 per 100,000 in 1992 (Duque and Klevens 1999,

p. 4). There are not a lot of alternatives to employment in the cocaine business because what other kind of investor would move to Medellin? Yet Medellin seems like it could be something of a comparative success story of restorative justice. Much of its crime problem is caused by 180 well-armed gangs, each with twenty to thirty mostly young members, many politicized as leftist or rightist "self-defense groups" (Duque and Klevens 1999, p. 5). For a decade the mayor's office has been working with these gangs, at times resorting to tough law enforcement but mostly working at negotiating peace treaties. Pacts are settled through a series of meetings culminating in a public ceremony of commitment to nonaggression, to refrain from demanding protection money, in the presence of civic and religious leaders. A "peace commissioner" organizes meetings between community leaders and gang members to analyze conflicts and their consequences. Reintegration is an important part of the process. Gang members get support for starting a new life, including "psychological support, job training and placement, and/or helping them to finish school" (Duque and Klevens 1999, p. 6). More recently, the mayor's office has been working with the private sector in Medellin, the World Bank, and the Inter-American Development Bank to fund a bottom-up crime prevention program in Medellin civil society that involves schools, workplaces, the media, reforms to institutions of law enforcement, and various approaches to child development. By no means have all of the preventive initiatives been restorative, yet much of the emphasis has been on restorative approaches even to very serious matters of gang violence. So far the results are encouraging: between 1992 and 1998, the homicide rate halved, which in the context of Medellin means the saving of several thousand lives each year (Duque and Klevens 1999, p. 4).

Papua New Guinea is another developing country with a gang problem that sometimes makes South Central Los Angeles look like a picnic. Papua New Guinea was once a stunning tourist destination of growing popularity. Today, fear of crime is a major reason there are few nations in the world less visited by tourists. Even the Peace Corps has pulled out. The past decade has seen more disinvestment than investment in Papua New Guinea. As in Colombia, however, out of desperation comes innovation. Raskol gang surrenders and gang retreats in Papua New Guinea have involved surrenders of up to 400 alleged gang members giving up arms and commiting to changes in their lives in return for help with employment (Dinnen 1996). Note the discussion in Chapter 4 of these surrenders and also of the Kulka Women's Club peacemaking at Box 3.3. While the writing of Sinclair Dinnen (1996, 2001) on the Papua New Guinea gang surrenders is illuminating, these surrenders are not being subjected to systematic evaluation as is beginning to happen in Colombia. Such little evidence as we have from the United States on the effectiveness of this kind of truce brokering with violent gangs is encouraging that crime is reduced (Torres 1981, cited in Klein 1995, p. 149). In 2001, the Papua New Guinea cabinet committed to a new National Law and Justice Policy and Plan of Action entitled Toward Restorative Justice: 2000–2005 (Law and Justice Sector Working Group 1999). The policy adopts restorative justice for the first time as the core rationale for the long-term future of the law-and-justice sector.

Streets that are safe enough for job creation are a minimal requirement for economic development. The next requirement is people who are equipped to fill the jobs that investment can create.

HUMAN AND SOCIAL CAPITAL DEVELOPMENT

This section develops the idea that restorative justice might fruitfully be applied to the holistic development of the learning potential of the young and the whole range of problems young people encounter—drug abuse, unemployment, homelessness, suicide, among others—in the transition from school to work.

The Late Modern Structural Dilemma of Human and Social Capital

In the new information economy, it is clear that human capital (the skills of people) and social capital (social skills for interacting with others, including dispositions such as trust and trustworthiness) are becoming progressively more important to economic development than physical captial (Dowrick 1993; Fukuyama 1995; Latham 1998). Young people whose human and social capital remains undeveloped are destined for unemployment. Families with high endowments of human and social capital tend to pass those on to their children. There is a strong correlation between parents' involvement in the education of their children and academic performance (Finn Report 1991, p. 151). For children whose families lack endowments of human and social capital, we rely on state-funded education systems to compensate.

Yet we quickly run up against the limits of the capabilities of formal education bureaucracies to make up for deficits that are profoundly informal (especially on the social capital side).[1] Our objective is to come up with a new policy solution to this limitation.[2] At the same time, we want to help solve the problem of children from families with high endowments, but where human and social capital development is interrupted by problems like drug addiction, bullying by peers, sexual abuse, depression, and suicide.

My hypothesis is that both the low family endowments problem and the interrupted transmission problem need a more informal yet more systematic solution than the formal education system can provide. Mentoring programs like Big Brothers and Big Sisters head in the right direction (reducing drug abuse and violence in one eight-site evaluation [Elliott 1998, p. xviii]). But they are insufficiently social, communal, and plural to deal with the kinds of deficits at issue with reducing youth unemployment, drug addiction, delinquency, and suicide.

In terms of social structure, I see the problem as one of a late modernity where:

1. nuclear families are isolated from extended families, which used to compensate for deficits of nuclear families; and
2. formal education bureaucracies are too formal to compensate for the social (informal) aspects of the deficits that thereby arise—for example, in teaching trust, love, respectfulness.

This structural dilemma of late modernity has crept up on us over the past century. Social historians have shown that early in the twentieth century parents much more commonly than today shared child-rearing obligations with extended families, churches, and other community networks (Lasch 1977; Zelizer 1985). Single parents, who in Western societies were more likely to be black and poor (LaFree 1998, pp. 147–48), were particularly likely to become "solo practitioners" of child rearing. Mothers struggling alone to educate their children without support from the village therefore worsened inequalities of race and sex. Remedial policies to spread burdens of informal education and support for children are thus imperative to tackling the inequalities arising from our dual structural dilemma of late modernity.

How the Education System Can Learn from the Criminal Justice System

The direction for a solution to this dual structural problem is captured by the African proverb that it takes a whole village to raise a child. But this of course begs the question raised by the structural problem; we do not live in villages in the West, nor in much of the East. Yet we have seen that recent experience with restorative justice innovation in the criminal justice system has come up with an interesting solution to a similar structural dilemma of crime control. Criminologists know that crime is a result of failures of informal community ordering (Sampson and Laub 1993; Sampson and Raudenbush 1999) and of social support for young people (Cullen 1994). Unfortunately, however, most remedial programs fail because of the structural impossibility of building village solutions in the city or suburb. Neighborhood Watch seems like a good idea, but the evidence shows that it is not very effective in reducing crime (Sherman et al. 1997). One reason is that most of us do not care enough about our community or are just too busy to turn up to Neighborhood Watch meetings. They work somewhat better in highly organized middle-class communities—where they are least needed in terms of crime.

To a degree, restorative justice circles are a way of resolving this problem. We train circle coordinators who report back that a young offender is totally isolated to try again, to work harder to discover people she likes or respects, even if it means bringing in the one sibling or uncle who is respected from another city. The late modern sense of community is fragmented across space, but it exists. What the restorative justice circle does is bring that community of care together for the first time in one room. In the quintessentially late modern case, one of the participants may be a friend from cyberspace whom the young offender physically meets for the first time. It is wrong to say that these faceless friendships are always artificial and meaningless. Community in the metropolis is in some ways more meaningful than community in the village because it can be based on casting a wide net among a very large group of people to find a few who have very similar interests to our own, such as an interest in the history of reggae music, which would be hard to share in a rural village.

The fact from the restorative justice evaluation literature I want to emphasize here is that when supporters are invited to attend these conferences, they generally come.

I do not go to Neighborhood Watch meetings, even though I think that would be a public-spirited thing to do. But if a young neighbor singled me out as someone he would like to have as a supporter at a conference after he had gotten into trouble with the police, I would attend. Why? The answer is that in the conference case I am honored to have been nominated by a human being as someone he respects. Second, I am personally touched by his predicament. He is in trouble and has made a personal appeal to me, so I feel it would be callous to be unwilling to give up my evening for the conference. In short, community fails with Neighborhood Watch but works with the restorative justice conference because it is an individual-centered communitarianism. This individual-centered communitarianism tugs at the sense of obligation that works in the late modern world of community based on geographically dispersed ties of respect and identification.

Now I will seek to translate to education as an institution this analysis from the sociology of crime about what mobilizes community. In doing so, I will also attempt to solve one of the problems of restorative justice circles identified in chapter 4—that the very act of assembling the community of care on the occasion of a youth being in trouble can stigmatize a young person as a troublemaker.

Youth Development Circles: The Idea

The basic idea is to translate the conference/circle from criminal justice into the arena of educational development. Unlike conferencing in the criminal justice system, the idea presented now has not been subjected to any piloting. The main difference is that the circle would be a permanent feature of the young person's life rather than an ad hoc group assembled to deal with a criminal offense. Initially, the circle would be constituted to replace parent-teacher interviews in high schools.

Twice a year from entry to high school at age twelve through to successful placement in a tertiary course or a job (modal age eighteen), the youth development facilitator (operating from an office in a high school) would convene a meeting of the young person's community of care. This meeting would be called a *youth development circle*.

The circle would have core members and casual members. Core members would be asked up front to commit as an obligation of citizenship and care to try to attend all circles *until the young person is successfully placed in a tertiary course or a job* and to continue to be there for him or her should the young person subsequently request a circle or get in trouble with the police or the courts. Core members would actually sign a contract to keep meeting and helping the young person until that tertiary or job placement was accomplished.

Core members would normally include

Parents or guardians
Brothers and sisters
One grandparent selected by the young person
One aunt, uncle, or cousin selected by the young person

A "buddy," an older child from the school selected by the young person

A pastoral adult carer from the school selected by the young person (normally, but not necessarily, a teacher)

A neighbor, sporting coach, parent of a friend, or any other adult member of the community selected by the young person as a mentor

Casual members could include

Current teachers of the young person

Current girlfriend or boyfriend

Closest mates nominated by the young person

Professionals brought in by the facilitator or parents (e.g., drug counselor, employer from an industry in which the young person would eventually like to work)

The victim of an act of bullying or delinquency and victim supporters

The circle would commence with the facilitator introducing new members and reading the young person's six-month and long-term life goals as defined by him or her at the last meeting (six months ago). The young person would then be invited to summarize how she had done with the six-month objectives and in what ways her life goals had changed over the past six months. In good circles, this would be followed by a series of celebratory speeches around the circle about what had been accomplished and the efforts that had been made. The crucial skill of the facilitator would be to elicit affirmation for accomplishment and offers of help (as opposed to criticism) when there was a failure of accomplishment. Gathering together for the ritual is all the communal signaling needed to show that accomplishment matters; personal criticism on top of this is only likely to foster rejection of the value of accomplishment. Indeed, through the ritual interpretation of poor accomplishment as a communal failure to give young persons the help they need, young people are less likely to interpret poor performance as reason for rejection by those they initially identify with. Rejection of the rejectors and devaluing accomplishment are less likely when there is a community of care that shares the burden to build accomplishment come what may—unconditional support.

Normally, expert adults relevant to the six-month life goals would then be invited to comment (the math teacher on a math improvement goal; the school counselor on improving relationships). Members of the circle who had undertaken to provide agreed help toward those goals would be asked to report on whether they had managed to deliver it (Auntie Pat reporting whether they had managed to get together for an hour a week to help with math homework). In light of this discussion, the young person would be asked her thoughts on goals for the next six months, and others would be invited to comment on this topic.

The facilitator would then ask first the young person and then all other participants if they saw any other challenges in the young person's life where care and support might be needed. There would be discussion of whether new goals were needed to respond to these challenges.

If no one else raised the question, the facilitator would ask the young person and then her peers, "Do your friends and other kids at school help you to achieve your goals, or do they sometimes tempt you to do the wrong thing?" Responses to this question are discussed by everyone, and suggestions for action might be raised.

The facilitator then announces a tea break during which relevant subgroups (e.g., the nuclear family, the young person's friends) might meet together informally to discuss a plan of action to propose to the circle. Everyone is asked to think during the break about whether any new objectives or plans should be considered after the break.

The circle reconvenes to discuss these topics and ends with the young person reading out her new goals and the names of members who have agreed in some way to provide help or support toward meeting them. With specific and important things, an adult member should be nominated as responsible for ensuring it is done on time. The facilitator checks that these adults are happy to take on these obligations. The meeting is closed with thanks to the participants for their care and citizenship.

Over the years, the emphasis of the circle would shift from educational and relationship challenges to the challenge of securing employment. With young people who were not doing well at school, special efforts would be made by the core members of the circle to bring in casual members who might be able to offer work experience, advice on skill training, and networking for job search.

A Ritual of Love

The foregoing makes the circle seem a dry affair—rather like an expanded parent-teacher interview. For it to change lives, however, it would have to break out of this formal bureaucratic mold to become a ritual of caring in the way good restorative justice circles work. The literature on restorative justice conferences shows that love is central to understanding what makes them succeed. Nathan Harris's (2001) research on Canberra conferences concludes that reintegration (as opposed to stigmatization) of offenders is critical to success. The attitude item with the highest loading on the reintegration factor in a factor analysis of offender attitudes toward the conference was "During the conference did people suggest they loved you regardless of what you did?" In court cases, this item had the lowest loading on the reintegration factor of all the reintegration items. In short, the feeling by offenders that they were in receipt of unconditional love seems a crucial ingredient for the success of circles. And so, it is hypothesized, with the youth development circle.

The key ingredient for social capital formation that neither good education systems nor dysfunctional families can adequately supply is love. In conditions of late modernity, even functional families lack sufficient ritual occasions to communicate how deeply they care about the child and how much they admire her efforts to develop her capacities. The rituals we do have—weddings, funerals, graduation, bar mitzvahs—are too few in the life of moderns. Village life had various low-key rituals around the campfire to compensate for this. Moderns must create new rituals of love and care that are meaningful in a modern setting and that can transmit modern endowments for success in life. This is the idea of youth development circles.

Theory of Why Youth Development Circles Might Succeed

There is a lot of failure in existing programs to deal with youth problems such as poor school performance, hatred of the school as an institution, truancy, bullying, dropout, drug abuse, delinquency, suicide, homelessness, and unemployment. They fail because they approach young people as isolated individuals. Youth development circles would not aspire to treat isolated individuals targeted because of their problems (and thereby stigmatizing them as individuals). They would seek to *help young people develop* in the context of their communities of care. The help would not stigmatize because it would be provided universally to young people in a school, not just to the problem students. The young people themselves would be empowered with a lot of say over who those supporters would be. Circles would be a move to find something better than seeking to solve educational problems by one-on-one encounters with the school counselor, drug problems by individual encounters with rehabilitation services, employment by one-on-one interviews at job placement services, or youth suicide by public funding of psychiatrists. Certainly, one of the aspirations of circles would be to embed choices to opt for such rehabilitative services in networks of support that build commitment to make them work (see chapter 4). But the aspiration is bigger than that.

Cultures of disadvantage are grounded in failures of families and peers to value and nurture learning. Regular out-of-school help with things as simple as reading stories improves literacy. The accumulated evidence of the discipline of criminology is that social support is one of the strongest predictors of crime prevention (Cullen 1994). The research on bullying in schools shows that it can be halved by restorative wholeschool approaches grounded in utilizing the social bonds that operate across a school (Olweus 1993). The evidence from studies of successful job search is that one-on-one job placement services are less important than access to personal networks of knowledgeable people who care enough about the unemployed person to help them with leads, contacts, and introductions (Granovetter 1974). Informal networking seems to be no less the stuff of getting professional, technical, and managerial jobs than of blue-collar jobs (Granovetter 1973, p. 1371). Crucial elements of social capital, such as trust and trustworthiness, are learned in trusting relationships. Yamagishi and Yamagishi's wonderful Japanese program of trust research shows that trust builds social intelligence, that you have to learn to take the risk of trusting others to learn how to make wise judgments about who is trustworthy (Yamagishi 2000). It is this kind of social intelligence that makes young people employable. Human and social capital, in short, are constituted by informal circles of social support. The theory of youth development circles is that an institutional infrastructure would be created to foster the emergence of this informal support, that this institutionalization would also build a citizenship obligation to participate in circles and that the circles would lend ritual power to informal support. We already know that gathering in the circle creates a sense of an occasion where it is appropriate to raise certain issues, to articulate certain emotions of concern or admiration.

Heimer and Staffen (1995) have shown that in contexts where those with power are dependent on people who are normally stigmatized, social regulation of those people is in fact highly reintegrative. In their study, hospital staff from intensive care wards treated young black single mothers highly reintegratively—because they were dependent on those young mothers to hang in with their unhealthy babies and take them off the hospital's hands. The Australian convict colony treated convicts in a highly reintegrative rather than stigmatizing way because there was a labor short-age, which meant the colony was dependent on convict labor (Braithwaite 2001). As a result of this reintegration, the convict colony became a low-crime society in the nineteenth century. The youth development circle is an attempt to lock people in to a similarly reintegrative institutional dynamic. The only way for the citizens in the circle to end the obligations to attend meetings and offer practical help to the young person is to get that person into a steady job or a tertiary institution. Stigmatizing him, giving up on him, will be seen in the circle as likely to delay that release.

Enriching Civil Society

Circles might help educate all our children for democracy itself. Democratic de-liberation is learned, but our society does not teach it to the young. Being a beneficiary of care, of cooperative problem solving when one is young, may be the best way to learn to become caring, dutiful democratic citizens as adults. Such citizens who are creative in cooperative deliberation not only build strong democracies but also con-stitute able workforces that attract investment (see Putnam 1993). The hidden cur-riculum of youth development circles would therefore be giving the young the lit-eracy to live in civil society, learning to listen, to accommodate the perspectives of others in setting their own goals. Democracy cannot flourish without citizens who are educated for excellence in governing their own lives (Barber 1992). Youth devel-opment circles are in sum an idea for deliberative education that democratizes ed-ucation as it serves as an education for democracy.

If a program of research and development of the idea showed that youth devel-opment circles did meet some of its aspirations in a major way, it would create a case for a new tripartite view of obligations of citizenship:

1. A citizenship obligation to be the primary supporter of the education and development of any child one parents
2. A citizenship obligation to be a secondary supporter of more than one child beyond one's own children until infirmity excuses us
3. An obligation of the state to assign a facilitator to ensure that no child misses the benefits of the obligations in 1 and 2

These are different from the mostly disrespected obligations to attend parents and citizens' association meetings and bake cakes for them. They are obligations to come along to help a particular child who they love, to whom they have a professional obligation, or who has nominated them as someone the child respects. The citizenship obligation to be a supporter of at least one child should not expire with retirement, only with infirmity. The special wisdom that comes with age incurs a special obligation to spend time with the young for passing on that wisdom to a new generation. As elders have lost their seat at the informal rituals of the campfire, respect for elders has been one of the most unfortunate casualties of modernity. Respect for the elders is the missing cement of modern civil society. Old people feel it and for this reason have enormous untapped reserves of willingness to serve the young.

At the other end of the age spectrum, older buddies of the child are especially important. Buddy selection should be driven by a combination of the child's preference for another she identifies with and by the objective of matching children with weak endowments with buddies having the strongest endowments. This is a strength of weak ties argument (Granovetter 1973). The child with a network low in human and social capital is given a bridge into the social capital of the network of the buddy with wonderful endowments. For the highly endowed buddy, who has few problems at school, a central issue in her own circle becomes setting objectives about helping her younger buddy to succeed—learning to lead, learning to be a builder of civil society. Endowed children would be taught in the circle how to mobilize their own networks to help less endowed buddies—partly through observing how adult leaders mobilize networks to help *them*. The key idea of the circle is generational help begets help as a dynamic in civil society.

Thinking about R and D on Youth Development Circles

In a sense R and D has already been under way since 1991 as restorative justice circles rather like these have been operating in Queensland schools to deal more narrowly with delinquency and behavior problems (Cameron and Thorsborne 2000). We found in chapter 3 that the preliminary evidence is most encouraging about these circles.

The first priority with R and D more specifically focused on youth development circles would be disadvantaged high schools. Success there could lead on to pilots in primary schools and high schools that are not disadvantaged. Preliminary trials should be qualitative and process oriented. Experimentation would be needed with different ways of running circles, different invitation lists, different kinds of follow-up, and different kinds of training for facilitators. Evaluation measures would have to be piloted.

Then perhaps ten to twenty volunteer pilot schools might learn how to manage youth development circles for at least 50 students. An independent review committee might then report to government on whether the preliminary R and D to that point was sufficiently encouraging to proceed with random assignment of, say, 2,000 grade 8 students, 1,000 to youth development circles, 1,000 to traditional parent-teacher interviews. Each school would then be able to compare at least 50 circle students with 50 students who continue with traditional parent-teacher interviews. Randomization would ensure that the two groups were identical in all respects except the circle intervention.

Data would be collected from these 2,000 students (with informed consent from students and parents) annually on

School marks
Self-reported enjoyment of school and learning
Truancy
Bullying and victimization by bullies
School-reported behavior problems
Dropout
Employment after dropout
Strength of family bonds
Homelessness
Self-reported drug use
Self-reported suicide proneness and depression that predict actual suicide and attempted suicide (though statistical power may not be sufficient in the latter case even over ten years for 2,000 cases)
Self-reported delinquency
Police-recorded delinquency

The process of monitoring these outcomes should continue until evidence of failure or success is clear. Clear failure can be revealed quite quickly under this methodology. Clear success on unemployment reduction would require a decade of follow-up for twelve-year-olds. At any point during this decade, it might be decided that the accumulated weight of the evidence was sufficient to resource the program beyond the experimental schools. In the first instance, these might be volunteer schools invited to innovate on improving the successful experimental protocol.

Why the Cost of Youth Development Circles Might Be Self-Liquidating

Youth development circles would be costly. The largest costs would be borne privately by the citizens who gave time to the circles, to being mentors to young people, to helping them find jobs, to helping them with their science experiments. A cadre of youth development facilitators would also be a substantial burden on the public purse. The offsetting saving on both fronts from replacing parent-teacher interviews would be modest.

However, the offsetting economic benefits of having a more employable workforce, a more socially skilled and committed workforce, might be massive in comparison. The most obvious benefits are with those children who have cost the criminal justice and youth welfare system over a million dollars by the time they are teenagers by virtue of their delinquency and drug abuse. As a universal program, circles would seek to give problem-free children the social support to set themselves ever-higher goals for excellence, to discover that it might not be uncool after all to be a "try-hard." The hope is for enhanced economic performance by nurturing innovation and accomplishment at the top of the curve as well.

The intangible benefits of job creation through acquiring more innovative business leaders with enhanced social intelligence and educational accomplishment acquired as a result of circles would be impossible to measure, except through the crude proxy of how wealthy these individuals are ten or twenty years on. However, the reduced levels of crime, drug abuse, and unemployment among 1,000 experimental children compared with 1,000 control children over ten years of follow-up could be readily costed and measured against the cost of running the circles for those 1,000 children.

Cultural Pluralism in Implementation

Obviously, there would be great cultural variation in the appropriate ways of implementing youth development circles. One of the depressing things about working on new approaches to tackling unemployment through education or nurturing capital investment in some other way is that they invariably seem more feasible in rich nations than in the poorest nations where investment is most needed. The institutional innovation therefore becomes another way the gap is widened between rich and poor nations. Youth development circles present a rare case where the reverse may be true. We have assumed the worst in our analysis—that there exists no village that can be mobilized as a resource to raise a child. But of course in the least developed nations there are still villages. Creative institutional design might link human and social capital development to persisting extrafamilial networks. These networks might be harnessed as an underexploited comparative advantage of premodern societies in modern conditions of capital formation.

I will use Bali as a brief case study for two reasons. First, many readers will be familiar with the culture because it is such a common tourist destination. Second, it is an extreme case of the comparative advantage I have in mind, since modernization came so late to Bali. Because of its lack of good ports, the Dutch did not bother colonizing the southern half of the island until 1906. In Bali *every* citizen is a member of a *banjar*, the traditional social hub of village life. This has been true since at least A.D. 914 (Eiseman 1990, p. 72). The *banjar* is both a physical meeting place and a social organization for cooperative work groups, education, Hindu religious instruction,[3] family and community health planning, management and conservation of the environment, and various other cooperative efforts in a village. But even in the large city of Denpasar everyone belongs to a *banjar*. Indeed, Eiseman (1990, p. 88) reports that *banjar* do such a good job of both adult and child literacy training that there are some *banjar* in Denpasar without a single illiterate member.

That said, things are far from rosy in Bali, especially with the collapse of the tourist industry in the wake of the Indonesian instability since 1997. While *banjar*-level commitment to basic education in literacy and Hindu teaching is high, motivating high levels of formal education, constant innovation to find more efficient practices to traditional economic activities (in agriculture, for example) often is not the stuff of *banjar* enthusiasm. Yet surely if the Indonesian state wants to enthuse the populace of Bali about encouraging their children into higher levels of educational accomplishment, into a learning-innovation culture, then the *banjar* stands ready as the vehicle for accomplishing that. In the Bali context, *banjar* could graft youth development circles as a *banjar* institution, and this might give them more clout in human and social capital formation than could ever be hoped for in Western cities.

In Summary

Youth development circles are a policy idea that addresses the dual structural problem of human and social capital formation in late modernity. This is that (1) intergenerational ties that compensated for human and social capital deficits of the nuclear family have unraveled and that (2) formal education bureaucracies cannot compensate for such deficits when they are informal, when they are about love and dependent on intimate circuits of endowment-building beyond the school. This is best accomplished by bringing into a circle around the young person a combination of those she most loves and those she most identifies with—in the hope that the latter will in time come to count among those she loves and those who most encourage her to strive for her goals. It is a hope for a world where funerals become rituals that honor us not only for the care we have extended to our children but also for the love and help we have granted to children in circles, children we have embraced into our own family, friendship, and economic networks, particularly during old age. The idea is to multiply the meaning of care and intimacy in a life through better institutional sharing of the burden of parents during their period of peak load by asking peers and older citizens to work harder at passing on their wisdom during the periods when their burdens of care are lowest. In turn, if circles succeed in extending ripples of love, we might hope that when youth blossom into young adults, some might share some of the burdens of care for the old folk who have shown love to them. At both ends, this might help relieve the inequitable burdens of care currently borne by postmotherhood women.

The program I am proposing would not be cheap. Problems such as youth crime and drug abuse involve a staggering cost to the community, and there is encouraging evidence now from meta-analyses that educational development may have a significant impact on these problems (Pearson and Lipton 1999). Moreover, youth development circles are a type of program amenable to random assignment of a sufficiently large number of cases to assess readily measurable costs (such as salaries) and benefits (such as crime reduction) with impressive statistical power. Hence, a government bold enough to spend an eight-figure sum on a decade of R and D would be in a position to ascertain with a high degree of confidence whether my hypothesis that benefits would far exceed costs is wrong. The magnitude of the policy objective of upgrading human and social capital might justify the boldness of the experimentation proposed.

Now we turn from building social capital in the young to its destruction by older people in positions of power who resort to corruption. We can achieve the most wonderfully educated populace through successfully implementing ideas like youth development circles, yet still opportunities for sustainable development can go begging when institutions have been corroded by corruption.

CORRUPTION

It is a mistake to see corruption as just another crime, or worse to apologize for it as grease necessary to keep the axles of commerce turning. Corruption is a central issue of sustainable development because it corrodes the core decision-making institutions on which sustainable development depends. Corruption destroys democracy, replacing the vote of the people with the vote of the dollar. And it manacles markets—success goes to the firm that pays the biggest bribe instead of to the most efficient producer. When corruption seriously corrodes both democratic and market decisions, nations have dim prospects of development. When corruption captures environmental regulation, they have dim prospects of sustainability. This is why the nations that score highest on Transparency International's Corruption Index (www.transparency) are mostly both economic and environmental basket cases (Cameroon, Azerbaijan, Honduras), while those that score lowest enjoy strong economies and the most impressive environmental stewardship of all nations (Denmark, Finland, etc).

Corruption has proved extraordinarily resistant to eradication throughout human history (Noonan 1984). This is because its most significant perpetrators are powerful and sophisticated men who are capable of corrupting the justice system itself and, even if not capable of that, are capable of terrorizing and tainting witnesses against them. Moreover, because a huge amount of corruption goes on even in societies near the bottom of Transparency International's Corruption Index, corruption enforcement falls into both the system capacity trap and the deterrence trap as discussed in chapter 4. Financial penalties cannot deter it because the returns are so large in comparison with the odds of detection. If the average returns are $100,000 and the odds of detection are less than one in a thousand, then the *average* case will only be deterrable by a fine over $100 million, and the *worst* cases will require fines so astronomical that they would bankrupt even Bill Gates. Given that it would rarely be in the interests of sustainable development to bankrupt large corporations as a punishment, the deterrence trap yawns so wide that extreme personal (as opposed to corporate) punishment, notably imprisonment, is the only way we are likely to effect classical deterrence. But then we are in the system capacity trap. As the O. J. Simpson trials illustrate, while it is possible to prove guilt on the balance of probabilities, it is extremely costly to impose a draconian sentence that demands a "beyond reasonable doubt" standard of proof on an extremely wealthy person who can hire the very best lawyers (Geis and Bienen 1998, pp. 169–204). With an offense like bribery that has consensual victims at the other end of the transaction (who themselves break the law), that is easy to conceal and easy to transact through a citizen of a second country in the territory of a third country via a secret bank account in a fourth country, collecting the evidence is prohibitively expensive.

While the deterrence and system capacity traps make corruption immune to traditional reactive criminal enforcement, the analysis of chapter 2 can be applied to how corruption might not be immune to restorative justice and responsive targeting. This is because of the character of corruption's modus operandi. While we have seen that corruption is difficult to prove beyond a reasonable doubt, it is not difficult for competent criminal intelligence agencies to know who is on the take, or at least to have formidable grounds for reasonable suspicion. This is because if you are on the take, it is important that potential partners in illicit payments know that you expect a bribe; if your corruptness is too big a secret, no one will know to offer you a bribe. So it is not hard for criminal intelligence operatives to pose as neophyte wealthy entrants into a market and inquire of knowledgeable local insiders who they have to take care of to get into the market. Once they know who the corruptors are, they can monitor their activities to discover which likely corruptees are doing deals with them.

When the police have reasonable suspicions as to who the corrupt are but lack the capability to prove this beyond reasonable doubt, we saw in chapter 2 that the commended strategy is to offer restorative justice circles to those subject to reasonable suspicion. These circles seek to embed organizational commitments to externally audited internal anticorruption programs, which may include temptation testing and polygraph testing of the individuals subject to the original reasonable suspicion. Those who spurn the offer are then targeted for intensive surveillance and Abscam-style covert facilitation: intelligence operatives posing as wealthy overseas businessmen offer bribes to the targets in the view of hidden cameras. Restorative justice and responsive targeting are, as argued in chapter 2, the affordable and effective way of tackling our most entrenched and serious crime problems. There is no serious offense type with a modus operandi that makes this analysis more true than corruption. My contention is that any society with the political will, whether generated internally or as a result of IMF conditionality, can root out corruption with restorative justice and responsive targeting.

Tax Integrity

Fiscal balance is critical to sustainable development; states do not attract investment when they run up deficits year in and year out, blowing out an unsustainable national debt. Fiscal balance can be accomplished by cutting public spending. Up to a point, all states, but especially states with a serious corruption problem, can find ways of cutting wasteful expenditure. The problem is that states that do have a debt and corruption problem tend to respond to IMF demands for cuts in public expenditure by keeping the featherbedding that is the product of corruption and cutting services that matter to the poor—such as education and public health. We saw in the last chapter that such basic cuts undermine the legitimacy of governments as well as posing a threat to sustainable development that increases risks of internal armed conflict, especially when cuts to basic services and essential infrastructure are compounded by decisions to withhold pay from the military.

An alternative path is to assist states struggling with a burden of debt to strengthen tax system integrity. In most countries value-added taxes and income that can be readily subject to withholding (pay-as-you-earn income where employers can be required to make deductions before pay reaches the hands of the employee; bank interest that can be subject to withholding by banks) can be made to work well (Kagan 1989). Equally, all nations have a substantial black economy, ranging, according to the best estimates (Schneider and Enste 1999), from over 60 percent of the total economy in the worst cases (Thailand, Nigeria, Egypt) to about 10 percent in the best cases (Japan, the United States, Austria, Switzerland). All states also have a huge and unquantifiable problem of wealthy individuals and corporations paying little or no tax as a result of using a variety of sophisticated tax planning strategies. While we cannot quantify this, it is clear that all states today confront a situation where many of their large corporations pay no company tax. It is unlikely that there exists a state without many high-wealth individuals who pay virtually no tax. While tax authorities mostly seek to conceal this situation from the public, many citizens are aware of the appallingly low levels of taxpaying by the rich. There is now evidence that when citizens perceive that others are not paying their fair share of tax, they are less willing to pay tax honestly themselves (Scholz 1998).

In this game of perceptions of compliance, the critical issue is that low- and middle-income earners will not desist from exaggerating their tax deductions and will not move economic activity they control from the black economy into the tax net unless they are convinced that the rich are paying something that they regard as approaching their fair share of tax. The most strategic objective toward increasing tax system integrity is therefore to tackle tax planning by the rich and to be seen to be doing so. When that is accomplished, improved tax compliance by low- and middle-income earners will follow.

The tax integrity dilemma with the rich is conceptually similar to the corruption enforcement dilemma. However, there is a major technical legal difference. Proving beyond reasonable doubt criminal wrongdoing by rich individuals and corporations that have paid no tax is almost always impossible because no law has actually been broken (as opposed to the situation with corruption, where a law has been broken that cannot be proved). The capacity of the rich for engineering of new financial products not previously covered by tax law, profit shifting around the globe, and a variety of other devices means that they can persistently and successfully play for the gray area of the law, never blatantly breaching it.

What wealthy nontaxpayers have in common with the corrupt is that they are beyond the reach of conventional criminal deterrence. Where they differ is that this problem mostly cannot be remedied by Abscam-style tactics because there is no technical breach of the criminal law. However, wealthy nontaxpayers can be much more easily moved by dialogue than the corrupt. In nations with credible tax administrations, when the tax commissioner issues a public ruling that a new aggressive tax planning arrangement is illegal, mostly the rich immediately cease using it. This is because if they did keep using it in full knowledge of this announcement, they would be in clear breach of the law. What they do instead is get their advisers to engineer a new aggressive tax planning arrangement for them. Then as soon as it is discovered and outlawed by the authorities, they will desist from it. There is absolutely no doubt that this is an area where "conversational regulation" (Black 1998) works. The problem for tax regulators is keeping up with understanding complex events so they can have something strategic to say in the regulatory conversation.

Solving this problem will not be easy. It is a key agenda item for our new Centre for Tax System Integrity at the Australian National University. Among our reasons for having some optimism about rising to this challenge are two facts. The first is that tax advice is highly patterned. Cutting-edge expertise in tax planning is not very widely diffused, so that strategies that target problem promoters are much less of a challenge than targeting problem taxpayers. Many of the wealthy taxpayers who are the biggest problem will be clients of the most aggressive advisers. An audit strategy of targeting the clients of the most aggressive advisers may cause (1) wealthy taxpayers to abandon those advisers and/or (2) targeted advisers to go to the tax authority asking how they need to change their behavior to get off the "A-list."

The second fact is that taxpayers frequently voluntarily and irrationally pay more tax than would be warranted by a calculative assessment of the probability of detection and punishment for nonpayment (Scholz 1998). Many businesspeople find excessive manipulativeness somewhat distasteful, at least when it results in the payment of no tax at all. To a degree it is my hypothesis that many do it only because they think everyone else is doing it, and they will put their business at an unfair disadvantage if they do not follow the predominant perceived tax morality. Many wealthy businesspeople neither want to pay more tax than they have to nor want to do anything extraordinary to avoid paying tax. It is when paying little or no tax is seen as normal in their industry sector that they can feel comfortable as nontaxpayers.

All this leads one to hypothesize that some deadly simple techniques of conversational regulation will prove the stuff of improved tax administration: writing to companies that pay little or no tax to advise them that they are paying much less than other companies of their size and politely inquiring whether their circumstances are likely to change so that they pay more tax next year. Hypothesis 1: companies in that circumstance which are randomly assigned to receiving such a letter will pay more tax in the next year than control companies randomly assigned to nonreceipt of the letter. Hypothesis 2: audits targeted on companies that fail to respond to such conversational regulation will further increase compliance. For some preliminary evidence that this can work with internationalized corporations see Braithwaite and Williams (2001).

If it is the case that some people in the business community feel uncomfortable about a situation where their company pays little or no tax, then the strategy of widening the circle (see chapter 4) is likely to work. If the tax authority goes to the company's tax manager with a plea for a less aggressive approach to tax obligations, this is unlikely to bear fruit because the tax manager is paid to be aggressive in delivering a low tax outcome. If, indeed, the plea fails to bear fruit, then make the plea to the tax manager's boss. If his boss is unresponsive, then go to her boss, then if necessary to the CEO, then to the chairman of the board. Move up the organization until conversational regulation strikes a responsive chord with an executive who has a wider vision of corporate obligation or of the sort of relationship the corporation is best to have with government.

I hypothesize that different kinds of conversations that seek to mobilize the professionalism and sense of responsibility of accountants and tax lawyers can also bear fruit, as can appeals to associations of, for example, accounting software manufacturers on matters like the self-accreditation of tax software to render manipulation more visible (Braithwaite and Williams 2001). In one recent case, the New South Wales Bar Association refused to listen to regulatory conversations about many of its members becoming serial bankrupts to avoid a need to pay any tax over many years, notwithstanding having incomes in some cases of a million dollars a year. The commissioner decided to move up the enforcement pyramid by naming some barristers as serial bankrupts in his 2000 annual report in an effort to encourage the media to ask of the Bar Association whether it had any concerns about the professional ethics at issue. In the event, legal objections stalled the strategy of naming in the annual report. But in the end the media did become aware of the conduct and pressured the Bar Association to take disciplinary action in such cases.

In short, there are many different circles in which conversational tax administration might be brought to life through the procedures and values of restorative justice. This could go right down to the level of the standard individual tax audit. Presentation of the results of a tax audit could be reconfigured as an educational encounter with all members of the taxpayer's family, or at least all members in respect of whom tax deductions have been claimed. The auditor would explain to the whole family the outcome of the audit, any irregularities that require the payment of a penalty, any advice on what family members need to do to keep receipts, ask for receipts when services are paid for in cash, and so on. The conference would also be told of taxpayer rights under the Taxpayers' Charter, and family members would be asked if they had any complaints about the way the audit had been conducted. Part of the idea here is that parents who prepare tax returns may be more honest in a world where dishonesty following a tax audit will be disclosed to their children. Conversational circles following audits may be especially effective for small family businesses. If the auditor secures a commitment from a conference of everyone who works in a family store to change the receipting practices at the cash register to assure future compliance, then any request from the family patriarch to adopt a different practice designed to evade tax will be seen as just that, and as a request to dishonor the commitment the employee signed at the conference.

It will take many years of hard empirical work before we know whether restorative and responsive tax administration can actually increase the integrity of tax systems. The attractive thing about this field is that theoretically informed evidence-based tax administration is so possible. Random assignment of large numbers of cases is more possible than with the more macroeconomic aspects of fiscal policy. So in six years we should be able to report whether restorative and responsive tax administration has actually changed tax outcomes and thereby assisted the pursuit of the fiscal balance so essential to sustainable development. And we will know whether theories on which the purported effectiveness of restorative and responsive regulation is predicated—theories of reintegrative shaming, procedural justice, defiance and disengagement, law-abiding social identities, and restorative deterrence—actually hold water.

REGULATION FOR SUSTAINABILITY

The restorative and responsive regulatory theories our research group is applying to tax compliance can be and have been applied to environmental regulation. I will not review the considerable literature on the effectiveness and limitations of environmental regulation because this has been done elsewhere. I simply refer readers to the most sophisticated and up-to-date discussion of that literature in Neil Gunningham and Peter Grabosky's *Smart Regulation: Designing Environmental Policy*, (1998). A way of summarizing that literature is to say that there are good reasons for believing that conversational regulation where multiple stakeholders (including environmental NGOs) are given voice can be effective, though only when it is backed up by the possibility of credible state enforcement.

That literature also suggests that there is not always a conflict between sustainability and development. Porter and van der Linde (1995a, p. 122) and Porter (1990) have shown that because pollution-prevention innovation allows firms to use a variety of inputs more efficiently—from raw materials to energy to labor—the resultant enhanced resource productivity can increase rather than reduce competitiveness. "When scrap, harmful substances, or energy forms are discharged into the environment as pollution, it is a sign that resources have been used incompletely, inefficiently, or ineffectively" (Porter and van der Linde 1995a, p. 122). For example, Porter and van der Linde (1995a, p. 125) report from their program of empirical work that of 181 waste prevention activities in twenty-nine chemical plants, only 1 resulted in a net cost increase, and, where specific data were available, the average increase in product yield was 7 percent. So we see companies like Dow initiating programs called Waste Reduction Always Pays.[4] It does not always pay, as Porter's critics point out (see Palmer, Oates, and Portney 1995; Portney 1995; and replies by Porter and van der Linde 1995b, 1995c). Yet at the very least it is clear that development and sustainability are not utterly irreconcilable.

The theoretical point I want to make is that while the trade-offs between environment and development can be both win-win and win-lose, the method for discovering the win-win path is restorative and responsive regulation. Pure restorative justice without the backing of an enforcement pyramid, according to the thinking in Gunningham and Grabosky (1998), is likely to result in a win for economic development and platitudinous commitments to green production that are always abandoned when the going gets tough. Command and control criminal enforcement of environmental wrongs is likely to both inhibit job creation through regulatory inflexibility and foster a regulatory culture of evasion, regulatory cat and mouse. It is the combination of restorative and responsive regulation that allows the weaknesses of the restorative model to be covered by deterrence and incapacitation (and vice versa), that creates a contracting space and a regulatory culture where management creativity can discover the win-win of sustainability and development (see further Ayres and Braithwaite 1992; Parker forthcoming).

RESTORING COMPETITION

Temptations to agree with competitors to eliminate price competition, to monopolize markets, are always a threat to the efficiency of economies. A competitive market is not one of those things that persists once we get the policy settings right. It is always under threat from new attempts at monopolization and cartelization. Restoring competition is a constant regulatory challenge that must be confronted at many different levels. At the micro level, a competition authority with strong investigative powers is needed to attack anticompetitive practices. At the national level, regulatory review is needed to tackle structural problems in the constitution of industries that inhibit competition, and at the international level the WTO is needed to tackle anticompetitive arrangements in international trade.

Chapters 1 and 4 highlighted some examples of restorative justice conferences convened by Australia's national competition and consumer protection authority, the Trade Practices Commission (now the Australian Competition and Consumer Commission; see also Ayres and Braithwaite 1992). While this Commission is able and willing to escalate up an enforcement pyramid to reasonably tough enforcement activity (though not imprisonment), it relies primarily on a conversational style of regulation at the base of the pyramid. Most merger activity is not inhibited, though conditions on mergers intended to maintain competition are commonly negotiated in a nonlitigious fashion. Many competition enforcement decisions are dealt with through a predecision conference. The Commission makes available on the Internet a draft decision to authorize an allegedly anticompetitive form of conduct, perhaps with a long list of conditions attached to the authorization. Interested parties can then call a predecision conference to discuss the proposed authorization. Consumer groups and other NGOs often participate in these conferences, as well as competitors, suppliers, and other business interests. Lawyers are rarely given permission to speak, though they attend quite often. These conferences typically proceed as a constructive dialogue that brings out considerations the Commission has not fully grasped. After contemplating these arguments, the Commission may bring out a final authorization or seek to broker a new kind of conciliation between the conflicting parties.

As I have argued elsewhere (Ayres and Braithwaite 1992), the virtue of such a restorative and responsive regulatory strategy compared with constant litigation is that it has better prospects of discovering creative win-win solutions that enhance competition while permitting economies of scale, consumer protection, environmental protection, and other public goods. My conclusion is that restorative and responsive competition enforcement is no less than crucial for sustainable and vigorous development.

But there is more to assuring the competitiveness of economies than firm-level decisions about mergers and restrictive trade practices enforcement. Structural industry-level policies, particularly legislative schemes, which guarantee one telecommunications operator a monopoly, one rail operator, one electricity operator, one or two airlines exclusive landing rights at a particular airport, and the like, need to be reviewed regularly, as do entire legal structures, such as intellectual property law, which through granting legal monopolies can drastically reduce the competitiveness of economies. Some such monopolies can of course be defended, but many persist because they are producer conspiracies against consumers and against national economic development. Australia, like many other countries, has established a transparent process for reviewing such structural arrangements. However, in some respects the current arrangements for regulatory review in Australia under the Productivity Commission's Office of Regulatory Review are inferior to the deliberative arrangements under the old Industries Assistance Commission (IAC). The IAC process was one of draft report followed by extensive public hearings to which all stakeholders were actively encouraged to make submissions (and received public funding to do so through, for example, the Australian Federation of Consumer Organizations). The public hearings were not set-piece affairs but amounted to a conversational regulation where, in public view of interested stakeholders and any member of the public who wished to attend, commissioners would argue back and forth with witnesses about the analyses they were submitting. Following the public hearings at different locations around the country, the IAC would issue a final report. Some Productivity Commission hearings in Australia follow this kind of open deliberative process with financial support for assuring the plurality of deliberation, but most contemporary regulation review in Australia advances the competitiveness of Australia in deliberation that is more restrictive, behind closed doors, and therefore less likely to secure either public confidence or creativity in the search for win-win regulatory innovation.

The Australian IAC approach was the model for the Trade Policy Review Mechanism at the WTO, one of the more neglected but more impressive features of that organization from the perspective of the restorative and responsive theoretical framework. A review staff of WTO economists produces a large report documenting the pace of liberalization and compliance with GATT obligations for the country under review. It covers all trade policies. The United States, the European Union, Japan, and Canada are on a two-year cycle for these reviews, the next sixteen largest traders on a four-year cycle, and the rest every six years.

Domestic transparency is an important objective of the Trade Policy Review, which is designed to help actors in the local economy see how their trade policies might be affecting national economic performance. But international transparency is a second objective; the reviews reveal to other countries when they are being victimized by protectionist measures of the reviewed country. All reports are public.

After both the secretariat and the contracting state have prepared reports, two half-day meetings are held in Geneva on the trade performance of the state before the Trade Policy Review Body. Two independent discussants are appointed for these meetings. Questions are directed at the reviewed state and the reviewers from the floor. The United States usually asks the best-prepared questions, having sent a questionnaire about the state under review to all relevant U.S. government departments. Questions in writing put on the first day must be answered in writing, preferably on the second day. The Trade Policy Review Body reacts to the report by raising concerns or complimenting the country where progress has been made.

Members of the WTO secretariat involved in the process see it as having an educative function, a transparency function, and a function of bringing peer pressure from the community of trade diplomats to bear on states with incoherent or GATT-inconsistent policies. "There is a competition to do well and pride at doing well," as one WTO official put it. Of course, if a protectionist practice made transparent by the process is bad enough, it may trigger bilateral retaliation (responsive escalation). For states that are not major traders, hardly anyone turns up to these review days. But for the major traders, up to three-quarters of contracting states will send observers. An average of about fifty sit in. Often ministers or deputy ministers of the reviewed state attend with a delegation of four or five.

Unfortunately, the trade negotiator's club does not have a culture of transparency. The norm is to speak platitudes in public while brutally beating up on other states in private meetings. The operant norm in this culture is reciprocity: trade diplomats fear frank talk in public because they believe those they talk frankly about will reciprocate when their turn comes. "In public when they notice an itch on someone else's back, their urge is to scratch it and invite them in turn to scratch theirs" (WTO official). In this important sense, while the process is procedurally restorative, it flouts restorative values.

Nevertheless, the educative part of the Trade Policy Review Process can work especially well with developing countries: "You pick up simplified customs procedures from one country and say have a look at that to other countries. Most voluntary change is not from a contest of analyses. It is more from educating them of things they have not seen or understood" (WTO official). In part, those in the Trade Policy Review Division of the WTO see it as educating domestic publics. Domestic trade ministries often will ask the reviewers to "please recommend" and make the case for X, which is a liberalization they cannot sell domestically. Sometimes they even say: "Please be critical of this. We'll get up and say the criticism is not balanced and in perspective. But it will help us in battles with other bureaucracies internally" (WTO official). Mexico and Iceland recently bought hundreds of copies of their own review so they could disseminate it to foment change in the domestic policy climate. Braithwaite and Drahos (2000, chap. 10) have argued for building upon the educative potential of the Trade Policy Review Process by expanding it into competition policy more broadly—developing performance indicators for national competition policy and auditing and publicly reporting on these on some regular cycle. The WTO's

Trade Policy Review Division itself has recommended that it "systematically" review bribery and corruption countermeasures and performance (Keesing 1997), an excellent suggestion for globalizing the restorative and responsive approach to corruption control commended in this chapter.

One of the intriguing features of the patterning of business regulation is that at the global level, because there is no sovereign, regulation tends to be less punitive and frequently substantially consistent with a restorative and responsive philosophical framework. In this respect global business regulation has much in common with the regulation of individuals in the premodern world before kings became sovereign over national territories (see chapter 1). Braithwaite and Drahos (2000) find considerable virtue and some effectiveness in difficult tasks of global business regulation with a variety of global deliberative processes of the style of the Trade Policy Review Mechanism. The unfortunate thing with many global regulatory challenges, human rights enforcement, for example, is that they do not have the resource investment that renders them as potent as the Trade Policy Review Mechanism.

In summary, through being deliberative, restorative, yet capable of responsive enforcement escalation, competition policy at firm level, at the level of national regulatory restructuring to enhance competition, and at the level of removing international impediments to competitive trade can greatly advance sustainable development. Determinedly litigious competition enforcement is less likely to do so.

A Less Crisis-Prone World Financial System

The Asian financial crisis of 1997–98 showed that economic growth even in powerhouse economies like Japan is vulnerable to financial crises in lesser economies with which they are heavily intertwined. Derivatives and the complexity of the new financial engineering do not really create new kinds of risk but rapidly accelerate the speed with which risk can feed on itself, making it hard to monitor and control. Old-fashioned national command and control regulation based on requiring banks to have so much gold in their vaults and other capital adequacy ratios help but are not enough to cope with the new risk environment. Banks that are international traders need to have sophisticated risk management systems above and beyond the minimum capital adequacy ratios.

Regulatory systems need to ensure that these risk management systems are up to the job in the specific international risk environment in which a particular bank moves. Enforcing inflexible capital adequacy rules can be both inadequate assurance of solvency and an unreasonable shackling of the competitiveness of banks that can deliver superior security in ways other than following these rules. Periodic regulatory conversations with groups of professional peers about the adequacy of risk management systems are what is needed. When a bank does get into financial difficulty, breaches minimum prudential standards, or violates its own compliance system, what is needed is a restorative justice conference that puts the problem—restoring solvency—in the center of the circle and makes the necessary repairs to its risk management systems. If it does not respond to needed reforms, then state regulators must escalate to threatening the license of the bank, imposing fines, temporarily suspending the bank's license, installing a state-appointed administrator of the bank, and other appropriate layers of a responsive enforcement pyramid.

But we also know from the Asian meltdown of 1997–98 that national regulation is not enough assurance for other nations whose own banks might collapse as a result of the insolvency of another nation's banks. They have seen what can be the consequences of privatization of banks into the hands of the Russian mafia or into the hands of family members of presidents or generals. It is one thing for nations to allow corruption in the banking sector to shackle their own development and yet another for them to allow it to threaten mass unemployment in other nations. So the Basle Committee on Banking Supervision should be asking for evidence from all states that all their banks that are large enough to pose any kind of knock-on international risk satisfy international prudential standards. At the moment the Basle Committee does not require reports from states that subscribe to its capital adequacy rules that their banks comply with them.

The Basle Committee needs a restorative and responsive regulatory process like the WTO's Trade Policy Review mechanism: banks having regulatory conversations with their regulators and consumer organizations on the adequacy of their risk management systems, states having regulatory conversations with the Basle Committee on the quality of their national regulatory conversations. What kind of regulatory pyramid could the Basle Committee erect above these restorative conversations? One would be direct intervention into the affairs of a state that is not delivering prudential regulation of its national banks—bypassing corrupt or incompetent state regulators through sending teams of experts in to audit the risk management systems of the national banks, reporting directly to the Basle Committee. If the state would not cooperate with this, the next stage of escalation could be to report the state of affairs to the World Bank, other development banks, and the IMF. The latter would likely demand putting the nation's prudential house in order as a condition of their support for the imprudent nation's debt. The next level of Basle Committee escalation could be to quietly advise the ratings agencies of the Committee's concerns. Lowered bond ratings would then increase the cost to the imprudent nation of servicing its national debt. A final escalation would be making public the Basle Committee's conclusion that it had no confidence in the security of the imprudent nation's banking system. This would likely cause a flight of private capital to safer economies.

Because the peak of such an international enforcement pyramid would have draconian consequences, the less severe interventions lower in the pyramid should be quite sufficient to assure adequate national auditing of risk management systems. Restorative and responsive regulation without any resort to the courts or formal punishment is quite possible with prudential integrity. And it is crucial for ensuring that all the world's people do not suffer for the imprudence or corruption of the leaders of a few nations.

CONCLUSION

Restorative justice cannot directly contribute to the deep capital markets, innovation, teamwork, and effort needed for sustainable development. But really there are not a lot of things governments can do directly to create the inspiration and perspiration needed for wealth creation. These are things that must blossom in civil society. What restorative justice and responsive regulation can contribute to are the conditions in which buds can form, conditions in which citizens can help develop the social and human capital of the young, as in youth development circles. But buds will not reach full bloom if they are planted in the soil of a financial system that is crashing around them, a world of cartels where prosperity is blocked to new entrants, a corrupt world where only those with the wealth to pay bribes get on, where the middle classes pay heavy taxes, and the rich pay none. In the economic policy debates on these matters, it is assumed that practical procedures for preventing these evils are just a matter of political will and economic incentives. The reform failures of postcommunist states instruct us otherwise. The crucial policy choices are about how to deliver these objectives on the ground.

I have attempted to show here that principles of restorative justice and responsive regulation are our best hope for transmitting the nuts and bolts of a stable and efficient financial system, for a competitive economy that prevents monopoly, a democracy, markets, and other institutions crucial for sustainable development that are not destroyed by corruption, for a tax administration that is evidence-based in the way it secures fiscal solvency, and a rule of law that attracts investment with safe streets, safe transport of traded goods, secure property rights, and contracts that are honored. When restorative, responsive institutions create spaces where states and civil society can collaborate to secure these objectives, sustainable development is in prospect.

Across the many economic policy arenas traversed in this chapter, I have made a case for culture change to a very different kind of institutional economics where rewards and punishments have a background but not a foreground importance. According to this new institutionalist culture for sustainable development, it is the restorative justice values articulated in chapter 1 that are in the foreground when we do good institution-building. There is open, critical, and plural deliberation in the circle, a focus on the problem in the center, not on who might be rewarded or sanctioned. Yet deliberation is framed in a way that makes it clearly understood that sticks and carrots will be invoked if the problem is not solved. The architecture of the kinds of restorative and responsive regulation I have described creates spaces for creativity in discovering win-win through cooperative engagement with the problem. It is the very solution of the problem that restores rewards to rationally restorative problem solvers. The irony is that if they foreground the pursuit of those rewards, instead of an ethic of care about curing the problem, the rewards will elude them. The great policy error of many in the discipline of economics is the instinct to foreground incentive. The values and practical procedures of restorative and responsive regulation have a remedy for it. That remedy is not so radical. It is actually embedded in institutions like the Trade Policy Review Body of the WTO, which economists mostly find unexceptionable in practice, if not in theory. That practice shows the need for a more dynamic kind of economic theory where the calculation of rewards and punishments is a middle-range fallback when other-regarding problem solving fails, a fallback that is itself abandoned for incapacitative governance of the economy when actors fail to respond to rational incentives. Within that dynamically conceived middle range, the methods and theories we have inherited from the discipline of economics have much to offer sustainable development.

NOTES

1. One alternative program that seeks to confront this challenge is the Responsible Citizenship Program in Canberra schools. It invites parents and supporters of children to participate in a process that makes conflict resolution an explicit part of the school curriculum. The program's hidden curriculum is building responsible citizenship (see Morrison 2001). Another is the Lewisham Primary School connect project in Sydney (Blood 1999).
2. And in doing so we do not seek to devalue existing approaches to building school-community, professional-public partnerships for problem solving, such as those mentioned in the previous footnote.
3. Non-Hindu *banjar* members are excused from these aspects of *banjar* obligations.
4. However, we also see Dow chairman Frank Popoff's qualifications to the Porter and van der Linde analysis, along with those of other CEOs, in *Harvard Business Review*, November–December 1995, pp. 194–208.

8

Transforming the Legal System

ALREADY THE POSSIBILITIES OF RESTORATIVE JUSTICE AND RESPONSIVE REGULATION have been explored in a remarkable variety of legal fields—criminal offending, school bullying, Indigenous justice, consumer complaints against nursing homes, nuclear regulation, financial regulation, other areas of business regulation, human rights, and the regulation of armed conflict. This chapter expands the ambit further to legal process across the entire legal system. The argument will be that (1) it is possible to transform the entire legal system to a more just one through a radical remake of the legal process according to the principles of restorative justice and responsive regulation; (2) such a project is not as utopian as it may seem, since major changes are already afoot that are spontaneously pushing the legal system in the direction of wider use of alternative dispute resolution; but (3) there is as much chance that the ultimate destination of this change will be an alternative dispute resolution (ADR) dystopia as a change for the good. Yet state and social movement steering of the growing wave of ADR holds out the possibility of a legal system that advances justice more than injustice. Equally, with radical transformation of the legal process, there is the prospect of enhanced economic efficiency through increasing the odds of win-win outcomes in a system where a culture of justice delivers principle-based certainty.[1]

It is doubtful that any Western society has such a legal system today. We have a legal system where even in a comparatively just society like Australia, 68 percent of the people in the workforce who suffer imprisonment are unemployed at the time of arrest, while almost all major corporate criminals are unpunished. It is a legal system that allows many profitable large corporations to get away with paying no company tax. It is a legal system that enacts a Trade Practices Act for the purposes of consumer protection yet finds that more than 90 percent of the private litigants under the act are businesses rather than consumers. Across the board when rights are created, those rights are used by large corporations for purposes such as avoiding their tax obligations, while poor and middle-class individuals almost never have the legal resources to enforce such rights in the courts. Systematically, the poor are denied access to the courts while wealthy corporations use the law as a weapon to advance their interests against public interests. Because the law is rarely a weapon of the weak but is often used against the weak, it actually does more to increase social injustice than to reduce it.

Notwithstanding the fact that we have allowed commercial interests to shape our justice system as an injustice system, I will reject the radical restorativist position that it is better totally to eschew formal law by building separatist institutions. While formal law does the terrible injustice that sees prisons in white societies with a majority of black faces, it also struggles to do some significant work of justice for the weak as well as the strong. We can keep the justice it does while crafting an ambitious strategy for correcting its injustices. Moreover, we have seen that we need formal law to protect against the injustices of informal justice (chapter 5). And we need formal law for capitalism to flourish and create employment—to give business a bedrock of certainty about the meaning of contracts, of property rights, so it can invest with confidence (chapter 7). A bedrock of certainty is not enough for private law to work with low transaction costs, however. Legal institutions that cultivate trust in business relationships, as opposed to adversarial legalism (Kagan 1991), are needed if capitalism is to flourish. Anderson and Kagan (2000) even argue that while capital flight is only ambiguously driven by substantively demanding environmental laws, plants are moved to other jurisdictions when the legal *process* of private and public environmental disputes is formalistic and adversarial.

To make the analysis more concrete, let us consider three types of private law disputes: business-business, individual-individual, and individual-business disputes.

A BUSINESS–BUSINESS DISPUTE

Mrs. Smith runs a successful company that manufactures electrical products. Mr. Brown runs a company that supplies its most important inputs, including widgets. Over the years the Smith and Brown companies flourished because when Smith wanted to do things differently, Brown was always innovative in modifying the design of widgets to improve the Smith products. Then one day disaster struck. Smith was hit with a consumer product recall because widgets were breaking in the new product line, posing a risk to safety. The costs of the recall were large enough to endanger the solvency of Smith's company. Smith's legal advice was therefore to sue Brown's company for the costs of the recall on grounds of Brown failing to meet the terms of their contract for the sale of widgets.

Brown's legal advice was to defend the suit. The Brown position was that the cause of the recall was that Smith had modified its new product line without appropriate consultation with Brown on whether the modifications would require widget design changes. The case goes to the court of Judge Ulose. Smith loses. Brown actually loses as well because he cannot recover his legal costs from a bankrupt Smith, and he has lost his biggest customer and a close friend.

In an alternative scenario the case goes to Judge Winwin's court. She sends Brown and Smith off to transformative mediation. At the mediation conference Brown is touched by the emotion and love of his old friend Smith's husband, who describes how it would destroy Smith to see her company collapse and her employees laid off.

Brown proposes that they stop wasting money on lawyers so they can come up with a way of spending their resources on solving the problem. It is agreed that Brown will redesign the widgets and resupply them without cost. Brown also offers to withhold a planned price rise until Smith recovers from the recall. The trust and mutual respect that the settlement consolidates between Smith and Brown help see them through many future difficulties that beset their businesses. The moral of this alternative tale is that wealth creation is based on generosity in relationships, working at mutual trust and responsiveness.

An Individual–Individual Dispute

David Williamson's intriguing play, *Face to Face*, is based on conferences Williamson had seen organized by John McDonald and David Moore of Transformative Justice Australia. In the play, Glen has intentionally rammed Barry's Mercedes, doing significant damage to both car and driver. It turns out that Barry is Glen's boss and has just fired him. Glen was sacked because he had severely assaulted his foreman after he discovered a prank workmates had played on him concerning the affections of the boss's personal assistant. As we peel back the many layers of resentment that ultimately lead to the ramming of Barry's Mercedes, we learn of violence, humiliation, sexual misconduct, racial vilification, misrepresentation of the accounts, and unfair labor practices in the firm. Each offender in this misconduct turns out to be a victim at some other level. And through the process of listening and engaging with the emotions of the other, to varying degrees they all come to see this about each other. In the end it seems arbitrary to define Glen as offender and Barry as victim. Both Glen and Barry and various others in the workplace agree to do certain things to restore respectfulness and fairness.

In this case an individual-individual dispute becomes a series of individual-business disputes about industrial relations, racial vilification, and other matters. This is the reverse of the previous case, where an individual-business tort claim (the product recall) becomes a business-business contract dispute, which becomes an individual-individual relationship issue between Smith and Brown.

An Individual–Business Dispute

An individual agrees to buy a neighbor's house in a private sale. Difficulties arise, and it looks certain the sale will fall through. The neighbor then lists the property exclusively with one real estate agent. Almost immediately the private buyer's difficulties are resolved, but the agent insists on his commission on the sale. Since the real estate agent has done no work to secure this sale, the vendor offers to pay half the normal commission for the private sale. This cannot be done, the real estate agent says, because the commission level is prescribed in the Real Estate Institute Code of Ethics. This code has been authorized by the Trade Practices Commission as something that protects the interests of consumers. The vendor lodges a complaint with the Trade Practices Commission. Because the Trade Practices Commission has received a lot of complaints from consumers about fixed commissions, it holds a conference to reconsider the authorization of the Real Estate Institute Code of Ethics. Both individual consumers and consumer organizations attend the conference, as do both individual real estate agents and representatives of the Real Estate Institute. One of the "consumer" interests at the conference is a representative of large businesses that are large vendors of real estate. After the conference the Code of Ethics is revised to strike out prescribed or recommended commission levels as an anticompetitive practice, and the real estate agent accepts the vendor's offer of half a commission.

What started out as an individual-business private law dispute over a real estate contract becomes a business-business dispute, a government-business and a government-industry-association dispute over public competition law and consumer protection law. As pointed out in chapter 7, these kinds of conferences with a diversity of interested parties who meet in the absence of lawyers are common in Australian competition law. I participated in a number during the 1980s that involved the ethics codes of the real estate institutes of various Australian states and territories. There were always complex and cross-cutting interests in the room. Often the dialogue would lead to quite lateral thinking about how to ensure price competition while finding new ways of achieving the consumer protection aspirations of industry codes of ethics.

The Nature of Disputes in Late Modern Economies

These three cases illustrate how private law disputes become public law ones, how a dispute based in tort leads to a contract dispute, how an industrial law dispute underpins a willful damage allegation, how a business-business dispute becomes an individual-individual and an individual-business dispute and vice versa, how other types of organizations like industry associations, consumer organizations, and trade unions can get involved as well. My hypothesis is that these are paradigmatic stories more than contingent stories about these three particular disputes. The divides between private, public, tort, criminal, and contract law are not neat.

Nils Christie (1981, p. 57) argues that training in law is training in simplification. It is training in how to pare a complex matter down to its legal essentials. That is a tort, this is a dispute over some feature of contract. Yet as Sutherland (1983) systematically showed more than fifty years ago, many of those things defined in the courts as tort matters also involve breaches of the criminal law.[2] As the Australian insurance cases discussed in chapter 1 illustrate, a contract dispute might also be a criminal fraud, a breach of consumer protection law, unconscionable exploitation of Aboriginal people who lack literacy in English, a problem of the public regulation of the insurance industry, a problem that might require reform of social security law, and, more important, a problem of business ethics and broken trust in human relationships.

The dispute emerges from the courts as a case of a certain type because the effects on peoples' lives have been legally narrowed. The move to restorative justice is a move in the opposite direction. As in *Face to Face*, the assault question is allowed in as the property damage to the Mercedes is discussed, as the insurance is discussed, as the racial vilification, the industrial relations, the sexual politics, and the relations of friendship are allowed in as relevant. Part of the restorative justice theoretical perspective is that disputes will rarely or never be lacking in important implications for human relationships and will often have their source in problems with human relationships. There is an essentialist claim here that human beings are relational animals. It is therefore hard to understand or resolve their disputes if relationships are excluded as legally irrelevant. It follows that restorative justice with tort, contract, labor or competition law may not be as conceptually different from restorative justice with criminal law as we might initially assume. Restorative justice is a whole of law issue, which is about widening the agenda of legal disputes to relational rifts that might be healed.[3] In a matter like personal injury tort cases, the relationship issues may be more profound with a family doctor who prescribed a dangerous drug recklessly, a supervisor at work who failed to show due care, than with criminal injury by a stranger. The tensions between winning in court and getting on with restoration may also be more profound:

> In civil practice in the US it is common for the motor vehicle accident traumatic brain injury plaintiff to have any rehabilitation efforts postponed until after the case has been tried/settled. This translates to a patient waiting 4+ years before participating in any programs that look to restoring lost functional/cognitive abilities, "reprogramming" attitudes and goals into realistic ones, and coordinating such processes with family members, coworkers, and friends.[4]

In cases like traumatic brain injury, the need to involve caregivers and children of the victim in a restorative justice process when their lives are also permanently and devastatingly tranformed is generally more profound than in a criminal shooting case, for example. And the need is greater for priority to be given to professional and family consensus on a restorative health and caregiving plan. The anger a woman directs at a large corporation when she believes it has destroyed her body through leakage of silicone from a breast implant can be greater and more self-destructive for the victim even than the anger a rape victim experiences toward the individual who has defiled her body. This is especially so because of the number of years that pass before a mass tort case may fizz to an unsatisfactory conclusion such as the corporation disappearing into bankruptcy.

The final lesson I wish to draw from thinking about the paradigmatic nature of these three legal stories is that because the late modern world is one where most individual action is embedded in matrices of organizational practice, legal disputes between two individuals very often acquire an organizational character. This is more than a matter of plaintiffs driving cases toward larger organizations with deeper pockets—why sue a nurse when you can sue a pharmaceuticals multinational? As in the real estate institute cases, when the disputes get legally or economically serious, organizational actors of wider sway choose to get involved—corporate complainants with the same grievance as the individual, government regulators, or industry associations. Hence private law cases become public law cases because if the dispute has wider implications, politically governments cannot afford to sit on the sideline. The original individual-individual dispute in *Face to Face* can be properly understood only in the context of the organization where the two individuals work and the organizational grievances it had induced. Even at the level of the narrowed disputes that are adjudicated in the courts, we saw during the twentieth century a shift from the situation where the overwhelming majority of litigants were individuals to one where from 1923 in New York State Court of Appeal cases the majority were corporations (Coleman 1982, p. 11). The simple fact is that most of the important things that are done in the world of the twenty-first century, for good or ill, are done by or through organizations. This fact, we will see, has profoundly important implications for the possibilities for transforming the legal system so that it can offer access to justice for all citizens.

In sum, I have identified three characteristics of our deepest disputes that will prove of strategic importance to this policy analysis: (1) they are complex in a way that means they would cascade across many areas of law were it not for the fact that lawyers tend to simplify them to the one category of law that courts can most productively (for their clients) digest; (2) our deepest disputes have disturbing relational meanings to litigants and are markers of identity; (3) legal disputes between two individuals are comparatively uncommon and when they do occur are usually disputes between individuals that are embedded in organizational action. The main exceptions to the last point are very important ones—family law disputes, disputes between neighbors, and crimes perpetrated by individual strangers.

From a Zero-Sum to a Win-Win Institution

Western legal institutions are designed to find for a plaintiff or a defendant. Declaring a draw is not a formal possibility, nor is it a possibility to transform the dispute into something radically different from that stated in the plaintiff's original claim. Win-lose is therefore deeply structured into the institutional design; creative redefining of disputes to open up win-win contract zones is proscribed, though less so in civil law than in common-law systems. While the certainty and security of property rights courts deliver are a huge plus for economic development, the institutional lock-in to win-lose and lock-out of win-win is a considerable economic minus. The minus is especially acute in areas like tort, where the transaction costs of delivering the win-lose outcome are so high. Under the English system of personal injury tort and insurance, "the administrative expenses of the system as a whole amount to about 85% of the value of the sums paid out, or about 45% of the total cost of the system . . . no other compensation system is anything like as expensive to operate as the tort system" (Cane 1999, p. 338). Legal costs are by no means the only reason for this. But even across a wider range of civil matters, the British Civil Justice Review found average legal costs in cases tried in the High Court to be between 50 and 75 percent of the amount recovered; in the county courts, between 125 and 175 percent! The smaller the claim, the bigger the percentage, a fundamental reason the civil courts are irrelevant to little people in most fields of law. Across U.S. asbestos tort cases, legal costs (including medical and other expert witnesses) have been estimated at 189 percent of recoveries (Felstiner and Dingwall 1999, p. 16). Of course, in those cases that are settled, recoveries regularly exceed legal costs by a wide margin. And this is the point. Restorative justice can both expand the realm of settlement and increase the justice of settlement processes. Restorative justice can make a contribution to transforming the legal system from one that is more certain but less efficient than the alternatives to one that is both more certain and more efficient than the alternatives. Since both the certainty and the efficiency of law are important to capital formation, this is a bold hypothesis.

There are doubtless many reasons that litigants go to court in circumstances where the odds are that a win will be more expensive than not fighting. One is that litigants get so angry that they do things against their own interests. Another is that they are misled by legal advisers who have more to gain from the fight. A third is that wealthy litigants can afford to use the courts as a weapon to sustain a kind of domination that reaches beyond the particular case. While it can never be economically rational for a worker to refuse to settle when the expected costs of suing the boss exceed the benefits, it can be rational for the boss to take a loss to teach this worker a lesson so that others will not do likewise.

A challenge for restorative justice is therefore to create institutions of disputing that are less dominated by lawyers, less dominated by the rich, and less dominated by anger. Previous chapters have discussed how to secure nondomination by lawyers (chapters 1 and 4) and nondomination by the powerful (chapter 5). They are not easy challenges. On anger, the evidence is that participants are less angry following restorative justice conferences than they are following court cases (Strang 2000).

But on anger, as on a lot of the other destructive effects disputants suffer, the theoretical claim of restorative justice is more than just that there will be less of it. Heather Strang (2000) finds that win-win for victims and offenders is several times more common in restorative justice conferences than in court. Win-win on emotional healing means that victims and offenders get more emotional healing after the crime. Lose-lose, which Strang finds to be more common in cases randomly assigned to court, means that victims suffer increased emotional hurts and offenders also suffer greater hurt. Strang thinks this result may occur because justice is relational. Healing for offenders begets healing for victims and vice versa. And hurt begets hurt. Whereas courtroom justice has a reciprocal negative dynamic of hurt begetting hurt, restorative justice is characterized by healing begetting healing (Zehr 1995). Strang's data are based on too small a sample to be definitive in testing this relational hypothesis, but they are suggestive that these empirical claims may be correct, especially in relation to emotional healing and hurting.

What is clear in Strang's data is that win-win is more common in restorative justice, and not just on emotional outcomes. What is not so clear is whether this is more a relational effect of healing for the victim begetting healing for the offender. It does look like some of this is going on. Or is it more an effect of expanding the agenda of issues in dispute, creating a bigger contract zone where win-win is a formal possibility?

The idea is that if X wants A, Y wants not-A but B, win-lose is the only option. But if it is also true that X wants P, and Y wants Q, then A and Q may be win-win if A is more important to X than P and Q is more important to Y than B. By widening the agenda of the dispute from A,B to A,B,P,Q settlement is more possible because creativity is used to open up a larger contract zone. As *Face to Face* illustrates, widening the agenda, especially onto an agenda about relationships, is precisely what restorative justice does. The relational hypothesis and the contract zone hypothesis as to why win-win is more common in restorative justice may therefore be related rather than separate hypotheses.

A third explanation of higher rates of win-win in restorative justice may have to do with the politics of identity. Adversarialism locks disputants into identities like victim versus gang member, business versus complaining consumer. What restorative justice encourages is the pursuit of shared superordinate identities that are a basis for cooperation—such as school member rather than school bully or victim (Eggins 1999; Morrison 2001). It may be that even conference participants who share no preexisting superordinate identity can discover a kind of shared identity as a group of people who work together to solve the problem that has been placed in the center of the circle. In these senses, restorative justice tends to be different from settlement mediations ordered by courts, which tend to shy away from widening the agenda of disputes into the (legally irrelevant) arena of human relationships between the disputants or the arena of shared identities. My rebuttable empirical claim is that if legally narrowed mediation/arbitration were replaced by restorative justice, we would see more settlement and less litigation.

From a longer term perspective, this may be even more true. We have seen that it is in the nature of disputes between human beings that they are connected to other disputes of a seemingly unrelated kind. Hence, a settlement to a legally narrowed dispute that sweeps deeper underlying disputes off the agenda may plant seeds of resentment that will burst into a broader dispute later.

The Rise of ADR

The legal system is being slowly transformed by alternative dispute resolution. Thus an agenda of radical transformation of the legal system by restorative justice is not totally utopian; it goes with a current already on the move. The next section argues that it is not clear that this current is now moving in a direction we should regard as good or bad. Certainly from a restorative justice perspective it must be steered onto a rather different course from its present one.

The 1970s was the time when ADR ideas began to have a substantial effect on practice. Many critiques of adversarial legalism were published, and mediation professionalism began to grow and spread into the legal profession. Particularly in areas like family law, where lawyers' fees were not as fat as in commercial law, diversion of disputes into pretrial mediation became a practice widely supported by judges and lawyers on both sides.

With commercial disputes, the impetus for ADR ran in the opposite direction. It was not the lawyers suggesting to the litigants that they would do better to mediate; it was the disputants themselves deciding to bypass the courts and go straight to mediation or commercial arbitration. At the big end of town, globalization gave a lot of impetus to the move to ADR. When deals crossed national boundaries, better to have an arbitration clause in a contract than to allow legal disputes to become even more complex as a result of battles over whether a French or German court should hear the matter. Major firms that experimented with ADR in their international business often found it cheaper, quicker, and more decisive (often there would be a clause forbidding appeal from the arbitration), so they moved many of their domestic disputes into mediation and arbitration rather than litigation. National legal systems then began to embrace ADR in commercial matters so they could more effectively compete with private arbitrators and mediators, especially when the competition was offshore.

More structural impacts of globalization on the nature of law are beginning to emerge that are pushing commercial law away from state command and control by rules and toward principles that set a framework for regulated self-regulation, what Gunther Teubner (1983) has called a shift from formal to reflexive law. Most international trade today is intracorporate, one subsidiary of a multinational selling something to a subsidiary of the same company in another country. So when a national tax authority negotiates with the company on how that transfer price should be set for tax purposes, it must take account of the law being applied by the national tax authority at the other end of the transaction. It is easier for states to negotiate such matters at the level of principles rather than at the level of complex sets of (incompatible) national rules (Braithwaite and Drahos 2000). And increasingly, national tax authorities are finding regulated self-regulation attractive—advanced pricing arrangements, protocols that set audited pricing rules for a particular multinational's business, eliminating messy cross-national litigation. A feature of globalization that is fueling a shift from formal law to regulated self-regulation is time-space compression (Bauman 1998). New technologies, particularly in computing, increase the instantaneousness and simultaneity of transnational economic processes. A cleverly engineered new derivative, for example, will quickly be traded across the globe (space compression) and can be designed to accumulate profits or losses at a velocity not seen before (time compression). As the half-life of formal national laws gets shorter as a result of dealing with such time-space compression, uniform formal law comes under attack as insufficiently dynamic. It is gradually jettisoned in favor of more reflexive forms of law, including ADR that is responsive to evolving business custom and the private justice systems of corporations (Collins 1999).

Other developments in corporate complaints management also steered disputes with customers and suppliers into ADR. The movements for preventive law and corporate compliance systems (Sigler and Murphy 1988) were about dispute prevention as well as more cooperative approaches to dispute resolution. Leaders like American Express funded research that showed responsive dispute resolution with consumers was good for the bottom line (TARP 1995). Business regulatory agencies, for their part, also encouraged these cooperative approaches, becoming less oriented to enforcement through the courts when businesses made their own compliance systems work to prevent problems and solve complaints cooperatively. Both developments fit Ulrich Beck's (1992) analysis of the emergence of a "risk society." Complex organizations became more concerned about seizing control of their own risks through private security, private forensic auditing, and privatized ADR rather than leaving these matters to public police and courts (Shearing and Stenning 1981). In such a risk society, for public regulators command and control executed through the courts made less sense than the audit of private risk management systems—the public risk management of private risk management.

The embrace of ADR by the legal system was accelerated by the case management movement in courts. Like most domains of state-funded activity in the last two decades of the twentieth century, the courts were called upon to do more with less. One of the easier ways for them to accomplish this was in effect to refuse to hear cases unless mediation had been attempted. In some jurisdictions around the world, for example, Saskatchewan in Canada,[5] legislatures actually enacted laws that prohibited the courts from hearing civil cases where there had not been a prior attempt at settlement through mediation.

An ADR Dystopia?

The case management movement illustrates the problems with the way the legal system has responded to these pressures to make it more economically efficient. Stephen Parker (1997) has documented a variety of instances of the legal profession corrupting case management reforms to reduce the cost of justice in Australia and the United Kingdom. One example is the removal of privilege from experts' reports in Australia so that all sides might digest the implications of such reports before going into battle over the surprises that emerge in expert testimony. In response, experts may give their opinion to the lawyer only orally (thereby reducing the efficiency of communication), committing them to writing only if and when it is strategic to do so. A similar reform in Britain on exchange of witness statements prior to trial seems not to have clarified the issues but muddied the waters: "Enormous resources are now apparently put into the preparation of these statements in language which is highly unlikely ever to have come from the witness, in the hope that the other side will be intimidated by the strength of the case" (Parker 1997, p. 9). Most worrying for restorative justice advocates is the corruption of ADR that sometimes has been the product of the new case management. Parker (1997, p. 9) cites the abuse of court-referred case appraisal (a form of ADR) by "the cynical litigant." He quotes Justice J. B. Thomas of the Queensland Supreme Court pondering

> how to prevent the coy or cynical litigant taking advantage of this procedure so that the true case is not run, and the procedure is used in order to get a good look at the opponent's case. Such a party will get a very poor result before the appraiser, and

will very easily better that result in the eventual challenge before the Court. In that situation the party who has played the game will be worse off than if no appraisal had occurred.

The deeper problem with the new case management from a restorative justice perspective is that the reforms tend to be about narrowing the issues, such as:

- changing the pleading rules, in an attempt to identify more clearly the main issues in dispute and to encourage bare denials
- changes to the discovery stage, so that documents which relate only to issues directly in dispute are to be disclosed (Parker 1997, p. 6).

Contrary to this legal common sense, restorative justice seeks to reduce the cost of justice by expanding the issues beyond those that are legally relevant, especially into underlying relationships. Court-annexed ADR and restorative justice could not be philosophically further apart on this question. The restorative justice critique of civil law ADR is that it is likely to fail when it is under the hegemony of lawyering for three reasons. First, the lawyer's reform instinct is to narrow the issues—a turn in the wrong direction. Second, the lawyer's practice instinct is to scheme to corrupt the narrowing so it conceals from the light of truth any bad aspects of her client's case. Third, lawyer domination of ADR means that ADR is used tactically and cynically to extract as much truth as possible from any noncynical truthful engagement by the other side while communicating deceptively to them in an attempt to put them on the wrong scent. Nontruth and nonreconciliation are the most likely results when the culture of adversarial lawyering captures both the convening of ADR and the presentation by both sides of the facts to be mediated. What seems most utopian about contemporary civil ADR is the hope that this culture of adversarial lawyering can be transformed.

Silencing lawyers in ADR is a more productive path than reforming them. This is the most shocking aspect of restorative justice for many lawyers, though not for the more visionary among them, and the reason that in some jurisdictions there has been so much opposition from the legal profession to restorative justice. In one famous encounter I witnessed on Sergeant Terry O'Connell's first speaking tour in the Northern Hemisphere, a flabbergasted London magistrate asked him where the participation of magistrates fit in to the then new idea of restorative justice conferences. O'Connell replied, "Magistrates can speak at conferences. When they commit a criminal offense, it is vital that they tell their side of the story in their own terms."

Top-down ADR ordered by courts is something restorative justice advocates support in certain circumstances even though it is likely to be colonized by lawyers and become "litigotiation" (Parker 1999b, p. 178). But the preferred path is bottom-up restorative justice that occurs before the lawyers take charge of the matter. While it is essential for lawyers to be allowed to advise their clients of their rights when they are involved in such bottom-up restorative justice practices, only in exceptional circumstances should they be allowed to speak at a conference. In my experience of chairing predecision conferences of the Australian Trade Practices Commission, I never found it to cause resentment to insist that the principals to the business dispute do the speaking face-to-face in their own terms, listening and responding directly to the other without having their responses mediated by legal counsel. And this was the general experience of my colleagues on the Commission. A contrast during the 1980s in Australia was the Australian Broadcasting Tribunal (ABT), which was dealing with rather similar questions about monopolization to those considered at Trade Practices Commission conferences, sometimes involving the same businesses and the same law firms. The ABT collapsed under the weight of legal adversarialism, in my view precisely because disputes were transacted through cross-examination of principals by lawyers rather than by face-to-face dialogue. It was costly; when it did decide anything, the decision was often appealed, sometimes all the way; and the ABT was ultimately abolished. In contrast, the Trade Practices Commission, now the Australian Competition and Consumer Commission, has gone from strength to strength as a result, I suggest (Ayres and Braithwaite 1992, chap. 1), of its more restorative and responsive approach to regulation.

The prescription advanced here is that ADR should not be convened by lawyers, should not normally hear from lawyers, should reject legal discourse of a sort that narrows the issues to the legally relevant, should resist domination by courts that instruct it to do so, and should attempt to outflank such legal domination by a preference for bottom-up face-to-face dialogue among a plurality of stakeholders before any lawyers start collecting fees. The social movement for restorative justice is unlikely to achieve this kind of transformation of ADR by persuading the legal profession at large to this view, though it will get invaluable support from some reforming lawyers who are engaged with new traditions such as therapeutic jurisprudence and holistic lawyering that share a great deal in common with restorative justice (Wexler and Winick 1996). Transformation will be achieved by persuading the business community, governments, and other organizations with deep pockets, which are the ultimate funders of the current ADR practices that serve them so badly, and by persuading ordinary citizens, who are hardly served at all by such practices. This should be in their interests, since the evidence is that simply introducing settlement processes within a litigation framework does not cut delay and cost (Cranston 1995), while alternatives that totally bypass the traditional court system, such as informal tribunals, have more chance of cost reduction (Sainsbury and Genn 1995). The early experience of collaborative law, an innovative approach that emerged in US divorce law during the 1990s, also supports this conclusion (Tesler 1999). Collaborative lawyers from both sides sign an agreement stating that they will remove themselves from the case if it goes to litigation; they also sign on to collaborative as opposed to adversarial values. Collaborative law is a genuine paradigm shift, congenial to restorative justice, that increases the prospects of settlement occuring in a cheaper non-litigation framework which is less emotionally damaging for people suffering a divorce. Collaborative law is now moving from family to employment and commercial law. It might give pause to my earlier reservations about lawyers speaking during restorative justice processes. Perhaps legal discourse will not dominate if the lawyers have signed a collaborative law agreement and been trained in collaborative law values and methods.

More generally the threat to lawyers' incomes that this reform agenda poses is not as dramatic as it first seems. Most commercial lawyering would continue to have nothing to do with litigation, involving advice to clients on what the law requires. And we will see as this chapter progresses some important new and expanded roles for lawyering that serves the poor.

MORE ADR DYSTOPIA

The more fundamental problem with the contemporary wave of civil justice reform through ADR is that it is not about justice. On this critique of ADR, the nonlawyer professional mediators are a bigger problem than the lawyers. The professional project of mediators is to distinguish their competence from that of judges as trained competence in suspending their values. Judges are seen as opinionated, indeed "judgmental," in opining that this is an injustice and that is not. The ideology of civil law mediation is that the mediator should be morally neutral. What the mediator deals with is a conflict; it would be inappropriately opinionated of a mediator to embark upon a mediation with a preconception that any aspect of the conflict involved an injustice.

On this issue the feminist critique of ADR has been most persuasive. Sarah Cobb (1997) and Donna Coker (1999, p. 75) speak of " 'domesticating' stories of violence so they become stories of conflict." Part of that domestication is reframing victim rights as victim needs. Coker (1999, p. 84) contrasts Navajo peacemaking as having "a strong antisubordination, antisexist" normative explicitness. For the Navajo peacemaker, "fairness need not mean neutrality" (Coker 1999, p. 104). The relevant values I argued in chapters 1 and 5 that facilitators should bring to restorative justice are nondomination, justice itself, respect for fundamental human rights and the development of human capabilities. The facilitator is an agent of justice first, conflict resolution second, because a restoration of harmony based on injustice makes mediation a tool of domination. Flowing from the neutrality ethic of professional family court mediation, Trina Grillo (1991) finds that informal rules are that disputants should focus on the future rather than the past and not be too emotional, especially not get angry. There is a sharp distinction here with the ideology of restorative justice where the ideal is exploration of all the emotions suffered as a result of looking backward to the truth before moving forward to reconciliation. Indeed, in restorative justice the emotions, the anger, are the most central focus. The objective is to get all the dimensions of how people feel into the circle so everyone in the circle can ask themselves if they can make any contribution to resolving those feelings. However, restorative justice should not eschew fact-finding and legal responsibility in the way much family court mediation has tended to. Truth before reconciliation, justice before healing, responsibility before forgiveness (unless a victim chooses, in nondominated speech, to seek her own grace through a gift of forgiveness to one who has not earned it through sincere apology). Values, values, values. Fairness, not neutrality.

A second strand of the feminist critique of ADR is that it tends to make the public private. Matters such as violence against women or giving women a fair financial share of the contribution made to the earning capacity of a family through child rearing or housework are dominations of public concern. Yet ADR in a sense "embodies the qualities of the private" (Astor 1994, p. 26) in that it is intimate, closed to outsiders, and confidential, reinscribing a problem like violence as a private, intimate matter that is best kept in the closet. The face-to-face risks depoliticizing what might be politicized through social movement politics, public interest law, or some other collective response that is frustrated by the informal disorganization of complainants (Abel 1981, 1982; Nader 1980). ADR's individualistic processing might mean that patterns of inequalities are missed that might be picked up by class actions in the courts. While we can agree with this critique of ADR that it tends to make the public private, we must rush also to recognize that there is an equally legitimate worry that ADR can make the private too public. This is the net-widening critique, which has had particular force in the arena of juvenile justice. The concern is that ADR is captured by the coercive apparatus of the state to widen nets of state control (see chapter 5). Moreover, instead of engaging with genuinely bottom-up participatory justice, as through grassroots community organizations, informality can be captured by the state (Pavlich 1996).

Without being clear about our values, we cannot resolve this dilemma of whether what is wrong with ADR is that it makes the public private or that it makes the private public. If we take the value of nondomination as our guide, we can conclude that patterns of domination have produced the result that family violence and corporate crime are public problems that have been wrongly hushed up behind closed doors. In these domains nets of social control need to be widened; a strategy is needed for making the private more public. Children, particularly children of oppressed racial minorities, obversely are more objects than subjects of domination. As a result, too many of their minor infractions that might be settled privately in civil society are the subject of public control by courts, public expulsion from school, and the like. For children nets of social control mostly need to be narrowed; a strategy is needed for making the public more private. The next section argues that restorative justice combined with responsive regulation has a principled strategy for removing us from the horns of that dilemma. Competing philosophies have ducked this challenge by focusing on one horn or the other, pretending that the dilemma cuts only in one direction.

The third major strand of the feminist critique of ADR is that it institutionalizes imbalances of power, in particular between men who control resources or the means of violence and women and children who do not. This critique also seems correct. A resource-poor woman who fears her violent husband's anger is structurally disadvantaged in a mediation with her husband. She has a more equal contest when a lawyer stands beside her in court to confront her husband and his lawyer. While there is still an imbalance of power in court, the addition of a lawyer to both sides of the contest diminishes imbalance. Of course, if the husband can afford excellent legal advice and the wife cannot afford any, the reverse is true; the addition of a lawyer to one side but not the other makes the power imbalance even worse.[6]

Too much of the writing on mediation versus court in family law juxtaposes the power imbalances involved rather than focusing on their integration. The power imbalance of a man being able to afford an excellent lawyer should the matter go to court is another whip he holds during the mediation. A nondominating alternative integration is needed: one that absolutely guarantees the woman a right to a contest in court with well-funded legal aid and one that guarantees her a restorative justice alternative where she confronts her husband not alone but with the advocacy of as many lay supporters as she chooses to have present, including publicly funded battered women's advocates if fear of battering is an issue for her. Pie in the sky, the battle-weary family lawyers say; the legal aid budget would never be provided to deliver this. This response that has been hardened by bitter experience may be unduly pessimistic in light of two possibilities. The first is that as a result of a move from dyadic mediation to pluralized restorative justice circles in family law disputes—involving aunts, uncles, grandparents, family doctors, and art teachers—women for good reason find the circle more satisfying and just than court for an overwhelming majority of disputes. Certainly the empirical evidence of how women react to court versus restorative justice in other arenas is that they find restorative justice more procedurally fair, more just in its outcomes, and more constructive and helpful to them, and they are more satisfied with the process (see the studies cited in chapter 3). So the optimism is not totally speculative here. The second possibility that could make the pessimism of the battle-hardened family lawyer misplaced arises from Christine Parker's proposals for sweeping reforms of access to justice. The next section argues that these reforms could free up the resources to make generous legal aid available in all cases where disputants of modest means wish to contest their rights in court.

The three central strands of the feminist critique of ADR—the domestication of injustice as conflict, the privatization of the public, and the institutionalization of imbalance of power—have their parallels in nonfeminist critiques that address the same concerns from the perspective of race, of consumers confronting giant corporations, and so on. But since the feminist critiques have been the most theoretically sophisticated and the best documented empirically, for our purposes there is no major advantage in replicating the story from these other angles.

I must apologize for not doing so, yet also ask the reader to be patient. In the next section, it may not seem that we are proceeding to a solution to these three pathologies of ADR—the domestication of injustice as conflict, the privatization of the public, and imbalance of power. Indeed, it may seem that we are moving in a direction that will make these problems worse—particularly the privatization of the public. But if we are to avoid the pathologies both of existing ADR and of a court system that is effectively available only to the rich and the handful who are sufficiently destitute or desperate to get legal aid, the lesson of the law and society tradition of research is that we have dim prospects of getting there through piecemeal change. A paradigmatic change is needed. The next section argues that Christine Parker has provided the big structural idea that can flip our justice paradigm systemically. It is a paradoxical idea in that it has privatizing dimensions that give it appeal within neoliberal discourses of governance. Yet ultimately its genius is that it posits the radical structural shift needed to solve the ADR pathology of privatizing injustices that should be matters for the public sphere.

PARKER'S PROGRAM FOR ACCESS TO JUSTICE

Although she does not explicitly frame her reform proposals in these terms, Christine Parker's (1999b) approach to access to justice implicitly relies on the empirical claim made in the opening pages of this chapter. This is that in late modernity, most legal disputes are embedded in an organizational context and if the disputes get really serious, affected organizations get involved with them. Parker (1999b, p. 174) says:

> People experience domination in the places where they spend their daily lives in the presence of more powerful others—families, schools, workplaces, shops, government departments and community organizations. Because commonplace dominations make up most injustice, it is in these institutional loci that citizens will frequently experience injustice (or be enriched by justice).

So what is the implication of the story about legal disputes between individuals ceasing to be the majority of disputes?

It opens up the possibility of the state "steering rather than rowing" (Osborne and Gaebler 1992) the justice system. In a variety of other arenas a "new regulatory state" has moved away from the direct provision of services (like health or justice) to the public regulation of the private provision of such services (Majone 1994; Loughlin and Scott 1997; Parker 1999b; Braithwaite 2000a). The core idea of the new regulatory state is regulated self-regulation, an idea it shares with reflexive law (Teubner 1983), as discussed earlier, and with responsive regulation itself. Justice, like health, can never be a perfect fit to the regulatory state paradigm because government itself will always be one of the organizational actors that is a principal site of injustice. In response to this, regulation of one part of the state by another (e.g., inspectors of prisons—some public, some private) is part of the new regulatory state scholarship (Hood et al. 1999).

Parker's responsive regulatory idea is that each organization (public or private) above a certain size would be required by law to prepare an access-to-justice plan in relation to all the kinds of injustices its activities are likely to touch—injustices to prisoners if it is a prison, to consumers if it is a business, to creditors, shareholders, suppliers, and so on. Very large organizations might be required to report annually on their performance under this plan, organizations with only 100 to 1,000 employees triennially (unless they had experienced special problems with access to justice). The key performance requirement would be continuous improvement in access to justice. The organization would have to demonstrate to independent auditors who examine all disputes touched by its activities that it had improved access to justice compared with the last reporting period. These auditors, who would be accredited as independent and competent by an accreditation agency, would examine complaint files, staff, student, or customer satisfaction surveys, practical availability of dispute resolution, evidence that disputants were advised of their rights to appeal outcomes to the courts, evidence of disputant satisfaction with the fairness of the dispute resolution they got, and evidence of the effectiveness of dispute prevention. The latter is particularly important because it will usually be the case that the most efficient way for an organization to continuously reduce the injustice for which it is responsible will be dispute prevention rather than dispute resolution.

A major economic efficiency argument for the access-to-justice plan is that it shifts most of the costs of dispute resolution into the hands of the actors who control dispute prevention. The idea is that the organizational sector of the economy would internalize most of the costs of the disputing externalities they cause. The cheapest way for them to internalize the costs of justice would be to prevent injustice. Parker (1999b, forthcoming) and others (Sigler and Murphy 1988; V. Braithwaite 1993) have written a great deal about what makes for excellence in intraorganizational access to justice, corporate integrity, and compliance systems and on the standards that have been set by industry associations, regulatory agencies, and voluntary standards bodies around the world on these matters. I will not traverse this research here. But it is important to note that requiring corporations to develop plans for increasing access to justice sets them a challenge of a kind they have a lot of experience in meeting.

When a lot of dissatisfied patients, workers, or shareholders were taking an organization to court, this would trigger heavier regulation of the organization by the access-to-justice accreditation agency. A second auditor might be sent in to directly observe the organization's dispute resolution processes, to work with the organization to prepare a dispute prevention plan. Implementing the agreed dispute prevention plan would be mandatory—heavy legal penalties would apply when there was a failure to implement. Parker (1999b, p. 190) also recommends that courts impose exemplary damages on organizational defendants that had failed to prevent the litigation by making their access-to-justice policies work.

A regime of access-to-justice plans would to some degree be self-enforcing. For example, firms in a chain of custody for a hazardous chemical—raw material supplier, manufacturer, reprocessor, distributor, retailer—would refuse to do business with a member of the chain that lacked a credible complaints resolution system lest the complaints from environmentalists or harmed consumers come to them instead.

What Parker is advocating in effect is responsive regulation of access to justice. Access to justice becomes less something the state provides, more something the state regulates others to provide.[7] I hypothesize that most of them would not hire lawyers to provide it, and this would prove a good thing. Here it is important to note that as in any responsive regulatory strategy, there is a critical residual role for direct state provision (in this case of access to justice). And while the radical effect of a regime of access-to-justice plans would be to take justice primarily out of the hands of lawyers, placing it in the care of restorative justice circles convened in factories, schools, and stock exchanges, lawyers would have an even more critical role to play than they do in our present system, albeit with fewer of them. On the latter question, Parker has some profound things to say. I take up her analysis of the interplay between the justice of the law and the justice of the people in the next section. But first there are some things to say about how individual-individual disputes would be dealt with under the reform proposal.

The key economic idea of Parker's approach is that by making the organizational sector of the economy pay for most of those disputes that are currently pricing the justice system beyond the reach of ordinary people, existing court and legal aid budgets would be freed up for individual-individual disputes. If we get most commercial litigation out of the courts, resources can be shifted to the family court. The most expensive parts of our present justice system are the tying up of the higher courts with commercial litigation for the rich and the tying up of the prisons system (and the lower, criminal courts) by the poor. A reform program of restorative criminal justice that reduces the latter cost and access-to-justice plans that reduce the former could therefore be self-funding. When much of the cost of commercial disputes is shifted to large companies and much of the cost of regulating criminals is shifted from prisons to the loving regulation and care of relatives and friends, the resources saved might fund a quantum increase in legal aid so battered women can be guaranteed quality legal advice when they choose to fight for their rights in the family court, so they can also be guaranteed the option of restorative justice circles as well—rather than just quick and dirty one-on-one mediation in the shadow of an unrepresented court appearance. The cost savings at the commercial and criminal ends of the system could also fund more community justice centers that can provide a restorative justice service for neighborhood disputes and other individual-versus-individual disputes.

The goals of the access-to-justice accreditation agency under the proposed transformation of the legal system would be to ensure that

1. Restorative justice becomes available for all genuine (nonvexatious)[8] grievances of injustice. This would be achieved by
    a. regulating for access-to-justice plans in organizations beyond a specified size; and
    b. government funding for restorative justice programs to cover grievances beyond the organizational sector.
2. Legal aid is allocated to ensure that citizens of modest means are legally represented when they confront a serious legal dispute (including all family law and criminal cases) that they cannot or do not wish to resolve through restorative justice.
3. Access-to-justice plans and state-subsidized restorative justice programs safeguard fundamental human rights and are responsively regulated to continuously improve the quality of access to justice.
4. Annual reports are produced on changes in the patterns of injustice revealed by the accreditation agency's oversight of the private and public provision of access to justice.

Points 3 and 4 are the goals the regulator would have to meet if the three major pathologies of ADR—the domestication of injustice as conflict, the privatization of the public, and imbalance of power—were to be dealt with. How this might be accomplished is the challenge for the next section.

CAN RESTORATIVE JUSTICE AND RESPONSIVE REGULATION CORRECT THE PATHOLOGIES OF ADR?

Chapter 5 argued that while the justice system will never be the most important institution for confronting social injustice, its role in that regard is not a trivial one. Moreover, part of the normative theory of restorative justice is that we view justice holistically so that social justice is part of legal justice. Indeed, it was argued that a concern for legal justice that is not connected to social justice lacks authenticity. While we must rely on other institutions, particularly those addressed in the previous chapter, to genuinely change imbalances of power, we have seen that legal institutions can and do worsen them. Indeed, there is a temptation to see this as inevitable, given the way the courts are institutions where the rich fight over money and the poor go to jail, given the way informal justice can make things even worse for the poor if they do not have even a legal aid lawyer in their corner.

The critique of both the courts and ADR is so pessimistic because it is so micro. It lacks a macrosociological imagination. Certainly, most individual court cases and most ADR cases can be pulled apart to reveal imbalances of power that play out so the transaction of the case helps the powerful more than the powerless disputant. But there is a fallacy of composition in arguing that therefore the sum of all those court and ADR cases increases imbalances of power. Engel and Munger (1996) show that people with disabilities almost never assert their rights in the courts. However, they do ask their workmates, teachers, and classmates to respect those rights in the organizations across which they move their wheelchairs. One of the reasons they often get a positive response is that the courts have declared rights of wheelchair access to buildings and like rights. Justice, as Galanter (1981) instructed us, must be seen as occurring in many rooms. While the courtroom is just one of those rooms, the public discourse of rights it articulates has an influence on the private justice systems in the many other rooms where the paraplegic seeks to maneuver her wheelchair.

The macrosociological challenge of transforming legal institutions into things that reduce imbalances of power is to work on the way the public justice of the courtroom influences the private justice that occurs in other rooms, and vice versa. The vice versa is critically important because commercial interests—of business, the legal profession, and the crime control industry (Christie 1993)—dominate the stage in courtrooms. Indigenous, womens', and disabled persons' groups do not dominate the courts. The macrolegal change needed is (1) to push out of the courts most of the cases those commercial interests are presently pushing into them; (2) to give voice to the interests of less powerful citizens through restorative justice; and (3) to open a communication channel between restorative justice and courtroom justice so the justice of the people influences the justice of the law. We must also keep open the communication channel from the justice of the courtroom downstairs to the private justice that occurs in so many other rooms. Indeed, we must improve it. Parker (1999b, p. 64) has theorized the macrochallenge beautifully as the pursuit of a culture of justice where every potential claimant has a choice of whether to pursue a dispute informally or formally, yet where "less disputing is necessary because justice is less frequently denied." But this will always be a romantic ideal unless we regulate organizational provision of access to informal justice so that disputants can always get it and its quality becomes so high that disputants actually prefer it to the justice of the courts. Once the courts are uncluttered with the disputes that arise in the organizational sector, an affordable right to the justice of the courts could become real. Yet the right to restorative justice is what most powerless citizens would actually choose because in most, but not all, cases it would be the superior justice for them (see the evidence in chapter 3 and in Parker 1999b).

Put another way, we must reframe the choice between courtroom justice and ADR as a debate about where the imbalance of power will be worse. The better ideal to pursue is a macrorestructuring of the legal process so that the powerless always have a choice of both and always have access to good legal advice so they can choose the venue where the imbalance of power will be less. Moreover, the macrochallenge is to change the nature of the power-imbalance dynamic between the two. Instead of a person being dominated in a family law mediation because the alternative is a court hearing in which her partner is legally represented and she is not, that person must be empowered by a transformed system wherein if she is dominated in the mediation she can walk away from it with assurance that she can fight in court with a lawyer to help her. The ideal is that the most powerless complainants must be able to regulate the other responsively. Restorative justice and responsive regulation are not simply twin capabilities that should be available to the state as dispenser of justice. They should be available to every potential player of the justice game. If our analysis is correct that restorative justice is a powerful tool for securing respect for legal rights, but more powerful if it is backed by the possibility of responsive escalation to litigated justice, then an important way of securing equal protection of rights is to make both restorative justice and responsive regulation as available to the most powerless citizens as they are to powerful corporations and state regulators.

Equal access to restorative justice and the courts (through legal aid) is not enough, however. The organizational sector of the economy will still have organization on its side. The remedy to this is organization of citizen groups—a consumer movement to stand behind consumers, an Indigenous rights movement to stand behind Indigenous people, a welfare rights movement to stand behind welfare claimants, a tenants' union to stand behind tenants, and so on. An important part of the function of these NGOs is simply to be a countervailing lobby against the power of corporate interests. Corporate interests will attempt to capture, corrupt, or politically influence the access-to-justice accreditation agency when it impacts upon their interests. When that happens, lobbying from a citizen group that exercises a countervailing power, putting the regulator in the middle, is needed if we are to avoid power imbalance (Ayres and Braithwaite 1992, chap. 3).

NGOs have a particularly important role in overcoming the pathology of privatized ADR of depoliticizing disputes that should be in the public arena, that should be given a collective as opposed to an individualized quality. If NGOs are resource-poor, they should be eligible for legal aid. They must have standing to sue. With a little re-sourcing they can then transform private troubles into public issues. They can do this through aggregating individual claims into high-profile class actions. They can do it by jumping in to defend a restorative justice settlement that is appealed to the courts by a more powerful actor in the system (as one would have liked to have seen re-storative justice and victim advocacy groups do with the *Clotworthy* case before the New Zealand Court of Appeal—see chapter 5). They can do it by appealing a re-storative justice settlement to the courts to establish a legal guideline that protects against domination. They can do it by monitoring the monitoring and reporting of patterns and concerns in disputes by the access-to-justice accreditation agency: guarding the guardians of access to justice. NGOs need better resourcing to do this—from tax-deductible citizen donations, foundations, and government funding. Braith-waite (1998, p. 364) has advocated a tax credit that would give every citizen a right to write checks from the taxes they pay to their favored NGOs up to a value of, say, $500.

Depending on how well resourced they are, NGOs can also play a role in respond-ing to invitations from less powerful or less articulate citizens for support in restorative justice circles. This is particularly important in an arena like nursing home regulation, where on one side of the circle you have a well-resourced business, doctors, and other health care professionals and on the other residents who are very old and sick, often unable to voice their concerns audibly and unable to sustain their attention on the negotiation.

It is hard for most advocacy NGOs to do a lot of this, however, unless they are given funding specially for this purpose. Volunteer nursing home visitors can nev-ertheless be effective advocates with a little training. The first line of defense against this kind of imbalance of power is auditors of organizational access-to-justice plans collecting interview data on whether circle participants felt disadvantaged or domi-nated because of their age, sex, disability, and so on, on whether circle facilitators work hard at getting a plural balance of supporters on both sides of a dispute. I will not repeat the issues around how circles might be designed to generate reduced im-balances of power compared with one-on-one mediation as discussed in chapter 5.

An important point to make here is that ADR is already widespread in both the organizational sector and civil society generally. Power imbalance in those programs is also widespread. Privatized, corporatized ADR is where making the private more public is imperative, where we must be on guard against victims of injustice being rendered quiescent by domination. So we need regulation of access to justice not only to expand and regulate new restorative justice options but also to regulate the quality of this large quantum of organizational ADR that is already provided. We need regulators who get out and discover what is happening in some of those extant programs, who blow the whistle on them so that appropriate NGOs get concerned and take their concerns up to be exposed to the justice of the courts. Or NGOs that simply counter quiescence by speaking truth to power.

The ideal, as articulated by Parker (1999b) and Braithwaite and Parker (1999), is for the justice of the law, particularly the fundamental human rights traversed in chapters 1 and 5, to filter down into restorative justice and for the justice of the people given voice in restorative deliberation to percolate up into the justice of the law. Advocacy groups that are politicized in their capacity to see a private trouble that should be turned into a public issue are critical to opening up both these channels of communication.

Our conclusion is not quite that restorative justice can deal with the three main pathologies of ADR better than mediation. Aspects of the microdesign and the value framing of restorative justice as justice surely do help with the domestication of injustice as conflict, the privatization of the public, and imbalance of power. However, the main conclusion is that these pathologies of ADR are not mainly addressed by measures internal to ADR design but by the way ADR is articulated to a macrorestructuring of access to justice where justice is no longer seen as something that falls out of a market for lawyering (with a bit of pro bono on the side). Rather, justice is seen as a responsive regulatory accomplishment. You get justice on this view by applying restorative justice and responsive regulation to the provision of justice itself. Justice is most unlikely to fall out of a system where we simply rely on lawyers to be trained in law schools to be ethical and then paid to be the guardians of it. Equally justice is unlikely to be a product of a market for commercial arbitration and other forms of ADR that constitute simply a competing professionalism to law. Many ADR advocates think it will. In this they are being starry-eyed, self-serving, or both. We can only transform our legal system from an injustice to a justice system if we reinstitutionalize justice with a framework of justice values (I would urge restorative justice values) that perhaps should be given a constitutional status (Braithwaite 1995a) and a set of responsive processes for regulating for justice, for ensuring that all the professional guardians of justice are guarded, for preventing ordinary citizens from being crowded out of the courts by those who pay the piper. Otherwise the tune becomes a lament for citizen justice corrupted as corporatized justice.

One of the paradoxes of corporatized justice, however, is that constant corporate game playing in the courts is actually not the best way to deliver the macrocertainty in the law that is in the interests of the economy and business as a whole (McBarnet and Whelan 1999). The complexly incomprehensible uncertainty of the domains of law most dominated by commercial lawyering—company law and tax—are adequate demonstrations of that. The text of these laws gets longer every year and further beyond the comprehension of businesspeople. That is the price of the courts becoming captured as a stage for the most creative legal entrepreneurs.

Under responsive regulation of access to justice, organizations have a right to test uncertain laws in the courts, even an obligation to do so in circumstances where such uncertainty is blocking the access to justice they would be required to provide. However, organizations that persistently opt for legal gamesmanship in the courts to evade the spirit of the law would increase the risk of failing to demonstrate to the accredited access-to-justice auditor that they have improved access to justice. This may escalate the regulatory oversight to which they are subject, shorten their audit cycle, expose them to exemplary damages when they lose cases in the courts, to being named in reports to the parliament as a firm that has failed to improve access to justice. If this responsive regulation worked in reducing the appeal of the entrepreneurs of legal obfuscation, business leaders would spend less time in court, more time running their businesses according to laws that might be more certain. Certainty might improve because law would mostly move up from the good-faith operation of private justice systems to the public courts because there genuinely was an issue of law that needed to be clarified. In general businesspeople who meet face-to-face with their suppliers, competitors, or customers want to keep life simple, respect their relationships with these others, by complying with the principles of fair play in the law (Collins 1999). If the other side is captured by a legal entrepreneur who advises them of a way of getting around the law, however, they tend to get angry and hire their own legal mouthpiece to do likewise. So often in that circumstance, business leaders are like Smith and Brown in the first story in this chapter and realize that litigation is not in their interests. An empirical literature on business disputing going back to Macaulay's (1963) classic study demonstrates that this is so. What is also true, however, is that it is not in the interests of business to have a legal *system* where the law is recurrently made more complex by other businesspeople engaging in this kind of disputing. Business has a profound interest in the kind of culture of justice Parker (1999b) advocates—a culture where it is poor form in the world of business relationships to be someone who seeks business advantage by corrupting the spirit of a just law. Notwithstanding the rise and rise of commercial ADR, business is far away from realizing that collective interest in legal certainty and a business culture of justice they can rely upon as shared by those they do business with. As Hugh Collins (1999) points out, one reason is that private law is insufficiently open to continual reconfiguration to absorb changing business expectations in domains like contract. Business gets more certainty when legal doctrine is continuously and contextually returned to business expectations.

Parker's (1999b) two-channel communication—top-down from the courts to business restorative justice and bottom-up from business restorative justice to the courts—would increase business demand and legal responsiveness for principle-based law, as opposed to complex and detailed rule-based law. If the law is to be a comprehensible guide to business principals who sort out disputes face-to-face, complex rules that can only be mediated through lawyers are not as useful as simple principles. Tax may be an exception where big business has a macrointerest in a hopelessly complex law as well as a micro interest in exploiting and adding to that complexity in specific disputes. It is the macrocomplexity in the law that makes it possible for big business to iteratively play for the area of the law left gray after each round of law reform (chapter 7). This enables many large corporations to pay only as much tax as they want to pay. It is common for them to want to pay some tax so their shareholders can be issued with franked dividends—on which the shareholders need pay no tax. Although a more principle-based tax law may not be in the interests of large businesses and very wealthy individuals, it is clearly in the public interest. In some domains, big business has come to the party with negotiated justice. The United States and Australia have shown a lead with the notion of advanced pricing arrangements, whereby the tax authority reaches a product-by-product agreement on how prices on international intracorporate sales will be set for the purpose of transfer pricing. The tax authority gets a guaranteed tax take from intracorporate sales, and the company is spared audits on this matter. To make restorative justice and responsive regulation work well in an area like this, however, two things are needed: a formidable capacity of the tax authority to audit and contest the transfer prices of multinationals that stay out of advance pricing arrangements and a willingness of the courts to respond to such challenges with a principle-based approach to the interpretation of tax law. There may be many areas of law where businesses will continue to pursue self-interest by exploiting an uncertainty that is against their collective interests, but tax may be the exception where business in some ways has a collective interest in an uncertain law. All the more reason that ordinary people should push for a structural transformation of the law that makes the wealthy pay their fair share of public provision.

GETTING STARTED

The program proposed in this chapter for transforming the legal system would involve something of a revolutionary change. Before this can happen, perhaps we need more of a crisis of confidence, more and nastier lawyer jokes, a deeper cost of justice crisis, a deeper collapse of the integrity of the tax system. But we can and are getting on with the job of bottom-up restorative justice programs in many corners of the justice system. Numerous companies are developing the sophistication and fairness of their internal justice systems and relying more heavily on restorative justice. Standards Australia and comparable organizations are developing complaints handling and compliance system standards for the private sector. Parker (1999b, p. 189) suggests following the example of the Australian Affirmative Action Agency strategy of paving the way for a new regime of enforced self-regulation by persuading lead companies to trial new affirmative action programs that can provide models for companies less confident of tackling a new access-to-justice challenge (V. Braithwaite 1993). So her idea is that the gradualist path to more radical change would involve a reforming state persuading lead companies and public sector bureaucracies to develop wide-ranging access-to-justice plans appropriate to their business. She adduces some persuasive empirical evidence that this would not be so difficult to do because it is in fact good business to give superior justice to customers than one's competitors, to hold and motivate excellent employees by treating them justly, and to be able to restructure in response to changes in a competitive environment by virtue of the trust one has built through just policies, to be able to keep at bay environmental and other NGOs that might threaten the firm's legitimacy. Parker believes the lead firms would show that improving justice would improve business. In time, the idea of mandating access-to-justice plans would not seem so threatening to business, and indeed the organizations that had already invested in them would press for others to be required to do so. In many domains of business regulation, such as environmental regulation (see Porter and van der Linde 1995a, 1995b, 1995c), we have seen this dynamic now—new forms of regulation that are bitterly resisted by most businesses are embraced by the innovative few, which then demonstrate them to be good for business in sophisticated markets. In deploying their management creativity to deliver the desired regulatory outcome, they discover innovative ways of doing so that had never occurred to state regulators. Parker (1999b, p. 188) notes, "Lawyers and political philosophers are disinclined to think of the challenge of justice as a challenge of management creativity." But we can actually get on with the task of creating simultaneously more efficient and just strategies of guaranteeing justice by talking to the innovators who might show the way at the healing edge of the organizational sector of the economy. In addition, we can educate the next generation of business and governmental leaders to an understanding of access to restorative justice by giving them direct experience of participating in restorative justice programs in schools that deal with problems such as bullying. This step is also now being taken in thousands of schools around the world.

Our argument is that real improvement in access to justice requires major structural change to the legal process so that there is both greatly expanded access to restorative justice and greatly expanded access to legal aid in the courts. The idea is that if there is quality in how the expansion of informal justice is done, demand upon the expanded access to legal aid will be modest and affordable. Research by Blankenburg (1994; see also Parker 1999b, p. 77) comparing litigation in the Netherlands and the neighboring German state of North Rhine–Westphalia shows that the analysis may hold up even when the revolutionary structural difference advocated is only partially in place. The Netherlands has much greater access of citizens to legal aid than North Rhine–Westphalia and more activist consumer organizations, which are more willing to pursue legal complaints. Yet the latter has a litigation rate thirteen to twenty times higher than that in the Netherlands. After eliminating a variety of other possible explanations for this difference, Blankenburg concludes that people litigate less in the Netherlands even though it is easier for them to do so because precourt ADR is much more satisfactorily available there. It follows that while radical structural change to the legal process is advocated in this chapter, this is not a case where no positive change can ever occur until the full revolutionary transformation is enacted. So long as the partial change is structurally significant, there is every reason to hope that the partial improvement in access to justice will be significant. An example of a more modest reformism that might be a stepping-stone to wider structural change is Hugh Collins's (1999, p. 353) suggestion of voluntary public certification of corporate ADR motivated by relief from the courts when the certification requirements were honored.

Finally, the best way to start transforming the legal system from an injustice to a justice system is to participate in building the social movements that we have found to be crucial to making decent transformation possible. These include all the social movements with an agenda of legal advocacy, of public interest law, to ameliorate the dominations less powerful actors experience in the society—the gay and lesbian rights movement; Indigenous rights; consumer, environmental, and animal rights; children's and aged care advocacy; the women's movement, and so on. In addition, of course, there is the work of building and enriching the social movement for restorative justice itself.

CONCLUSION

The late twentieth century saw a rise in the importance of ADR across the legal system driven by quite a long list of structural shifts: global competition with national court systems for commercial disputing business from arbitrators and mediators, a crisis of the cost-efficiency of formal legalism in managing the risks of time-space compression manifest in developments such as global derivatives trading, a shift toward responsive regulation by business regulatory agencies; a privatization of security and compliance auditing in "risk society," fostering a privatization of dispute resolution and dispute prevention; declining citizen trust in the courts and lawyers; the growth of mediation as a quasi profession; and pursuit of efficiency via the new case management by the courts themselves.

This means that a restorative and responsive transformation of the entire legal system is not as utopian as it first seems; it goes with the grain of these cultural shifts and can be defended in the neoliberal discourses that are dominant at the end of the millennium. Yet it is not clear whether the growth in ADR has been good or bad from the perspective of restorative justice values. Informed by the feminist critique of ADR, there are three key restorative justice concerns: the domestication of injustice as conflict, the institutionalization of imbalance of power, and the privatization of what should be matters of public concern. On the latter there is also a worry about the expansion of public coercion into domains that should be private—such as ADR net widening for juvenile offenders and video cameras in workplace toilets to detect and confront drug abuse.

The moral neutrality, the nonjudgmentalism of mediation professionalism provides it with no normative basis for concluding what should be private issues and what should be public concerns. Restorative justice, which values fairness and justice rather than neutrality, can develop the value framework for deliberating these judgments in a principled way. Nondomination and deliberation itself seem the most useful values for guiding what should be public or private. Public accountability of restorative justice in terms of these values is needed to guard against the domestication of injustice as mere conflict (Roche 2001).

Of course nondomination as a value also requires restorative justice to be on guard against imbalance of power. As we saw in chapter 5, restorative justice processes that engage a wide plurality of stakeholders in the circle are structurally more able to remedy imbalances of power than mediations that engage only two principals to a conflict. However, the more fundamental shift needed is one where ADR with an imbalance of power is not coerced because a disputant cannot afford a lawyer. And litigation that involves an imbalance of power has the alternative of guaranteed access to restorative justice. The deepest source of the imbalance of power in our contemporary legal system is that the rich have effective access to both litigation and ADR, while the poor are forced to lump one or the other. The Indigenous criminal defendant is forced to lump the white man's court (while the corporate criminal can opt for ADR). The woman in a family law dispute is forced to lump ADR. The structural inequality in the availability of options means that a wealthy man can dominate in the family law ADR because he can go to court with the support of competent counsel, but his wife cannot; the white-collar criminal can get criminal proceedings dropped in exchange for offers of compensation to victims and organizational reform, but the unemployed offender cannot. A universal guarantee to rich and poor of access to both court and restorative justice for any serious claim of injustice seems a utopian structural shift.

Parker (1999b) has shown how it could be fiscally possible. It is possible because in late modernity most serious disputes involve large organizations on one side or the other. Hence, Parker's idea of responsively regulating large organizations to continuously improve access-to-justice plans would cause the organizational sector of the economy to internalize most of the current public costs of civil disputing. This huge cost shift would increase the competitiveness of economies for three reasons. First, most of the internalization of the costs of disputing in a risk society would be dealt with by dispute prevention rather than dispute resolution. Second, where commercial dispute resolution was necessary, it would be rational to institutionalize win-win restorative justice options more than the win-lose and lose-lose options that Heather Strang's research suggests to be more common in adversarial justice. Third, courtroom commercial law that was driven by the need to solve the problems thrown up by access to justice plans would be more principle-based, less costly, than the proliferation of complex rules driven by legal formalism. Because thickets of rule complexity built up by adversarial legalism ultimately cause a collapse in the certainty of commercial law, a move toward principle-based law ironically increases the legal certainty required for efficient capitalism (Braithwaite and Braithwaite 1995; McBarnet and Whelan 1999; Anderson and Kagan 2000).

More important than the economic efficiency argument, a rule of law that grows from the impulses bubbled up from the restorative justice of the people, a legal system where the justice of the law has a conduit for filtering down to the justice of the people and vice versa, will be a more democratic rule of law than one shaped by legal entrepreneurs who work only in the service of the rich and powerful (Parker 1999b). The most crucial determinant of the quality of justice in societies is neither the quality of their state justice system nor the quality of the culture of justice in private dispute resolution; it is the relationship between the two. When the people are imbued with a culture of justice learned in part from a principled law that filters down to them (and that law is shaped by the principles that bubble up from their indigenous deliberation of disputes), when weaknesses of indigenous disputing can be remedied by legal enforcement of rights, then justice has the deepest meaning. It is not that the "balance" between restorative justice and state justice has been got right, it is that the one is constantly enriching and checking the other.

Once the state had been relieved of the burden of funding most of the commercial litigation that dominates its civil dockets, most of its criminal litigation and prison beds, it would have the resources to guarantee restorative justice to all individuals who want it, legal aid to all of modest means who are not satisfied with their restorative justice. Corporate access-to-justice plans would also have saved the economy the resources to fund an access-to-justice accreditation agency to hold both private access-to-justice plans and publicly funded restorative justice programs accountable for continuous improvement in equality of access to justice. Annual reports would be debated in the legislature on changes in the patterns of injustice revealed by the accreditation agency's oversight of the private and public provision of justice. The accountability required by the restorative justice value of nondomination would also imply public funding for advocacy groups to monitor the accreditation agency and directly monitor justice providers that fail to guard against the domination of the groups they represent. While this is a radically transformative agenda, all its elements are susceptible to incremental development.

It should now be clear that restorative justice might be more than a variation on an old theme about how to do disputing, more than a reform at the margins of the criminal justice system. If we marry it to responsive regulation, there is potential for it to transform the place of regulation and law in sustaining the economy, managing relationships between nations, reinventing education and building a richer democracy. This longer term ambition must be restrained for the moment by a debate about the content we want restorative values to have and by the learning we acquire about the mistakes we are making in our experimentation with restorative justice and responsive regulation.

NOTES

1. While restorative and responsive transformations are to the legal process rather than to the content of the law, it will be argued that they will have consequences for the content of law, particularly on the question of whether law should be more principle-based or more rule-based.
2. Since Sutherland's time the transformation of criminal disputes into civil ones has become more institutionalized by the work of private security professionals such as forensic accountants: "A corporation that's getting ripped off, they [private forensic accountants] can do the work for you and you don't have to report to the police . . . They're going to go into the civil courts and that's where the criminal courts want it to go. They don't want to charge anybody. It's too costly on taxpayers . . . The days of the long-winded long-trial paper crime are gone . . . Courts don't want to do them . . . so what you do is put together a case that's got all the best evidence rules, you pick your best case and give full disclosure" (Ericson and Haggerty 1997, p. 206).
3. I am thankful to Angus Corbett via Christine Parker for this characterization.
4. Personal communication with U.S. plaintiff lawyer L. Virginia McCorkle.
5. The Queens's Bench Act, Statutes of Saskatchewan, 54.2, 1994, c.20, s.2. Under the Queen's Bench Civil Mediation Program, all parties to a lawsuit are required to meet with a mediator at a very early stage in the legal process.
6. The quality of the lawyering that can be funded is highly relevant to power imbalance beyond gendered disputes. For example, Genn (1987) found that in personal injury set-

tlement negotiations, plaintiffs mostly used nonspecialist solicitors who were outgunned in negotiations with insurance company solicitors. However, Peter Cane pointed out to me that with personal injury lawyering being much more specialized in Britain today, this particular difference may now be much less profound.

7. In the first instance, justice is not something to provide; it is something to do. But once injustice has been done or alleged, access to justice is something to provide, according to Parker.

8. Even for vexatious grievances, it is generally best to sort them out so the vexatiousness does not lead to other injustices.

References

Abel, R. 1981. "Conservative Conflict and the Reproduction of Capitalism: The Role of Informal Justice." *International Journal of the Sociology of Law* 9:245–67.

———. 1982. "The Contradictions of Informal Justice." In *The Politics of Informal Justice: The American Experience*, Vol. 1, edited by R. Abel. New York: Academic Press.

Aboriginal Corrections Policy Unit. 1997a. *The Four Circles of Hollow Water*. Aboriginal Peoples Collection. Ottawa, Canada: Solicitor General.

———. 1997b. *Responding to Sexual Abuse: Developing a Community-Based Sexual Abuse Response Team in Aboriginal Communities*. Ottawa, Canada: Solicitor General.

Acharya, Amitrav. 1999. "Preventive Diplomacy: Background and Application to the Asia-Pacific Region." In *The Next Stage: Preventive Diplomacy and Security Cooperation in the Asia-Pacific Region*, edited by D. Ball and A. Acharya. Canberra: Australian National University.

Agnew, R., and A. A. Peters. 1986. "The Techniques of Neutralization: An Analysis of Predisposing and Situational Factors." *Criminal Justice and Behavior* 13:81–97.

Ahmed, Eliza. 2001. "Part III—Shame Management: Regulating Bullying." In *Shame Management through Reintegration*, by Eliza Ahmed, Nathan Harris, John Braithwaite, and Valerie Braithwaite. Cambridge: Cambridge University Press.

Ahmed, Eliza, Nathan Harris, John Braithwaite, and Valerie Braithwaite. 2001. *Shame Management through Reintegration*. Cambridge: Cambridge University Press.

Allison, Graham T. 1971. *Essence of Decision: Explaining the Cuban Missile Crisis*. Boston: Little, Brown.

Alvarez, Jose E. 1999. "Crimes of States/Crimes of Hate: Lessons from Rwanda." *Yale Journal of International Law* 24:365–483.

American Bar Association. 1994. "Victim-Offender Mediation/Dialogue Program Requirements." Resolution adopted by the American Bar Association House of Delegates.

Anderson, C. Leigh, and Robert A. Kagan. 2000. "Adversarial Legalism and Transaction Costs: The Industrial Flight Hypothesis Revisited." *International Review of Law and Economics* (20):1–19.

Anderson, Elijah. 1999. *The Code of the Streets*. New York: Norton.

Andrews, Don. 1995. "The Psychology of Criminal Conduct and Effective Treatment." In *What Works: Reducing Reoffending—Guidelines from Research and Practice*, edited by J. McGuire, New York: Wiley.

Andrews, Don, and James Bonta. 1998. *The Psychology of Criminal Conduct*. 2d ed. Cincinnati: Anderson.

Asmal, Kader. 2000. "Truth, Reconciliation and Justice: The South African Experience in Perspective." *The Modern Law Review*, 63(1):1–25.

Astor, Hilary. 1994. "Swimming against the Tide: Keeping Violent Men Out of Mediation." In *Women, Male Violence and the Law*, edited by Julie Stubbs. Annandale, NSW: Federation Press.

Austin, W. T. 1984. "Crow Indian Justice: Strategies of Informal Social Control." *Deviant Behavior* 5:31–46.

Australian Department of Foreign Affairs and Trade. 1999. "Approaches to Peace-Building and Preventive Diplomacy in the Asia-Pacific Region." In *The Next Stage: Preventive Diplomacy and Security Cooperation in the Asia-Pacific Region*, edited by D. Ball and A. Acharya. Canberra: Australian National University.

Ayres, I., and J. Braithwaite. 1992. *Responsive Regulation: Transcending the Deregulation Debate*. New York: Oxford University Press.

Ball, R. A. 1983. "Development of Basic Norm Violation: Neutralization and Self-Concept within a Male Cohort." *Criminology* 21:75–94.

Ban, Paul. 1996. "Implementing and Evaluating Family Group Conferences with Children and Families in Victoria Australia." In *Family Group Conferences: Perspectives on Policy and Practice*, edited by Joe Hudson, Allison Morris, Gabrielle Maxwell, and Burt Galaway. Sydney: Federation Press and Criminal Justice Press.

Barber, Benjamin R. 1992. *An Aristocracy of Everyone: The Politics of Education and Future of America*. New York: Oxford University Press.

Bardach, E., and R. A. Kagan. 1982. *Going by the Book: The Problem of Regulatory Unreasonableness*. Philadelphia: Temple University Press.

Bargen, J. 1996. "Kids, Cops, Courts, Conferencing and Children's Rights: A Note on Perspectives." *Australian Journal of Human Rights* 2:209–28.

Barnes, Geoffrey. 1999. "Procedural Justice in Two Contexts: Testing the Fairness of Diversionary Conferencing for Intoxicated Drivers." Ph.D. diss., Institute of Criminal Justice and Criminology, University of Maryland.

Barnett, R. 1977. "Restitution: A New Paradigm of Criminal Justice." In *Assessing the Criminal: Restitution, Retribution and the Legal Process*, edited by R. Barnett and J. Hagell, Cambridge, Mass.: Ballinger.

———. 1981. "Restitution." In *Perspectives on Crime Victims*, edited by Burt Gallaway and Joe Hudson. St. Louis: Mosby.

Bauman, Zygmunt. 1998. *Globalization: The Human Consequences*. Cambridge U.K.: Polity Press.

Baumrind, D. 1973. "The Development of Instrumental Competence through Socialization." In *Minnesota Symposium of Motivation*, edited by A. D. Pick. Vol. 7. Minneapolis: University of Minnesota Press.

———. 1978. "Parental Disciplinary Patterns and Social Competence in Children." *Youth and Society* 9:239–76.

Bayart, Jean-François, Stephen Ellis, and Beatrice Hibou. 1999. *The Criminalization of the State in Africa*. Bloomington: Indiana University Press.

Bayley, David H. 1976. *Forces of Order: Police Behavior in Japan and the United States*. Berkeley: University of California Press.

Bayley, D., and C. Shearing. 1996. "The Future of Policing." *Law and Society Review* 30:585–606.

Bazemore, Gordon. 1999a. "After Shaming, Whither Rehabilitation: Restorative Justice and Relational Rehabilitation." In *Restorative Juvenile Justice: Repairing the Harm of Youth Crime*, edited by G. Bazemore and L. Walgrave. New York: Criminal Justice Press.

————. 1999b. "Communities, Victims, and Offender Rehabilitation: Restorative Justice and Earned Redemption." In *Civic Repentance*, edited by A. Etzioni. Lanham, Md.: Rowman and Littlefield.

Bazemore, G., and M. Umbreit. 1994. *Balanced and Restorative Justice: Program Summary: Balanced and Restorative Justice Project*. Washington, D.C.: U.S. Department of Justice, Office of Juvenile Justice and Delinquency Prevention.

Bazemore, G., and C. Washington. 1995. "Charting the Future of the Juvenile Justice System: Reinventing Mission and Management." *Spectrum*, spring:51–66.

Beck, Guy L. 1997. "Fire in the Atman: Repentance in Hinduism." In *Repentance: A Comparative Perspective*, edited by Amitai Etzioni and David E. Carney. New York: Rowman and Littlefield.

Beck, Ulrich. 1992. *Risk Society: Toward a New Modernity*. London: Sage.

Benson, M. L. 1989. "Emotions and Adjudication: A Study of Status Degradation among White-Collar Criminals." Unpublished paper, Department of Sociology, University of Tennessee.

Berman, Harold J. 1983. *Law and Revolution: The Formation of the Western Legal Tradition*. Cambridge, Mass.: Harvard University Press.

Birchall, P., S. Namour, and H. Syme. 1992. "Report on the Midland Pilot Reparation Scheme." Unpublished paper, Western Australia.

Black, Julia. 1998. "Talking about Regulation." *Public Law*, spring: 77–105.

Blagg, Harry. 1997. "A Just Measure of Shame? Aboriginal Youth and Conferencing Australia." *British Journal of Criminology* 37:481–501.

————. 1998. "Restorative Visions and Restorative Justice Practices: Conferencing, Ceremony and Reconciliation in Australia." *Current Issues in Criminal Justice* 10:5–14.

Blankenburg, E. 1994. "The Infrastructure for Avoiding Civil Litigation: Comparing Cultures of Legal Behavior in the Netherlands and West Germany." *Law and Society Review* 28:789–808.

Blight, J., J. Nye Jr., and D. Welch 1987. "The Cuban Missile Crisis Revisited." *Foreign Affairs* 66:170–88.

Blood, Peta. 1999. *Good Beginnings: Lewisham Primary School Connect Project*. Sydney: Lewisham Primary School.

Boden, Leslie I. 1983. "Government Regulation of Occupational Safety: Underground Coal Mine Accidents 1973–1975." Unpublished manuscript, Harvard School of Public Health.

Boggiano, A. K., M. Barrett, A. W. Weiher, G. H. McLelland, and C. M. Lusk. 1987. "Use of the Maximal-Operant Principle to Motivate Children's Intrinsic Interest." *Journal of Personality and Social Psychology* 53:866–79.

Bond, Michael H., and Wang Sung-Hsing. 1983. "China: Aggressive Behavior and the Problem of Maintaining Order and Harmony." In *Aggression in Global Perspective*, edited by Arnold P. Goldstein and Marshall H. Segall. New York: Pergamon Press.

Bonta, James, Jennifer Rooney, and Suzanne Wallace-Capretta. 1998. *Restorative Justice: An Evaluation of the Restorative Resolutions Project*. Ottawa: Solicitor General Canada.

Boulton, D. 1978. *The Grease Machine*. New York: Harper and Row.

Boutros-Ghali, Boutros. 1992. *An Agenda for Peace: Preventive Diplomacy, Peace-Making and Peace-Keeping*. New York: United Nations.

Bovens, Mark. 1998. *The Quest for Responsibility*. Cambridge: Cambridge University Press.

Box, S. 1981. *Deviance, Reality and Society*. London: Holt, Rinehart and Winston.

Braithwaite, John. 1984. *Corporate Crime in the Pharmaceutical Industry*. London: Routledge and Kegan Paul.

————. 1985. *To Punish or Persuade: Enforcement of Coal Mine Safety*. Albany: State University of New York Press.

————. 1989. *Crime, Shame and Reintegration.* Cambridge: Cambridge University Press.

————. 1991. "Thinking about the Structural Context of International Dispute Resolution." In *Whose New World Order: What Role for the United Nations?* edited by M. R. Bustelo and P. Alston. Sydney: Federation Press.

————. 1993a. "Beyond Positivism: Learning from Contextual Integrated Strategies." *Journal of Research in Crime and Delinquency* 30:383–99.

————. 1993b. "The Nursing Home Industry." In *Beyond the Law: Crime in Complex Organizations, Crime and Justice: A Review of Research,* edited by M. Tonry and A. J. Reiss. Vol. 18. Chicago: University of Chicago Press.

————. 1993c. "Shame and Modernity." *British Journal of Criminology* 33:1–18.

————. 1995a. "Community Values and Australian Jurisprudence." *Sydney Law Review* 17: 351–72.

————. 1995b. "Corporate Crime and Republican Criminological Praxis." In *Corporate Crime: Ethics, Law and State,* edited by F. Pearce and L. Snider. Toronto: University of Toronto Press.

————. 1995c. "Inequality and Republican Criminology." In *Crime and Inequality,* edited by J. Hagan and R. Peterson. Palo Alto, Calif.: Stanford University Press.

————. 1995d. "Reintegrative Shaming, Republicanism and Policy." In *Crime and Public Policy: Putting Theory to Work,* edited by Hugh Barlow. Boulder, Colo.: Westview Press.

————. 1996. "Restorative Justice and a Better Future." Dorothy J. Killam Memorial Lectures, Dalhousie University, 17 October.

————. 1997a. "Institutionalizing Distrust, Enculturating Trust." In *Trust and Democratic Governance,* edited by V. Braithwaite and M. Levi. New York: Russell Sage Foundation.

————. 1997b. "On Speaking Softly and Carrying Sticks: Neglected Dimensions of Republican Separation of Powers." *University of Toronto Law Journal* 47:1–57.

————. 1998. "Linking Crime Prevention to Restorative Justice." In *Conferencing: A New Response to Wrongdoing,* edited by T. Wachtel. Pipersville, Pa.: Real Justice. *www.realjustice.org.*

————. 1999. "Restorative Justice: Assessing Optimistic and Pessimistic Accounts." In *Crime and Justice: A Review of Research,* edited by M. Tonry. Vol. 25. Chicago: University of Chicago Press.

————. 2000a. "The New Regulatory State and the Transformation of Criminology." *British Journal of Criminology* 40: 222–38.

————. 2000b. "Restorative Justice and Social Justice." *Saskatchewan Law Review* 63:185–94.

————. 2000c. "Survey Article. Repentance Rituals and Restorative Justice." *Journal of Political Philosophy* 8:115–31.

————. 2001a. "Crime in a Convict Republic." *Modern Law Review,* 64:11–50.

————. 2001b. "Reconciling Models: Balancing Regulation, Standards and Principles of Restorative Justice Practice." In *International Perspectives on Restorative Justice Conference Report,* edited by H. Mika and K. McEvoy. Belfast: School of Law, Queens University.

————. Forthcoming. "Domination, Quiescence and War Crimes" In *Handbook on Multi-National Policy toward Peace, Prosperity and Democracy,* edited by S. Nagel. Lexington, Ky.: Lexington Books.

————. Forthcoming. "Principles of Restorative Justice." In *Restorative Justice,* edited by A. Von Hirsch. Oxford: Hart Publishing.

Braithwaite, J., and D. Biles. 1984. "Victims and Offenders: The Australian Experience." In *Victimization and Fear of Crime: World Perspectives,* edited by R. Block. Washington, D.C.: U.S. Department of Justice.

Braithwaite, John, and Valerie Braithwaite. 1995. "The Politics of Legalism: Rules versus Standards in Nursing-Home Regulation." *Social and Legal Studies* 4:307–41.

———. 2001. "Part I—Shame, Shame Management and Regulation." In *Shame Management through Reintegration*, by Eliza Ahmed, Nathan Harris, John Braithwaite, and Valerie Braithwaite. Cambridge: Cambridge University Press.

Braithwaite, J., and D. Chappell. 1994. "The Job Compact and Crime." *Current Issues in Criminal Justice* 5:295–300.

Braithwaite, John, and K. Daly. 1994. "Masculinities, Violence and Communitarian Control." In *Just Boys Doing Business*, edited by T. Newburn and E. Stanko. London: Routledge.

Braithwaite, John, and Peter Drahos. 2000. *Global Business Regulation.* Melbourne: Cambridge University Press.

Braithwaite, John, and Brent Fisse. 1985. "Varieties of Responsibility and Organizational Crime." *Law and Policy* 7:315–43.

Braithwaite, J., and T. Makkai. 1993. "Can Resident-Centred Inspection of Nursing Homes Work with Very Sick Residents?" *Health Policy* 24:19–33.

———. 1994. "Trust and Compliance." *Policing and Society* 4:1–12.

Braithwaite, J., T. Makkai, V. Braithwaite, and D. Gibson. 1993. *Raising the Standard: Resident Centred Nursing Home Regulation in Australia.* Canberra: Australian Government Publishing Service.

Braithwaite, John, and S. Mugford. 1994. "Conditions of Successful Reintegration Ceremonies: Dealing with Juvenile Offenders." *British Journal of Criminology* 34:139–71.

Braithwaite, John, and Christine Parker. 1999. "Restorative Justice Is Republican Justice." In *Restoring Juvenile Justice: An Exploration of the Restorative Justice Paradigm for Reforming Juvenile Justice*, edited by Lode Walgrave and Gordon Bazemore. Monsey, N.Y.: Criminal Justice Press.

Braithwaite, John, and Philip Pettit. 1990. *Not Just Deserts: A Republican Theory of Criminal Justice.* Oxford: Oxford University Press.

———. 2000. "Republicanism and Restorative Justice: An Explanatory and Normative Connection." In *Restorative Justice: Philosophy to Practice*, edited by Heather Strang and John Braithwaite. Aldershot: Ashgate Dartmouth.

Braithwaite, John, and Declan Roche. 2000. "Responsibility and Restorative Justice." In *Restorative Community Justice*, edited by M. Schiff and G. Bazemore. Cincinnati, Ohio: Anderson.

Braithwaite, John, and Rob Williams. 2001. *Meta Risk Management.* Canberra: Centre for Tax System Integrity, Australian National University.

Braithwaite, Valerie. 1993. "The Australian Government's Affirmative Action Legislation: Achieving Social Change through Human Resource Management." *Law and Policy* 15:327–54.

Braithwaite, V., J. Braithwaite, D. Gibson, and T. Makkai. 1994. "Regulatory Styles, Motivational Postures and Nursing Home Compliance." *Law and Policy* 16:363–94.

Brehm, Sharon S., and Jack W. Brehm. 1981. *Psychological Reactance: A Theory of Freedom and Control.* New York: Academic Press.

Brewer, D. D., J. D. Hawkins, R. F. Catalano, and H. J. Neckerman. 1995. "Preventing Serious, Violent, and Chronic Juvenile Offending: A Review of Evaluations of Selected Strategies in Childhood, Adolescence, and the Community." In *A Sourcebook: Serious, Violent, and Chronic Juvenile Offenders*, edited by J. C. Howell, B. Krisberg, J. D. Hawkins, and J. J. Wilson. Thousand Oaks, Calif.: Sage.

Bridgeforth, Carol A. 1990. "Predicting Domestic Violence from Post-arrest Suspect Interviews." Master's thesis, Institute of Criminal Justice and Criminology, University of Maryland.

Bridgeman, C., and L. Hobbs. 1997. *Preventing Repeat Victimisation: The Police Officers' Guide.* London: Police Research Group.

Brown, B. 1977. "Face-Saving and Face-Restoration in Negotiation." In *Negotiations: Social Psychological Perspectives*, edited by D. Druckman. Beverly Hills, Calif.: Sage.

Brown, Jennifer Gerada. 1994. "The Use of Mediation to Resolve Criminal Cases: A Procedural Critique." *Emory Law Journal* 43:1247–309.

Brown, M., and K. Polk. 1996. "Taking Fear of Crime Seriously: The Tasmanian Approach to Community Crime Prevention." *Crime and Delinquency* 42:398–420.

Buckley, Ross P. 2000. "National Sovereignty in the Era of Hot Money: Strategic Options for Asian Nations." Unpublished paper.

Burford, G., and J. Pennell. 1998. "Family Group Decision Making Project: Outcome Report Volume I." St. John's: Memorial University, Newfoundland.

Burley, A. 1992. "Toward an Age of Liberal Nations." *Harvard International Law Journal* 33: 393–405.

Burnside, Jonathan, and Nicola Baker, eds. 1994. *Relational Justice: Repairing the Breach*. Winchester: Waterside Press.

Bush, Robert A. Baruch, and Joseph P. Folger. 1994. *The Promise of Mediation: Responding to Conflict Through Empowerment and Recognition*. San Francisco: Jossey-Bass Inc.

Bushie, Berma. 1999. "Community Holistic Circle Healing: A Community Approach." Proceedings of Building Strong Partnerships for Restorative Practices conference, Vermont Department of Corrections and Real Justice, Burlington, Vermont.

Butts, J., and Snyder, H. 1991. *Restitution and Juvenile Recidivism*. Pittsburgh: National Center for Juvenile Justice.

Cameron, Rita, and Margaret Thorsborne. 2000. "Restorative Justice and School Discipline—Mutually Exclusive?" In *Restorative Justice and Civil Society*, edited by H. Strang and J. Braithwaite. Melbourne: Cambridge University Press.

Campbell, Bea. 1993. *Goliath: Britain's Dangerous Places*. London: Methuen.

Campbell, Tom. 1988. *Justice*. Hampshire: Macmillan.

Cane, Peter. 1999. *Atiyah's Accidents, Compensation and the Law*. 6th ed. London: Butterworths.

Carnevale, Peter J., and Dean G. Pruitt. 1992. "Negotiation and Mediation." *Annual Review of Psychology* 43: 531–82.

Chamlin, M. B., and J. K. Cochran. 1997. "Social Altruism and Crime." *Criminology* 35: 203–28.

Chan, Wai Yin. 1996. "Family Conferences in the Juvenile Justice Process: Survey on the Impact of Family Conferencing on Juvenile Offenders and Their Families." In *Subordinate Courts Statistics and Planning Unit Research Bulletin*. Singapore.

Chatterjee, Jharna. 2000. *RCMP's Restorative Justice Initiative*. Ottawa: Research and Evaluation Branch, Community, Contract and Aboriginal Policing Services, Royal Canadian Mounted Police.

Cheyne, J. A., and R. H. Walters. 1969. "Intensity of Punishment, Timing of Punishment, and Cognitive Structure as Determinants of Response Inhibition." *Journal of Experimental Child Psychology* 7:231–44.

Christie, Nils. 1977. "Conflicts as Property." *British Journal of Criminology* 17:1–26.

———. 1981. *Limits to Pain*. New York: Columbia University Press.

———. 1993. *Crime Control as Industry: Towards Gulags, Western Style?* London: Routledge.

Clairmont, Donald. 1994. "Alternative Justice Issues for Aboriginal Justice." Paper prepared for the Aboriginal Justice Directorate, Department of Justice, Ottawa.

Clinard, Marshall, and Peter C. Yeager. 1980. *Corporate Crime*. New York: Free Press.

Coats, R., and J. Gehm. 1985. *Victim Meets Offender: An Evaluation of Victim Offender Reconciliation Programs*. Valparaiso, Ind.: PACT Institute of Justice.

———. 1989. "An Empirical Assessment." In *Mediation and Criminal Justice*, edited by M. Wright and B. Galaway. London: Sage.

Cobb, Sara. 1997. "The Domestication of Violence in Mediation." *Law and Society Review* 31: 397–440.

Coffee, J. C., Jr. 1981. "No Soul to Damn, No Body to Kick: An Unscandalized Essay on the Problem of Corporate Punishment." *Michigan Law Review* 79:413–24.

Cohen, A. K. 1955. *Delinquent Boys: The Culture of the Gang.* Glencoe, Ill.: Free Press.

Coker, Donna. 1999. "Enhancing Autonomy for Battered Women: Lessons from Navajo Peacemaking." *UCLA Law Review* 47:1–111.

Coleman, James S. 1982. *The Asymmetric Society.* Syracuse, N.Y.: Syracuse University Press.

Collier, Paul. 2000. *Economic Causes of Civil Conflict and Their Implications for Policy.* Washington, D.C.: World Bank.

Collins, Hugh. 1999. *Regulating Contracts.* New York: Oxford University Press.

Collinson, J. L. 1978. "Safety: Pleas and Prophylactics." *Mining Engineer,* July:73–83.

Confucius. 1974. *The Philosophy of Confucius.* Trans. James Legge. New York: Crescent Books.

Craig, Gordon A., and Alexander L. George. 1990. *Force and Statecraft.* 2d ed. New York: Oxford University Press.

Cranston, Ross. 1995. " 'The Rational Study of Law': Social Research and Access to Justice." In *Reform of Civil Procedure: Essays on "Access to Justice,"* edited by A. Zuckerman and R. Cranston. Oxford: Clarendon Press.

Crawford, Adam. 1996. "Victim/Offender Mediation and Reparation in Comparative European Cultures: France, England and Wales." Paper presented at the Australian and New Zealand Society of Criminology Conference, Wellington, January–February.

———. 1997. *The Local Governance of Crime: Appeals to Community and Partnerships.* Oxford: Clarendon Press.

Cullen, Francis T. 1994. "Social Support as an Organizing Concept for Criminology: Presidential Address to the Academy of Criminal Justice Sciences." *Justice Quarterly* 11:527–59.

Cullen, Francis T., and Paul Gendreau. 2000. "Assessing Correctional Rehabilitation: Policy, Practice, and Prospects." In *Policies, Processes, and Decisions of the Criminal Justice System.* Vol. 3, edited by J. Horney. Washington, D.C.: U.S. Department of Justice.

Cullen, Francis T., John Paul Wright, and Mitchell G. Chamlin. 1999. "Social Support and Social Reform: A Progressive Crime Control Agenda." *Crime and Delinquency* 45: 188–207.

Cummings, William K. 1980. *Education and Equality in Japan.* Princeton: Princeton University Press.

Cunneen, C. 1997. "Community Conferencing and the Fiction of Indigenous Control." *Australian and New Zealand Journal of Criminology* 30:292–312.

Daly, K. 1996. "Diversionary Conferences in Australia: A Reply to the Optimists and Skeptics." Paper presented at the annual meeting of the American Society of Criminology, 20–23 November.

Daly, K., and R. Immarigeon. 1998. "The Past, Present, and Future of Restorative Justice: Some Critical Reflections." *Contemporary Justice Review* 1:21–45.

Davies, Norman. 1997. *Europe: A History.* London: Pimlico.

Davis, G. 1992. *Making Amends: Mediation and Reparation in Criminal Justice.* London: Routledge.

Davis, Robert T., and R. W. Stahl. 1967. "Safety Organization and Activities of Award-Winning Companies in the Coal Mining Industry." In *Bureau of Mines Information Circular 8224.* Washington, D.C.: Bureau of Mines.

De Greiff, Pablo. 2000. "Deliberative Democracy, Punishment and Truth-Telling." Unpublished manuscript.

De Haan, W. 1990. *The Politics of Redress: Crime, Punishment and Penal Abolition.* London: Unwin Hyman.

DeMichiei, John M., John F. Langton, Kenneth A. Bullock, and Terrance C. Wiles. 1982. *Factors Associated with Disabling Injuries in Underground Coal Mines.* Washington, D.C.: Mine Safety and Health Administration.

de Waal, Alex. 1997a. *Famine Crimes: Politics and the Disaster Relief Industry in Africa.* Bloomington and Indianapolis: Africa Rights and the International African Institute, Indiana University Press.

———. 1997b. *Times Literary Supplement,* 21 February.

Diamond, A. 1935. *Primitive Law.* London: Longmans, Green.

Dienstbier, R. A., D. Hillman, J. Lenhoff, and M. C. Valkenaar. 1975. "An Emotion-Attribution Approach to Moral Behavior: Interfacing Cognitive and Avoidance Theories of Moral Development." *Psychological Review* 82:229–315.

Dignan, J. 1990. *An Evaluation of an Experimental Adult Reparation Scheme in Kettering, Northamptonshire.* Sheffield, United Kingdom: Centre for Criminological and Legal Research, University of Sheffield.

———. 1992. "Repairing the Damage: Can Reparation Work in the Service of Diversion?" *British Journal of Criminology* 32: 453–72.

Dingwall, Robert, J. Eekelaar, and T. Murray. 1983. *The Protection of Children: State Intervention and Family Life.* Oxford: Basil Blackwell.

Dinnen, Sinclair. 1996. "Challenges of Order in a Weak State." Ph.D. diss., Australian National University.

———. 2001. "Restorative Justice and Civil Society in Melanesia: The Case of Papua New Guinea." In *Restorative Justice and Civil Society,* edited by H. Strang and J. Braithwaite. Melbourne: Cambridge University Press.

Dix, T., and Grusec, J. E. 1983. "Parental Influence Techniques: An Attributional Analysis." *Child Development* 54:645–52.

Djalal, Dino Patti. 1999. "The Indonesian Experience in Facilitating a Peace Settlement between the Government of the Republic of the Philippines and the Moro National Liberation Front." In *The Next Stage: Preventive Diplomacy and Security Cooperation in the Asia-Pacific Region,* edited by D. Ball and A. Acharya. Canberra: Australian National University.

Dobash, R. E., and R. P. Dobash. 1979. *Violence against Wives: A Case against Patriarchy.* New York: Free Press.

Dolling, D., and A. Hartman 2000. "Reoffending after Victim-Offender Mediation in Juvenile Court Proceedings." Paper to Fourth International Conference on Restorative Justice for Juveniles, Tübingen, Germany.

Donnelly, Jack. 2000. *Realism and International Relations.* Cambridge: Cambridge University Press.

Doob, A., and J. Roberts. 1983. *Sentencing: An Analysis of the Public's View of Sentencing. A Report in the Department of Justice, Canada.* Canada: Department of Justice.

———. 1988. "Public Attitudes towards Sentencing in Canada." In *Public Attitudes to Sentencing,* edited by N. Walker and M. Hough. Aldershot: Gower.

Dowrick, Steve. 1993. "New Theory and Evidence on Economic Growth and Their Implications for Australian Policy." *Economic Analysis and Policy* 23: 105–21.

Doyle, M. 1983. "Kant, Liberal Legacies and Foreign Affairs." *Philosophy and Public Affairs* 12:205–35; 323–53.

———. 1986. "Liberalism and World Politics." *American Political Science Review* 80:1151–69.

Dunford, F. 1990. "System-Initiated Warrants for Suspects of Misdemeanour Domestic Assault: A Pilot Study." *Justice Quarterly* 7:631–53.

Dupont, Alan. 1999. "Preventive Diplomacy and Transnational Security Issues." In *The Next Stage: Preventive Diplomacy and Security Cooperation in the Asia-Pacific Region,* edited by D. Ball and A. Acharya. Canberra: Australian National University.

Duque, Luis F., and Joanne Klevens. 1999. "Medellin, Colombia: A Case Study in Violence Prevention Efforts." Paper presented to the annual meeting of the American Society of Criminology, 10 November, Toronto.

Durkheim, E. 1961. *Moral Education: A Study in the Theory and Application of the Sociology of Education*. Trans. E. K. Wilson and H. Schnurer. New York: Free Press.

Eckel, Malcolm David. 1997. "A Buddhist Approach to Repentance." In *Repentance: A Comparative Perspective*, edited by Amitai Etzioni and David E. Carney. New York: Rowman and Littlefield.

Eggins, R. A. 1999. "Social Identity and Social Conflict: Negotiating the Path to Resolution." Ph.D. diss., Australian National University.

Eglash, Albert. 1975. "Beyond Restitution: Creative Restitution." In *Restitution in Criminal Justice*, edited by J. Hudson, and B. Galaway. Lexington, Mass.: Lexington Books.

Eiseman, Fred B. 1990. *Bali: Sekala and Niskala*, Vol. 2. Singapore: Periplus Editions.

Elliott, D. S. 1998. *Blueprints for Violence Prevention*. Boulder: Institute of Behavioral Science, University of Colorado.

Elliott, D. S., and H. L. Voss. 1974. *Delinquency and Dropout*. Lexington, Mass.: Lexington Books.

Emler, N., and S. Reicher. 1995. *Adolescence and Delinquency: The Collective Management of Reputation*. Oxford: Blackwell.

Engel, D., and Munger, F. 1996. "Rights, Remembrance and the Reconciliation of Difference." *Law and Society Review* 30:7–53.

Ericson, Richard V., and Kevin D. Haggerty. 1997. *Policing the Risk Society*. Oxford: Clarendon Press.

Ervin, L., and A. Schneider. 1990. "Explaining the Effects of Restitution on Offenders: Results from a National Experiment in Juvenile Courts." In *Criminal Justice, Restitution and Reconciliation*, edited by B. Galaway and J. Hudson. New York: Willow Tree Press.

Esbensen, Finn-Aage, and David Huizinga. 1993. "Gangs, Drugs and Delinquency in a Survey of Urban Youth." *Criminology* 31:565–87.

Evans, Gareth. 1999. "Preventive Diplomacy: Concepts and Practice." In *The Next Stage: Preventive Diplomacy and Security Cooperation in the Asia-Pacific Region*, edited by D. Ball and A. Acharya. Canberra: Australian National University.

Farrington, David P. 1993. "Understanding and Preventing Bullying." In *Crime and Justice: Annual Review of Research*, edited by M. Tonry. Vol. 17. Chicago: University of Chicago Press.

Felstiner, William L. F., and Robert Dingwall. 1999. *Asbestos Litigation in the United Kingdom: An Interim Report*. Chicago: American Bar Foundation, Centre for Socio-Legal Studies.

Findlay, Mark. 1998. "Decolonising Restoration and Justice." *Current Issues in Criminal Justice* 10:85–88.

Finn Report. 1991. *Young People's Participation in Post-compulsory Education and Training*. Canberra: Australian Government Publication Service.

Fishkin, James, and Robert C. Luskin. 1999. "The Quest for Deliberative Democracy." Paper presented to the European Consortium for Political Research, University of Mannheim, Bermand, 26–31 March.

Fisse, B. 1983. "Reconstructing Corporate Criminal Law: Deterrence, Retribution, Fault, and Sanctions." *Southern California Law Review* 56: 1141–246.

Fisse, B., and J. Braithwaite. 1983. *The Impact of Publicity on Corporate Offenders*. Albany: State University of New York Press.

———. 1993. *Corporations, Crime and Accountability*. Cambridge: Cambridge University Press.

Fitzpatrick, Peter. 1992. "The Impossibility of Popular Justice." *Social and Legal Studies* 1: 199–215.

Forsythe, Lubica. 1995. "An Analysis of Juvenile Apprehension Characteristics and Reapprehension Rates." In *A New Approach to Juvenile Justice: An Evaluation of Family Conferencing in Wagga Wagga*, edited by David Moore, with Lubica Forsythe and Terry O'Connell. A Report to the Criminology Research Council. Wagga Wagga, Australia: Charles Sturt University.

Foucault, Michel. 1977. *Discipline and Punish: The Birth of the Prison*. London: Pantheon.

Fry, Don. 1997. *A Report on Diversionary Conferencing*. Alice Springs, Australia: Northern Territory Police.

Fukuyama, Francis. 1995. *Trust: The Social Virtues and the Creation of Prosperity*. New York: Free Press.

Fuller, Lon. 1964. *The Morality of Law*. New Haven, Conn.: Yale University Press.

Galanter, Marc. 1981. "Justice in Many Rooms." In *Access to Justice and the Welfare State*, edited by M. Cappelletti. Alphen aan den Rijn, Netherlands: Sijthoff.

Galaway, B. 1992. "The New Zealand Experience Implementing the Reparation Sentence." In *Restorative Justice on Trial: Pitfalls and Potentials of Victim-Offender Mediation—International Research Perspectives*, edited by H. Messmer and H. U. Otto. Dordrecht and Boston: Kluwer Academic Publishers.

Galaway Burt and Joe Hudson, eds. 1975. *Considering the Victim*. Springfield: Ill.: Charles C. Thomas.

Garland, D. 1985. *Punishment and Welfare*. Aldershot: Gower.

———. 1990. *Punishment and Modern Society*. Oxford: Clarendon Press.

Geertz, Clifford. 1983. *Local Knowledge*. New York: Basic Books.

Gehm, John. 1990. "Mediated Victim-Offender Restitution Agreements: An Exploratory Analysis of Factors Related to Victim Participation." In *Criminal Justice, Restitution, and Reconciliation*, edited by B. Galaway and J. Hudson. Monsey, N.Y.: Willow Tree Press.

Geis, Gilbert, and Leigh B. Bienen. 1998. *Crimes of the Century*. Boston: Northeastern University Press.

Gendreau, Paul. 1996. "The Principles of Effective Intervention with Offenders." In *Choosing Correctional Interventions That Work: Defining the Demand and Evaluating the Supply*, edited by Alan T. Harland. Newbury Park, Calif.: Sage.

———. 1998. "Keynote Speech: What Works in Community Corrections: Promising Approaches in Reducing Criminal Behavior." In *Successful Community Sanctions and Services for Special Offenders*, edited by B. J. Auerbach and J. C. Castellano. Lanham, Md.: American Correctional Association.

Gendreau, Paul, Kathleen Clark, and Glenn A. Gray. 1996. "Intensive Surveillance Programs: They Don't Work." *Community Corrections Report* 3(3):1–15.

Gendreau, Paul, Claire Goggin, and Francis T. Cullen. 1999. "The Effects of Prison Sentences on Recidivism." Report to the Corrections Research and Development and Aboriginal Policy Branch, Solicitor General of Canada, Ottawa.

Genn, Hazed. 1987. *Hard Bargaining*. Oxford: Oxford University Press.

Gentry, Deborah B., and Wayne A. Benenson. 1993. "School-to-Home Transfer of Conflict Management Skills among School-Age Children." *Families in Society*, February:67–73.

Gernet, Jacques. 1982. *A History of Chinese Civilization*. Cambridge: Cambridge University Press.

Geudens, Hilde. 1998. "The Recidivism Rate of Community Service as a Restitutive Judicial Sanction in Comparison with the Traditional Juvenile Justice Measures." In *Restorative Justice for Juveniles: Potentialities, Risks and Problems for Research*, edited by Lode Walgrave. Leuven: Leuven University Press.

Goffman, E. 1956. "Embarrassment and Social Organization." *American Journal of Sociology* 62:264–71.

Goldgeir, James, and Michael McFaul. 1992. "A Tale of Two Worlds: Core and Periphery in the Post–Cold War Era." *International Organization* 46:467–92.

Goleman, D. 1995. *Emotional Intelligence*. New York: Bantam Books.

Goodes, T. 1995. *Victims and Family Conferences: Juvenile Justice in South Australia*. Adelaide: Family Conferencing Team.

Gottfredson, Denise. 1997. "School-Based Crime Prevention." In *Preventing Crime: What Works, What Doesn't, What's Promising. A Report to the United States Congress*, edited by Lawrence Sherman, Denise Gottfredson, Doris MacKenzie, John Eck, Peter Reuter, and Shawn Bushway. Washington, D.C.: National Institute of Justice.

Gottfredson, S. D., and D. M. Gottfredson. 1994. "Behavioural Prediction and the Problem of Incapacitation." *Criminology* 32:441–74.

Gottfredson, Stephen D., and Ralph B. Taylor. 1987. "Attitudes of Correctional Policymakers and the Public." In *America's Correctional Crisis: Prison Populations and Public Policy*, edited by Stephen D. Gottfredson and Sean McConville. New York: Greenwood Press.

Grabosky, P. N. 1990a. "Citizen Co-production and Corruption Control." *Corruption and Reform* 5:125–51.

———. 1990b. "Professional Advisors and White Collar Illegality: Towards Explaining and Excusing Professional Failure." *University of New South Wales Law Journal* 13(2):1–24.

———. 1992. "Law Enforcement and the Citizen: Non-governmental Participants in Crime Prevention and Control." *Policing and Society*. 2:249–71.

———. 1994. "Green Markets: The Environmental Regulation by the Private Sector." *Law and Policy* 16: 419–48.

———. 1995. "Using Non-governmental Resources to Foster Regulatory Compliance." *Governance* 8:527–50.

Granovetter, Mark S. 1973. "The Strength of Weak Ties." *American Journal of Sociology* 78: 1360–80.

———. 1974. *Getting a Job: A Study of Contacts and Careers*. Cambridge, Mass.: Harvard University Press.

Green, Ross Gordon. 1998. *Justice in Aboriginal Communities*. Saskatoon: Purich Publishing.

Griffiths, Curt Taylor, and Ron Hamilton. 1996. "Sanctioning and Healing: Restorative Justice in Canadian Aboriginal Communities." In *Restorative Justice: International Perspectives*, edited by Burt Galaway and Joe Hudson. Monsey, N.Y.: Criminal Justice Press.

Grillo, Trina. 1991. "The Mediation Alternative: Process Dangers for Women." *Yale Law Journal* 100:1545.

Gunningham, Neil. 1995. "Environment, Self-Regulation and the Chemical Industry: Assessing Responsible Care." *Law and Policy*. 17:57–109.

———. 1996. "From Adversarialism to Partnership? ISO 14000 and Regulation." Paper presented to the Australian Centre for Environmental Law, Australian National University, Conference on ISO 14000, Canberra.

Gunningham, Neil, and Peter Grabosky. 1998. *Smart Regulation: Designing Environmental Policy*. Oxford: Clarendon Press.

Habermas, Jurgen. 1996. *Between Facts and Norms: Contributions to a Discourse Theory of Law and Democracy*. London: Polity Press.

Hagan, J. 1991. "Destiny and Drift: Subcultural Preferences, Status Attainments, and the Risks and Rewards of Youth." *American Sociological Review* 56:567–82.

Hagan, John, and Bill McCarthy. 1997. *Mean Streets: Youth Crime and Homelessness*. Cambridge: Cambridge University Press.

Haines, Fiona. 1997. *Corporate Regulation: Beyond "Punish or Persuade."* Oxford: Clarendon Press.

Haines, Kevin. 1998. "Some Principled Objections to a Restorative Justice Approach to Working with Juvenile Offenders." In *Restorative Justice for Juveniles: Potentialities, Risks and Problems for Research*, edited by Lode Walgrave. Leuven: Leuven University Press.

Haley, John. 1996. "Crime Prevention through Restorative Justice: Lessons from Japan." In *Restorative Justice: International Perspectives*, edited by Burt Galaway and Joe Hudson. Monsey, N.Y.: Criminal Justice Press.

———. 1999. "Apology and Pardon: Learning from Japan." In *Civic Repentance*, edited by A. Etzioni. Lanham, Md.: Rowman and Littlefield.

Haley, John, assisted by A. M. Neugebauer. 1992. "Victim-Offender Mediations: Japanese and American Comparisons." In *Restorative Justice on Trial: Pitfalls and Potentials of Victim-Offender Mediation—International Research Perspectives*, edited by H. Messmer and H. U. Otto. Dordrecht and Boston: Kluwer Academic Publishers.

Halliday, Fred. 1999. *Revolution and World Politics*. London: Macmillan.

Hamilton, V. Lee, and Joseph Sanders. 1992. *Everyday Justice: Responsibility and the Individual in Japan and the United States*. New Haven, Conn.: Yale University Press.

Harmon, Michael M. 1995. *Responsibility as Paradox: A Critique of Rational Discourse on Government*. Thousand Oaks, Calif.: Sage.

Harris, M. K. 1991. "Moving into the New Millennium: Toward a Feminist Vision of Justice." In *Criminology as Peacemaking*, edited by H. E. Pepinsky and R. Quinney. Bloomington: Indiana University Press.

Harris, Nathan. 2001. "Part II—Shaming and Shame: Regulating Drink-Driving." In *Shame Management through Reintegration*, by Eliza Ahmed, Nathan Harris, John Braithwaite, and Valerie Braithwaite. Cambridge: Cambridge University Press.

Harris, Nathan, and Jamie Burton. 1997. *The Reliability of Observed Reintegrative Shaming, Shame, Defiance and Other Key Concepts in Diversionary Conferences*. RISE Working Papers. Canberra: Australian National University.

Hassall, Ian. 1996. "Origin and Development of Family Group Conferences." In *Family Group Conferences: Perspectives on Policy and Practice*, edited by Joe Hudson, Allison Morris, Gabrielle Maxwell, and Burt Galaway. Sydney: Federation Press and Criminal Justice Press.

Hawkins, Keith. 1984. *Environment and Enforcement: Regulation and the Social Definition of Pollution*. Oxford: Clarendon Press.

Hay, D. 1975. "Property, Authority and the Criminal Law." In *Albion's Fatal Tree*, edited by D. Hay, P. Linebaugh, J. G. Rule, E. P. Thompson, and C. Winslow. London: Allen Lane.

Hayes, Hennessey, Tim Prenzler, with Richard Wortley. 1998. *Making Amends: Final Evaluation of the Queensland Community Conferencing Pilot*. School of Criminology and Criminal Justice, Griffith University.

Heidensohn, Frances. 1986. "Models of Justice: Portia or Persephone? Some Thoughts on Equality, Fairness and Gender in the Field of Criminal Justice." *International Journal of the Sociology of Law* 14:287–98.

Heimer, Carol A., and Lisa R. Staffen. 1995. "Interdependence and Reintegrative Social Control: Labelling and Reforming 'Inappropriate' Parents in Neonatal Intensive Care Units." *American Sociological Review* 60:635–54.

———. 1998. *For the Sake of the Children: The Social Organization of Responsibility in the Hospital and the Home*. Chicago: University of Chicago Press.

Heinze, A., and W. Kerstetter. 1981. "Pretrial Settlement Conference: Evaluation of a Reform in Plea Bargaining." In *Perspective on Crime Victims*, edited by B. Galaway and J. Hudson. St. Louis, Mo.: Mosby.

Hesse, Carla, and Robert Post. 1999. "Introduction." In *Human Rights in Political Transitions: Gettysburg to Bosnia*, edited by C. Hesse and R. Post. New York: Zone Books.

Hibou, Beatrice. 1999. "The 'Social Capital' of the State as an Agent of Deception." In *The*

Criminalization of the State in Africa, edited by J.-F. Bayart, S. Ellis, and B. Hibou. Bloomington: Indiana University Press.

Hindelang, M. J., M. R. Gottfredson, and J. Garofalo. 1978. *Victims of Personal Crime: An Empirical Foundation for a Theory of Personal Victimization*. Cambridge, Mass.: Ballinger.

Hobbes, T. 1949. *De Cive*. New York: Appleton-Century-Crofts.

Hoffman, M. L. 1970. "Moral Development." In *Carmichael's Manual of Child Psychology*, edited by P. H. Mussen. New York: Wiley.

———. 1983. "Affective and Cognitive Processes in Moral Internalization." In *Social Cognition and Social Development*, edited by E. T. Higgins, D. N. Rubble, and W. W. Hartup. New York: Cambridge University Press.

Hogg, Russel, and David Brown. 1985. "Reforming Juvenile Justice: Issues and Prospects." In *Juvenile Delinquency in Australia*, edited by A. Borowski and J. Murray. Sydney: Methuen Australia.

Homel, R., M. Hauritz, R. Wortley, G. McIlwain, and R. Carvolth. 1997. "Preventing Alcohol-Related Crime through Community Action: The Surfers Paradise Safety Action Project." In *Crime Prevention Studies*, edited by R. V. Clarke. Vol. 7. Monsey, N.Y.: Criminal Justice Press.

Hood, C., C. Scott, O. James, G. W. Jones, and A. J. Travers. 1999. *Regulation inside Government: Waste-Watchers, Quality Police and Sleaze-Busters*. Oxford: Oxford University Press.

Hooper, Stephen, and Ruth Busch. 1996. "Domestic Violence and Restorative Justice Initiatives: The Risks of a New Panacea." www2.waikato.ac.nz/law/wir/special.

Hough, Michael, and Julian Roberts. 1998. "Attitudes to Punishments: Findings from the British Crime Survey." *Home Office Research Study 179*. London: Home Office.

Howley, Patrick. 1999. *Report on Bougainville for the Year 1999*. Melbourne: Peace Foundation.

———. 2000. *Breaking Spears and Mending Hearts*. Canberra: Research School of Pacific and Asian Studies, Australian National University.

Hoyle, Carolyn, and Richard Young. 1998. "A Survey of Restorative Cautioning with the Thames Valley Police." Oxford: Centre for Criminological Research, University of Oxford.

Hsien, Lim Li. 1996. "Family Conferencing Good for Young Delinquents: Report." *Straits Times*, 6 March.

Huang, Ray. 1988. *China: A Macro History*. Armonk, N.Y.: M. E. Sharpe.

Hudson, Joe. 1998. "Conducting the Family Group Conference Process: An Overview." In *Conferencing: A New Response to Wrongdoing*, edited by T. Wachtel. Pipersville, Pa.: Real Justice.

Hughes, Gordon. 1996. "Convergent and Divergent Discourses of Communitarian Crime Prevention: A Meditation on Current Developments in Europe, the USA, Australia and New Zealand." Paper presented to the Australian and New Zealand Society of Criminology Annual Conference, Wellington.

Hume, D. 1963. "Of the Independency of Parliament." In *Essays, Moral, Political and Literary*. Vol. 1. Oxford: Oxford University Press.

Ignatieff, Michael. 1999. *The Warrior's Honour: Ethnic War and the Modern Conscience*. London: Vintage Books.

Iivari, J. 1987. "Mediation as a Conflict Resolution: Some Topic Issues in Mediation Project in Vantaa." Paper presented to the International Seminar on Mediation, Finland, September.

———. 1992. "The Process of Mediation in Finland: A Special Reference to the Question 'How to Get Cases for Mediation.' " In *Restorative Justice on Trial: Pitfalls and Potentials of Victim-Offender Mediation—International Research Perspectives*, edited by H. Messmer and H. U. Otto. Dordrecht and Boston: Kluwer Academic Publishers.

Jabbour, Elias J. 1997. *Sulha: Palestinian Traditional Peacemaking Process*, edited by Thomas C. Cook Jr. Montreal: House of Hope Publications.

Jaccoud, M. 1998. "Restoring Justice in Native Communities in Canada." In *Restorative Justice for Juveniles: Potentialities, Risks and Problems for Research*, edited by Lode Walgrave. Leuven: Leuven University Press.

Jackson, Moana. 1987. "The Maori and the Criminal Justice System: A New Perspective— He Whaipaanga Hou." Report for New Zealand Department of Justice. Wellington, New Zealand: Policy and Research Division, Department of Justice.

Jacobs, James B. with Coleen Friel and Robert Radic 1999. *Gotham Unbound: How New York City Was Liberated from the Grip of Organized Crime*. New York: New York University Press.

James, T. M. 1993. *Circle Sentencing*. Supreme Court of the Northwest Territories: Canada.

Jenkins, Ann L. 1997. "The Role of Managerial Self-Efficacy in Corporate Compliance with Regulatory Standards." Ph.D. diss., Australian National University.

Johnson, Paul. 1998. *A History of the American People*. London: Phoenix.

Kaczynska-Nay, Eliza. 2000. "Compliance and Community at the International Level: A Case Study of the Treaty on the Non-proliferation of Nuclear Weapons." Ph.D. diss., Australian National University.

Kagan, Robert A. 1989. "On the Visibility of Income Tax Law Violations." In *Taxpayer Compliance: Social Science Perspectives*, edited by Jeffrey A. Roth and John T. Scholz. Philadelphia: University of Pennsylvania Press.

———. 1991. "Adversarial Legalism and American Government." *Journal of Policy Analysis and Management* 10:369–406.

Kaldor, Mary. 1999. *New and Old Wars: Organized Violence in a Global Era*. Cambridge U.K.: Polity Press.

Karstedt-Henke, Susanne, and Bernhard Crasmoller. 1991. "Risks of Being Detected, Chances of Getting Away." In *The Future of the Juvenile Justice System*, edited by J. Junger-Tas, L. Boendermaker, and P. van der Laan. Leuven: Acco.

Katz, I., D. Glass, and S. Cohen. 1973. "Ambivalence, Guilt and the Scapegoating of Minority Group Victims." *Journal of Experimental Social Psychology* 9:423–36.

Keen, David. 1998. *The Economic Functions of Violence in Civil Wars*. Adelphi Paper 320. Oxford: Oxford University Press.

Keesing, Donald B. 1997. *Trade Practices Laid Bare: Further Improving the WTO's Trade Policy Review Mechanism*. Geneva: World Trade Organization.

Kelling, George, and Catherine M. Coles. 1996. *Fixing Broken Windows: Restoring Order and Reducing Crime in Our Communities*. New York: Touchstone Books.

Kelman, Steven. 1984. "Enforcement of Occupational Safety and Health Regulations: A Comparison of Swedish and American Practices." In *Enforcing Regulation*, edited by Keith Hawkins and John M. Thomas. Boston: Kluwer-Nijhoff.

Kennedy, David M. 1997. "Pulling Levers: Chronic Offenders, High-Crime Settings, and a Theory of Prevention." *Valparaiso University Law Review* 31:449–85.

Kennedy, Robert. 1969. *Thirteen Days: A Memoir of the Cuban Missile Crisis*. New York: Norton.

Keohane, Robert O., and Joseph S. Nye. 1987. "Power and Interdependence Revisited." *International Organization* 41:725.

Kerner, H., E. Marks, and J. Schreckling. 1992. "Implementation and Acceptance of Victim-Offender Mediation Programs in the Federal Republic of Germany: A Survey of Criminal Justice Institutions." In *Restorative Justice on Trial: Pitfalls and Potentials of Victim-Offender Mediation—International Research Perspectives*, edited by H. Messmer and H. U. Otto. Dordrecht and Boston: Kluwer Academic Publishers.

Kigin, R. and S. Novack. 1980. "A Rural Restitution Program for Juvenile Offenders and Victims." In *Victims, Offenders and Alternative Sanctions*, edited by J. Hudson and B. Galaway. Lexington, Mass.: Lexington Books.

Kinsey, Karyl A. 1986. "Theories and Models of Tax Cheating." *Criminal Justice Abstracts*, September:402–25.

Kleiman, Mark A. R. 1993. "Enforcement Swamping: A Positive-Feedback Mechanism in Areas of Illicit Activity." *Mathematical and Computer Modelling* 17:65.

———. 1997. "Managing Drug-Involved Offenders." *Drug Policy Analysis Bulletin*, January: 3.

———. 1999. "Getting Deterrence Right: Applying Tipping Models and Behavioral Economics to the Problems of Crime Control." Paper presented to the annual meeting of the American Society of Criminology, 11 November, Toronto.

Klein, Malcolm. 1995. *The American Street Gang: Its Nature, Prevalence and Control*. New York: Oxford University Press.

Knight, T. 1985. "Schools and Delinquency." In *Juvenile Delinquency in Australia*, edited by A. Borowski and J. M. Murray. Melbourne: Methuen.

Koh, Angeline Cheok Eng. 1997. "The Delinquent Peer Group: Social Identity and Self-Categorization Perspectives." Ph.D. diss., Australian National University.

Kolko, Gabriel. 1994. *A Century of War: Politics, Conflicts, and Society since 1914*. New York: New Press.

Kraakman, R. H. 1984. "Corporate Liability Strategies and the Costs of Legal Controls." *Yale Law Journal* 93:857–898.

Krawll, M. B. 1994. *Understanding the Role of Healing in Aboriginal Communities*. Ottawa: Solicitor General, Canada Ministry Secretariat.

Kressel, Kenneth, Dean C. Pruitt, and associates. 1989. *Mediation Research: The Process and Effectiveness of Third-Party Intervention*. San Francisco: Jossey-Bass.

Krushchev, N. 1970. *Krushchev Remembers*. Vol. 1. Edited and translated by S. Talbott. Boston: Little, Brown.

Kuhn, A. 1987. "Koperverletzung als Konflift, Zwischenbericht 1987 zum Project Handschlag." Unpublished paper cited in T. Trenczek, "A Review and Assessment of Victim-Offender Reconciliation Programming in West Germany." In *Criminal Justice, Restitution and Reconciliation*, edited by B. Galaway and J. Hudson. Monsey, N.Y.: Willow Press.

Lacey N. 1988. *State Punishment: Political Principles and Community Values*. London: Routledge.

LaFree, Gary. 1998. *Losing Legitimacy: Street Crime and the Decline of Social Institutions in America*. Boulder, Colo.: Westview Press.

Lajeunesse, T. 1993. *Community Holistic Circle Healing: Hollow Water First Nation, Aboriginal Peoples Collection*. Canada: Supply and Services.

Lam, J. A. 1989. *The Impact of Conflict Resolution Programs on Schools: A Review and Synthesis of the Evidence*. Amherst, Mass.: National Association for Mediation in Education.

Langbein, L., and C. M. Kerwin. 1985. "Implementation, Negotiation and Compliance in Environmental and Safety Regulation." *Journal of Politics* 47:854–80.

LaPrairie, C. 1994. *Seen but Not Heard: Native People in the Inner City*. Victimisation and Domestic Violence, Report 3. Ottawa: Department of Justice.

———. 1995. "Altering Course: New Directions in Criminal Justice and Corrections. Sentencing Circles and Family Group Conferences." *Australian and New Zealand Journal of Criminology*, December: 78–99.

———. 1999. "Some Reflections on New Criminal Justice Policies in Canada: Restorative Justice, Alternative Measures and Conditional Sentences." *Australian and New Zealand Journal of Criminology* 32: 139–52.

Lasch, Christopher. 1977. *Haven in a Heartless World.* New York: Basic Books.

Latham, Mark. 1998. *Civilising Global Capital: New Thinking for Australian Labor.* St. Leonards, Australia: Allen and Unwin.

Latimer, Jeff, Craig Dowden and Danielle Muise. 2001. *The Effectiveness of Restorative Justice Practices: A Meta-Analysis.* Ottowa: Department of Justice, Canada.

Laue, James H. 1991. "Contributions of the Emerging Field of Conflict Resolution." In *Approaches to Peace: An Intellectual Map*, edited by W. S. Thompson, K. M. Jensen, Richard N. Smith, and Kimber M. Schraub. Washington, D.C.: United States Institute of Peace.

Law and Justice Sector Working Group. 1999. *The National Law and Justice Policy and Plan of Action: Toward Restorative Justice, 2000–2005.* Port Moresby, Papua New Guinea.

Lee, Kelly. 1999. "Globalization, Communicable Disease and Equity: A Look Back and Forth." International Roundtable on "Responses to Globalization: Rethinking Equity in Health," 12–14 July. Geneva: World Health Organization.

Lepper, M. R. 1973. "Dissonance, Self-Perception and Honesty in Children." *Journal of Personality and Social Psychology* 25:65–74.

Lepper, M. R., and D. Greene. 1978. *The Hidden Costs of Reward.* Hillsdale, N.J.: Erlbaum.

Levrant, Sharon, Francis T. Cullen, Betsy Fulton, and John F. Wozniak. 1999. "Reconsidering Restorative Justice: The Corruption of Benevolence Revisited?" *Crime and Delinquency* 45: 3–27.

Lewis, C. 1989. "Co-operation and Control in Japanese Nursery Schools." In *Japanese Schooling: Patterns of Socialisation, Equality and Political Control*, edited by James Shields. University Park: Pennsylvania State University Press.

Lewis, David. 1986. "Causation" and "Postscript: Redundant Causation." In *Philosophical Papers*. Vol. 2. Oxford: Oxford University Press.

Lewis, Helen B. 1971. *Shame and Guilt in Neurosis.* New York: International Universities Press.

Lewis-Beck, Michael S., and John R. Alford. 1980. "Can Government Regulate Safety: The Coal Mine Example." *American Political Science Review* 74:745–56.

Lin, L. 1996. "The Effectiveness of Outside Directors as a Corporate Governance Mechanism: Theories and Evidence." *Northwestern University Law Review* 90:898–976.

Lind, E. Allan, and Tom R. Tyler. 1988. *The Social Psychology of Procedural Justice.* New York: Plenum Press.

Lipsey, M. W. 1990. "Juvenile Delinquency Treatment: A Meta-analytic Inquiry into the Variability of Effects." Unpublished paper prepared for the Research Synthesis Committee of the Russell Sage Foundation.

Little, Michael 2001. "ISSP: An Experiment in Multi-Systemic Responses to Persistent young offenders known to children's services." Unpublished paper, University of Chicago.

Longclaws, Lyle, Burt Galaway, and Lawrence Barkwell. 1996. "Piloting Family Group Conferences for Young Aboriginal Offenders in Winnipeg, Canada." In *Family Group Conferences: Perspectives on Policy and Practice*, edited by Joe Hudson, Allison Morris, Gabrielle Maxwell, and Burt Galaway. Sydney: Federation Press and Criminal Justice Press.

Losel, Friedrich. 1995. "The Efficacy of Correctional Treatment: A Review and Synthesis of Meta-Evaluations." In *What Works: Reducing Reoffending*, edited by Hames McGuire. West Sussex: Wiley.

Loughlin, M., and C. Scott. 1997. "The Regulatory State." In *Developments in British Politics*, Vol. 5, edited by P. Dunlevy, I. Holliday, and G. Peele. London: Macmillan.

Lu, Hong. 1998. "Community Policing—Rhetoric or Reality? The Contemporary Chinese Community-Based Policing System in Shanghai." Ph.D. diss., Arizona State University.

———. 1999. "Bang Jiao and Reintegrative Shaming in China's Urban Neighbourhoods." *International Journal of Comparative and Applied Criminal Justice* 23: 115–25.

Macaulay, S. 1963. "Non-contractual Relations in Business: A Preliminary Study." *American Sociological Review* 28:55–69.

Mackay, Robert E. 1998. "Restorative Justice: Natural Law, Community and Ideal Speech." In *Law, Justice and Culture. Proceedings of the 17th World Congress of the International Association for Philosophy of Law and Social Philosophy*, edited by A.-J. Arnaud and P. Koller. Vol. 2. Stuttgart: Franz Steiner Verlag.

MacKenzie, D. L. 1997. "Criminal Justice and Crime Prevention." In *Preventing Crime: What Works, What Doesn't, What's Promising: A Report to the United States Congress*, edited by Lawrence Sherman, Denise Gottfredson, Doris MacKenzie, John Eck, Peter Reuter, and Shawn Bushway. Washington, D.C.: National Institute of Justice.

Majone, G. 1994. "The Rise of the Regulatory State in Europe." *West European Politics* 17: 77–101.

Makkai, T., and J. Braithwaite. 1991. "Criminological Theories and Regulatory Compliance." *Criminology* 29:191–220.

———. 1993a. "The Limits of the Economic Analysis of Regulation." *Law and Policy* 15: 271–91.

———. 1993b. "Praise, Pride and Corporate Compliance." *International Journal of the Sociology of Law* 21: 73–91.

———. 1994a. "Reintegrative Shaming and Regulatory Compliance." *Criminology* 32: 361–85.

———. 1994b. "The Dialectics of Corporate Deterrence." *Journal of Research in Crime and Delinquency* 31: 347–73.

———. 1996. "Procedural Justice and Regulatory Compliance." *Law and Human Behavior* 20(1): 83–98.

Maoz, Z., and N. Abdolali. 1989. "Regime Types and International Conflict, 1816–1976." *Journal of Conflict Resolution* 33(1): 3–36.

Marshall, T. F. 1985. *Alternatives to Criminal Courts*. Aldershot: Gower.

———. 1992. "Restorative Justice on Trial in Britain." In *Restorative Justice on Trial: Pitfalls and Potentials of Victim-Offender Mediation—International Research Perspectives*, edited by H. Messmer and H. U. Otto. Dordrecht and Boston: Kluwer Academic Publishers.

Marshall, T. F., and S. Merry. 1990. *Crime and Accountability: Victim Offender Mediation in Practice*. London: Home Office.

Masters, Guy. 1995. "The Family Model of Social Control in Japanese Secondary Schools." Unpublished manuscript, Lancaster University.

———. 1997. "Reintegrative Shaming in Theory and Practice." Ph.D. diss., Lancaster University.

Masters, Guy, and David Smith. 1998. "Portia and Persephone Revisited: Thinking about Feeling in Criminal Justice." *Theoretical Criminology* 2: 5–28.

Matza, D. 1964. *Delinquency and Drift*. New York: Wiley.

Maxwell, Gabrielle M. 1993. "Arrangements for Children after Separation? Problems and Possibilities." In *Women's Law Conference Papers: 1993 New Zealand Suffrage Centennial*. Wellington: Victoria University of Wellington.

Maxwell, Gabrielle M., and Allison Morris. 1993. *Family, Victims and Culture: Youth Justice in New Zealand*. Social Policy Agency and Institute of Criminology, Victoria University of Wellington, New Zealand.

———. 1996. "Research on Family Group Conferences with Young Offenders in New Zealand." *In Family Group Conferences: Perspectives on Policy and Practice*, edited by Joe Hudson, Allison Morris, Gabrielle Maxwell, and Burt Galaway. Sydney: Federation Press and Criminal Justice Press.

Maxwell, Gabrielle M., Allison Morris, and T. Anderson. 1999. *Community Panel Adult Pretrial Diversion: Supplementary Evaluation.* Research Report, Crime Prevention Unit, Department of Prime Minister and Cabinet and Institute of Criminology, Victoria University of Wellington, New Zealand.

McBarnet, Doreen, and Christopher Whelan. 1999. *Creative Accounting and the Cross-Eyed Javelin Thrower.* Chichester: Wiley.

McCold, Paul. 1997. "Restorative Justice: Variations on a Theme." In *Restorative Justice for Juveniles: Potentialities, Risks and Problems for Research,* edited by Lode Walgrave. Leuven: Leuven University Press.

McCold, Paul, and Benjamin Wachtel. 1998. "Restorative Policing Experiment: The Bethlehem Pennsylvania Police Family Group Conferencing Project." Pipersville, Pa.: Community Service Foundation.

McCold, Paul and Ted Wachtel. 2000. "Restorative Justice Theory Validation." Paper presented to the Fourth International Conference on Restorative Justice for Juveniles, Tübingen, Germany. (www.restorativepractices.org)

McDonald, J., D. Moore, T. O'Connell, and M. Thorsborne. 1995. *Real Justice Training Manual: Coordinating Family Group Conferences.* Pipersville, Pennsylvania: Pipers Press.

McGarrell, Edmund F., K. Olivares, K. Crawford, and N. Kroovand. 2000. *Returning Justice to the Community: The Indianapolis Juvenile Restorative Justice Experiment.* Indianapolis: Hudson Institute.

Meima, M. 1990. "Sexual Violence, Criminal Law and Abolitionism." In *Gender, Sexuality and Social Control,* edited by B. Rolston and M. Tomlinson. Bristol, England: European Group for the Study of Deviance and Social Control.

Meister, Robert. 1999. "Forgiving and Forgetting: Lincoln and the Politics of National Recovery." In *Human Rights in Political Transitions: Gettysburg to Bosnia,* edited by C. Hesse and R. Post. New York: Zone Books.

Melton, Ada Pecos. 1995. "Indigenous Justice Systems and Tribal Society." *Judicature* 79: 126.

Michael, Franz. 1986. *China through the Ages: History of a Civilization.* Taipei: SMC Publishing.

Miller, Seumas, and John Blackler. 2000. "Restorative Justice: Retribution, Confession and Shame." In *Restorative Justice: Philosophy to Practice,* edited by Heather Strang and John Braithwaite. Aldershot: Ashgate Dartmouth.

Mine Enforcement and Safety Administration. 1977. *A Report on Civil Penalty Effectiveness.* Washington, D.C.: Mine Enforcement and Safety administration.

Ministry of Justice, Western Australia. 1994. *Juvenile Justice Teams: A Six-Month Evaluation.* Perth: Ministry of Justice.

Minor, Kevin I., and J. T. Morrison. 1996. "A Theoretical Study and Critique of Restorative Justice." In *Restorative Justice: International Perspectives,* edited by Burt Galaway and Joe Hudson. Monsey, N.Y.: Criminal Justice Press.

Minow, Martha. 1990. *Making All the Difference: Inclusion, Exclusion and American Law.* Ithaca, N.Y.: Cornell University Press.

Mitchell, R. 1993. "Intentional Oil Pollution of the Oceans." In *Institutions for the Earth: Sources of Effective International Environmental Protection,* edited by P. M. Haas, R. O. Keohane, and M. A. Levy. Cambridge, Mass.: MIT Press.

———. 1994a. "Compliance Theory: A Synthesis." *Receil* 2: 327–34.

———. 1994b. "Regime Design Matters: International Oil Pollution and Treaty Compliance." *International Organization* 48: 425–58.

Miyazawa, Setsuo. 1992. *Policing in Japan: A Study on Making Crime.* Albany: State University of New York Press.

Moore, David B. 1994. "Public Anger and Personal Justice: From Retribution to Restoration—and Beyond." Paper presented to Silvan S. Tomkins Institute Colloquium, "The Experience and Expression of Anger," Philadelphia.

Moore, David B., with L. Forsythe. 1995. *A New Approach to Juvenile Justice: An Evaluation of Family Conferencing in Wagga Wagga*. Wagga Wagga: Charles Sturt University.

Moore, David, and John M. McDonald. 2000. *Transforming Conflict*. Bondi: Transformative Justice Australia.

Moore, David B., and Terry O'Connell. 1994. "Family Conferencing in Wagga Wagga: A Communitarian Model of Justice." In *Family Conferencing and Juvenile Justice*, edited by Christine Alder and Joy Wundersitz. Canberra: Australian Studies in Law, Crime and Justice, Australian Institute of Criminology.

Morris, Allison, Gabrielle Maxwell, Joe Hudson, and Burt Galaway. 1996. "Concluding Thoughts." In *Family Group Conferences: Perspectives on Policy and Practice*, edited by Joe Hudson, Allison Morris, Gabrielle Maxwell, and Burt Galaway. Sydney: Federation Press and Criminal Justice Press.

Morris, Ruth. 1995. "Not Enough!" *Mediation Quarterly* 12: 285–91.

Morrison, Brenda E. 2000. "The Role of Affect and Identity in Resolving Social Dilemmas: Insights from Restorative Justice." Paper presented at the annual conference of Australasian Social Psychologists, Perth, Western Australia, 27–30 April.

———. 2001. "Affect, Identity and the Self: A Field Theory of Restorative Process." Manuscript held at the Centre for Restorative Justice, Australian National University.

Mugford, S., and N. Inkpen. 1995. "The Implementation of Shaming Conferences as a New Policy Strategy: The Case of Drink Drivers." Paper presented to the American Society of Criminology Conference, Boston.

Murphy, Jeffrie G., and Jean Hampton. 1989. *Forgiveness and Mercy*. New York: Cambridge University Press.

Nader, Laura, ed. 1980. *No Access to Law: Alternatives to the American Judicial System*. New York: Academic Press.

Nagin, Daniel. 1978. "Crime Rates, Sanction Levels and Constraints on Prison Population." *Law and Society Review* 12: 341–66.

Nathanson, Donald L. 1992. *Shame and Pride: Affect, Sex and the Birth of the Self*. New York: Norton.

———. 1998. "From Empathy to Community." In *Conferencing: A New Response to Wrongdoing*, edited by T. Wachtel. Pipersville, Pa.: Real Justice.

Newman, Graeme. 1983. *Just and Painful*. London: Macmillan.

Nicholl, Caroline G. 1998. *Implementing Restorative Justice*. Washington, D.C.: Office of Community Oriented Policing Services, U.S. Department of Justice.

Noonan, John T., Jr. 1984. *Bribes*. New York: Macmillan.

North, Douglass. 1990. *Institutional Change and Economic Performance*. Cambridge: Cambridge University Press.

Novack, S., B. Galaway, and J. Hudson. 1980. "Victim and Offender Perceptions of the Fairness of Restitution and Community-Service Sanctions." *In Victims, Offenders and Alternative Sanctions*, edited by J. Hudson and B. Galaway. Lexington, Mass.: Lexington Books.

Nugent, W. R., and J. B. Paddock. 1995. "The Effect of Victim-Offender Mediation on Severity of Reoffense." *Mediation Quarterly* 12:353–67.

Nugent, W. R., M. S. Umbreit, L. Wiinamaki, and G. Paddock. Forthcoming. "Participation in Victim-Offender Mediation and Re-Offense: Successful Replications?" *Journal of Research on Social Work Practice*.

Nussbaum, Martha 1995. "Human Capabilities: Female Human Beings." In *Women, Culture, and Development*, edited by M. C. Nussbaum and J. Glover. Oxford: Clarendon Press.

Obonsawin-Irwin Consulting Inc. 1992a. *An Evaluation of the Attawapiskat First Nation Justice Project*. Ontario: Ministry of the Attorney General.

———. 1992b. *An Evaluation of the Sandy Lake First Nation Justice Project*. Ontario: Ministry of the Attorney General.

O'Collins, Maev. 2000. "Images of Violence in Papua New Guinea: Whose Images? Whose Reality?" In *Reflections on Violence in Melanesia*, edited by Sinclair Dinnen and Allison Ley. Annandale, NSW, and Canberra: Hawkins Press/Asia Pacific Press.

Offer, A. 1994. "Going to War in 1914: A Matter of Honour?" Paper presented to the Australian War Memorial Conference, Australian National University.

Okidi, C. 1978. *Regional Control of Ocean Pollution: Legal and Institutional Problems and Prospects*. Alphen aan den Rijn, Netherlands: Sijthoff and Noordhoff.

Olweus, Dan. 1993. "Annotation: Bullying at School-Basic Facts and Effects of a School-Based Intervention Program." *Journal of Child Psychology and Psychiatry* 35:1171–90.

Osborne, D., and T. Gaebler. 1992. *Reinventing Government: How the Entrepreneurial Spirit Is Transforming the Public Sector*. Reading, Mass.: Addison-Wesley.

Palk, Gerard, Hennessey Hayes, and Timothy Prenzler. 1998. "Restorative Justice and Community Conferencing: Summary of Findings from a Pilot Study." *Current Issues in Criminal Justice* 10:138–55.

Palmer, Karen, Wallace E. Oates, and Paul R. Portney. 1995. "Tightening Environmental Standards: The Benefit-Cost or the No-Cost Paradigm?" *Journal of Economic Perspectives* 9(4):119–32.

Parke, R. D. 1969. "Effectiveness of Punishment as an Interaction of Intensity, Timing, Agent Nurturance and Cognitive Structuring." *Child Development* 40:213–35.

Parker, Christine. 1998. "Public Rights in Private Government: Corporate Compliance with Sexual Harassment Legislation." *Australian Journal of Human Rights* 5:159–93.

————. 1999a. "Compliance Professionalism and Regulatory Community: The Australian Trade Practices Regime." *Journal of Law and Society* 26:215–39.

————. 1999b. *Just Lawyers*. Oxford: Oxford University Press.

————. Forthcoming. *The Open Corporation*.

Parker, Stephen. 1997. "Islands of Civic Virtue? Lawyers and Civil Justice Reform." *Griffith Law Review* 6:1–29.

Parliament of New South Wales, Standing Committee on Social Issues. 1998. "Hepatitis C: The Neglected Epidemic." Sydney: NSW Parliament.

Pate, K. 1990. "Victim-Offender Restitution Programs in Canada." In *Criminal Justice, Restitution and Reconciliation*, edited by B. Galaway and J. Hudson. New York: Willow Tree Press.

Paternoster, Raymond, Robert Brame, Ronet Bachman, and Lawrence W. Sherman. 1997. "Do Fair Procedures Matter? The Effect of Procedural Justice on Spouse Assault." *Law and Society Review* 31:163–204.

Paternoster, Raymond, and Sally Simpson. 1996. "Sanction Threats and Appeals to Morality: Testing a Rational Choice Model of Corporate Crime." *Law and Society Review* 30: 549–83.

Patterson, G. R. 1982. *Coercive Family Process*. Eugene, Ore.: Castalia Publishing.

Pavlich, George. 1996. "The Power of Community Mediation: Government and Formation of Self-Identity." *Law and Society Review* 30:707–33.

PEACE Foundation. 1999a. *PEACE Foundation's Involvement in the Reconciliation of BRA Factions in Buin*. Port Moresby, Papua New Guinea: PEACE Foundation Melanesia.

————. 1999b. *Report on Bougainville for the Year 1999*. Port Moresby, Papua New Guinea: PEACE Foundation Melanesia.

Peachey, D. E. 1989. "The Kitchener Experiment." In *Mediation and Criminal Justice: Victims, Offenders and Community*, edited by M. Wright and B. Galaway. London: Sage.

Pearson, Frank S., and Douglas S. Lipton. 1999. "The Effectiveness of Educational and Vocational programs: CDATE Meta-Analyses." Paper presented to Annual meeting the American Society of Criminology, Toronto.

Pease, Ken. 1998a. "Crime, Labour and the Wisdom of Solomon." *Policy Studies* 19:255–66.

————. 1998b. "Repeat Victimisation: Taking Stock." *Police Research Group Crime Detection and Prevention Series Paper 90*. London: Home Office.

Pennell, J., and G. Burford. 1995. *Family Group Decision Making: New Roles for 'Old' Partners in Resolving Family Violence*. Implementation Report, Vol. 1. St. John's: Family Group Decision Making Project, School of Social Work, University of Newfoundland.

————. 1996. "Attending to Context: Family Group Decision Making in Canada." In *Family Group Conferences: Perspectives on Policy and Practice*, edited by Joe Hudson, Allison Morris, Gabrielle Maxwell, and Burt Galaway. Sydney: Federation Press and Criminal Justice Press.

————. 1997. "Family Group Decision Making: After the Conference—Progress in Resolving Violence and Promoting Well-Being." St. John's: Family Group Decision Making Project, School of Social Work, University of Newfoundland.

————. 2000. "Family Group Decision Making: Protecting Children and Women." *Child Welfare* 79:131–58

Pepinsky, H. E., and R. Quinney, eds. 1991. *Criminology as Peacemaking*. Bloomington: Indiana University Press.

Pepler, Debra J., Wendy Craig, Suzanne Ziegler, and Alice Charach. 1993. "A School-Based Antibullying Intervention." In *Understanding and Managing Bullying*, edited by Delwin Tattum. London: Heinemann.

Perry, Charles S. 1981a. "Dying to Dig Coal: Fatalities in Deep and Surface Coal Mining in Appalachian States, 1930–1978." Unpublished manuscript, Department of Sociology, University of Kentucky.

————. 1981b. "Safety Laws and Spending Save Lives: An Analysis of Coal Mine Fatality Rates 1930–1979." Unpublished manuscript, Department of Sociology, University of Kentucky.

Pettit, P. 1993. "Liberalism and Republicanism." *Australian Journal of Political Science* 28:162–89.

————. 1997. *Republicanism*. Oxford: Clarendon Press.

Phillips, A. 1991. *Engendering Democracy*. Cambridge: U.K. Polity Press.

Pitts, John, and Philip Smith. 1995. "Preventing School Bullying." *Police Research Group Crime Detection and Prevention Series Paper 63*. London: Home Office.

Polanyi, Karl. 1957. *The Great Transformation: The Political and Economic Origins of Our Time*. Boston: Beacon Hill.

Polanyi, Michael. 1951. *The Logic of Liberty*. Chicago: University of Chicago Press.

Polk, Ken. 1994. "Family Conferencing: Theoretical and Evaluative Questions." In *Family Conferencing and Juvenile Justice*, edited by Christine Alder and Joy Wundersitz. Canberra: Australian Studies in Law, Crime and Justice, Australian Institute of Criminology.

Pontell, Henry. 1978. "Deterrence: Theory versus Practice." *Criminology* 16:3–22.

Porter, Michael. 1990. *The Competitive Advantage of Nations*. New York: Macmillan.

Porter, Michael, and Claas van der Linde. 1995a. "Green *and* Competitive: Ending the Stalemate." *Harvard Business Review*, September–October:120–34.

————. 1995b. "Reply to Portney's Critique of Porter and van der Linde (1995) 'Green *and* Competitive: Ending the Stalemate.' " *Harvard Business Review*, November–December: 206–8.

————. 1995c. "Toward a New Conception of the Environment-Competitiveness Relationship." *Journal of Economic Perspectives* 9(4):98–118.

Portney, Paul R. 1995. "Critique of Porter and van der Linde (1995) 'Green *and* Competitive: Ending the Stalemate.' " *Harvard Business Review*, November–December:204–6.

Posner, Richard A. 1977. *Economic Analysis of Law*. 2d ed. Boston: Little, Brown.

Power, Patrick. 2000. "Restorative Conferences in Australia and New Zealand." Ph.D. diss., Law School, University of Sydney.

Pranis, K. 1996. "A State Initiative toward Restorative Justice: The Minnesota Experience." In *Restorative Justice: International Perspectives*, edited by B. Galaway and J. Hudson. Monsey, N.Y.: Criminal Justice Press.

————. 2000. "Democratizing Social Control: Restorative Justice, Social Justice, and the Empowerment of Marginalized Populations." In *Restorative Community Justice*, edited by G. Bazemore and M. Schiff. Cincinnati Ohio: Anderson.

Pratt, John. 1996. "Colonization, Power and Silence: A History of Indigenous Justice in New Zealand Society." In *Restorative Justice: International Perspectives*, edited by Burt Galaway and Joe Hudson. Monsey, N.Y.: Criminal Justice Press.

Putnam, Robert D. 1988. "Diplomacy and Domestic Politics: The Logic of Two-Level Games." *International Organization* 42:425–60.

————. 1993. *Making Democracy Work: Civic Traditions in Modern Italy*. Princeton, N.J.: Princeton University Press.

Putnam, Robert D., and Nicolas Bayne. 1987. *Hanging Together: Cooperation and Conflict in the Seven Power Summits*. Cambridge, Mass.: Harvard University Press.

Putnam, Robert D., and C. Randall Henning. 1989. "The Bonn Summit of 1978: A Case Study in Coordination." In *Can Nations Agree? Issues in International Economic Cooperation*, edited by Richard N. Cooper, Barry Eichengreen, C. Randall Henning, Gerald Holtham, and Robert D. Putnam. Washington, D.C.: Brookings Institution.

Reed, P. 1986. "Developmental Resources and Depression in the Elderly." *Nursing Research* 36:368–74.

————. 1987. "Spirituality and Well-Being in Terminally Ill Hospitalized Adults." *Research in Nursing and Health* 10:335–44.

————. 1992. "An Emerging Paradigm for the Study of Spirituality in Nursing." *Research in Nursing and Health* 15: 349–57.

Rees, Joseph V. 1988. *Reforming the Workplace*. Philadelphia: University of Pennsylvania Press.

————. 1994. *Hostages of Each Other: The Transformation of Nuclear Safety since Three Mile Island*. Chicago: University of Chicago Press.

Reiss, A. J., Jr. 1980. "Understanding Changes in Crime Rates." In *Indicators of Crime and Criminal Justice: Quantitative Studies*, edited by S. E. Feinberg and A. J. Reiss. Washington, D.C.: U.S. Government Printing Office.

Rensselaer, W. L., III. 1992. "Colombia's Cocaine Syndicates." In *War on Drugs: Studies in the Failure of US Narcotics Policy*, edited by A. McCoy and A. Block. Boulder, Colo.: Westview Press.

Retzinger, Suzanne. 1991. *Violent Emotions*. Newbury Park, Calif.: Sage.

Retzinger, Suzanne, and Thomas J. Scheff. 1996. "Strategy for Community Conferences: Emotions and Social Bonds." In *Restorative Justice: International Perspectives*, edited by Burt Galaway and Joe Hudson. Monsey, N.Y.: Criminal Justice Press.

Richardson, James L. 1994. *Crisis Diplomacy: The Great Powers since the Mid–nineteenth Century*. Cambridge: Cambridge University Press.

Rigby, Ken. 1996. *Bullying in Schools and What to Do about It*. Melbourne: Australian Council for Educational Research.

Rigby, Ken, Alison Whish, and Garry Black. 1994. "School Children's Peer Relations and Wife Abuse." *Criminology Australia*, August:8–12.

Roach, Kent. 1999. *Due Process and Victims' Rights: The New Law and Politics of Criminal Justice*. Toronto: University of Toronto Press.

Roberts, Julian V., and Loretta J. Stalans. 1997. *Public Opinion, Crime, and Criminal Justice*. Boulder, Colo.: Westview Press.

Robertson, Jeremy. 1996. "Research on Family Group Conferences in Child Welfare in New Zealand." In *Family Group Conferences: Perspectives on Policy and Practice*, edited by Joe Hudson, Allison Morris, Gabrielle Maxwell, and Burt Galaway. Sydney: Federation Press and Criminal Justice Press.

Roche, Declan 2001. *"Restorative Justice and Deliberative Accountability."* Ph.D. diss., Australian National University.

Ross, Rupert. 1996. *Returning to the Teachings: Exploring Aboriginal Justice*. London: Penguin.

Rouche, Michel. 1987. "The Early Middle Ages in the West." In *A History of Private Life*, edited by Phillipe Ariès and Georges Duby. Cambridge, Mass.: Harvard University Press.

Rumsey, Alan. 2000. "Women as Peacemakers in the New Guinea Highlands: A Case from the Nebilyer Valley, Western Highlands Province." In *Reflections on Violence in Melanesia*, edited by Sinclair Dinner and Allison Ley. Leichhardt, NSW: Hawkins Press.

Said, E. W. 1995. *Orientalism: Western Conceptions of the Orient*. Harmondsworth: Penguin.

Sainsbury, R., and H. Genn. 1995. "Access to Justice: Lessons from Tribunals." In *Reform of Civil Procedure: Essays on "Access to Justice,"* edited by A. Zuckerman and R. Cranston. Oxford: Clarendon Press.

Sampson, Robert, J., and John H. Laub. 1993. *Crime in the Making: Pathways and Turning Points through Life*. Cambridge, Mass.: Harvard University Press.

Sampson, Robert, and Stephen W. Raudenbush. 1999. "Systematic Social Observation of Public Spaces: A New Look at Disorder in Urban Neighbourhoods." *American Journal of Sociology* 105:603–51.

Sandor, Danny. 1993. "Juvenile Justice: The Thickening Blue Wedge." *Alternative Law Journal* 18: 104–8.

Schedler, G. 1980. "Can Retributivists Support Legal Punishment?" *The Monist* 63: 185–98.

Scheff, Thomas J. 1990. *Microsociology: Discourse, Emotion, and Social Structure*. Chicago: University of Chicago Press.

———. 1994. *Bloody Revenge: Emotions, Nationalism and War*. Boulder, Colo.: Westview Press.

Scheff, Thomas J., and Suzanne M. Retzinger. 1991. *Emotions and Violence: Shame and Rage in Destructive Conflicts*. Lexington, Mass.: Lexington Books.

Scheingold, Stuart A., Jana Pershing, and Toska Olson. 1994. "Sexual Violence, Victim Advocacy, and Republican Criminology: Washington State's Community Protection Act." *Law and Society Review* 28: 501–33.

Schiff, Mara F. 1998. "The Impact of Restorative Interventions on Juvenile Offenders." In *Restoring Juvenile Justice*, edited by Lode Walgrave and Gordon Bazemore. Monsey, N.Y.: Criminal Justice Press.

Schneider, A. 1986. "Restitution and Recidivism Rates of Juvenile Offenders: Results from Four Experimental Studies." *Criminology* 24:533–52.

———. 1990. *Deterrence and Juvenile Crime: Results from a National Policy Experiment*. New York: Springer-Verlag.

Schneider, Friedrich, and Dominik Enste. 1999. "Shadow Economies around the World: Size, Causes, and Consequences." Unpublished manuscript, Department of Economics, Johannes Kepler University of Linz.

Scholz, John T. 1998. "Trust, Taxes and Compliance." In *Trust and Governance*, edited by V. Braithwaite and M. Levi. New York: Russell Sage Foundation.

Scholz, John T., and Wayne B. Gray. 1990. "OSHA Enforcement and Workplace Injuries: A Behavioral Approach to Risk Assessment." *Journal of Risk and Uncertainty* 3:283–305.

Scott, Margaret. 1997. *Port Arthur: A Story of Strength and Courage*. Sydney: Random House.

Sen, Amartya K. 1999. *Development as Freedom*. New York: Alfred A. Knopf.

Sessar, Klaus. 1990. "Tertiary Victimisation: A Case of the Politically Abused Crime Victims."

In *Criminal Justice, Restitution and Reconciliation*, edited by B. Galaway and J. Hudson. Monsey, N.Y.: Willow Tree Press.

———. 1998. "Punitive Attitudes of the Public: Reality and Myth." In *Restoring Juvenile Justice*, edited by Lode Walgrave and Gordon Bazemore. Amsterdam: Kugler Publishers.

Sessar, K., A. Beurskens, and K. Boers. 1986. "Wiedergutmachung als Konfliktregelungsparadigma?" *Kriminologisches Journal* 18:86–105.

Shapland, J., J. Willmore, and P. Duff. 1985. *Victims in the Criminal Justice System.* Cambridge Studies in Criminology. Brookfield, Vt.: Gower.

Shawcross, William. 2000. *Deliver Us from Evil: Warlords and Peacekeepers in a World of Endless Conflict.* London: Bloomsbury.

Shearing, Clifford. 1995. "Reinventing Policing: Policing as Governance." *Privatisierung staatlicher Kontrolle: Befunde, Konzepte, Tendenzen. Interdisziplinare Studien zu Recht und Staat* 3: 69–88.

———. 1997. *Violence and the Changing Face of Governance: Privatization and Its Implications.* Cape Town: Community Peace Foundation.

———. 2001. "Transforming Security: A South African Experiment." In *Restorative Justice and Civil Society*, edited by H. Strang and J. Braithwaite. Melbourne: Cambridge University Press.

Shearing, Clifford, and Philip Stenning. 1981. "Modern Private Security: Its Growth and Implications." In *Crime and Justice: An Annual Review of Research*, edited by M. Tonry and N. Morris. Vol. 3. Chicago: University of Chicago Press.

Sherman, L. W. 1992. *Policing Domestic Violence.* New York: Free Press.

———. 1993. "Defiance, Deterrence and Irrelevance: A Theory of the Criminal Sanction." *Journal of Research in Crime and Delinquency* 30:445–73.

———. 1998. "American Policing." In *The Handbook of Crime and Punishment*, edited by M. Tonry. New York: Oxford University Press.

Sherman, L. W., and G. Barnes. 1997. "Restorative Justice and Offenders' Respect for the Law." RISE Working Paper 3. Canberra: Law Program, RSSS, Australian National University.

Sherman, L. W., and R. A. Berk. 1984. "The Specific Deterrent Effect of Arrest for Domestic Assault." *American Sociological Review* 49:261–72.

Sherman, Lawrence, Denise Gottfredson, Doris MacKenzie, John Eck, Peter Reuter, and Shawn Bushway. 1997. *Preventing Crime: What Works, What Doesn't, What's Promising: A Report to the United States Congress.* Washington, D.C.: National Institute of Justice.

Sherman, L. W., and H. Strang. 1997a. "Community Policing and Restorative Justice." Press Release, Australian National University, 21 April.

———. 1997b. "Restorative Justice and Deterring Crime." RISE Working Paper 4. Canberra: Law Program, RSSS, Australian National University.

———. 1997c. "The Right Kind of Shame for Crime Prevention." RISE Working Paper 1. Canberra: Law Program, RSSS, Australian National University.

Sherman, L. W., H. Strang, G. C. Barnes, J. Braithwaite, N. Inkpen, and M. M. Teh. 1998. *Experiments in Restorative Policing: A Progress Report.* Canberra: Law Program, RSSS, Australian National University.

Sherman, L. W., H. Strang, and D. Woods. 2000. *Recidivism Patterns in the Canberra Reintegrative sharing Experiments (RISE).* Canberra: Centre for Restorative Justice, Australian National University.

Shover, Neal. 1996. *Great Pretenders: Pursuits and Careers of Persistent Thieves.* Bolder, Colo.: Westview Press.

Sigler, Jay A., and Joseph E. Murphy. 1988. *Interactive Corporate Compliance: An Alternative to Regulatory Compulsion.* New York: Quorum Books.

Skinner, Q. 1984. "The Idea of Negative Liberty: Philosophical and Historical Perspectives." In *Philosophy in History: Essays on the Historiography of Philosophy*, edited by R. Rorty, J. Schneewind, and Q. Skinner. Cambridge: Cambridge University Press.

Smith, D., H. Blagg, and N. Derricourt. 1985. "Victim-Offender Mediation Project." Report to the Chief Officers' Group, South Yorkshire Probation Service. Cited in *Crime and Accountability: Victim-Offender Mediation in Practice*, edited by T. Marshall and S. Merry. London: Home Office, 1990.

Snyder, Glenn H., and Paul Diesing. 1977. *Politics among Nations: Bargaining, Decision Making and System Structure in International Crises*. Princeton, N.J.: Princeton University Press.

Sonnekus, Eon, and Cheryl Frank. 1997. "Reconstructing and Developing Juvenile Justice in the New South Africa: Towards Restorative Juvenile Justice." Paper presented to the conference on Restorative Justice for Juveniles, Leuven, Belgium, 12–14 May.

Sparrow, Malcolm K. 2000. *The Regulatory Craft: Controlling Risks, Solving Problems, and Managing Compliance*. Washington, DC: Brookings.

Stanko, E. 1995. "Policing Domestic Violence: Dilemmas and Contradictions." *Australian and New Zealand Journal of Criminology*, special supplementary issue:31–44.

Stewart, Trish. 1993. "The Youth Justice Co-ordinator's Role: A Personal Perspective of the New Legislation in Action." In *The Youth Court in New Zealand: A New Model of Justice*, edited by B. J. Brown and F. W. M. McElrea. Auckland: Legal Research Foundation.

Strang, Heather. 2000. "Victim Participation in a Restorative Justice Process: The Canberra Reintegrative Shaming Experiments." Ph.D. diss., Australian National University.

Strang, Heather. 2001. *Victim Participation in a Restorative Justice Process*. Oxford: Oxford University Press.

Strang, H., G. Barnes, J. Braithwaite, and L. Sherman. 1999. "Experiments in Restorative Policing: A Progress Report." Canberra: Australian National University. www.aic.gov.au/rjustice/rise/index.html#papers.

Strang, Heather, and John Braithwaite, eds. Forthcoming. *Restorative Justice and Family Violence*. Melbourne: Cambridge University Press.

Strang, H., and L. W. Sherman. 1997. "The Victim's Perspective." RISE Working Paper 2. Canberra: Law Program, RSSS, Australian National University.

Stringer, A. 1999. "The Findings of the Prison and Debt Project." Brisbane: Prisoners' Legal Service.

Stubbs, J. 1995. " 'Communitarian' Conferencing and Violence against Women: A Cautionary Note." In *Wife Assault and the Canadian Criminal Justice System*, edited by Mariana Valverde, Linda MacLeod, and Kirsten Johnson. Toronto: Centre of Criminology, University of Toronto.

Sutherland, E. H. 1983. *White Collar Crime: The Uncut Version*. New Haven, Conn.: Yale University Press.

Sutherland, E. H., and D. R. Cressey. 1978. *Criminology*. 10th ed. New York: Lippincott.

Sykes, G., and D. Matza. 1957. "Techniques of Neutralization: A Theory of Delinquency." *American Sociological Review* 22:664–70.

Tangney, June Price. 1995. "Recent Advances in the Empirical Study of Shame and Guilt." *American Behavioral Scientist* 38:1132–145.

TARP. 1995. *American Express–SOCAP Study of Complaint Handling in Australia*. Geelong: Society of Consumer Affairs Professionals in Business.

Tauri, Juan. 1998. "Family Group Conferencing: A Case Study of the Indigenisation of New Zealand's Justice System." *Current Issues in Criminal Justice* 10:168–82.

Tauri, Juan, and Allison Morris. 1997. "Re-forming Justice: The Potential of Maori Processes." *Australian and New Zealand Journal of Criminology* 30:149–67.

Tavuchis, N. 1991. *Mea Culpa: A Sociology of Apology and Reconciliation*. Stanford, Calif.: Stanford University Press.

Tay, Simon S. C. 1999. "Preventive Diplomacy: Concept, Theory and Strategy." In *The Next Stage: Preventive Diplomacy and Security Cooperation in the Asia-Pacific Region*, edited by D. Ball and A. Acharya. Canberra: Australian National University.

Taylor, Natalie. 2000. "When Disagreement Strikes: Incorporating Compliance, Conversion, Resistance and Reactance into a Model of Social Response." Ph.D. diss., Australian National University, Canberra.

Tesler, Pauline H. 1999. "Collaborative Law: What It Is and Why Family Law Attorneys Need to Know About It." *American Journal of Family Law* 13(4):215–25.

Teubner, Gunther. 1983. "Substantive and Reflexive Elements in Modern Law." *Law and Society Review* 17:256.

Thurman, Q. C. 1984. "Deviance and the Neutralization of Moral Commitment: An Empirical Analysis." *Deviant Behavior* 5:291–304.

Ting-Toomey, Stella, and Mark Cole. 1990. "Intergroup Diplomatic Communication: A Face Negotiation Perspective." In *Communicating for Peace: Diplomacy and Negotiation*, edited by Felipe Korzenny and Stella Ting-Toomey. Newbury Park, Calif.: Sage.

Tomkins, Sylvan. 1962. *Affect/Imagery/Consciousness*. New York: Springer.

Touval, Saadia, and I. William Zartman. 1985. *International Mediation in Theory and Practice*. Boulder, Colo.: Westview Press.

———. 1989. "Mediation in International Conflicts." In *Mediation Research*, edited by Kenneth Kressel, Dean G. Pruitt, and associates. San Francisco: Jossey-Bass.

Trenczek, T. 1990. "A Review and Assessment of Victim-Offender Reconciliation Programming in West Germany." In *Criminal Justice, Restitution and Reconciliation*, edited by B. Galaway and J. Hudson. Monsey, N.Y.: Willow Press.

Trevelyan, G. M. 1973. *English Social History: Chaucer to Queen Victoria*. London: Book Associates.

Trimboli, Lily. 2000. *An Evaluation of the NSW Youth Justice Conferencing Scheme*. Sydney: NSW Bureau of Crime Statistics and Research.

Turner, John C., with Michael A. Hogg, Penelope J. Oakes, Stephen D. Reicher, and Margaret S. Wetherell. 1987. *Rediscovering the Social Group: A Self-Categorization Theory*. London: Basil Blackwell.

Tutu, Desmond. 1999. *No Future without Forgiveness*. London: Rider.

Tyler, Tom. 1990. *Why People Obey the Law*. New Haven, Conn.: Yale University Press.

Tyler, Tom, and Steven Blader. 2000. *Cooperation in Groups: Procedural Justice, Social Identity, and Behavioral Engagement*. Philadelphia: Psychology Press.

Tyler, Tom, and Robyn M. Dawes. 1993. "Fairness in Groups: Comparing the Self-Interest and Social Identity Perspectives." In *Psychological Perspectives on Justice: Theory and Applications*, edited by Barbara A. Mellers and Jonathan Baron. Cambridge: Cambridge University Press.

Tyler, Tom and Yuen J. Huo 2001. *Trust and the Rule of Law: A Law-Abidingness Model of Social Control*. New York: Russel Sage.

Umbreit, Mark. 1985. *Crime and Reconciliation: Creative Options for Victims and Offenders*. Nashville, Tenn.: Abington Press.

———. 1990a. "The Meaning of Fairness to Burglary Victims." In *Criminal Justice, Restitution and Reconciliation*, edited by B. Galaway and J. Hudson. Monsey, N.Y.: Willow Tree Press.

———. 1990b. "Mediation in the Nineties: Pushing Back the Boundaries." *Mediation* 6:27–29.

———. 1992. "Mediating Victim-Offender Conflict: From Single-Site to Multi-site Analysis in the US." In *Restorative Justice on Trial: Pitfalls and Potentials of Victim-Offender Media-*

tion—International Research Perspectives, edited by H. Messmer and H. U. Otto. Dordrecht and Boston: Kluwer Academic Publishers.

———. 1998. "Restorative Justice through Juvenile Victim-Offender Mediation." In *Restoring Juvenile Justice*, edited by Lode Walgrave and Gordon Bazemore. Monsey, N.Y.: Criminal Justice Press.

Umbreit, M., and R. Coates. 1992. *Victim-Offender Mediation: An Analysis of Programs in Four States of the US*. Minneapolis, Minn.: Citizens Council Mediation Services.

Umbreit, M., with R. Coates and B. Kalanj. 1994. *Victim Meets Offender: The Impact of Restorative Justice and Mediation*. Monsey, N.Y.: Criminal Justice Press.

Vagg, Jon. 1998. "Delinquency and Shame: Data from Hong Kong." *British Journal of Criminology* 38:247–64.

Van Ness, Daniel. 1986. *Crime and Its Victims: What We Can Do?* Downers Grove, Ill.: Intervarsity Press.

———. 1993. "New Wine and Old Wineskins: Four Challenges of Restorative Justice." *Criminal Law Forum* 4:251–76.

———. 1998. "Legal Principles and Process." In *Restoring Juvenile Justice*, edited by Lode Walgrave and Gordon Bazemore. Monsey, N.Y.: Criminal Justice Press.

Van Ness, Daniel, and Karen Heetderks Strong. 1997. *Restoring Justice*. Cincinnati, Ohio: Anderson Publishing.

Wachtel, Ted. 1997. *Real Justice. How We Can Revolutionize Our Response to Wrongdoing*. Pipersville, Pennsylvania: Piper's Press.

Wachtel, Ted, and Paul McCold. 2001. "Restorative Justice in Everyday Life: Beyond the Formal Ritual." In *Restorative Justice and Civil Society*, edited by H. Strang and J. Braithwaite. Melbourne: Cambridge University Press.

Walgrave, Lode. 1993. "In Search of Limits to the Restorative Justice for Juveniles." Paper presented at the International Congress on Criminology, Budapest, 23–27 August.

———. 1995. "Restorative Justice for Juveniles: Just a Technique or a Fully Fledged Alternative?" *Howard Journal* 34: 228–49.

Warhaft, E. Barry, Ted Palys, and Wilma Boyce. 1999. " 'This Is How We Did It': One Canadian First Nation Community's Efforts to Achieve Aboriginal Justice." *Australian and New Zealand Journal of Criminology* 32: 168–81.

Warner, K. 1994. "The Rights of the Offender in Family Conferences." In *Family Conferencing and Juvenile Justice: The Way Forward or Misplaced Optimism?* edited by C. Alder and J. Wundersitz. Canberra: Australian Institute of Criminology.

Warner, S. 1992. *Making Amends: Justice for Victims and Offenders*. Aldershot: Avebury.

Waters, Andrew. 1993. "The Wagga Wagga Effective Cautioning Program: Reintegrative or Degrading?" B.A. honors thesis, University of Melbourne.

Weitekamp, E. 1989. "Restitution: A New Paradigm of Criminal Justice or a New Way to Widen the System of Social Control?" Ph.D. diss., University of Pennsylvania.

———. 1998. "The History of Restorative Justice." In *Restoring Juvenile Justice*, edited by Lode Walgrave and Gordon Bazemore. Monsey, N.Y.: Criminal Justice Press.

West, D. J., and D. P. Farrington. 1973. *Who Becomes Delinquent? Second Report of the Cambridge Study in Delinquent Development*. London: Heinemann Educational.

Wexler, D. B., and B. J. Winick, eds. 1996. *Law in a Therapeutic Key: Developments in Therapeutic Jurisprudence*. Durham, N.C.: Carolina Academic.

White, Rob. 1994. "Shame and Reintegration Strategies: Individuals, State Power and Social Interests." In *Family Conferencing and Juvenile Justice*, edited by Christine Alder and Joy Wundersitz. Canberra: Australian Studies in Law, Crime and Justice, Australian Institute of Criminology.

Whyte, Ian D. 1995. *Scotland before the Industrial Revolution*. London: Longman.

Wilson, J. Q., and R. Herrnstein. 1985. *Crime and Human Nature*. New York: Simon and Schuster.

Wilson, William Julius. 1987. *The Truly Disadvantaged: The Inner City, the Underclass and Public Policy*. Chicago: University of Chicago Press.

Wong, Dennis. 1996. "Paths to Delinquency: Implications for Juvenile Justice in Hong Kong and China." Ph.D. diss., University of Bristol.

———. 1999. "Delinquency Control and Juvenile Justice in China." *Australian and New Zealand Journal of Criminology* 32:27–41.

Wormwald, Jenny. 1980. "Bloodfeud, Kindred and Government in Early Modern Scotland." *Past and Present* 87:54–97.

Wright, M. 1982. *Making Good: Prisons, Punishment and Beyond*. London: Hutchinson.

———. 1992. "Victim-Offender Mediation as a Step towards a Restorative System of Justice." In *Restorative Justice on Trial: Pitfalls and Potentials of Victim-Offender Mediation—International Research Perspectives*, edited by H. Messmer and H. U. Otto. Dordrecht and Boston: Kluwer Academic Publishers.

———. 1999. *Restoring Respect for Justice: A Symposium*. Winchester: Waterside Press.

Wundersitz, Joy, and Sue Hetzel. 1996. "Family Conferencing for Young Offenders: The South Australian Experience." In *Family Group Conferences: Perspectives on Policy and Practice*, edited by Joe Hudson, Allison Morris, Gabrielle Maxwell, and Burt Galaway. Sydney: Federation Press and Criminal Justice Press.

Wynne, Jean. 1996. "Leeds Mediation and Reparation Service: Ten Years Experience with Victim-Offender Mediation." In *Restorative Justice: International Perspectives*, edited by Burt Galaway and Joe Hudson. Monsey, N.Y.: Criminal Justice Press.

Yamagishi, Toshio. 2000. "Trust as a Form of Social Intelligence." In *Trust in Society*, edited by K. Cook. New York: Russell Sage Foundation.

Yazzie, Robert, and James W. Zion. 1996. "Navajo Restorative Justice: The Law of Equality and Justice." In *Restorative Justice: International Perspectives*, edited by Burt Galaway and Joe Hudson. Monsey, N.Y.: Criminal Justice Press.

Yeats, Mary Ann. 1997. " 'Three Strikes' and Restorative Justice: Dealing with Young Repeat Burglars in Western Australia." *Criminal Law Forum* 8: 369–85.

Young, Iris. 1995. "Communication and the Other: Beyond Deliberative Democracy." In *Justice and Identity: Antipodean Practices*, edited by Margaret Wilson and Anna Yeatman. Wellington, New Zealand: Bridget Williams Books.

Young, Richard. 2000. "Integrating a Multi-victim Perspective into Criminal Justice through Restorative Justice Conferences." In *Integrating a Victim Perspective within Criminal Justice: International Debates*, edited by A. Crawford and J. Goodey. Aldershot: Ashgate Dartmouth.

Youth Justice Coalition. 1990. *Kids in Justice: A Blueprint for the 90s*. Sydney: Law Foundation of New South Wales.

Zahn-Waxler, C. Z., M. R. Radke-Yarrow, and R. A. King. 1979. "Child Rearing and Children's Prosocial Initiations towards Victims in Distress." *Child Development* 50:319–30.

Zehr, Howard. 1985. *Retributive Justice, Restorative Justice*. New Perspectives on Crime and Justice: Occasional papers of the MCC Canada Victim Offender Ministries Program and the MCC, U.S. Office of Criminal Justice. Vol. 4. Elkhart, Ind.: Mennonite Central Committee; Kitchener, Ontario: Canada Victim Offender Ministries Program.

———. 1990. *Changing Lenses: A New Focus for Criminal Justice*. Scottsdale, Pa.: Herald Press.

———. 1995. "Rethinking Criminal Justice: Restorative Justice." Unpublished paper.

Zelizer, Viviana A. Rotman. 1985. *Pricing the Priceless Child: The Changing Social Value of Children*. New York: Basic Books.

Zimring, F. E. 1981. "Kids, Groups and Crime: Some Implications of a Well-Known Secret." *Journal of Criminal Law and Criminology* 72: 867–85.

Index

Abel, R., 252
Aboriginal communities, Australia, 22–4, 95–6, 143, 242. *See also* Indigenous peoples
Aboriginal Consumer Education Fund, 23
Aboriginal Corrections Policy Unit, 11, 134
access to justice, 128–9, 253, 254–7, 258–9, 261, 262, 265–6
accountability, 110, 147, 164, 166, 264, 266
adat law, in Indonesia, 130, 186
Adbolali, N., 171
advocacy groups, 166, 260, 266
affect theory, 79–80
African American circles, Minneapolis, 103, 140
Agenda for Peace, 170, 172
Agnew, R., 85
agreements from restorative justice processes, 51–2, 67, 102, 123, 160
Ahmed, Eliza, 77, 80, 132, 190, 193
Alford, John R., 63
Alliance of NGOs on Crime Prevention and Criminal Justice, 11
Allison, Graham, 189, 191
alternative dispute resolution (ADR), 239, 259, 261, 263, 264–5; development of, 246–8; feminist critique, 251–3, 264; pathologies of, 257–62; problems of, 248–54
Alvarez, Jose E., 203
American Bar Association, 165
American Express, 247

Anderson, 85
Anderson, Admiral (chief of US naval operations), 189
Anderson, C. Leigh, 240, 265
Anderson, Pastor Allan, 92
Anderson, T., 58, 61, 125
Andrews, Don, 97, 101
anger, 103–4; and incapacitation, 83; and international relations, 184, 187, 207; and the legal system, 243, 245, 251; shame–rage spiral, 79, 80, 190; victim, 139–40, 141
Annan, Kofi, 200
antisocial behavior, 98, 99
apology: and healing, 15, 36, 152, 208, 251; and shame, 81; and victim satisfaction, 52
Arnold, Thurman, 150
Arthur Young (auditors), 113
ASEAN, 173
Asian economic crisis, 185, 234–5
Asmal, K., 208
Association of Muslim Professionals, 89
Astor, H., 252
Aug San Suu Kyi, 3
Australian Broadcasting Tribunal, 250
Australian Competition and Consumer Commission, 231, 250
Australian Federation of Consumer Organizations, 232
Ayres, I.: corruption and capture, 91; deterrence, 65, 120, 124; power imbalance, 258–9; regulatory pyramid,

legal system, 239, 244–6, 248;
  transformation of, 239, 246, 250, 256,
  257, 260, 262
legitimacy, 33–4, 146, 198, 200; of rulers,
  130; of states, 197, 205–6, 226
Lepper, M. R., 106
Levrant, Sharon, 101
Lewis, C., 19
Lewis, David, 116
Lewis, Helen B., 79
Lewis-Beck, Michael S., 63
liberty, 127, 131. *See also* freedom
licenses, 94, 123
Lin, L., 113
Lincoln, Abraham, 5, 206
Lind, E. Allen, 78
Linde, Claas van der, 230, 263
Lipsey, M. W., 99
Lipton, Douglas S., 224
listening, 15, 78, 220
literacy, 220, 223, 224
Little, Michael, 59, 61
Lockheed bribery, 113, 116
Losel, Friedrich, 100
Loughlin, M., 254
love, 53, 214, 218–19, 224, 256
Lu, Hong, 20
Luskin, Robert C., 132

Macaulay, S., 261
Mackay, Robert E., 167
MacKenzie, D. L., 122
Madison, James, 127
Mafia, in New York, 94, 123
Magna Carta, 130
Majone, G., 254
Makkai, Toni, 17–18, 77–8, 104, 112, 120,
  124
mana, Maori concept of, 53
Mandela, Nelson, 5, 166, 175, 197, 198,
  206
Manual of Naval Regulations, 189
Maori culture, 11, 24, 25, 53, 76, 88, 143;
  concept of justice in, 68, 76
Maoz, Z., 171
markets, 182, 197, 212, 225, 231–4, 236
Marks, E., 50, 148
Marshall Plan, 184, 206

Marshall, Tony, 8, 11, 172
Masters, Guy, 8, 11, 18, 19, 59
Matza, D., 85, 87
Maxwell, Gabrielle, 8; conferences, 10,
  49, 97, 126, 147, 158; evaluation of
  adult restorative justice programs, 58,
  125; net-widening, 148–9; recidivism,
  58, 61, 81
McBarnet, Doreen, 260, 265
McCarthy, Bill, 82, 142
McCold, Paul, 11, 49, 50, 52, 54, 55, 56,
  67, 74, 86, 148, 163
McDonald, John, 8, 24, 86, 241
McElrea, Fred, 8
McFaul, Michael, 171
McGarrell, Edmund F., 50, 52, 54, 56, 61,
  62, 67, 159
McNamara, Robert, U.S. Secretary of
  Defense, 189
Medellin, Colombia, 212, 213
mediation, 190, 251; elite, 175, 187–8;
  international, 172–80
mediation programs, 50, 51, 54, 55–6, 59,
  148
mediation, transformative, 133, 240
Meima, M., 11
Mein Kampf, 184, 188
Meister, Robert, 206
Melton, Ada Pecos, 25
mentoring programs, 214, 222
mercy, 12, 15, 119, 129
Metternich, K., 172, 187
Michael, Franz, 22
microcommunity-building, 67–9
Midland Pilot Reparation Scheme, Western
  Australia, 49
Mika, Harry, 15
Mikac, Walter, 92
Miller, Phillip, 177
Miller, Seumas, 53
Mine Safety and Health Administration,
  63, 122
Ministry of Justice, Western Australia, 49,
  54, 67
Minor, Kevin I., 148
Minow, Martha, 155
Mitchell, Ronald, 114
Miyazawa, Setsuo, 18

Printed in the United States
17650LVS00005B/117